Victor Duruy

History of Rome, and of the Roman People

From its Origin to the Invasion of the Barbarians: Vol. VII.- Section II.

Victor Duruy

History of Rome, and of the Roman People
From its Origin to the Invasion of the Barbarians: Vol. VII.- Section II.

ISBN/EAN: 9783337249410

Printed in Europe, USA, Canada, Australia, Japan

Cover: Foto ©rinafisch / pixelio.de

More available books at **www.hansebooks.com**

By VICTOR DURUY,

MEMBER OF THE INSTITUTE, EX-MINISTER OF PUBLIC INSTRUCTION, ETC.

TRANSLATED BY M. M. RIPLEY AND W. J. CLARKE.

EDITED BY

THE REV. J. P. MAHAFFY,

PROFESSOR OF ANCIENT HISTORY, TRINITY COLLEGE, DUBLIN.

Containing over Three Thousand Engravings, One Hundred Maps and Plans,

AND NUMEROUS CHROMO-LITHOGRAPHS.

VOLUME VII. — SECTION II.

PUBLISHED BY

C. F. JEWETT PUBLISHING COMPANY,

BOSTON.

of some accomplices, assassinated, during a banquet, both Odenathus and Herodes.[1]

Zenobia had shared in the power and in the labors of her husband.[2] She claimed descent from the Macedonian kings of Egypt, which made her the woman of highest rank in the East; she was called also the most beautiful, and she was the most virtuous.[3] Ambition had stilled in her heart the vices which the harem nourishes. She knew all the languages spoken from Palmyra to Athens, and from Athens to Memphis, even Latin;[4] she read Homer and Plato; with Longinus — whose claims as author of the treatise on the Sublime are questionable, but who knew how to die bravely — she discussed questions of philosophy and literature; with the famous Archbishop of Antioch, Paul of Samosata, questions of theology; and she gave her two elder sons such able instructors that it was

ZENOBIA.[5]

said of one of them, Timolaos, that had he lived longer he might have taken rank with the great Latin orators. The desert had, like Athens and Rome, its academy of learned men; but Palmyra had not all the tastes of the Western world, for we find there no trace of those amphitheatres which all truly Roman cities made haste to build.

Zenobia accompanied her husband in war and the chase; she aided him in conquering the Persians, and essayed without him to conquer Egypt. Some accuse her of having been in the conspiracy which cost the Palmyrene Caesar his life; but we have reason to doubt this. She had a son by a former marriage, to whom Herodes barred the way to power, and whom the latter's death would make heir to the kingdom. Doubtless the mother thought of this, it may be she hoped for it; but to share in a plot against

---

[1] Zonaras, xii. 24.

[2] M. de Vogüé (*Inscr. sém.* p. 29) translates the Semitic name of Zenobia, Batzebinah, by *mercatoris filia.* But it may also be said that Zenobia is a Greek name, which the queen assumed on account of her kinship with the Zenobii, who were very numerous at Palmyra, and also to gratify her Greek subjects.

[3] Treb. Pollio, *T'yr. triq.* 20.

[4] *Ibid.* 30. This author adds that Zenobia had read a history of Rome written in Greek, — doubtless that of Dion Cassius, and that she had composed an abstract of the history of Alexander and of the East.

[5] Zenobia, queen of Palmyra, wearing the diadem. (Small bronze.)

Odenathus would have been to conspire against herself.   Maeonios had assassinated his uncle through revenge, and with the design of taking his place, not of leaving it to Zenobia; neither had it been necessary to urge him to rid himself of Herodes, whom Odenathus had associated with himself in the supreme power,[1] the first crime making the second necessary.   But we admit that the young prince's stepmother must have seen without regret this death, which freed her son from a rival.   The tragedy being accomplished, she aroused against the murderer the very soldiers who had proclaimed him king, and who now, doubtless for a little

BRONZE.[3]

money, laid his head at Zenobia's feet; after which they saluted her eldest son, Waballath, with the title of Augustus, and the two others as Caesar.[2] She presented these boys, clad in the Roman purple, to the people and to the army, while she kept for herself the real power, with the title *basilissa*, queen, —equivalent, doubtless, in the minds of the Palmyrenes, to that of Augusta.

In the midst of the confusion which had prevailed for nearly forty years, no one was surprised at all these Caesars emerging from an Arab city.   But it must have seemed strange to behold these children of the desert, who had been accustomed to hold the sex in subjection, thus quietly accepting a woman's sway. The East, it is true, had so many goddesses reigning in heaven that it might easily, without too great a sacrifice, allow women to reign upon earth,[4] and its legends always spoke of Semiramis, the mighty sovereign of Babylon, of Dido, the famous Carthaginian, and of that Queen of Sheba who had wished to behold in all his glory the king of the Jews, the founder of Tadmor.   Zenobia took pleasure in remembering Cleopatra, whom she equalled in beauty and in power, but whose masculine resolution at the last hour she perhaps

---

[1] Treb. Pollio, *Tyr. trig.* 14, 15.

[2] The Latin legend of the coins of Waballath is V. C. R. I. D. R., which M. de Sallet reads, *vir consularis, rex imperator, dux Romanorum*.   At Palmyra he did, in fact, bear the title of king, and in Lower Egypt was called βασιλεύς, king.   In the fifth year of his reign (August 29, 270, to August 28, 271) he took the title of Augustus.

[3] Bronze of Waballath Augustus, son of Zenobia.

[4] The Great Goddess of Byblos was considered superior in power to the male gods, — her father and brothers, for example (Halévy, *Inscr. de Byblos*, a paper read before the Academy of Inscriptions, May 3, 1878).

did not possess.[1] Her court was modelled after that of the Emperors, with Oriental forms of homage borrowed from Persia, which Diocletian later imitated, and the diadem which he assumed. With bared arm and helmeted head, she harangued her troops in a loud and musical voice, going along with them usually on horseback, but some-times even on foot, and shared in the prolonged banquet-ings of her generals, though never forget-ting her rank and dignity. Aurelian does her justice. "Those who say," he writes, "that I have conquered only a woman, have no idea what this wo-man was,—how wise in counsel, resolute in carrying out her plans, firm with her soldiers, and, accord-ing to the situation, gentle or severe. Through her aid Odenathus subdued the Persians, and through fear of her

ZENOBIA.[2]

arms the Arabs, the Saracens, and the Armenians have been kept in tranquillity."[3]

Zenobia was a formidable adversary. She entertained the design of adding to her territory in the East two countries as

[1] Treb. Pollio, *Tyr. trig.* 30. We say "perhaps," for Cleopatra had the opportunity for suicide, which Zenobia, who was very carefully guarded, probably did not have; see later.

[2] Bust of the Vatican (Museo Chiaramonti, No. 263).

[3] Treb. Pollio, *Tyr. trig.* 30.

its outposts and bulwarks. — Egypt, whither she sent an army which seized Alexandria, and Asia Minor, whose peoples, "unable to say no," accepted her sway. The Bithynians alone refused, and this refusal caused the failure of the whole plan; for Bithynia, lying between the Propontis and the Bosphorus, was the great highway for armies passing from Europe into Asia; and this highway remained open to Aurelian.

The Egyptian campaign began brilliantly. The historian Zosimus speaks of an army of seventy thousand men which seized upon

WABALLATH AND AURELIAN.[2]

the country, or at least upon the northern provinces. A general of the name of Probus[1] had been sent against the pirates, who, taking advantage of the wide-spread disorder produced by the great Gothic invasion, were now infesting the coasts of Asia Minor and Syria. He landed, with what troops he had, in the Delta, where the Palmyrenes had left only a garrison of five thousand men, increased his small army by some volunteers, and would have defeated Zenobia's troops, when he was surprised near Memphis. Falling into the enemy's hands, he took his own life,[3] and the queen remained mistress of Lower Egypt.

Alexandrian coins bear the heads of Aurelian and Zenobia's son, as if they had been colleagues; and the latest of them, belonging to the seventh year of the reign of Waballath, show that this situation lasted till into the year 272.[4]

---

[1] Or Probatus (Treb. Pollio, *Claud.* 11).

[2] VABALATHVS V. C. R. IM. D. R. and the laurelled head of Zenobia's son. On the reverse: IMP. C. AVRELIANVS AVG. and the radiate head of Aurelian. (Bronze coin.)

[3] . . . *Paquavit . . . ὅ mare ut pacem imperator* (Vopiscus, *Prob.* 9). Zonaras says even that he was taken . . . *Ζωσίμαν . . . Ηραῖον Λοίκαν* (xii. 27). According to M. de Sallet (*Die Fürsten von Palmyra*, p. 11). Probus was a usurper who attempted to seize Egypt while Claudius was fighting against the Goths. Zenobia defeated him; after which the Egyptians acknowledged the authority of the *imperator Romanus*, that is to say, Waballath, who swore fidelity to the Roman Augustus, Claudius. In respect to this individual we have followed the story of Zosimus, who seems to have been well informed as to the affairs of the Palmyrenes. (See Waddington, *Inscr. de Syrie*, 195.)

[4] Eckhel, vii, 496. So long as Zenobia ruled Egypt as the deputy of Claudius, the name of this Emperor appears alone on the Alexandrian coins; upon the death of Claudius she caused to be struck, in Alexandria, coins bearing the effigies of Aurelian and Waballath, and also others with the head of Aurelian alone. After the rupture, in 271–272, the head of Aurelian disappears from the Alexandrian coins, and the name of Waballath is followed by the title Σεβαστός, Augustus (De Vogüé, *op. cit.* p. 32).

In the spring of this year Aurelian left Italy with a numerous army for the purpose of regulating the affairs of Asia. On the way he drove out from Illyria, Thrace, and Moesia the Gothic bands who still lingered there or had returned thither; he pursued some of them across the Danube, and compelled them to give him as hostages a number of young girls of noble family, whom he placed at Perinthus. He wrote to the legate of Thrace to furnish for the support of these hostages a certain sum, but to keep them in communities of seven, so that the expense to the state should be less, while the young girls might still be suitably maintained. We have already seen that hostages such as these were very useful to the imperial policy. One of them, we are told, married a Roman general (and doubtless others did the same), and the Emperor furnished the dowry.

In Bithynia Aurelian was welcomed as a liberator; hostilities began in Galatia, where it was necessary to take Ancyra by storm. Tyana, an important city of Cappadocia, which covered the Cilician Gates of Mount Taurus, would have made a long resistance if one of its richest citizens had not indicated an ill-fortified and ill-guarded point. Aurelian put the traitor to death, without, however, confiscating his property, — a virtue rare among the monarchs of that time. The soldiers expected to plunder this wealthy city, but Aurelian forbade them to do it. Apollonius of Tyana still had his admirers; the biographer of Aurelian is one of them, and he declares that an apparition of the hero prevented the Emperor from destroying this city. Policy counselled moderation, and Aurelian understood that in those troublous times indulgence was due to those who did not know on which side the right lay, and where obedience was due.[1] When he gave out that Apollonius had prohibited the sack of his native city, the soldiery, who might have refused obedience to their Emperor, dared not refuse it to "the divine man," and a well-told lie saved a great city.

The passes of the Taurus were not at all guarded,[2] and the legions came down into Cilicia, turned the Gulf of Issus, and,

---

[1] See later the amnesty that he granted.

[2] The Taurus, or Bulghar-Dagh, has peaks which rise to a height of 11,500 feet; but the pass is only 3,170 feet. Thence, by way of Adana and Mopsuesta, Aurelian could reach the road which crossed a spur of the Amanus (*Pylae Amanides*), then turn at Alexandretta to the point where the Amanus, which runs parallel to the coast at a height of about

arriving at the Syrian Gates, saw beneath them the Lake of Antioch, — the city itself luxuriously reposing on the bank of the

THE PASSES OF MOUNT AMANUS.

Orontes, and Daphne, the sanctuary of licentious rites. Zenobia was there with a portion of her cavalry. An action, which does not seem to have cost many lives,[1] gave the city into the power

---

6,560 feet, leaves between it and the sea only those two famous defiles called the Cilician and the Syrian Gates, at 2,625 and 2,950 feet above the sea. (See in the *Bulletin de la Soc. de Géogr.*, January, 1878, the map of Messrs. Favre and Mandrot.)

[1] . . *Pexit apud Dafacm certamine* (Vopiscus, *Aur.* 25). Zosimus (i. 51) represents it as more severe; but it was only a cavalry engagement and a skirmish of outposts.

of the Romans; they entered it. while the Palmyrenes fell back towards Chalcis. Aurelian continued his plan of clemency. Many inhabitants of Antioch, fearing that they should be treated as partisans of the queen, had escaped from the city with the Arab army; but a proclamation guaranteed them life and property, and almost all returned.

In another affair. which has been made very conspicuous, he showed the same spirit of conciliation. Paul of Samosata enjoyed at Antioch both the office of bishop and that of *procurator ducenarius*, or steward of Zenobia's finances. The city contained many Jews and Christians; among the latter were men who, while accepting the Gospel, rejected the divinity of Christ, or at least understood it otherwise than the Church did. According to them. Jesus was but a man in whom the Spirit of God. the *Logos*, resided, as formerly in Moses and the Prophets.[1] They recognized the union of the Divine Word and the human nature in the person of Christ, and admitted that he might well be called God. But this attempt at a rational explanation destroyed the doctrine of God made man, and diminished the religious fruitfulness of Christianity. Paul thought as they did. In 264 his faith had already become an object of suspicion : however, a numerous synod of bishops. priests, and deacons. assembled to examine into his views. had found them not heretical. Five years later his adversaries convoked another assembly. whither came seventy-six bishops, and he was cut off from the Church. A synodal letter addressed " to the bishops of Rome and Alexandria. to all the bishops, priests, and deacons forming the Church under the heavens." announced to them the deposition of the Bishop of Antioch. Paul, however. supported by Zenobia, did not resign the episcopal dignity. The case was brought before Aurelian, who, with a good sense which we must admire, avoided giving a decision. and carefully abstained. while speaking of these disputes. from making any reference to the fact that there existed imperial edicts against the Christians. " These matters concern bishops." he said ; " let him hold the see of Antioch with whom the bishops of Rome and Italy are in fellowship." The brother of Seneca. the tribune at Jerusalem, had

---

[1] At the same time admitting his miraculous birth, ἐκ παρθένου (Saint Athan., *Contra Apollin.* i. 3).

also made answer on the subject of Saint Paul accused by the Jews:
"I am not minded to be a judge of these matters." The brave
and honest soldier whose history we are writing had discovered
for himself this admirable truth, which so many monarchs have
overlooked, and still at this day even fail to recognize.[1] He at
once reaped the fruit of it. The bishop's friends had been, like
Paul himself, the queen's partisans; Aurelian punished them indi-
rectly, at the same time conciliating the Christian community, —
numerous in that great city.

An attempt has been made to see in the Emperor's response
an acknowledgment of the primacy of the Roman See. It was,
however, natural that Aurelian, having to decide a point of doctrine between Christians, should address himself to the metropolitan
bishops, and that he should constitute the heads of the Christian
communities of Italy arbitrators of the dispute, without attaching
other importance to the affair. His judgment nevertheless constituted a precedent extremely useful to the pontifical authority.

Affairs being regulated at Antioch, Aurelian set out in pursuit
of the enemy. He came up with their rear-guard not far from
Chalcis, and dislodged it from a height where it had been posted.
The Palmyrenes made no further halt till they arrived under the
walls of Emesa; here Zenobia had gathered seventy thousand
men, resting on a securely fortified place, and having in front of
them a wide plain suited for cavalry movements. The battle this
time was desperate. In the one army the ancient renown of
Rome, in the other the new fame of Palmyra, fired the hearts
of all. For a moment Aurelian had reason to fear that his
soldiers might give way before the shock; his cavalry was almost
destroyed; but a vigorous charge, which he led in person against
the centre of the too-extended line of the enemy, decided the
victory. It had been so dearly bought, however, that the Romans
were not in a condition to pursue the vanquished. In the heat of
the combat Aurelian had vowed a temple to the Sun, and it was
related afterwards that the god himself had been seen in the midst
of the legions, restoring their disordered lines. The Sun was the

---

[1] Euseb. *Hist. eccl.* vii. 27 and 29. The synodal letter is quoted by Eusebius. It contains,
as was customary, many complaints, true or false, against the bishop, on the subject of his
morals. Hefele (*Conciliengeschichte*, i. 102–117) enumerates three synods of Antioch on this
affair, but he is unable to give the date of the second, and we do not mention it.

THE TEMPLE OF THE SUN AT ROME (RESTORATION BY GERHARD, ÉCOLE DES BEAUX-ARTS).

great divinity of Palmyra; it now appeared that he had abandoned his people. But the gods, it is well known, are always on the side of the heavy battalions; and with a sentiment made up both of pride and humility, the victors took pleasure in transforming into divine assistance the aid which they had found in their own courage.[1]

In a council of war held by Zenobia at Emesa it had been decided to fall back upon Palmyra. It was confidently believed that the heavy Roman army could not traverse "the land of thirst," or at least that it would subsist there with difficulty, exposed as it would be to incessant attacks from the nomads. The "Syrian robbers," as Vopiscus calls them, did, in fact, much harm to the Romans, but were not able to prevent their reaching the desert capital. Palmyra was surrounded by a deep moat and a wall covered with innumerable machines of war, which sent off an incessant shower of arrows, darts, and flames.[2] The Emperor had not expected a defence so determined. On arriving in sight of the city, he wrote to the queen: "Aurelian, Emperor of the Roman world and conqueror of the East, to Zenobia and those who are engaged in her cause. You ought to have done willingly that which I order in this letter. I command you to surrender, and I promise to spare your lives. You, Zenobia, will withdraw with your family into a place which I shall indicate to you, by the advice of the honorable Senate. You will surrender to the Roman treasury all that you possess of precious stones, gold, silver, silk, horses, and camels. The Palmyrenes will preserve their rights."[3]

The reply was no less proud: "Zenobia, Queen of the East. No person has ever dared to demand what your letter asks. You wish me to surrender myself, as if you did not know that Queen Cleopatra preferred to die rather than owe her life to a master. I am momentarily expecting assistance from the Persians; the Saracens and Armenians are on my side. The Syrian robbers have defeated your army, Aurelian; what then will be your situation when we have received the reinforcements which are coming to us from all sides? You will then abandon this proud tone with which you demand my submission, as if your arms were everywhere victorious."[4]

---

[1] See in Zosimus (i. 57–58) the numerous oracles made to speak in all the temples of Syria
[2] Doubtless employing the bitumen with which the region abounds.
[3] Vopiscus, *Aur.* 26.   [4] *Ibid.* 27.

After this interchange of haughty language nothing remained but to storm the city or to reduce it by famine. The Roman army invested the place. Zenobia counted on Persia; but Persia had changed rulers three times in as many years, amidst conspiracies of the nobles, and religious quarrels agitating the people. Sapor. the conqueror of Valerian. had died in 271. His son Hormisdas, devoted to peace, reigned fourteen months, and the successor of Hormisdas, Bahram Varanes. less than four years. Of Hormisdas is related an anecdote worthy of the *Arabian Nights*. Being suspected of entering into some conspiracy with the satraps. who

were discontented at the protracted duration of Sapor's reign (thirty years). the prince cut off his hand and sent it to his father as a sign of his fidelity. It was contrary to custom that a person in any way mutilated should succeed to the throne;

COIN OF BAHRAM, OR VARANES I.[1]

but Sapor, to honor his son's heroism. bequeathed to him the royal authority. This legend has preserved to us the memory of Hormisdas; at Ram Hoormuz, which he built. the Persians still show an orange-tree — an object of veneration to them — which he is said to have planted.[2]

Bahram was on the Persian throne when Aurelian appeared before Palmyra. But the kingdom was agitated by the preaching of Manes, who sought to blend in one the religions of Christ and of Zoroaster. The people. and even the court. were divided between the old and the new doctrines. Sapor had banished the sectary; Hormisdas had favored him. The magi, anxious for their authority, succeeded in re-establishing their influence over the mind of Bahram. who condemned Manes to be flayed alive. and was shortly after himself assassinated by a partisan of the reformer. This double tragedy came later than the siege of Palmyra; but domestic dissensions of this nature explain the reserved attitude

---

[1] Legend: *The worshipper of Ormuzd, the excellent Varanes, king of kings, of Iran and Turan, celestial germ of the gods,* around the head of the king. On the reverse: *The divine Varanes;* in the centre. a pyre: on the left, Varanes. standing; at the right, another figure. (Silver coin.)

[2] Malcolm, *History of Persia,* i. 100.

of the nation which had but recently held a Roman Emperor in captivity. They contented themselves with sending some slight reinforcements to Palmyra, which were, however, intercepted on the way. In respect to Armenia, we have already indicated the reasons which made the friendship of Rome indispensable to this country, while the Arabs and the Saracens were either bought or intimidated, and at very slight expense in either case.

Zenobia, then, stood alone. When she knew that she could no longer count on those whom she had believed her allies, and when she saw that her provisions were rapidly decreasing, she resolved

RUINS OF THE TEMPLE OF DIANA AT PALMYRA.

to escape to the Persians and endeavor to persuade them to make a vigorous effort, while her own army still held out. Mounted on a rapid dromedary, she made her way to the Euphrates, and was nearly at its bank when the horsemen who had been sent in her pursuit came up with her. This sad news caused great confusion in Palmyra. Some were disposed to prolong the defence, but the larger number threw down their arms and opened the gates. Aurelian made no change in the terms he had at first offered; he treated the city with mildness, left it in undisturbed possession of its rights, and contented himself with taking the treasures of Zenobia.

Returning to Emesa, where from the resources of a rich province the troops could compensate themselves for the privations they had lately suffered, the Emperor constituted a tribunal to judge Zenobia and her ministers. In her first interview with Aurelian she asserted herself as proudly as ever. "How dared

GATE OF ZENOBIA'S PALACE (ACTUAL CONDITION).

you," he said, "insult the majesty of the Roman Emperors?" And she replied: "I acknowledge you as an Emperor, since you are able to conquer; but the Gallieni, the Aureoli, and others like them, were not emperors." The compliment was not excessive. It is said, however, that before the tribunal she basely threw upon her councillors the responsibility of the war. This is probably a calumny of the victors, or it may have been a rumor set in circu-

lation by Aurelian. The soldiers were eager for blood, and he
had determined not to put the queen to death, for he proposed to
have this second Cleopatra as an ornament to his triumph. The
judges were directed, therefore, to find only the ministers guilty;
and these persons were put to death, — among them Longinus, who
met his fate with the serenity of a sage (273).

The fall of the Queen of the East produced a great impres-
sion, and the desertion of all her allies proved the fear which
the resuscitated Empire inspired. Aurelian therefore had quitted

RUINS OF THE TEMPLE OF THE SUN AT PALMYRA

Syria with a mind freed from anxiety, and had traversed Asia
Minor, and even a portion of Thrace, when the news came to him
that the Palmyrenes were again in arms, that the Roman garrison
and its commander Sandarion had been murdered, and that, finally,
one Antiochus had been proclaimed emperor.[1] Palmyra had not
been willing to submit to fall back from her rank as an imperial
city to the condition of a mere trading mart. She had for a
moment drunk of the cup of grandeur, and was intoxicated by
it still, and her dreams were haunted by the memory of her
caravan leaders made Caesars of Rome. The act of folly which
she had just now committed was cruelly expiated. Aurelian's anger
was terrible; his severity in Rome had been already manifested.

---

[1] Vopiscus, Aur. 31; cf. Zosimus, i. 60, 61.

and at Palmyra, as he had been more clement, he was now even more pitiless. We know not who the troops were to whom he intrusted his vengeance, but a letter shows that this revenge had been, as it were, the execution of an entire people. "Aurelian Augustus to Ceionius Bassus. Let the soldiers use their swords no longer: enough Palmyrenes have been killed. We have not even

spared mothers; we have slain children and old men, and put to death the inhabitants of the country. To whom shall we now leave the country and the city? It is proper to spare the few who remain, and believe them corrected by the sight of so much punishment. I desire that the temple of the Sun, pillaged by the eagle-bearer of the tenth legion, by the standard-bearers, by the dragon - bearer,[1] and by the trumpeters, be restored as it was. You have in the treasures of Zenobia three hundred pounds weight of gold: you have also eighteen hundred pounds of silver, obtained from the possessions of the Palmy-

THE DRAGON-BEARER
(BAS-RELIEF OF THE TRAJAN COLUMN).

renes; and you have also the royal jewels. Employ all this in the ornamentation of the temple; you will thus do a thing agreeable to the immortal gods and to me. I will write to the Senate to send a priest to make the dedication of the temple."[2]

Palmyra never recovered from this blow. The families who had made her fortune doubtless perished in the massacre, and of the inhabitants who survived none were able to take their place.

---

[1] The soldier who bore the standard representing a dragon's head, terminated by a red streamer, which in the wind resembled the tortuous folds of the serpent. Cf. Treb. Pollio, *Gall.* 8, and Amm. Marcellinus, xvi. 12: . . . *Purpureum signum draconis summitati hastae longioris aptatum.* It seems to have resembled a Chinese flag.

[2] Vopiscus, *Aur.* 31.

Commerce became used to other routes, the sand invaded this de-populated oasis, and for ten centuries the world knew not even the place where the Queen of the East had built her palaces of marble; but a spring which still flows has preserved through the ages, it has been conjectured, the name of him who made this vast desolation.[1]

After the tragedy of Emesa, Aurelian had hastened his return to Europe without stopping in Egypt, whence Probus, as brave a

RUINS OF THE PALACE OF ZENOBIA.

soldier as himself, had expelled the Palmyrenes. Believing this country pacified, he had not thought it advisable to appear there: but when it was understood that the Emperor was on his way to Gaul, a merchant enriched by traffic in the papyrus of Egypt and the commodities of India, Firmus, a Greek, whom the political for-tunes of the sheiks of Palmyra had dazzled, undertook to repeat their enterprise. He secured the aid of the Blemmyes and of the Saracens, stirred up Alexandria, ever ready for riots, and detained the corn-bearing fleet, — which was a serious matter. Firmus assumed the purple at the moment when Palmyra revolted, — whence it may

---

[1] The *Ain Ournus*, to be seen near Palmyra. It has been conjectured that *Ournus* is an altered abbreviation of Aurelianus (*Récit de Fatalla Sayeghri*, discovered by Lamartine, *Voyage en Orient*, ii. 382).

be concluded that the two movements were concerted.[1]   Aurelian had no difficulty in confining the usurper within one of the four quarters of Alexandria, the Bruchium, separated by a wall from the rest of the city, which will be remembered as the position where Julius Caesar so long braved all the forces of Egypt.   There stood the palace of the Ptolemies, the museum, — which a long portico, made of the most precious marble, connected with the royal residence, — and the palace of the Caesars, built in the place where once stood the two obelisks called Cleopatra's Needles.[2] Aurelian did not undertake to storm this peculiar position; but famine eventually delivered Firmus into his hands, and he caused the rebel to be crucified.   He then dismantled the Bruchium, the royal palace, and all that could serve as protection in case of a new disturbance, that the provisioning of Rome might never again be at the mercy of this seditious city.[3]   This time at least his anger was directed towards the city itself rather than its inhabitants;[4] but he augmented by one twelfth the frumentary tax of Egypt, and laid upon the country a new annual tribute, — namely, the sending to Rome of a certain quantity of glass, papyrus, linen, hemp, and other products of the country.[5]

Zenobia being a captive, "the robber Firmus" having been crucified, and the populace of Alexandria being held in check by a Roman garrison, order began to be restored throughout the East, which had twice within a few months been overrun by a great and victorious army.   From every side came in embassies, protestations

[1] The *Augustan History* does not say this; but the narrative of Vopiscus is extremely confused.   I give what is probable, but not certain.   A few words in the letter of Aurelian to the Senate and the Roman people, after the defeat of Firmus, would lead us to suppose that the subjugation of Egypt had been preceded by that of the Gauls: . . . *Pacato toto orbe terrarum* (Vopiscus, *Firm.* 5); but other information furnished by the *Augustan History*, by Zosimus (i. 61), by medals and by the course of events, is contrary to this view.   There are coins of the fifth year of the reign of Tetricus; that is to say, 272–273.

[2] In respect to this temple of the Caesars, constructed in the time of Augustus, see *Bull. de corresp. hellén.*, 1878, p. 175.

[3] Amm. Marcellinus, xxii. 16.

[4] He permitted the women and children and the old men to go out of the Bruchium.   At least, Eusebius (*Hist. eccl.* vii. 32) relates this fact, on the authority of Anatolius, an eye-witness, who later was the bishop of Laodicea, but he does not name Aurelian; and as he represents Anatolius as after this attending the Council of Antioch, held to examine Paul of Samosata, we perhaps ought to place this event in the time of Claudius, when Probus expelled the Palmyrenes from Alexandria and the Delta.

[5] Vopiscus, *Aur.* 44.

of friendship, and presents; among other things, as a gift from
the king of Persia, a purple mantle, which seems to have been the
predecessor of our Indian cashmeres.[1]   Nothing, therefore, detained
Aurelian longer in this part of the Empire, and he was at liberty
to turn his attention at last towards the Western provinces, where
Tetricus had been reigning for more than five years.[2]

Victorina, "the mother of the camps," was dead,[3] and her
resolute soul no longer sustained the courage of the gentle senator
whom she had made Emperor of Gaul. Having made his
residence at Bordeaux, so that he might not be disturbed by the
uproar on the frontier and the clamor of the legions, he waited
till Aurelian should come to relieve him of his imperial functions.
Medals represent him wearing, not the cuirass, but the toga, and
holding in one hand a sceptre, and in the other a cornucopia.
When, as they received their pay, the soldiers saw their Emperor
represented on the coin with the attributes of peace, and a
legend signifying that moderation in success makes a ruler great,
they must have regarded this gentle personage as unworthy to
have the command of men. They retained him, however; their
pride was gratified in maintaining the Gallic empire which they
had created. Both they and their chiefs had all their interests in
these provinces, where they had spent their whole lives, and they
said to each other that Tetricus would never disturb their tranquil
existence by leading them to the opposite end of the Empire to
fight with Persians or Blemmyes. Moreover, Gaul was also their
domain; they conducted themselves in it as masters, with all
the insolence of a soldiery commanding its officers. To resist
their demands, on one occasion Autun closed its gates; they
besieged the city for seven months, and Tetricus made no attempt
to end this strange war. Claudius, to whom Autun appealed,
was too much occupied by the Goths to listen to these far-off
complaints; the unhappy city was sacked,[4] and many of its

[1] Vopiscus, Aur. 29.
[2] See De Boze, Tetricus, in the Mem. de l'Acad. des inscr. xxxvi. 515 et seq. Numerous medals of this Emperor bear the words: ubertas, lætitia, felicitas publica, and milestones prove that he repaired the roads in Gaul in order to facilitate commerce.
[3] Certain accounts represent her as having been put to death by Tetricus,— which is improbable. He instituted solemn funeral ceremonies in her honor, and decreed her apotheosis (consecratio).
[4] Eumenes (Pan. vet. vii. 4; Gratiarum actio Constantino, and Pro Restaur. scholis, 11:

citizens perished (269). One of them fled as far as to the foot of the Pyrenees. to Tarbes, "which the Adour traverses, which hears afar the roar of angry Ocean;" the fugitive married there, and was the ancestor of the poet Ausonius, one of the last literary names of the Empire.[1] Other cities were of the same mind with Autun; an inscription at Barcelona attests the fidelity of this city to Claudius and to the Empire.[2]

The self-interested fidelity of the Gallic legions did not at all reassure their Emperor. We have reason to believe that he sought

ELEPHANTS ATTACHED TO A CHARIOT AND BEARING A TOWER.[3]

the confidence of Claudius by secret messages, and we know that, quoting Vergil. he wrote to Aurelian: "Invincible hero, deliver me from these miscreants."[4] An understanding was readily established between two men, one of whom had no wish for a colleague, while the other was eager to be again a subject. When the armies met, near Châlons-sur-Marne, Tetricus communicated his order of battle to Aurelian; and just as the action began, deserted his troops, who at once disbanded.[5] The whole Empire was again

represents certain Bagaudes, or insurgent peasants, as mingled with these soldiers (latrocinium Bagaudicæ rebellionis).

[1] Auson., Parent. 4. The poet states this flight as occurring under Victorinus.
[2] Orelli, No. 1.020.   [3] Engraved stone (La Chausse, Recueil, etc. vol. ii. pl. 129).
[4] Eripe me his, invicte, malis (words of Palinurus in the Aeneid, vi. 265).
[5] Aur. Victor, De Cæs, 35.

SARCOPHAGUS OF ALEXANDER SEVERUS AND MAMÆA (SO CALLED), MUSEUM OF THE CAPITOL. BOOK II.

united under a single chief (274); it was now twenty-one years since this had been the situation.

Aurelian celebrated the great event by a triumph, where he endeavored to surpass in magnificence those ancient solemnities which Rome had not for a long time seen.[1] Slowly there passed under the eyes of the dazzled crowd the innumerable wreaths of gold offered by the Roman cities; twenty elephants and giraffes, tamed animals; the chariot of a Gothic king drawn by four stags: that of the Queen of Palmyra, made of chased gold and silver, and gleaming with a thousand gems; pictures representing the battles won, the cities taken, and representations of conquered nations. Then followed the Senate, the magistrates, and the pontiffs; the people in white togas,

GOLD COIN.[2]

and the colleges or corporations, preceded by their banners; the army with its standards; the *cataphracti* with their heavy armor, and the soldiers with their military decorations; lastly, eight

THE YOUNGER TETRICUS.[3]

hundred pair of gladiators, followed by the crowd of captives of all nations adjacent to the Empire, some in chains, others bearing the captured spoils; and among them women of Gothic race who had been taken fighting among their fathers and husbands. But all eyes were fixed upon Tetricus and his son, who walked clad in the scarlet chlamys and wearing the Gallic braccae, that the crowd might recognize the Emperors of Gaul. Zenobia followed them, laden with precious stones, a gold chain on her feet, another on her hands, a third about her neck; and, as a last insult, it was a Persian buffoon who held up these chains, whose weight would have overwhelmed her, to recall to the fallen queen in what a vain hope she had trusted. We cannot doubt that Aurelian enjoyed his victory. More clement, however, than Marius and Caesar, he did

---

[1] Orosius (vii. 9) enumerates, from Romulus to Vespasian, three hundred and twenty triumphs, and Pitiscus (*Lex. Ant.*, s. v. *Triumphus*) has made out only thirty from Vespasian to Belisarius, who celebrated the last of them.

[2] The Elder Tetricus on Horseback.

[3] C. PIVS ESVVIVS TETRICVS CAES. Bust of the younger Tetricus, bare-headed, from a bronze medallion found on the banks of the Rhône at Andancette, the ancient *Figlinae*. (Museum of Grenoble, J. de Witte, *op. cit.*, pl. xlv. No. 4.)

not, as he went up to the Capitol, give the fatal sign ordering his captives to the Tullianum, where Jugurtha and Vercingetorix had perished.[1]

The pageant being ended, he gave back to Tetricus his honors, bestowed upon him a palace on the Caelian Mount, and appointed him governor of Lucania,[2] telling him it was better to rule over an Italian province than to reign on the other side of the Alps, — which the ex-Augustus did not contradict. The Emperor often called Tetricus his colleague, sometimes his comrade-in-arms, and even imperator; and these distinctions authorized the Senate, after the death of Aurelian, to place Tetricus among the *divi*.[3] Vercingetorix ended otherwise; but he had lived differently.

To Zenobia Aurelian also gave a villa near Tibur, in the neighborhood of that of Hadrian. She lived there like a Roman lady of rank, her daughters married into the most illustrious houses, and two centuries later some of the nobles of Rome called themselves descendants of the Queen of Palmyra; among them we know of one who was a contemporary of Saint Ambrose, Saint Zenobius, Bishop of Florence.[4]

The triumph had been the Emperor's festival; later the people had theirs, — scenic representations, great hunts, mock sea-fights, combats between gladiators, and gratuitous distributions. Aurelian decided that, for the future, citizens should receive every day a loaf of wheat bread and a piece of pork. All distributions were increased by an ounce; that is to say, a twelfth. He even formed the design of buying lands in Etruria and establishing a vast vineyard, so that he could give the people a measure of wine, as he did a measure of oil, daily.   A counsellor wiser than the

---

[1] It has been asserted that the arch of triumph whose remains are seen at Besançon was erected on occasion of this pageant.

[2] Treb. Pollio (*Tyr. trig.* 24) says "of all peninsular Italy." It is probable that we ought to read *corrector Italiae regionis Lucaniae*, as in the case of Postumius Titianus, consul in 301, who was *corrector Italiae regionis Transpadanae* (*C. I. L.* vi. 1418, 1419). Borghesi (*Œuvres*, ii. 416) forms out of the eleven *regiones* of Augustus in Italy eight provinces, which Diocletian retained.

[3] This at least seems to be inferable from the coins of Tetricus bearing the word *consecratio* (Cohen, v. 144.)   Cf. De Boze, *Hist. de Tétricus* in the *Mém. de l'Acad. des inscr.* xxvi. 521. Eckhel (vii. 457) differs from this opinion.

[4] Zosimus mentions only a son of Zenobia brought with her to Rome, but does not give his name, and says that the other captives were drowned in the Bosphorus. What was the end of Wahballath is not known; Eckhel (vii. 493) supposes that Aurelian gave him a principality in Syria.

Emperor opposed this project. "After this," said the praetorian prefect, "we should be obliged to give them also chickens and geese." Aurelian yielded; but he caused the treasury to offer wine at reduced price, — a measure of political economy almost equally objectionable. After food, clothes; he distributed tunics of Afri-

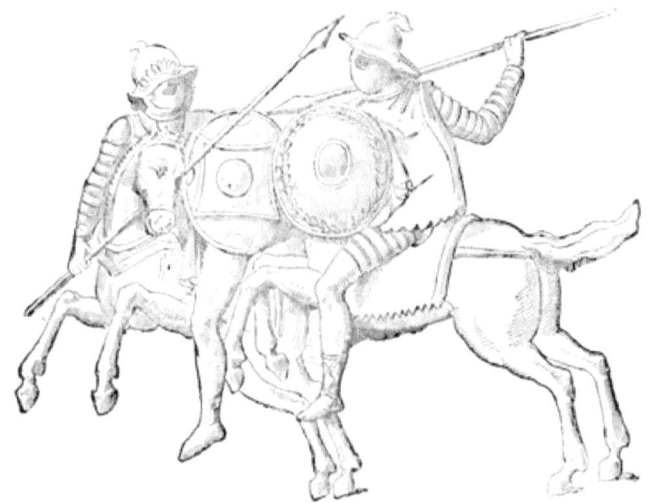

GLADIATORS ON HORSEBACK (POMPEII).

can linen, and long strips of cloth, "which they were to use in the circus, waving them to indicate their approbation."[1]

We have to remark here that these largesses to the populace were not actuated by a desire to win their favor. Aurelian's strength lay in the armies, it did not depend upon Rome; and in spite of his liberality towards the Romans, he was indifferent as to their good or ill will.

At Emesa Aurelian had come upon his mother's god, and he had attributed his victory to the Sun. The extravagances of Elaga-balus had not brought this divinity into disfavor; it was held in great honor. And this was natural; for as the pagan world

[1] . . . *Quibus uteretur populus ad favorem* (Vopiscus, *Aur.* 47). Formerly it had been a corner of the toga that was waved in sign of applause. After Aurelian's time the distribution of mere corn was certainly resumed. Theodoric gave a hundred and twenty thousand *modii* annually. Cf. Hirschfeld. pp. 20, 21.

was tending more and more to a belief in the divine unity, the Sun, shedding light, heat, and life through all nature, seemed the author of these gifts.[1] Aurelian had offered stately sacrifices to the Sun in Emesa, and he created at Rome a new priest-hood in the honor of this deity,[2] building a temple which was esteemed by contemporaries the most splendid in Rome, especially

THE SUN.[3]

on account of the vast wealth deposited in it, — a great quantity of gems, and fifteen thou-sand pounds weight of gold. Through fear of the jealousy of the other gods, Aurelian of-fered gifts in the temple of each.

So many prodigali-ties — not to speak of the money given to the people and the soldiers, or of the expense for the fortifications of Rome, for the cleansing of the Tiber, for the quays

which he constructed at certain points along the river, for the construction of thermae along the right bank, for that of a forum at Ostia, for the increase of the flotilla bringing to Rome the corn of the frumentary provinces — compel us to admit that the successful wars which Aurelian had carried on had placed great resources in his hands. Historians tell us only of the pillage of Palmyra; but Alexandria must have furnished large booty. Antioch, Ancyra, Tyana, the cities of Syria, at that time so prosperous, large ransoms, and Gaul, like Egypt, certainly paid for its return into the Empire by an increase in the taxes.

[1] This was Pliny's faith (*Hist. nat.* ii. 4), a philosopher who did not believe in many things.
[2] Vopiscus, *Aur.* 35.
[3] Marble medallion representing in relief the masque of the Sun, according to the type of the Rhodian coins (Roman sculpture in the Museum of the Louvre, Fröhner, *Notice de la sculpt. ant.*, etc., No. 421).

Aurelian's economy procured him other resources.   He lived simply, and required the persons around him to do likewise.   He kept his slaves in the same humble position they had held before his accession, and required the Empress to superintend the affairs of the palace; he refused her a silk mantle because at this time that material was worth its weight in gold, and he made his friends presents which gave them comfort, but not wealth, that envy might not be excited against

THE EMPRESS
SEVERINA.[1]

them.[2]   He himself never had a silver vase weighing over thirty pounds; the gods came into possession of the presents that were

SILVER VASE FROM THE HILDESHEIM TREASURE.[3]

made him.   All the magnificent objects displayed at his triumph were carried into the temples, as in the old days of republican virtue, to serve as resources in case of extreme peril.

Sumptuary laws were an evil common at Rome, and Aurelian did not fail to establish many.[4]   Thus, to guard against a scarcity of the

[1] SEVERINA AVG[usta].   Diademed bust of the Empress Severina, wife of Aurelian, placed on a crescent.   (Coin of copper alloy. Antoninianus of the weight of 4.05).

[2] . . . *Donarium insidiam patrimonii moderatione citarent* (Vopiscus, *Aur.* 45).

[3] Reproduction in the Museum of Cluny.

[4] Vopiscus, *Aur.* 45-6. Cf. Lamprid., *Elagabalus*, 4. He limited the number of eunuchs, etc.

precious metals, he forbade the use of gold on furniture and garments. His biographer goes so far as to assert that he renewed the women's senate to which Elagabalus had given the duty of regulating the matrons' toilettes,—a puerility which this soldier would never have copied from the effeminate Syrian. But he displayed great pomp in religious solemnities, where he appeared wearing a crown, and attired in garments covered with gold and precious stones. This Oriental luxury was the fashion of the day, reappearing even in the works of art,

AURELIAN.[1]

whose decline it marks, and Diocletian carried it much farther. These Emperors both believed they should be more respected if an imposing ceremonial marked distinctly to the eye the distance between the subject and the ruler.

This ostentation, often regarded as necessary, and really so in a certain social condition, has never been able, however, to protect any others than those who protected themselves by their personal valor, or whom the faith of nations surrounded with a sure though invisible defence. From this point of view Aurelian could have done without it, for he had the people and the troops on his side. An absolute ruler, however, is never secure against

FIGHTING HERO.[2]

---

[1] DEO ET DOMINO NATO AVRELIANO. Radiate head of the Emperor. (Small bronze.)

[2] Fighting hero, found near Vienna, in Dauphiny (*Gazette archéol.*, 1876). Clarac (*Musée de sculpt*, pl. 826, No. 2,083 B) has given this statue the name of Deiphobus.

conspiracies, and one was shortly to be formed among those immediately about him. The magnificent entertainment which he had just given the Romans preceded his death by only a few months.

Aurelian employed this time in consolidating the work of restoration which he had pursued so vigorously for the five years preceding. A sedition in Gaul called him into that country.[1] It is not known what he did there. We hear of a success of Probus over the Franks, near the mouths of the Rhine, and of a victory gained over the Alemanni near Vindonissa (Windisch) by Constantius Chlorus on the day when his son Constantine was born.

COIN OF
AURELIAN.[2]

Later traditions attribute to Aurelian the reconstruction of Dijon and of Genabum, which seems to have taken his name, *Civitas Aurelianorum*. These were two important positions for commerce and war: at Orléans, the geographic centre of Gaul, ended the principal military roads of the country, and Dijon was the great station between the valley of the Rhône and that of the Seine. Forum Julii and the Viennese province owed him perhaps some favor; inscriptions found there celebrate the Restorer of the World.

Aurelian doubtless revisited the banks of the Rhine, the theatre of his earliest successes; then he repaired to the upper Danube, for we find him afterwards in Vindelicia and Illyricum. He wished to inspect personally this frontier, which had been lately so disturbed, where it was well also from time to time to exhibit the imperial crown, especially when worn by a conqueror. Aurelian had the intention of doing more than this, and was about to go as far as Ctesiphon for the purpose of visiting upon the allies of Zenobia the injuries they had done the Empire; but he was stopped by a conspiracy before reaching Byzantium.

Ecclesiastical authors assert that divine justice put a stop to his evil designs against the Church.[3] The Emperor's conduct in

[1] Zonaras, xii. 27.

[2] Reverse of a coin (small bronze) of Aurelian, bearing the legend: GENIVS ILLVR.

[3] Euseb., *Hist. eccl.* vii. 30, and Zonaras, xii. 27. In book viii. chap. iv. Eusebius says that from the time of Decius and Valerian until the last years of Diocletian, the devil slept, and Sulpicius Severus, who lived in Gaul, makes no mention of the great persecution which has been placed in Aurelian's reign.

the affair of Paul of Samosata, the peace which the Christians
enjoyed during his reign, forbid us to believe that he was proposing to undertake a persecution: and to account for his death
it is not necessary to employ the method which in all ages has
been used to explain sudden catastrophes. Following the example
of Septimius Severus, whom he seems to have taken for a model,
he maintained discipline in the administration as well as in the
army; he kept watch over the imperial agents in the provinces,
and punished extortioners rigorously, even going so far as to put
them to death by crucifixion. Having cause for displeasure against
one of his secretaries, Mnestheus, he threatened him with punishment. The freedman knew that the Emperor spoke no idle words;
he counterfeited Aurelian's handwriting, prepared a list of persons
known to be out of favor, placing his own name on the list to
make the story more credible, and exhibited it to the persons
whose names were inscribed thereon, as an order of death which
he had discovered. To escape from the punishment which they
believed impending over them, these persons conspired and assassinated Aurelian (January or March, 275). He was but sixty-one
years of age, and had reigned five years.

During the reign of Aurelian there was a sedition of a peculiar
character. We have seen [1] how greatly in these times the gold
and silver coins had been altered. The master of the Roman
mints, Felicissimus, had formed the idea of sharing in the profits
which the Emperors believed they were making by this scandalous
operation. Very little gold and silver was furnished him for the
coin he had to make; he put into it even less, and doubtless
associated with himself as sharers in the profits those who were
employed under him. Otherwise it is difficult to understand why a
sedition should have broken out when Aurelian sought to bring this
abuse to an end.[2] The revolt was formidable; the manufacturers
interested in the trade in precious metals, the silversmiths and
goldsmiths, the bankers, and all who handled silver, threatened

---

[1] pp. 209 et seq.

[2] . . . *Monetae opifices qui, quum, auctore Felicissimo rationali, nummariam notam cor-*
rasissent, poenae metu bellum fecerunt (Aur. Victor, *Caes.* 35). Cf. Vopiscus, *Aur.* 38. The
procurator monetae, of equestrian rank, commanded a whole army of workmen. Upon this
organization, see *Mém. de l'Acad. des inscr.* ix. 218; Fr. Lenormant, *La Monnaie dans*
l'Antiquité, i. 251; and Cuq, the *Examinator per Italiam*, p. 36.

with reforms which were likely to unsettle the market, appear
to have made common cause with the officers of the mint; and
the people, as usual, interested themselves in the quarrel, through
hatred of the police. A battle actually took place in Rome, on the
Caelian hill, and seven thousand soldiers perished in it, — which
implies great carnage among the rebels.

We are very ignorant in respect to this affair.[1] Was the
Senate concerned in it? Possibly; for old authors mention the
execution of many senators, without telling us the cause, and
the Senate itself lost at this time the right it had possessed since
the time of Augustus to coin bronze money. At least we find no
longer, after the reign of Aurelian, the letters S. C. on coins, — a
proof that the senatorial mints were united after this time to those
of the Emperor.[2] The biographer of Aurelian adds that the Emperor
afterwards coined better money, and withdrew the false from
circulation. Aurelian had not time to accomplish this double
work, which Tacitus took up after him,[3] and to which succeeding
Emperors devoted much care, — without, however, completing it
until the reigns of Diocletian and Constantine.

These measures prove the resolution of Aurelian to introduce
order everywhere. The same spirit manifests itself in other acts.
He caused to be burned in Trajan's forum, as Hadrian had done
before him, the registers containing the accounts of the debtors of
the state, — bad debts, and for the most part irrecoverable, but
holding over a number of private individuals the perpetual fear of
a judicial execution. The lodging of information against those
violating the fiscal laws was forbidden. The *quadruplatores* —
always so numerous at Rome — did not disappear at once, but their
odious trade ceased to be encouraged. It is impossible that the

---

[1] The letter of Aurelian to the Roman people after the defeat of Firmus (see Vol.
VI. p. 211) gives reason to suppose that the Senate, the knights, the people, and the praetorians were not amicable towards one another, since the Emperor recommends concord to
them.

[2] The *triumviri monetales* disappeared at the same time; the last known, with certain date,
was consul in 225 (Willmans, No. 1,211).

[3] . . . *Cavit* (Tacitus) *ne si quis argenti publici privatimque aes miscuisset, si quis aere
argentum, si quis aeri plumbum, capitale esset cum bonorum proscriptione* (Vopiscus, *Tac.* 9).
From this attempt resulted a little more regularity in the coinage. The Antoniniani of
Aurelian, of Tacitus, and of Claudius II. are somewhat more valuable than those of their
predecessors. Cf. Mommsen, *Geschichte des röm. Münz.* iii. 96.

author of these measures could have put to death, in order to fill his treasury, senators guilty only of wealth.

Aurelian is however accused of cruelty, and as early as the fourth century this reproach rested upon his memory. Certainly he was not a mild ruler; but the times were not suited for mild government, and in a monarch responsible for the tranquillity of an empire, indulgence towards the guilty was treason towards the innocent. To confirm the reproaches made against him we need to have the names and number of the victims, the motives or the pretexts of their condemnation; for we have learned in the course of this history, from more than one instance, how little is left of these vague and often contradictory accusations when examined narrowly. Vopiscus, who had conversed with contemporaries of the Emperor whose memoir he writes, dares not affirm anything. "It is said," he relates, "that to rid himself of many senators he imputed to them designs of revolt;" but according to John of Antioch and Suidas, some men of rank were condemned on the revelations of Zenobia,—which gives us reason to think that during the war in the East plots had been formed at Rome, as in the time of Severus during the war in Gaul.[1] One fact justifies our hesitations. It is certain that a catastrophe took place in the imperial family, one member of it being condemned to death. Who was this person? Some say the niece, and some the nephew of Aurelian; others maintain that both perished; and still others assert that the person condemned was the daughter-in-law of the Emperor.[2] If this last story be the true one, it would seem that Aurelian, by this execution, avenged some stain upon the honor of his house. In any case, it was a domestic tragedy having some grave cause, for Aurelian was not one of those madmen who for a caprice shed the blood of their own family.

The Emperor Titus is not our ideal of a ruler: and we shall therefore not reproach Aurelian with having chastised offenders like the accomplices of Felicissimus, or promoters of revolution like those who doubtless intrigued with Zenobia. We shall commend him for having given up his freedmen and slaves to

---

[1] We have also seen that Zosimus speaks of many plots, admitting their existence.

[2] Suidas, s. v. Aurel. But another difficulty arises; for, according to Vopiscus, Aurelian had no children except one daughter.

the ordinary judge when they were guilty, for the imperial household had need to be always held strictly in hand, that they
should not avail themselves of the numerous means of doing harm
which came within their reach; and we shall accept the judgment of the Emperor Julian, who was not inclined to be favorable
towards a ruler whose glory eclipsed that of Claudius, the head
of his own house. In the *Cæsars*, when Aurelian appears before
the Olympian areopagus to be judged, the Sun takes up his
defence. "The accused," he says to the gods, "is even with
Justice, or you have forgotten my oracle of Delphi: a man ought
to suffer the woes he has caused others to endure."[1]

This judgment seems even too severe; for at the side of
the strict right, Aurelian often placed clemency for those who
had gone astray. We have seen him accord pardon to all the
inhabitants of Antioch, and to the Palmyrenes after the first siege;
we have seen that even after the second revolt he put a stop to
the massacre; and at Alexandria he allowed part of those who
were besieged to go out from the Bruchium,[2] although their
departure must have permitted the resistance to be prolonged.
His conduct in respect to Tetricus, Zenobia, and Antiochus[3]
contrasts favorably with that of his predecessors, and he violated
Roman customs even more evidently when he proclaimed an
amnesty for political offences.[4] It was a worthy completion of
the restoration of the Empire thus to efface the traces of twenty
years of civil wars, during which many more persons had been
unfortunate than criminal.

[1] Vopiscus says nearly the same thing (*Aur.* 37): *Aurelianus fuit princeps necessarius magis quam bonus.*

[2] See p. 310, note 4, which explains that this act of clemency was not perhaps Aurelian's.

[3] Antiochus is that Palmyrene Cæsar "whom he sent away," says Zosimus, "not deigning to punish."

[4] *Amnestia sub eo delictorum publicorum decreta est* (Vopiscus, *Aur.* 39).

CHAPTER XCVIII.

TACITUS, PROBUS, AND CARUS (275-284 A.D.).

I.— An Attempt at a Senatorial Restoration ; Tacitus and Florianus (Sept. 25, 275, to July, 276).

THE death of Aurelian was followed by a strange situation, — for six months the Empire remained without a head. He had restored order with so vigorous a hand that all things went on as if he were still alive: the magistrates remained in the exercise of their functions ; the people in their respective occupations ; and, strangest of all, the army in a state of subordination. This peace during a long interregnum — the first and only one that the Empire ever knew — speaks more in praise of Aurelian than all our eulogies. At last men recognized in him the restorer of the Empire, the ruler who had put an end to usurpations, had pacified the provinces, had given back their military honor to the legions, and to Rome its grandeur. There was for the moment something like a new birth of public spirit and patriotism. The army, ashamed that it had not been able to preserve its illustrious chief from a vulgar conspiracy, punished itself by refusing to exercise the right which seemed to have become its recognized prerogative, — namely, that of electing an emperor ; and the Senate received with amazement the following communication:[1] "The Brave and Fortunate Legions to the Senate and People of Rome: The crime of one man and the inconsiderateness of many have deprived us of our late Emperor Aurelian ; you, whose paternal cares direct the state, honored men, deign to place this Emperor among the number of the gods, and to designate the successor whom you judge most worthy of the imperial purple ; none of those

---

[1] By letter (Vopiscus, *Aur.* 41), or by a deputation from the army (Aur. Victor).

whose crime or whose misfortune has caused our loss shall reign
over us."

The Conscript Father to whom his rank gave the right of express-
ing his opinion first, an old man of consular rank, by name Tacitus,[1] believed to be a descendant of the great historian, proposed to
gratify the wish of the legions in respect to the honors to be
decreed to the dead Emperor, and Aurelian was deified upon
the spot; but in the matter of the second request, the prudent
senator knew that to yield to it would be dangerous for the man
whom the Senate should choose, perhaps even for the Senate itself,
since the soldiers would not long maintain this attitude of repent-
ance and humility. The choice was therefore sent back again to
the army; but the latter persisted in its determination, — a way of
commanding under a new form.

A few patriotic generals — to whom, moreover, the number of
imperial deaths in so few years made it evident that the purple
was likely to change quickly into a shroud — had been the determining agents in this conduct of the army, and now made the
soldiery persevere in it. The senators were even less covetous
of this perilous honor. Tacitus, the one among them who was
most likely to be chosen, by reason of his name, his honors, and
his fortune,[2] had taken shelter, after the session of the Senate,
in one of his villas in Campania. The consul's order convoking
the assembly for the 25th of September drew him reluctantly
thence. In his address the consul Gordianus spoke with some
discreet doubt of the persevering moderation of the soldiers.
"Let us give a leader to the armies," he said; and he prudently added: "Either they will accept him whom you have
chosen, or they will name another." He then called attention to
the Barbaric nations, which lay around the Empire, making new
efforts to break into it, — Persia, so lately threatened by Aurelian,
perhaps meditating an attack, while the Syrians, a fickle race, were
ready to guide her squadrons across the provinces; the Egyptian
and Illyrian frontiers endangered; the Rhine crossed by the

---

[1] Upon coins and inscriptions he is called M. Claudius Tacitus.

[2] It seems impossible to accept the statement in the *Augustan History* with respect to the
fortune of Tacitus, *quod habuit in reditibus, sestertium bis milies oetingenties* (*Tac.* 10.), but we
are not able to substitute another. It is certain, from what afterwards occurred, that the
fortune was immense.

Franks, and once flourishing Gallic cities now in ashes. "We need an emperor," he exclaimed; and turning to Tacitus, with all the other senators, he added: "It is you whom we require." Vainly did the old man of seventy-five plead his age, his enfeebled health, and his pacific tastes. "You need a soldier," he said; "and you choose me, who am hardly able to fill the peaceful office of senator. The very unanimity of your choice will be fatal to me." But the senators would not listen to him; acclamations, twenty or thirty times repeated, hailed him Emperor; and the report of this session of the Senate, which to some seemed to open a new era, was written, according to custom, on an ivory tablet, which the new Augustus signed, his soul filled with sad presentiments.[1]

No doubt it was an error to give the Empire a chief like this; and since, as a result of the decree of Gallienus,[2] there could be found in the Senate no bold soldier, it would have been the proper course to seek one in the armies. Probus, Carus, Diocletian, had none of them been concerned at all in the murder of Aurelian, and the army would have been grateful to have its momentary disinterestedness applauded, without such action on the part of the Senate as must have caused the soldiery immediately to repent of their late conduct. The choice of an eminent soldier at this time made by the Senate would have been to seal, at least for the moment, a reconciliation between the civil and the military orders. But living, as they did, remote from public affairs, in their idle grandeur and their gilded servitude, the senators had lost their grasp of the actual world, and no man reminded them of the day — which many among them had seen, however — when the soldiers dragged to the Gemoniae Maximus and Balbinus, and shouted: "These are the Senate's Emperors!" At first rendered anxious and uneasy by the political duties which fell to them again, they had ended by resuming their old illusions, and abandoned themselves to the puerile delight of again grasping a power which they were incapable of retaining.

The senator next in rank to Tacitus, Falconius Nicomachus, reminded the Senate of the woes that Rome had suffered under too

---

[1] Vopiscus (*Tac.* 5) read this report in the Ulpian library.   [2] See p. 239.

youthful rulers, — which was at once a truth and a flattery; then addressing himself to Tacitus, whose sons were only boys, Falconius besought him, if the fates should soon snatch him from the state, to choose a successor, not from his own family, but from outside, "for the reason that it would not be right to dispose of the Empire as of a private estate." Falconius meant to imply that the electoral power should remain with the Senate; and the general opinion was with him. Loud cries of assent were heard from all parts of the curia.

The Conscript Fathers were enraptured at the turn events had taken. In the excess of his joy and of his hopes, one of them wrote to a less enthusiastic colleague: "Lay aside your indolence; come forth from your retreat at Baiae or Puteoli. Give yourself back to the city, the Senate. Rome flourishes, and with Rome the whole state. Let us give a thousand thanks to the army, which is a truly Roman army. Our just authority, that object of all our desires, is at last

THE EMPEROR TACITUS, LAURELLED.[1]

re-established. We receive appeals, we appoint emperors, we make kings. Can we not also unmake them? You understand me without further speech; to the wise, a word is enough."[2] This word was repeated by all the writer's colleagues. "I shall rule with and through you," Tacitus had said. When he asked the consulship for his brother Florianus, it was objected that the list was full; and he contented himself with replying: "The Senate knows well the Emperor it has made." Notwithstanding his new title, the feeble old man was really to the Senate only its first member, and it was said openly that the true ruler was now the Senate itself.[3]

Official letters made known this restoration of the Roman Republic to the chief cities of the Empire, — Milan, Aquileia, Athens, Corinth, Thessalonica, Antioch, Alexandria, Carthage, and Trèves. Two of these we have; the following is the one addressed to the capital of Roman Africa: —

[1] Bronze medallion.   [2] Vopiscus, Tac. 6 and 7; Flor. 6.
[3] ... Ipsum senatum principem factum (Vopiscus, Tac. 12).

" The honorable Senate of Rome to the decurions of Carthage:

" Peace and happiness, security and prosperity, to the Republic and to the Roman world.

" We have recovered the right of conferring the imperial authority of appointing the ruler, the Augustus; it is to us, therefore, that you will submit affairs of importance. Appeals from proconsular decisions and from all the tribunals of the Empire will be laid before the urban prefect. Your own authority is restored to its former condition, since in recovering its own rights the first body of the Republic protects the rights of others." And men clothed themselves in holiday attire, and sacrificed white victims to thank the gods for the return of the ancient liberty;[1] medals were struck whereon it was promised to this Emperor, who already had one foot in the grave, that in due time the *decennalia*[2] should be celebrated for him. Alas! the election of Tacitus, these ostentatious messages and these vain promises, were the last political act of the Roman Republic.

The praetorians, the people, and the armies accepted the Emperor chosen by those who had in earlier days been the masters of Rome,[3] and the inhabitants of the Empire swore fidelity to him. All things seemed to go well. But the Alani, seeing the Empire without a leader and defenceless, had invaded Asia Minor, whither the Goths, encamped in the vicinity of the Palus Maeotis, followed them. Tacitus was obliged to journey in haste to the scene of action. In Thrace he presented himself before Aurelian's army, which must have been astonished to see this feeble old man in the place where they had seen so long the martial figure of the iron-handed hero. Accordingly, the praetorian prefect essayed by humble words to prevent discontent. " Most virtuous comrades,"[4] he said, " you have asked the Senate to give you an Emperor; the very illustrious assembly has obeyed your will and command. It is not fitting for me to say more in the presence of the Emperor who will watch over us. Listen to him with the respect that he merits." Tacitus in his turn was extremely

---

[1] . . . *Antiquitatem sibi redditam* (Vopiscus, *Flor.* 6).   [2] Eckhel, vii. 498.

[3] In addressing the praetorians, Tacitus said *sanctissimi milites*, and in speaking to the plebeians he called them *sacratissimi Quirites*.   Oriental bombast extended to all men. Modern Italy has preserved something of it to this day.

[4] *Sanctissimi commilitones* (Vopiscus, *Tac.* 8).

modest; he feigned to consider himself the choice of the soldiers, and spoke in fitting terms on the subject of his age: it did not permit him, he said, to imitate the great exploits of his predecessors, but would inspire him with wise counsels. " Trajan also was an old man when he came to the Empire, and was called to it by the choice of one individual. Now it is by you first, most virtuous comrades, by you who know how to judge the worth of a ruler, and in the second place by the Senate, that I have been esteemed worthy of this title." It was imprudent to evoke in the midst of these troops the grand figure of the conqueror of the Dacians, the Germans, and the Parthian Empire; but the liberal *donativum*, which Tacitus paid with his own money, made the address seem eloquent.

The Barbarians made pretence that they had been summoned by the late Emperor as auxiliaries to give help against Persia. Not receiving the pay promised for an expedition which had not been made, they indemnified themselves by the pillage of Pontus, Galatia, and Cappadocia. Bold predatory bands penetrated even into Cilicia before Aurelian had been many months dead. What incessant vigilance was needful to keep in check those innumerable freebooters who prowled around the Empire, and, under Gallienus, had become familiar with all its roads! Tacitus negotiated; he paid and sent home some of these Barbarians; others fell under the swords of his soldiers. But the latter were already becoming weary of obedience; they murdered one of the Emperor's kindred whom Tacitus had intrusted with the government of Syria, and after that, to escape punishment, the Emperor himself. A six months' reign, and a colossal fortune dissipated in gifts to the soldiery or abandoned to the state,[1] were what the Senate's election had procured for Tacitus and his family.

He was a man of upright character and religious mind; never did he omit to have served in his house the meat of the sacrifices, — a sort of communion with the god to whom the sacrifice had been offered. He punished some of the murderers of his predecessor, and it cannot be denied that his intentions were of the best. His biographer attributes to him many statutes; but statutes are easily made, and he had neither the ability nor the time to bring out good results

---

[1] *Patrimonium suum publicavit* (Vopiscus, *Tac.* 10).

to the state.   For one act. however, we owe him special gratitude, — he caused the works of Tacitus to be placed in all the public libraries, and ordered ten copies of them to be made every year.   In mul-

tiplying thus the copies of the *Annals* and the *Histories* he increased the chance of their preservation; and while we cannot say that the single manuscript which has saved this great writer's work is derived from one of these, it is at least possible that without them we should have lost the tragic history of the Caesars.[1]

BRONZE MEDALLION.[2]

Tacitus had appointed as praetorian prefect his brother, M. Annius Florianus, and the latter now obtained the purple from his soldiers, who were themselves desirous not to leave the Senate time again to appoint an Emperor.   But the army of the East had at this time as general a brave soldier whose services had always been greater than his honors.   At the

news that Tacitus was dead. the troops of Probus proclaimed their general Emperor. and those of Florianus rid themselves at Tarsus of him whom they had chosen (July, 276). He had reigned three months. Upon their estate near Interamna was raised to the two brothers a cenotaph and statues thirty feet high   Doubtless to console their descendants. whom these nine months of the imperial dignity had deprived of the heads of their family and reduced to in-

BRONZE MEDALLION.[3]

digence. some friend of the Senate put in circulation this prophecy. which Vopiscus hands down to us: "A thousand years hence a mighty prince of the blood of Tacitus. after a glorious reign. will give back to the Conscript Fathers their authority. and, a true son of early Rome. will live submissive to the good old customs of the country."   "I do not anticipate." says Vopiscus modestly. "that my book will live long enough for men to read this prediction

---

[1] Two mediæval MSS. are the sole authorities for the text of his works, each containing a portion only; and they do not duplicate each other, so that we depend on one MS. for all that we have.

[2] M. ANN[ius] FLORIANVS, crowned with laurel.

[3] The Emperor Probus, laurelled, with pike and buckler.

at the time when it will either be seen to be fulfilled or will take its place among fables." Vopiscus was mistaken: his book has lived much longer than a thousand years, although without greatly deserving to do so; but the avenger of the Senate has never appeared.[1]

II. — PROBUS (JULY, 276, TO SEPTEMBER OR OCTOBER, 282).

THE reigns of Tacitus and Florianus had been only a continuation of the interregnum. The real successor of Aurelian was one of his compatriots and his bravest comrade in arms. M. Aurelius Probus.[2] We already know him; two letters of Valerian, drawn from the imperial archives, show in what esteem he was held by this Emperor, one of whose relatives Probus had with his own hand rescued from the Quadi: "In accordance with the opinion I have always had of young Probus, and the testimony of the most honorable citizens, who

COIN OF PROBUS.[3]

call him the man of his name, I have appointed him tribune, contrary to the ordinance of the divine Hadrian,[4] and have intrusted to him six cohorts of Saracens, the Gallic auxiliaries, and the Persian cavalry brought to us by the Syrian Artavasdes." Aurelian and Tacitus had had like confidence in him. The former wrote to him: "To show you how greatly I value your merits, I intrust to you my Tenth legion, which I myself received from Claudius. By a sort of happy accident this corps has always had future Emperors for leaders;" and the latter: "The Senate has appointed me Emperor; but know this, that the greater part of the burden

---

[1] I have followed the rendering some have given to the words *talis historia*, but without certainty whether it be not to the prediction itself that they apply rather than to the book of Vopiscus. It is, however, unimportant.

[2] Probus was born at Sirmium (Vopiscus, *Prob.* 3). Aurelius Victor (*Ep.* 37) makes him a Dalmatian. His father was a centurion, and later a tribune. One of his coins bears the words *Origini Aug.*, with the she-wolf, *Lupa geminos lactans*; whence it may be inferred that he claimed to be of Roman origin (Eckhel, vii. 505).

[3] Reverse of a coin of Probus, of the type of the she-wolf coins, and bearing the legend: ORIGINI AVG. (Small bronze.)

[4] The one which prohibited the appointment of too youthful tribunes (*sine barba*). Some sentences from the two letters of Valerian are here put together (Vopiscus, *Prob.* 4). The second contains the enumeration, always curious and significant, of the articles furnished See p. 190, note 2.

will rest upon your shoulders. We all know your worth. Aid us then in our times of need. I have given you the command of the army in the East.[1] I have increased your emoluments five-fold,[2] doubled your military decorations, and you will share with me the consulship of the coming year."

Probus did not desire the Empire. "You make a mistake," he said to the soldiers who saluted him, "for I shall never flatter you." He said the same to the praetorian prefect of Florianus, whom he did not remove from office. "I did not wish for this title, and it is contrary to my desire that it is given me. But I am not at liberty to refuse the burden which the army lays upon me; it is now a question of fulfilling my duty well." He was in the prime of life, forty-four years of age, and to his military abilities he joined uncommon good sense, which preserved him from being dazzled at his elevation. What took place upon the death of Aurelian shows that a reaction against military saturnalia had begun in the minds even of the generals.[3] Probus was one of those who felt most keenly the necessity of raising the civil order, humiliated since the time of Cara-calla by the arrogance of the soldiery. This appears from his letter, in which, while notifying the Senate of his accession, he seems to await from it the conferring of authority. "When you made choice of one of your own number, Conscript Fathers," he wrote, "to succeed the Emperor Aurelian, you acted in conformity with your usual rectitude and wisdom; for you are the lawful rulers of the world, and the authority which you hold from your ancestors you will transmit to your posterity. Would to the gods that Florianus, instead of seizing upon his brother's purple as an inheritance, had waited until your sovereign will had decided either in his favor or for some one else! The legions have done well to punish him for his rashness; they have offered me the title of Augustus, but I submit to your clemency my claims and my services."

---

[1] *Dereta totius Orientis ducatu* (Vopiscus, *Prob.* 7).

[2] *Salarium.* According to a letter of Valerian (*id., Prob.* 4), the *salarium* would include all the material advantages attached to the grade, and probably also the pay.

[3] It is perhaps another sign of this same reaction in men's minds that the name of Marcus Aurelius had been borne by most of the Emperors after Claudius Gothicus. Notwithstanding his wars, Marcus Aurelius was eminently the representative of civil order.

This letter does honor to the statecraft of this soldier. He knew the Senate's weakness, and was perfectly aware that he had nothing to fear from it; but this decrepit body had still the grandeur of ancient memories, and Probus deemed it wise to restore, before the eyes of the soldiery, some splendor to this overclouded majesty, that they might see that outside of them and above them there existed, if not a power, at least a right.

It is needless to say with what acclamations the senators welcomed this letter. Probus was likened to Alexander and to Trajan; he was accredited with all the virtues of the Antonines and all the talents of Claudius and Aurelian, and he merited these eulogies. What joy again when a second message announced that the Senate was to receive appeals, to appoint proconsuls and their legates, and finally (which was a more important thing), that it was to confirm the imperial ordinances! This the Conscript Fathers had never gone so far as to claim. Probus granted them more than they themselves had sought to take upon Aurelian's death; and the senatorial restoration seemed complete. In reality no change at all was made. The Emperor employed towards the venerable assembly gentle words instead of an air of displeasure: the Fathers no longer trembled; they seemed more active in their curule chairs, and they praised in good faith the unselfishness of the new Emperor. Probus asked nothing more than this, and he did not feel that with a few acts of deference he paid too dearly for this good under-

PROBUS.[1]

---

[1] Marble bust. Museum of Naples. No. 32 of the Catalogue.

standing. The reality of power remained where the public weal demanded that it should be, — in his hands;
and we shall see that he used it well.

Upon the death of Aurelian the Barbarians had fallen upon Gaul and had devastated many Gallic cities.[1] Probus went
thither with a large army. While his
generals were driving back the Franks into
the marshes of Batavia and Frisia, he himself drove the Alemanni across the Rhine,
pursued them into the valley of the
Neckar and over the slopes of the Suabian
Alps, taking from them their booty and the
captives whom they were carrying away.
In the hope of closing the road against new
incursions, he repaired the line of defence
which protected the Decumatian lands from
Ratisbon to Mayence; that is to say, from
the Danube to the Rhine.[2] Like Marius
and Hadrian, he believed that to keep the
soldiers busy was the best means of preserving discipline; he therefore caused them to
construct or repair a stone wall having large
towers at regular intervals, — an excellent
precaution if there were always a strong
army behind this rampart, ready to repulse
any assailants who might attempt to
break through it, but a useless measure
when the Empire, assailed on all sides,
was able to leave there only detachments

TRIUMPHAL COLUMN.[3]

too feeble to guard this immense line.[4] The wall, in fact, crum-

[1] Vopiscus, *Probus*; in chap. xv. it is said seventy; in chap. xiii., sixty. Vopiscus adds
that Probus destroyed four hundred thousand Barbarians; I am disposed to read *quadraginta*
instead of *quadringenta*. These four hundred thousand men killed would suppose a more formidable invasion than that of the Goths in the time of Claudius II, and nothing indicates
that this was so.

[2] On the subject of these works, see Vol. V. p. 190, and the map on p. 185.

[3] Column commemorative of the victories of Probus over the Alemanni (?), found at
Merten, near Metz (restoration from the *Revue archéol.*).

[4] At the present day the republic of Buenos Ayres adopts the same method of defence

bled under the feet of the invaders, like Hadrian's wall in Britain before the advancing Picts. But as late as the Middle Ages the Suabian peasant, building his hovel with the stones taken from these ruins, marvelled at the grandeur of the work, crossing valleys and passing over hill-tops; he attributed its construction to demons, and it has always been called the Devil's Wall.

These gigantic works, and the presence of the Emperor and his army, intimidated the Barbarians; nine tribes sought for peace, and gave hostages and corn, cattle and horses, their sole wealth. Probus received into pay sixteen thousand of their warriors, whom he scattered through his legions in small bands, so that they might be a power and not a danger; and he expressed this in words: " It is well to feel them, but not to see them " (277). Thus the Empire, on the side of the Rhine, again assumed a vigorous defensive.

The following year Probus visited Rhaetia, Illyricum, and Moesia, where the Alemanni, the Burgundians, the Vandals, the Sarmatians, and the Goths had reappeared; he drove out these unimportant bands, and once more restored security to these countries, where for the last forty years life had been so perilous. On the middle or lower Danube he encountered a German nation, the Lygians, whom Tacitus represents as having a frightful aspect, which in the hand-to-hand encounters of ancient war might well intimidate the adversary. " They blacken their shields, their bodies, their faces, and choose the darkest night to make their attack. The surprise, the horror produced by darkness, the mere aspect of this terrific host, which seems to have emerged from the infernal regions, chill with fear the bravest heart: for in battle it is always the eyes which are conquered first." [1] These black warriors did not, however, prevail against Roman discipline. From the time of this collision their name disappears from history, as if the nation itself had been utterly destroyed. Probus had promised his soldiers a piece of gold for each head of an enemy brought to him. In the case of the prisoners taken from all these barbarous tribes, he gave them lands in Britain, where they proved faithful to the master

against the Indians of the pampas; and China has done the same for centuries with her great wall. These lines of defence do not always prevent incursions, but they embarrass the invaders' return.

[1] Tac., *Germania*, 43.

who would have been able to punish them with severity in case
of disobedience.

After having tranquillized Thrace, long harassed by the
barbarous tribes of this country, whom Graeco-Roman civilization had not yet been able to transform into ,peaceful labor-
ers, he passed over into Asia Minor (279), and put an end to
the exploits of Palfurius, a famous brigand, and especially to those
of the Isaurians, inveterate freebooters, who pillaged by land and
sea, and who up to this time had never been subjugated. Probus
organized an expedition against them, penetrated into their mountains, searched through all their valleys, and when he withdrew
left behind him a force of veterans.[1]   These soldiers he established
in the principal haunt of the bandits, and distributed lands among

COIN OF BAHRAM OR
VARANES II.[2]

them, with the condition that their sons, on attaining the age of eighteen, should serve in the legions. This was like instituting military fiefs.
He probably imposed similar conditions on the
captives whom he had transported into Britain.
Severus had set an example of this tenure of land,
and the usage was destined to increase.

In Syria, Probus received a Persian embassy.
Bahram II., who had reigned since 275, had had
time to learn the value of the legions led by a brave and able
general. He begged for the friendship of Probus, and sent him
presents, which the Emperor scornfully refused. "I am surprised,"
Probus said, "that you send me so little, when all that you have
will one day belong to me. Keep it until it suits my convenience
to come and take it." This was bluster, but it was suited to the
Oriental taste; and the condition of the Roman fortresses in Mesopotamia, together with the menacing[3] preparations which were going
forward, decided Bahram not to resent this insolence, — and it even
appears that a treaty was concluded between the two empires.[4]

---

[1] Zosimus, i. 69-70. This author relates at length the desperate resistance made by Lydios,
one of the Isaurian chiefs, at Cremna, in Pisidia.

[2] Heads of Varanes or Bahram II. and the queen, with the legend: The worshipper of
Ormuzd, the excellent Varanes, king of the kings of Iran and Turan, germ of the gods. The
reverse bears: The divine Varanes, and a pyre between two figures. (Silver coin.)

[3] A coin of Probus bears on the reverse: *Exercitus Persicus* (Eckhel, vii. 504).

[4] *Facta pace cum Persis* (Vopiscus, *Prob.* 18).

Did the Emperor then proceed into Egypt, or did he send one of his lieutenants to call to account Coptos, Ptolemais, and the Blemmyes for assistance rendered some years before to Firmus? This we do not know; but Rome shortly beheld in her streets negro captives who had been taken on the borders of Ethiopia.

Probus had now completed, as Aurelian, Severus, and Hadrian had done, the review of the frontiers, — those of Africa excepted, where all was tranquil. This had become a periodical necessity, since the Barbaric world was astir, and always ready to attack the provinces.

The Emperor was recalled into Thrace to effect an important work. The invasions and battles which for half a century had been incessant along the whole line of the Danube had made many parts of these provinces desolate. Probus resolved to call the Barbarians into this portion of the Empire and give them lands, cattle, and farming implements. He had already transported Lygians and Vandals into Britain, and had advised the Alemanni to settle in the Decumatian lands. The hostility of the Goths of Dacia towards the Bastarnae, who occupied the eastern Carpathians, gave him the occasion to bring into the Empire this latter tribe, the remnant of that great mass of Gallic nations whom we have seen, in the time of Alexander and Perseus, established in the valley of the Danube.

A hundred thousand Bastarnae, with their wives and children, came down into Thrace, where, happy at escaping from their enemies, they adapted themselves readily to this new life. Rome rejoiced. "For us the Barbarians labor," it was said; "for us they sow."[1] The same attempt was made in the case of the Gepidae, the Guthunges (Goths), and the Frankish prisoners. It was a dangerous system; thus to fill the frontier provinces with foreign elements was equivalent to making the Barbarians the warders at the gates of the Empire. This peaceful invasion, which the Emperor himself organized, far from hindering the other, which was made with violence a century later, facilitated it. Ancient Rome had had a different policy: she Latinized conquered regions; Probus Germanized Roman provinces.[2]

These Barbarians established in the provinces did not always

---

[1] *Barbari nobis arant, nobis serunt* (Vopiscus, *Prob.* 15).

[2] See, pp. 188 *et seq.*, the paragraph relative to the army.

quietly accept their exile. The Gepidae and the Guthunges desired
to continue in Thrace their nomadic life; they ranged through the
cultivated lands, and committed such ravages that it became necessary to kill a great number, and adopt rigorous measures against
the rest. The Franks did more. Relegated to the lands about
the Euxine, they seized some vessels, says Zosimus,[1] crossed the
Bosphorus, and having ravaged along their way the coasts of Asia
Minor and Greece, and pillaged Athens, Syracuse, and Carthage,
they passed through the Straits of Hercules, coasting Spain and
Gaul, and came back to the mouths of the Rhine, where they
related to their amazed fellow-countrymen how they had with
impunity traversed the whole of the great Empire. This was a
fatal revelation, too well understood by the Frisians and Saxons,
who began about that time to ravage with their piracies the
coasts of the Western provinces. Other dangers were to be feared
from the Barbarians destined for the games of the circus. These
men who were so ready to shed their blood did not take kindly
to the trade of amusing the populace. Probus had reserved a
large number of them for the shows which he was to furnish to
the city after his victories; but they broke their chains, and
some hard fighting was necessary before they were subdued.

About this time the turbulent population of Alexandria proclaimed as emperor Saturninus, an able general, valued by Aurelian
and Probus, but of volatile mind and restless disposition, — like
that Gallic race, says the historian, whence he sprang.[2] At first
he yielded to the popular whim; but later, seized with fear, he
fled into Palestine to escape the dangerous honor offered him;
finally, however, believing that there was no longer safety for
him in a private station, he took off a purple veil from a statue
of Venus and made himself an imperial mantle of it. But he said,
weeping, to the soldiers who dragged him to this honor: "Alas,
how useful a citizen is lost to the state! I have restored the
Gallic provinces, I have taken Africa from the Moors, and I have
pacified Spain. To what profit is it all? In one day I lose all
that I had gained. In calling me to the imperial power you

---

[1] i. 71.

[2] . . . Oriundo fuit Gallus, ex gente hominum inquietissima et avida semper vel faciendi
principis vel imperii (Vopiscus, Saturn. 7). Zosimus and Zonaras consider him a Moor.

sentence me to death." Probus attempted to spare him, addressing to him friendly letters, with promises of pardon; but the soldiers, who hoped to profit by his promotion, compelled him to persevere in his usurpation. On the arrival of the imperial troops he sought shelter in a fortress, but was captured and put to death.

At Lyons a similar occurrence took place. Ever since the armies, under the strong hand of their new leaders, had resumed obedience, the populace of the great cities had seemed to inherit the former's turbulence. The Lyonnese proclaimed Proculus, — a rude soldier whom Probus had but to touch with his finger to overthrow. Bonosus, another veteran, revolted to escape the responsibility of a misdemeanor: he had suffered the Germans to burn the Roman flotilla on the Rhine, of which he had been left in charge. Defeated by the imperial troops, aided by German auxiliaries, he attached a rope to a tree, and hung himself. His body was an object of derision. "This is not a man hanging here," it was said, "but only a skin of wine;"[1] and the reproach was merited. Probus had spared the family of Proculus, and he did the same in the case of Bonosus, granting to Hunila, his wife, a pension for life.

Again, a revolt broke out in Britain. A friend of the Emperor had persuaded him to give the government of this province to some individual whose name has not been preserved; learning that the fidelity of his *protégé* was wavering, and fearing to be regarded as his accomplice, the Emperor's friend feigned to have fallen into disgrace at court, exiled himself into Britain, and being cordially welcomed by the governor, assassinated him.

All these attempts had failed miserably; none the less, however, were they a dangerous symptom. The bad instincts, which had for a moment given way before a feeling of the public disasters, were re-awakening. Probus owed his elevation to war; notwithstanding this, he greatly preferred to be occupied only with works of public utility, and condemned his soldiers to this. The troops were not unwilling to be employed in repairing military roads and rebuilding dilapidated fortifications, as their predecessors had so often done; but Probus would have them construct temples and porticos, regulate the course of rivers and drain marshes, break

---

[1] Vopiscus, *Bonos.* 15. He was a Breton of Spanish origin, and his mother a Gaul. His father had been a schoolmaster. In respect to his habits of intoxication, see above, p. 196.

up the ground and plant the vine in Gaul, Pannonia, and Moesia, where these vineyards, longer of life than the Empire, still exist; and there was current a dangerous saying of his: "The day will come when Rome will no longer need an army." Our sympathy is due to this gallant soldier who did not underrate the share of the civil authority in an established community, who in the midst of arms was mindful of the labors of peace, and employed his legions therein while maintaining among them severe discipline. He was yet in the prime of life,[1] beloved of the Senate, feared by the Barbarians, and had he lived would have secured prosperous days to the Empire; but he was not suffered to live. The Roman army was composed of too rough material for ideas of devotion to the public weal taking any other form than that of courage in battle to be comprehensible to these men, who were in no respect Romans. One summer day, in a torrid heat which rendered fatigue greater than usual, and men's minds more excitable, the soldiers, employed in draining a marsh in the neighborhood of Sirmium threw down their implements, seized their swords, and forcing an entrance into a tower where Probus was overlooking the work, they murdered him[2] (September or October, 282). The deed being done, they wept over the man whom they had just killed, and upon his tomb were inscribed these words: "Here lies the Emperor Probus, a truly upright man, who conquered all barbarous nations and all tyrants."[3] Carus, whom he had loaded with honors, avenged his death upon the murderers.

We may add one title more to those which Aurelian and Probus

---

[1] Fifty years of age (Orelli, No. 1,104).

[2] This tower was protected with iron (*turris ferrata*), whence it may be inferred that murmurs had already been heard, and that Probus guarded himself against a surprise. Zonaras represents this murder as preceded by a revolt of other troops, who had constrained Carus to assume the purple and march upon Italy. Cf. Vopiscus, *Prob.* 21; Aur. Victor, 37; Eutropius, ix. 17; Orosius, vii. 24; the Syncellus, etc. The authority of none of these writers being great, I adopt that version of the story which seems to me most probable.

[3] The coins of Probus have for their legend: *Bono imp. C. Probo*, — an epithet rare upon imperial coins. An inscription (Wilmanns, No. 1,048) bears the following: *Pietate justitia fortitudine et plane omnium virtutum principi vero Gothico veroque Germanico ac victoriarum omnium nominibus inlustri, M. Aur. Probo*. Mommsen concludes from the words *vero Gothico veroque Germanico* that Probus had refused these two titles. It seems to me that the general character of the inscription gives another meaning to these words. The people of Valentia, in engraving these words, wish to contrast the important victories of Probus over the Goths and Germans with the pretended successes of so many other Emperors who were anything but real conquerors.

possess to the esteem of history: these valiant Emperors created the great military school whence emerged Carus, Diocletian and his three colleagues, Constantine, Licinius, and the generals who for more than a half century protected the frontiers from invasion.

III. — CARUS (SEPTEMBER, 282, TO DECEMBER, 283); CARINUS AND NUMERIANUS (DECEMBER, 283, TO APRIL, 285).

M. AURELIUS CARUS also was an Illyrian:[1] but he had been brought up in the capital, he called himself a Roman, and had filled military and civil offices, having been proconsul of Cilicia, consul *suffectus*, and praetorian prefect. He was therefore a senator; but he had less consideration for the Senate than had Probus, and contented himself with announcing to the Conscript Fathers his accession, and congratulating them that the Emperor was this time one of their own order.

COIN OF CARUS.[2]

He had two sons, of very different characters and tastes, — Carinus, violent and profligate; and Numerianus, of gentle manners and cultivated mind. If we may believe the flatteries of the Senate, who caused a statue to be erected to him in the Ulpian library,[3] the latter was a great orator, and his verses were compared with those of the most famous poet of his time, Nemesianus. The new Emperor appointed his two sons Caesars, and, sharing the Empire with Carinus, gave him — perhaps not without hesitation — the government of the Western provinces. It is at least asserted that the Emperor soon repented of this act, and sought to withdraw the authority from his son in order to bestow it upon Constantius Chlorus.[4] He himself, resuming the project formed by Probus of striking a heavy blow at Persia, the hereditary enemy, directed his steps towards the East, at

---

[1] At least he was born in Illyria; one of the chroniclers represents him as the son of a Carthaginian. *Punis parentibus* (Vopiscus, *Carus*, 4); Zonaras calls him a Gaul.

[2] DEO ET DOMINO CARO INVIC. AVG. Radiate busts; the Sun and Carus facing each other. (Small bronze.)

[3] This statue bore the following inscription: *Numeriano Caesari oratori temporibus suis potentissimo* (Vopiscus, *Num.* 12).

[4] Vopiscus, *Carin.* 16.

the head of a formidable army; his second son accompanied him (January, 283).

CARUS, CROWNED WITH LAUREL.[1]

At the news of the death of Probus the Quadi had crossed the Danube and overrun the whole of Pannonia.[1] Carus killed sixteen thousand of them, and took a large number of prisoners, among them many women.

He then advanced with rapid marches into Mesopotamia. Bahram II., whose principal army was at that time employed at the opposite extremity of his kingdom, essayed by a humble embassy to avert the storm. When the envoys arrived in the camp they were conducted into the presence of an old man, who, seated on the ground and clad in a simple woollen tunic, was eating some peas cooked with a little salt meat. This old man said to them that he was the Emperor, and that if the Persians did

COIN COMMEMORATIVE OF VICTORIES OVER THE QUADI.[3]

not acknowledge the majesty of Rome he would make their country as bare as his head; upon which, removing his cap, he showed it

---

[1] Eutropius (ix. 6) places the Quadi in the eastern Carpathians; but this must be an error, for we have always found them in the vicinity of the Marcomanni.

[2] Intaglio of the *Cabinet de France* (nicolo, 14 millim. by 12), No. 2,106 of the Catalogue; not a likeness; Carus was older and bald, if the words attributed to him are authentic.

[3] IMP. NVMERIANVS P. F. AVG. Laurelled bust holding a spear and a globe. On the reverse: TRIVNF. VQVADOR; Carinus and Numerianus in a quadriga. (Bronze medallion, Cohen, No. 19.) But neither the father nor the younger son ever returned to Rome, and of this triumph, all that was seen were the coins which bore its emblems (Eckhel, vii. 512).

to them perfectly bald. "Are you hungry?" he then said. "If you are, eat from this dish; otherwise, you may go."[1] A victory gave him the road to Seleucia, and he entered that region without difficulty; he crossed the Tigris, took Ctesiphon, and was making ready to execute his threats, when one day during a storm his tent was seen to be in flames. Aper, his praetorian prefect, declared it to have been set on fire by a flash of lightning, which had also killed the Emperor. The lightning was probably not the real culprit. Carus was a hard master, and his soldiers and officers, fatigued by this summer cam-paign under a burning sun, saw them-selves with alarm dragged away by him into the heart of Asia. A prophecy was put in circulation that no Roman Empe-ror could go beyond Ctesiphon, and some one took advantage of the storm to strike the blow. The oracle was fulfilled, and the flames concealed all traces of the crime (end of December, 283). The Em-peror's secretary wrote to the urban pre-fect: "Our beloved Emperor Carus was ill in his bed when a furious storm burst

BAHRAM II. (VARANES).[2]

over the camp. The sky became so darkened that we could not see each other's faces, and in the general confusion incessant peals of thunder prevented our being aware of what was going on. Immediately after a very heavy burst of thunder the outcry was raised that the Emperor was dead. It appeared that in the trans-ports of their grief the household officers had set on fire the imperial tent, whence has arisen a report that the Emperor had been killed by lightning; but, so far as we have been able to investigate the matter, we believe that his death was caused by the illness from which he was suffering."[3]

Numerianus inherited the title of Augustus, which his brother Carinus also assumed at Rome; and the army, abandoning its con-

---

[1] These words have been also attributed to Probus.

[2] Intaglio of the *Cabinet de France* (sardonyx of 15 millim. by 11), No. 1,357 of the Cat-alogue. Under No. 1,359 the same collection possesses an intaglio cut on both sides: the reverse of the head of Bahram II. is a lion surmounted by a scorpion.

[3] Vopiscus, *Car.* 8.

M. AUR. CARINUS.[1]

endure the fatigues of this expedition, and the sun and the burning sands of the desert had brought on an affection of the eyes
which made it necessary for him to live in darkness. He was
always either in his tent or in his litter, and the soldiers became
accustomed to not seeing him. Thus slowly the army crossed
Mesopotamia, the Syrian provinces, and Asia Minor. The prae-

[1] Bust of the Capitol, Hall of the Emperors, No. 79.

torian prefect, Aper, father-in-law of Numerianus, was in command. At the beginning of September they reached the shores of the Bosphorus. A part of the army had already crossed the straits when a rumor was put in circulation that Numerianus was dead. The soldiers rushed to the Emperor's tent, and found there a dead body, from which life had departed some days before. This secret, . kept so long, directed suspicion upon the man whose duty it was to reveal it instantly; the soldiers surrounded Aper, accused him of his son-in-law's murder, loaded him with chains, and the generals, assembled at Chalcedon, on the Asiatic side, formed themselves into a tribunal to judge the murderer whose crime no man doubted. Before the decision they chose one of their number as chief; he was the son of a freedman, and himself a soldier of fortune, the captain of the household troops,[1] Diocles by name, a man who must have been an honored soldier, since without canvassing or the intervention of the soldiery he was the choice of his companions in arms. He ascends the tribunal, and swears by the Sun, the divinity who sees all things, even the secret thoughts of men, that he has in no way been concerned in the murder, nor has desired the imperial power; then, turning towards Aper, he exclaims, " This man is the assassin," and plunges his sword into the prefect's heart, as the priest immolates the victim devoted to the infernal gods. As supreme judge he had pronounced sentence ; as soldier he executed it (Sept. 17, 284).

Diocletian is emperor; a new era is about to open: the history of Republican and Imperial Rome ends, and that of the Later Empire begins.

---

[1] *Domesticus regens* (*Id.*, *Numer.* 13). The *domestici*, who are mentioned as early as the time of Caracalla, were companies of the body-guard; their captains naturally took the rank and authority given them by the confidence of the Emperor, whose life was in their hands. An inscription found at Nicomedeia mentions a body-guard of protectors (*protectores divini lateris*) under Aurelian (*C. I. L.* iii. 327). Another mentions an officer of this guard who was consul in 261 (Perrot, *La Galatie*, etc., i. 6). In an inscription of the time of Claudius II. the *protectores* are mentioned (*Bull. épigr.* No. 1, p. 5).

CHAPTER XCIX.

DIOCLETIAN; WARS AND ADMINISTRATION.

I. — DIOCLETIAN AND MAXIMIAN; THE DYARCHY (284–293).

DIOCLES, who after his accession gave to his Greek name a Roman and more sonorous form, Diocletianus,[1] was a Dalmatian from the environs of Scutari, whose father had been a slave.

DIOCLETIAN.[3]

Entering the service at an early age, he attracted the notice of his superior officers less by brilliant achievements than by his acute and penetrating mind, which always found the wisest measure to adopt and the best means of carrying it into execution.[2] At the time of the death of Claudius Gothicus, Diocletian was twenty-five years old, — an age well suited to profit by the lessons of the great military school of Aurelius and Probus.[4] In those stormy times advancement was rapid; he rose quickly to the higher grades in the army, was made consul *suffectus*, governor of Moesia, and commander of the palace-guard, — a post of confidence which gave him very high rank. To set in circulation the report that in taking the life of Aper he had executed a decree of Heaven, Diocletian related that a Druidess of Tongres, in Belgium, had promised him that he should be Emperor after he had killed a wild boar. "From that day," he said, "I

---

[1] His name in inscriptions is C. (or M.) Aurelius Valerius Diocletianus (Wilmanns, Nos. 769 and 824). He was born in 245 at Doclea, in Dalmatia, near Podgoritza, below Montenegro, and was but thirty-nine at the time of his accession.

[2] Aur. Victor, who lived not long after Diocletian, filling high offices under Julian, says that the former was chosen *ob sapientiam*, and calls him *magnus vir* (Caes. 39).

[3] IMP. C[aesar] Caius] VAL[erius] DIOCLETIANVS P[ius] F[elix] AVG[ustus]. Laurelled bust, with cuirass and aegis. (Bronze medallion.)

[4] . . . *Usumque bonæ militiæ quanta his Aureliani Probique instituta fuit* (Aur. Victor, 39).

sought the wild boar everywhere, and I have killed many; but other men have eaten them." Aurelian, indeed, and then Probus, Tacitus, and Carus, successively ascended the throne, and still Diocletian remained in the ranks. On the 17th of September, 284, the designated wild boar[1] fell at last beneath his blows, and the son of the Dalmatian slave became Emperor of Rome.

The rare documents which we possess in relation to Diocletian do not give those inner details which permit us to understand the

CHASE OF THE WILD BOAR.[2]

true nature of the man. However, notwithstanding gaps and obscurities, it is clearly to be seen that he was something more than a soldier of fortune. But he did not come from one of those rich and intellectual communities in which the Antonines had acquired the elegant tastes and refined manners of the Roman world. Accordingly, not possessing their natural or acquired distinction as a means to keep the crowd at a distance, he surrounded himself with a cold and solemn ceremonial, regulated by the strictest etiquette. In the arts his taste inclined to the massive constructions, the heavy ornamentation of periods of natural decline; and

---

[1] *Aper* is the Latin word signifying "wild boar." It has been believed that by this precipitate murder Diocletian intended to prevent compromising revelations, since he, as commander of the body-guard, must have known what was taking place in the tent of Numerianus. But as father-in-law of the Emperor, as well as praetorian prefect, Aper had a superior authority, which would have permitted him to send away all persons who might have prevented the carrying out of his designs.

[2] Bas-relief from a sarcophagus found at Salona, the subject of which is regarded as an allusion to the murder of Aper.

while Hadrian's villa at Tivoli has preserved to us a great number of valuable works of art, from the palace of Diocletian at Salona — an enormous mass of marble, granite, and porphyry — none whatever have come down to us.

In respect to literature his taste would seem to have been better. We know that he gave to Nicomedeia a school of higher instruction, to which he called Lactantius, the most eloquent rhetorician of his time;[1] that he excused students, up to their twenty-fifth year, from municipal burdens;[2] that he took as his model the philosopher Marcus Aurelius,[3] — a greater man than himself, but not so great a ruler; that, finally, he caused biographies of the Emperors to be written.[4] Unfortunately the lessons that he learned from history, although they revealed to him the points truly important for an administration, did not teach him gentleness. Throughout his reign he showed himself pitiless towards armed insurrections, and even towards those that were not armed; and while in his retirement he showed much practical philosophy, he appears never to have had a very lively interest in intellectual matters: at Salona his garden was far more attractive to him than were his books. His religion was that of the peasant, — for his infirmities, a healing deity, Aesculapius; for his fortunes, a protecting deity, Jupiter, and the voice of the oracles, listened to more attentively in certain cases than the utterance of human wisdom.

But Diocletian possessed the qualities which make the ruler, — a knowledge of men, a comprehension of the needs of the state, and the firm resolve to devote his thoughts and himself

[1] Lactan., *Div. Inst.* v. 2, and Saint Jerome, *De Vir. illustr.* 80: . . . *Arnobii discipulus, sub Diocletiano principe accitus cum Flavio grammatico.* Another writer, Hierocles, was vicar of the diocese of Bithynia.

[2] . . . *Ut studiis non avocentur* (*Code Just.* x. 49, 1). See in the reign of Valentinian I. an ordinance concerning the schools of Rome. Diocletian also said: *Artem geometriæ discere, atque exercere publice interest* (*Code Just,* ix. 11, 2).

[3] *Augustan History, Marc. Ant.* 19. He blamed the savage temper of Maximian (*asperitatem*), and said of Aurelian that he was better suited to be a general than to be an Emperor (*Ibid., Aurel.* 43). Lactantius (*De morte pers.*) speaks of his moderation: . . . *Hanc moderationem tenere conatus est.*

[4] A part of the *Augustan History.* Cf. Teuffel, *Geschichte der röm. Literatur,* No. 388. Capitolinus says to him (*In Macrino,* 15, *ad fin.*): . . . *Quae de plurimis collecta Serenitati Tuae . . . detulimus, quia te cupidum veterum imperatorum esse perspeximus.* The saying of Diocletian, that the best of rulers is in danger of being sold by his courtiers, seems to have been borrowed from letters exchanged between Timesitheus and Gordian III. (*Hist. Aug., Gordianus III.* 24–25.)

to the cares of government. It might be thought that this creator of the Byzantine court was an effeminate person; on the contrary, he

GATE OF THE PALACE OF DIOCLETIAN, CALLED THE GOLDEN GATE, AT SALONA.

manifested, in respect to the provinces, the frontiers, and the armies, all the masculine energy of Hadrian. Like that indefatigable travel-ler, he was incessantly on the road throughout the Empire. He weighed his plans carefully, determined them long in advance, in order to have time to secure their success, and executed with energy what he had prudently prepared. His bust in the Capitol shows plainly this patient tenacity. By the broad, square forehead,

AESCULAPIUS.[1]

the cold and tranquil face, we recognize a man master of himself, — which is the first condition for becoming master of others.

Lactantius accuses him of cowardice and of avarice, — strange reproaches to address to the soldier who had gained his promotions on fields of battle, and to the frugal ruler who was the most ostentatious of emperors only because he believed this ostentation necessary to the new monarchy he was founding. Neither do we agree with Lampridius when he calls Diocletian the "Father of the Golden Age;"[2] the fourth century has no right to this title. The history of his reign, which with but a brief exception gave to the Roman world a long period of domestic peace, and to the Empire forty years of security, will make us know him better than the words of doubtful veracity spoken by his enemies or by his flatterers.

The man chosen by the army of the East had a dangerous com-

[1] Marble in the Museum at Naples.   [2] Aug. Hist., Heliog. 34.

petitor in Carinus, who, proud of a brilliant success over the
Jazyges, had no idea of abandoning his paternal inheritance. But,
detested by the Senate,[1] — a matter, it is true, of but little importance,
— Carinus was despised for his sensuality by the rough comrades
in arms of the later Emperors, and dreaded by the soldiers on
account of his cruelty; and this disaffection of the army was serious
for an aspirant to the throne who had to encounter a competitor.

On both sides many months were employed in making ready
for the struggle. Carinus first defeated
Julian, governor of Venetia, who had
assumed the purple; and he gained also
some partial advantages over the ad-
vance-guard of Diocletian. In March or
April, 285, the armies met for a decisive

COIN OF THE USURPER JULIAN.[2]

engagement at Margus, on the Morawa, not far from the confluence
of that river with the Danube. As always, the Asiatic legions
gave way before the onset of the legions of Europe; but Carinus
was killed by one of his own officers whose wife he had outraged.[3]

His death seems to have been a deliverance for every one.
On the conqueror's part there were no confiscations, no exiles; each
man retained his office, even the urban and praetorian prefects,
one of whom Diocletian took for his colleague in the consulship.
It is probable an agreement had been entered into before the
battle, and that the officers of the Western Emperor had sold him
to his competitor. Eutropius says that Carinus was betrayed, or
at least abandoned.[4] Later we shall see similar defections in the
armies of Vetranio, Magnentius, Maximus, and Eugenius, — doubtless
brought about by the gold of Constantius and Theodosius. In
these days, when Rome had only mercenaries for soldiers, the best
of all war-engines was a well-filled treasury.

This great commotion had unsettled the Empire, encouraged
the Barbarians, and impaired the fidelity of the subject-nations,
whom Rome imperfectly protected, and ruined by her exactions.

---

[1] Carinus had one day said to the Roman populace that the wealth of the aristocracy
belonged to them, for the reason that they were the true Roman people (*Hist. Aug., Carinus*, 1).

[2] IMP. C. IVLIANVS P[ius] F[elix] AVG[ustus] and the laurelled bust of Julian. On
the reverse: LIBERTAS PVBLICA, surrounding a figure of Liberty. (Gold coin.)

[3] *Suorum ictu interiit quod libidine impatiens, militarium nuptas affectabat . . . sese ulti
sunt* (Aur. Victor, 39).

[4] ix. 20.

The taxes were heavy both in themselves and by reason of the exhaustion of the sources of production.[1] What has been said[2] of the hardships which oppressed manufactures, trade, and agriculture, of the disappearance of the small landowners, and the desolation of the country, even in its most fertile regions, explains why in the midst of these populations driven wild by suffering (*Gallias efferatas injuriis*),[3] insurrections should have broken out. That of the Bagaudae[4] was for the moment formidable. Fugitive slaves, husbandmen oppressed by their landlords, vagrant peasants, insolvent debtors, became freebooters, and at last formed an army, which gave itself two Caesars, Aelianus and Amandus (285). We have coins struck for these peasant-emperors;[5] on the reverse of one is the word *Spes*. Using anything as weapons, they flung themselves upon the villages and unwalled cities with the savage ardor of evil instincts when unchained, ravaging, burning, and killing.[6] Autun, lately the pride of Gaul, was a second time devastated.[7] Brigand chiefs are often popular favorites, the war they make upon the rich seeming to the poor but legitimate reprisal. The Bagaudae remain in the memory of the people as defenders of the unfortunate. A tradition which took shape in the following centuries even represents this outbreak as a Christian insurrection. It would be no cause for surprise if some Christians were among these insurgents, as there were some in the Gothic bands which had ravaged Asia Minor. Were they not also sufferers from oppression, and might not the spirit of

---

[1] Julius Caesar required from the Gauls only forty million sesterces (about two million dollars). This was a tax which it was for his interest to render light. Augustus, after reorganizing the pacified Empire, had required from Gaul nearly the same tribute as from Egypt, — twelve thousand five hundred talents (Vell. Paterc., ii. 39, and Strabo, XVII. i. 13), or nearly fourteen million dollars. Savigny believes that in the time of Constantine the tribute had quintupled (Marquardt, *Handb.* ii. 288).

[2] p. 206.

[3] *Paneg. veteres*, vi. 8, edit. of 1676. The word *efferatas* signifies literally "rendered wild or savage."

[4] According to Ducange, the Celtic word *bagad* signifies "a band." Gallic peasants had already mingled in the tumults of the soldiery in the time of Tetricus (Eumenes, *Paneg. veter.* vii. 4, and *Pro rest. scholis*, 14). For twenty years (254–274) Gaul had been a prey to the devastations of the Barbarians and to civil war.

[5] But these coins are either counterfeit or else re-minted.

[6] . . . *Hostem barbarum suorum cultorum rusticus vastator imitatus est* (*Paneg. veter.* ii. 4). Was it to conceal from these plunderers the wealth of the temple of Mercury that the treasure of Bernay was at that time buried? See many objects of this collection, Vol. II. p. 395, and Vol. VI., frontispiece, and pp. 128, 129.

[7] *Ibid.* iv. 4.

vengeance, which was forbidden to the saints, arm against a world which oppressed them, those who had more wrath than resigna-

DIOCLETIAN.[1]

tion?[2]   While Northern Gaul was in a blaze, the Saxons were scouring the North Sea and the British Channel and devastating

[1] Bust of the Capitol, Hall of the Emperors, No. 80.
[2] In the middle of the second century, Christianity counted in Gaul only the small but fervent community of Lyons. The great mission, organized a century later, founded churches

the coasts, the Franks were astir along the Rhine, other Germans on the Danube, the Moors in Africa, the Persians behind the Tigris; the whole line of the frontiers was threatened, and the Empire shaken to its foundations. Diocletian spent twelve years in securing upon its base the shaken colossus.

He had seen some of the bravest Emperors, men who had saved the state, murdered by their soldiers, and others fall victims to the machinations of their generals. Insurrections of the soldiery, treasonable designs on the part of ambitious men, and attacks from without, were the triple peril which must be averted. If to arrive at the supreme authority there was only one man to overthrow, many would still make the attempt; but it would be difficult to destroy two emperors at the same moment, and this difficulty would be likely to cause the disaffected to hesitate. In the interests of the Empire and of himself, Diocletian therefore had need of a colleague who, having no further personal ambition, would aid in controlling that of others, and at the same time keep the Barbarians in check. From the first century of the Empire this necessity had been recognized. Piso had been adopted by Galba, Trajan by Nerva; in the time of Marcus Aurelius, Severus, the Gordians, Valerian, and Carus,[1] there had been several Emperors at once; and the history of the Thirty Tyrants, which Diocletian studied, had shown him that the enfeebled Empire was exposed to dangers too many for one hand to be sufficient to ward off all the blows. This was the solution of the future, — the one imposed by geography, which is a mighty force; by the natural division of the Empire into two halves, the one Greek, the other Latin; and lastly by the weakness of a state which, no longer able to conquer, was now reduced to self-defence. Surrounded by Barbarians, whom in the days of her strength she had not cared to subjugate and civilize, Rome was now, as it were, a prey in the midst of devouring wolves. The time had come, therefore, to organize a vigorous

in Arles, Narbonne, Toulouse, Limoges, Clermont, Tours, and Paris, which prospered after the edict of toleration issued by Gallienus in 260. In respect to the tardy evangelization of the Gallic provinces, see the publications of the Abbé de Meissas, who boldly combats the wild assertions of the legendary school.

[1] When Carus appointed his two sons Caesars, and intrusted to the elder the government of the Western provinces, while he took the younger with him into the East, he was already anticipating the system of Diocletian, — with this advantage to the latter, that, having no sons, he was able to choose his Caesars from among his ablest officers.

defensive, making, by a division of the power, the imperial action present and effective in all the provinces.   As to the rebel legionaries and the usurping generals, it would probably be easier to prevent their revolts by bestowing a share of power on the most ambitious or most able among them.

DIOCLETIAN.[1]

Diocletian had that clear view of the public needs which in politics denotes the man of great ability.   On the first day of May, 285, he invested with the purple, not one of his own kindred, but a comrade in arms, Maximian; and on this occasion he himself took a new name, Jovius, which may be translated as "devoted to Jupiter."   He specially adored this divinity whose name was the beginning of his own;[2] he placed the figure of Jupiter upon his coins, and the statue of the god upon the column before which he presently invested Galerius with the imperial insignia; he built him a temple in the palace of Salona, and made it his study to appear in public ceremonies with the calm majesty of the father of gods and men.   To Maximian, whom he adopted as his son,[4] he gave the name of Herculius, in memory of the assistance afforded by the son of Alcmene to his divine father during the war of the giants.[5]   These appellations were well chosen to characterize the part each was destined to play, — the one as the ruling thought, the other, the executing

MAXIMIAN HERCULES.[3]

---

[1] Diocletian, with the name of Jovius.   IOVIO DIOCLETIANO AVG.   (Bronze medallion.)

[2] *Dios* is the genitive of Zeus, the Greek Jupiter.   Diocletian probably regarded this accidental circumstance as a sign pledging him to the worship of the god.

[3] HERCVLIO MAXIMIANO AVG.   Maximian and Hercules seated; between them, a Victory.   Reverse of the same medallion.   (Cohen, No. 105.)

[4] This adoption seems to be proved by the names M. Aurelius Valerius assumed by Maximian.   (Wilmanns, Nos. 769, 1,060, 1,062.)

[5] *Eadem auxilii opportunitate, qua tuus Hercules Jovem vestrum quondam Terrigenarum bello laborantem magnâ victoriae parte juvit* (Paneg. ii. 1).   The inhabitants of Fano and Pisaurum had already made Hercules the companion and colleague of Aurelian: *Herculi Augusto consorti Domini nostri Aureliani* (Orelli, No. 1,031).

strength.   Maximian was not proclaimed Augustus; his title of
Caesar marked a subordinate rank, and the surname which he had
accepted pledged him to filial obedience.

From the time of Claudius II., Illyricum, the region of the
Empire where there was most fighting, had held the right to
provide emperors,[1] as Spain, Gaul, Africa, and Syria had done in
their turn.   Maximian was the son of a Pannonian colonist in the
neighborhood of Sirmium.   He was a brave soldier and an experienced general, but of coarse manners, and of mind so uncultivated
that he who recaptured Carthage knew nothing of Hannibal, of
Scipio, or of Zama; he felt himself the inferior of Diocletian, and
was not angry at this consciousness.   The Augustus had chosen,
therefore, not so much a colleague as a docile lieutenant.

Carus had taken Ctesiphon; but the Persians had quickly recovered possession of it, so that there was only one victory more for
Rome, but not an enemy the less.   Detained in Asia by the hostile
attitude of the Persians, Diocletian despatched the Caesar to Gaul,
there to restore order and to give security to the western frontiers.
The Seine and the Marne at their junction form a peninsula which
the Bagaudae had cut with deep trenches (Saint-Maur-les-Fossés):
this was their fortress and camp of refuge; there they collected
their booty, and they believed themselves secure against attack.
But their bands, undisciplined and poorly armed, could not stand
before the legions; in a few weeks this Jacquerie, shut up in its
camp of Saint-Maur, perished there.[2]

The pacification of Gaul gave to the Caesar the title of
Augustus (286).[3]   Diocletian had not ventured to incur the risk
that the victorious army, giving to their leader the supreme title,
should make of him a rebel.   But to this elevation he added the
condition that Maximian Hercules should lay aside the purple
whenever he himself should set the example, and a solemn oath
on the altar of Jupiter consecrated this engagement.[4]

[1] *Indie . . . gentium domina gloriae vetustate, sed Pannonia virtute* (*Paneg.* i. 2).   . . . *In
quibus provinciis omnis vita militia est* (*ib.* iii.).

[2] *Paneg. veteres*, ii. 8; . . . *Levibus praeliis agrestes domuit* (Eutrop. ix. 20).

[3] A rescript of June 21, 286, gives him that title.   As Augustus, he became " the brother
of Diocletian " (Wilmanns, No. 739),   a title which modern sovereigns interchange with each
other.

[4] This pledge is mentioned twice (in 307 and in 310) by the authors of the *Paneg. veter.*
vi. 9: . . . *Consilii olim inter vos placiti constantia et pietate fraterna*, and vii. 15: . . . *Illum in*

The new Augustus had already possessed, as Caesar, the tribunitian and proconsular authority; he now received the title of Pontifex Maximus, which had been shared but once before, namely, by Pupienus and Balbinus. He had his own praetorian prefect, his army, his treasury; and he promulgated decrees which were valid everywhere, although he was intrusted only with the administration of the Western provinces. The unity of command was maintained by the deference that Maximian had promised to his colleague; it was manifested to all eyes by the unity in legislation (all edicts being issued in the name of the two Emperors), and by that of the coinage, which was the same from the banks of the Euphrates to the Rhine. Inscriptions commemorative of public works executed by either bore the names of both;[1] in a word, the administration was divided, but the government was not, Diocletian alone possessing the supreme authority.[2] In public documents his name preceded that of Maximian, as, later, Constantius was always mentioned before Galerius. This unvarying order proves that, in the system of Diocletian, a certain pre-eminence was reserved to the first Augustus.

For the expedition against the Bagaudae, the posts on the Rhine had been stripped of their garrisons; taking advantage of this situation, the Heruli and Chaviones on the north[3] and the Burgundians and Alemanni on the south, crossed the river. But they arrived too late; Maximian had brought his troops back to Mayence, and from this strong position he kept watch on the movements of the Barbarians. The Burgundians and Alemanni seemed too numerous for him to attack in front, and he allowed them to advance into the desolated provinces, where famine and disease soon reduced their numbers; and when their diminished bands came again within his reach he easily van-

---

Capitolini Jovis templa jurasse. It is also referred to by Eusebius in his *Life of Constantine,* book i. chap. xviii. The fact is certain, therefore, though not the date. It seems to me probable that it occurred on the day when, receiving from Diocletian the imperial dignity, Maximian could refuse nothing to his benefactor.

[1] Orelli, Nos. 1,052, 1,054.

[2] *Cujus nutu omnia gubernabantur* (Aur. Victor).

[3] The Chaviones originally occupied northern Holstein. The great movement of the Germanic tribes towards the South, of which we have already spoken (pp. 179 *et s.*), had brought to the Rhine the Chaviones, the Heruli, and some Burgundians, the main body of the latter nation having stopped in the valley of the Saale.

quished them. The Heruli, less dangerous, had been arrested on
their first advance and driven back across the river. These were
far from glorious victories; but men cared little what devastation
the Barbarians might have made. The Roman dignity at that time
was satisfied when the Emperor could say: "The enemy is no
longer within the limits of the Empire."

Trèves had become the Rome of the Gallic provinces. It had
a palace for the Emperor, arsenals and workshops for the armies, a
circus and a forum for the people. On the first of January, 288,

GLASS CUP FOUND AT TRÈVES, REPRESENTING THE GEAT CIRCUS.[1]

a public ceremony had attracted thither vast crowds. Maximian
for the second time assumed the consular dignity. According to
custom, he was about to address the assembly, when a cry was
heard from the ramparts: "The Barbarians are at the gates!"
The Emperor threw off the consular toga, put on his cuirass, and
hastened to meet the foe. It proved to be some German horsemen
who had made their way between the outposts, and were on a
plundering expedition.[2] Such was life upon this frontier.

To give chase to the Saxon and Frankish pirates who were
ravaging the coasts of Britain and Gaul, Maximian had collected

---

[1] Wilmowski, *Inchung. Frennde in Trier und Umgegend*, 1873, p. 18, pl. ii., and Fröhner,
La Verrerie antique, Descript. of the Coll. Charvet, 1879, p. 96.

[2] Or some Alemannic band astray after the late invasion, who had escaped the soldiers of
Maximian (*Paneg.* ii. 6).

RUINS OF HOT BATHS IN A ROMAN VILLA, DISCOVERED IN 1811 AT BOGNOR, IN SUSSEX,
ENGLAND (LYSON'S RELIQUIAE BRITANNIAE ROMANAE, PL. XXV. VOL. III.)

at Boulogne, under the Menapian Carausius, a fleet designed to close the straits. This Carausius, once a galley-slave, had not improved in character with his advance in fortune. He made it his plan to plunder the freebooters who were his compatriots, suffering them to pass freely, but on their return detaining them, and compelling them to share their booty with him. In this manner he collected money enough to buy his officers and crews; and when Maximian pronounced against him sentence of death, no man could be found to execute it. Carausius placed himself out of reach by going over into Britain, where he cor-

COIN OF CARAVSIVS.[1]

rupted the troops and assumed the title of Augustus (287). With a remarkable appreciation of the resources offered by the possession of the island, he organized a powerful marine, which caused his standard to be respected as far as the Pillars of Hercules, and his alliance with the Saxons and Franks secured him soldiers and sailors. Many cities on the Gallic sea-coast preserved their old and profitable commercial intercourse with Britain, and Boulogne even re-

SMALL BRONZE.[2]

mained in his hands. Carausius therefore was master of his island and of the sea, and Maximian could effect nothing against him. The Emperor made an attempt, however, to reduce him to obedience. A fleet was constructed at the mouths of the Gallic rivers, and on the festival of the Palilia (21st of April, 289) the official panegyrist[3] celebrated in Trèves the approaching fall of "the chief of the pirates." The details of the conflict are not in our possession; but we know that the brigand chief came out of it a legitimate emperor, in virtue of a treaty which admitted his title of Augustus, and left to him the kingdom of which he had taken possession (290). The British mints issued coins with the figure of Hercules, "preserver of the three Augusti;" and others bear the words: "Carausius and his brothers."

This treaty was a confession of impotence; but Diocletian considered it as an armistice necessary until more propitious days

---

[1] Coin of Carausius, with the legend: VIRTVS CARAVSI. (Cohen, No. 35.)

[2] Carausius, Diocletian, and Maximian Hercules. CARAVSIVS ET FRATRES SVI. Radiate head of Carausius, with the bare heads of Diocletian and Maximian Hercules.

[3] He is known as Mamertinus, but the name is not given by the older manuscripts.

should come. He was not willing that Maximian should withdraw his attention and his troops from Germany: he himself had been obliged to go into Syria, in order to keep watch upon Egypt,—where turbulent Alexandria was causing anxiety,—and upon the Persians, whose courage had been revived by the death of Carus. The prolonged sojourn of the Emperor and an army so near the Persian frontier, together with a civil war caused by a competitor for the throne, decided king Bahram to avoid all disagreements with the Romans. His envoys came to meet Diocletian as the Emperor drew near the Euphrates, bringing presents from their master and soliciting his friendship.

Diocletian for the moment asked nothing more, preoccupied as he was with an affair more important for the security of the Empire than any new victory over cavalry impossible to capture. For the last twenty-seven years Armenia had been a Persian province: and since the time of Augustus, even since that of Pompey, the traditional policy of Rome had been to retain this country under her influence. An heir to the Armenian crown, Tiridates, was now living at the imperial court, where by his amiable deportment he had gained the regard of the most important men, and by his courage, his strength, and his skill in martial exercises, the esteem and respect of the soldiers. This prince was an invaluable instrument for the execution of a design suggested to the mind of Diocletian by the anarchy prevailing in Persia. Given up to all the woes of a foreign rule, Armenia had been wounded in her religion and in her patriotism: the statues of her kings had been thrown down, the objects of her worship profaned, her nobles excluded from public office; and an intense hatred brooded in the hearts of all. Everything was ready, therefore, for a revolution, and the domestic troubles of Persia rendered success probable. Tiridates set out, with the instructions and good wishes of Diocletian, but without ostensible assistance. This was, in fact, not needed, and would moreover have been a violation of the promised friendship lately granted to king Bahram. As soon as the new claimant appeared, defections occurred in every direction. Tiridates ascended the throne of his fathers, and thenceforth held in the interest of Rome that great fortress of Armenia which protected against the Persians Asia Minor and a part of the Syrian provinces (287).

This bloodless victory, gained by statecraft, was an important success. To avoid all complaints on the part of the Persian king, Diocletian had quitted Syria before the departure of Tiridates on

MAXIMIAN.[3]

this expedition. A rescript shows him to have been in Thrace in the middle of October, 286 ;[1] thence he went into Pannonia, which was ravaged by Sarmatian bands, and into Rhaetia, where it was needful to show the eagles. Following the example of the great Emperors, he visited the frontiers, to restore security with the restoration of respect for the name of Rome; and everywhere he repaired the line of defences which had been trodden down under the feet of the Barbarians.[2]

Maximian had come from Gaul to meet his colleague; in their conference doubtless were concerted the measures against Carausius which that skilful usurper was able to defeat the following year. The rare and confused documents of this period do not enable us to reconstruct its life ;[4] we are reduced to deriving from the panegyries or the

[1] Mommsen, Ueber die Zeitfolge der in den Rechtsbüchern enthaltenen Verordnungen Diocletians, in the Journal of the Academy of Sciences of Berlin, 1860, pp. 349–447. Tillemont, in his learned history, began the work of placing the rescripts in their chronological order, and Godefroy gives a chronology of the laws of the Theodosian Code, i. 5–214, edit. of 1737.

[2] . . . Omnia quae priorum labe conciderant . . . resurgentia, tot urbes diu silvis obsitas . . . instaurari moenibus . . . castra toto Rheni et Istri et Euphratis limite restituta (Eumenes, Paneg. veter. iv. 18). Suidas (s. v. ἀρχαία) speaks in the same way: ὁ Διοκλητιανὸς λόγον ποιούμενος τῶν πραγμάτων, ᾠήθη δεῖν δυνάμενον ἀμείνους ἑκάστην ἀρχαίαν ὀχυρῶσαι καὶ φησὶ να ποιῆσαι.

[3] Half figure of marble; fragment of an armed statue found in the capital of Carinthia (Clarac, Musée de sculpt. pl. 980, No. 2,526).

[4] Aurelius Victor, Eutropius, and Zonaras give each of them but a few lines to Diocletian, and scarcely more can be extracted from the bad rhetoric of the panegyrists or the eloquent invectives of Lactantius. What Zosimus says of Diocletian has been lost.

political pamphlets — two very imperfect sources — a few isolated
facts, without being able to establish between them that connection
of cause and effect which forms the solid texture of history. The
rescripts issued by the Emperors show indeed the cities where they
were at the time, but give no hint of the interests which had called
them thither; these interests can only be conjectured by placing
beside the dates inscribed on these decrees the legend of some coin,
or a word let fall by the poor writers of the time. Thus we find
in February, 291, Maximian at Rheims, at Trèves, and in the country of the Nervii, where, carrying out the disastrous policy of Augustus and Tiberius, he established Frankish prisoners as colonists.[1]
In January, 290, Diocletian is at Sirmium, in February at Adrian-
opolis, in April at Byzantium, in May at Antioch. He drives out
of Syria the Saracens who had come in to pillage, and we find him
again at Sirmium in the middle of July. This was like the activity
of Julius Caesar.[2] It has not been usual to recognize this diligence
and this laborious life in the Emperor who established that severe etiquette whose supreme expression came to be the immovable
majesty of the Byzantine Emperors.

The occurrences which recalled Diocletian in so great haste
to the shores of the Danube, where he remained till the close of
this year, 290, were the great national movements then agitating
Germany. Sanguinary encounters were taking place: the Goths
were falling upon those of the Burgundians who had followed them
in the East, the Taifales and the Thervinges upon the Gepidae and
the Vandals.[3] It was impossible to say what might arise out of
this confusion, — possibly a new invasion. But the Emperors
guarded the frontier, and nothing could pass.

---

[1] Also, possibly, Sarmatian. Ausonius, in his poem on the Moselle, speaks of Sarmatian
colonies established near Trèves.

[2] . . . *Illum modo Syria viderat, jam Pannonia susceperat* (Paneg. vetr. iii. 4).

[3] *Paneg. vetr.* iii. 16 and 17: *Ruunt omnes in sanguinem suum populi . . . obstinataeque
feritatis poenas, nunc sponte persolvunt.*

II. — THE TETRARCHY.

EARLY in the year 291 the two Augusti crossed the Alps in all the severity of winter to have another conference at Milan.[1] Diocletian was meditating a reorganization of the state. The division of power made in 286 had been only partially successful, because the part assigned to each Emperor was still too great for the action of the government to be everywhere prompt and effectual. Dangers were increasing. In the East, the pacific Bahram was dying, and the Persians would again become a source of danger. In the North, the Barbaric world was pushing forward its turbulent tribes towards the Rhine and the Danube. The Chemavi and the Frisones had seized upon Batavia, at the mouths of the Rhine, — a tract half land, half sea, a domain divided with even less certainty between the Germans and the Empire. At this time all the shore of the North Sea, from the Meuse to Jutland, was bordered with a population who sailed the seas in search of Gallic merchant vessels. In the interior, extensive provinces were becoming detached from the Empire; Egypt was about to proclaim an Emperor. Britain had already done this, — which signified that both countries were aspiring to independence, — and the Moors of Africa were claiming their liberty, sword in hand. Diocletian considered it wise to complete his political system; he decided that the two Augusti should take to themselves, under the title of Caesars, two lieutenants, who should be regarded as heirs. It was his hope that the Empire would thus be better guarded, the ambition of subalterns more certainly controlled, and the grave question of the succession settled, without giving opportunity in future for the soldiers to intervene with their caprices and their demands. The first day of March, 293, Constantius and Galerius were proclaimed Caesars.[2]

Theoretically, this conception was a happy one; with Diocletian it could succeed, thanks to the authority which his wisdom proved

[1] The remembrance of this occasion was perpetuated by coins bearing the words: *Concordia Augg.*

[2] Orelli, No. 467, and *C. I. L.* vol. ii. No. 1,439. The two Caesars were designated consuls for the year 294, and must have been so from the first year after their elevation.

by ten years of firm and successful rule, gave him; and it is with good reason that contemporaries have praised the harmony which he knew how to maintain among princes of characters so different. But in this system he had not taken into account the rivalries which would inevitably break out after his time, the impatient

CONSTANTIUS CHLORUS.[1]

ambition of the Caesars and the mutual jealousy of the Augusti who should succeed the founders of the tetrarchy. His plan met the fate of so many other projects inspired by political sagacity, which passion or unfavorable circumstances have shipwrecked. However, when to this reform in the constitution of the government we add that which Diocletian also made in the administration, we shall be obliged to recognize in this ruler a very high order of intellect, and to place him in the first rank of Roman Emperors. The name of Charlemagne has remained great, although his work also failed; it is true that it lasted for a longer time.[2]

Galerius was a Dacian who had been a shepherd in his youth.

[1] Bust of the Capitol, Hall of the Emperors, No. 80.

[2] Charlemagne pursued the same plan as did Diocletian, in giving three of his sons the title of kings, while holding them subject to his superior will. At the division of 817 the sons of Louis le Débonnaire were similarly placed. Charlemagne also organized his army on the Roman principle, that the military service was a charge on property. Again, like the Romans, he laid the keeping up of roads and bridges upon the adjacent landowners, who were bound, moreover, to furnish subsistence for the Emperor or his agents when passing over their lands. One of the injunctions of Charlemagne to his counts in respect to their fiscal vigilance is a sentence from two of Justinian's *novellæ* (viii. 8. and xvii. 1); and his bishops were like Constantine's, — state functionaries. How many Roman institutions we find in the Middle Ages if we examine them closely!

and whose family, fleeing before the invasion of the Carpæ, had taken refuge near Sardica (Sophia) in the Dacia of Aurelian. From a shepherd he became a soldier. He was another Maximian, rude and coarse; but like him, also, obedient and faithful, without education, but not without courage, of violent and cruel nature, useful in a secondary position if held there, but wholly unsuited to the highest rank.[1] With Constantius, on the contrary, reappeared qualities that had been long unknown in the Emperors, — gentle and elegant manners, a cultivated mind, an amiable character, and (a thing always of importance among these new men) a noble

SILVER COIN.[2]   SMALL BRONZE.[3]   MEDIUM BRONZE.[4]

lineage, his mother being a niece of Claudius Gothicus, and his father belonging to an old Macedonian family. Under Aurelian he had distinguished himself by defeating the Alemanni near Windisch (274), and Carus, it is said, had thought of adopting him. The pallor of his countenance had caused him to be called by the Greeks Chlorus, or the "Yellow;" and to claim kinship with him, all the Emperors, down to Theodosius, took his family name, Flavius,[5] as Severus and his successors had taken those of the Antonines. Being appointed Cæsar before Galerius, Constantius was to succeed that one of the two Augusti who should first quit the world or the political stage.

Constantius and Galerius were married. They now repudiated their wives, of whom one, Helena, who had been united to

---

[1] Church writers have accumulated all forms of accusation against Galerius. According to them he was made up entirely of vices and cruelties. Eutropius speaks otherwise of him: *Vir et probe moratus et caecquius in re militari* (x. 2). As administrator, the Empire owed him a new province, Valeria, which he formed in Pannonia by turning a forest into cultivated land and causing the Danube to flow into Lake Pelso (Aur. Victor, *Caes.* 40).

[2] GAL. VALERIA AVG. [n-ta], daughter of Diocletian, and wife of Galerius.

[3] FL. MAX. THEODORA AVG., second wife of Constantius Chlorus.

[4] CONSTANTIVS ET MAXIMIANVS AVG. Laurelled heads.

[5] The usurper Maximus gave this *gentilicium* to his son Victor (Wilmanns, No. 824). Eugenius took it, and Valentinian III. again bore it (*ibid.* 615).

Constantius by that marriage of the second order which the
Romans called concubinage,[1] has remained famous as the mother
of Constantine and a zealous Christian. After this sacrifice made
to policy, the Caesars married the daughters of the two Augusti.
—Galerius the daughter of Diocletian, whose lieutenant he was;
Constantius the daughter of Maximian, under whose orders he
was placed. Each was subordinated to that Emperor whose faults
he balanced or whose virtues he complemented by opposite merits:
warlike energy was joined with wisdom, mildness with strength.
Diocletian took with him the youth Constantine, then nineteen
years of age. This was as a pledge of the father's fidelity, — a
needless precaution in the case of such a man as Constantius, but
one long practised at the imperial court.[2]

Diocletian had reserved to himself the administration of the

---

[1] Zosimus, Orosius, and the *Alexandrian Chronicle* affirm this, Saint Ambrose implies it,
the Benedictines, his editors, admit it (note to the *Opera S. Ambrosii*, ii. 1210), and we find
no weight in the objections which Tillemont draws from the virtuous character of Constantius
Chlorus, and Gibbon from the condition of illegitimacy which would have prevented Constantine from being his father's heir. It has been already explained (Vol. VI. p. 460, note 1) that
no disgrace attached to marriages of this kind. Many reasons gave cause for them, among
others the inferior condition of the woman; and we know that Helena was an innkeeper's
daughter (*stabularia*, says Saint Ambrose). Constantine had also, before his elevation, a concubine, Minervina, who was the mother of Crispus (Zosimus, ii. 20, the author of the *Epitome*,
41, and Zonaras, xiii. 2). Concubinage was a real marriage, — *conjugium inaequale*, says
Theodosius, *licita consuetudo*, says Justinian; and it was as well accepted by the legists and
by the Church as is in our days the morganatic marriage of the Germans. The Bishop of Seville, Saint Isidore, wrote: *Christiano non duas simul habere licitum est, aut uxorem, aut certe
loco uxoris concubinam;* and the Fathers of the First Council of Toledo, in 400, think the same
in their seventeenth canon: *Qui non habet uxorem et pro uxore concubinam habet a communione
non repellatur.* Similar decisions were made by the Councils of Mayence, 815, and of Tibur,
895. The condition of the children of these unions was not in civil law the same with that of
children born of full legal marriages. Thus Libanius, in his twelfth discourse, asserts that the
brothers of Constantine, born of Theodora, had more right than he to the Empire, — which
would confirm Gibbon's opinion. But Constantius Chlorus and Constantine did not feel themselves bound by these ancient rules. Each of them had a son grown to manhood, capable of
succeeding his father, and meanwhile of being useful to him, and also children of a second
marriage who were still very young. The eldest was useful — necessary, even; the others
were not so; and the omnipotence of the two Augusti sanctioned all. Constantine, so severe
on "unequal marriages" (law of 337, *Code Just.* v. 27, 1), made a law giving all the rights of
legitimate children to those born while their parents were living in concubinage, if the latter
should afterwards contract *justae nuptiae* (*ibid.* v. 27, 5). It would seem as if this law, whose
date is unknown, may have been suggested to Constantine by the memory of his mother and
of his first wife.

[2] When Maxentius demanded of the viceroy of Africa that the latter should give him his
son as a hostage, he refused to do it (Zosimus, ii. 12). Aur. Victor says of Galerius that he
detained Constantine at his court, *ad vicem obsidis* (*Caes.* 40). Commodus retained at Rome
the sons of the governors of provinces (Herodian. iii. 1). Before the news of his proclamation
as emperor arrived at Rome, Severus caused his children to be removed from the city.

East, with Egypt, Libya, the islands, and Thrace; Galerius was to take charge of the Danubian provinces and Illyricum, with Macedon, Greece, and Crete. In the West, Maximian had the government of Italy, Africa, and Spain, and Constantius had Gaul and Britain.[1]

The Caesars, being invested with the tribunitian power[2] and the military *imperium*, were treated as royal personages, and wore the diadem.[3] Their names were often placed with those of the Augusti at the head of edicts, but they issued none by their own authority; and in the case of an ordinance made for a part of the Empire governed by a Caesar, the act bore indeed with the names of the two Augusti that of the Caesar concerned in its execution, but never the name of the other Caesar. The legislative power remained undivided between the two Augusti, as it had been between Severus and Caracalla, and between Valerian and Gallienus; or rather, it was entirely in the hands of him who was the soul of this government, Diocletian.[4] The Augusti entered the Caesarian provinces at their pleasure, and exercised there a supreme authority. Thus, in the absence of the Gallic Caesar, Maximian guarded the Rhenish frontier, and Diocletian in residing at Sirmium was not outside his imperial domain; most of his rescripts are dated from Illyricum or from Thrace. The Caesar received orders and even reprimands from the Augustus. We shall see that Diocletian called Galerius into the East after a defeat which the latter had suffered, and treated him with the severity of early times.[5] There seem to reappear, under other names and with a great difference in the duration of the authority, the ancient dictator and his master of the horse.

Each one of the four rulers selected a capital. The two Caesars established themselves on the frontier. — Galerius at Sirmium, the central point of defence in the middle valley of the Danube; Constantius by turns at Trèves or at York, to protect Gaul or Britain.

[1] Lactantius (*De Morte pers.* 8) gives Spain to Maximian; referring to the persecution by Diocletian, he says further (chap. xvi.): *Verabatur universa terra, praeter Gallias,* where Constantine was in command. Tingitanian Mauretania formed part of the district of Spain.

[2] Wilmanns, No. 1,061, and *Paneg. retor.* x. 1: . . . *Cum apud majestatem tuam divina virtutum restaurum vicaende prudiceram.* The Caesars were called *nobilissimi.*

[3] Euseb., *Life of Constantine,* i. 18.

[4] . . . *Valerium ut parentem suspiciebant* (Aur. Victor, 39).

[5] Under Constantius the Caesars, Gallus and Julian, were merely lieutenants of the Emperor

The two Augusti placed themselves in the second line. — Maximian
at Milan,[1] behind the Alps, but having within reach the Germans,
who were making an attempt to establish themselves in Rhaetia
and the upper valley of the Rhine; and Diocletian at Nicomedeia,

ROMAN GATE, CALLED THE BLACK GATE, AT TRÈVES.

on the shore of the Sea of Marmora, whence he kept watch at once
upon the Tigris, the lower Danube, and the Euxine, by way of
which so many dangerous invasions had come in. At the same
time no one of them confined himself to the city which he had

[1] Here Maximian built a palace and baths, of which there remain the sixteen columns
which decorate San Lorenzo. The church itself, of octagonal form and surmounted with
a cupola, like the so-called temple of Jupiter at Salona, seems also to have been one of the
great halls of the palace or of the thermae of Maximian mentioned by Ausonius in his little
poem, *Ordo nobilium urbium*.

MILAN: THE SIXTEEN ANTIQUE COLUMNS OF SAN LORENZO (FROM A PHOTOGRAPH).

made his chief residence ; incessantly they were in motion along
the frontier. which was well guarded : and if the Barbarians did
not fall back. at least they no longer advanced.

Constantius had orders to resume against Carausius the expedition which had failed in 289. The treaty signed after the
Roman defeat had been violated
by the usurper's alliance with
the Franks. to whom he promised the islands of the Batavi
and all the coast as far as the
River Scheldt ; the plundering of
the Gallic coast had doubtless
been recommenced.[1] Carausius
had a garrison at Boulogne and
a squadron in the harbor ; Constantius closed the port by a
dyke, and both garrison and
vessels were obliged to surrender.
Before attempting a descent into
Britain he made an expedition
against the Franks. pursuing
them into their marshes between
the Wahal. the Rhine. and Lake
Flevo, — a submerged territory
easy to defend, but badly defended,
however, by the Barbarians.[2] He
drove them back into Germany,

ROMAN VASE.[3]

and distributed his numerous captives, under the title of colonists.
through certain portions of the territory of Amiens. Beauvais.
Troyes. and Langres, which had been laid waste by the Bagaudae.[4]

Carausius was assassinated in 293 by his praetorian prefect
Allectus, who took his place and kept it three years ; but the
new master of Britain had neither the skill nor the power of

---

[1] . . . *Bellum quod cunctis provinciis videbatur* (Pan. vet. v. 7).

[2] *Illa regio . . . terra non est* (Pan. vet. v. 8).

[3] Roman vase found in the neighborhood of Amiens. This bronze vase is part of the
collection of M. Danicourt of Péronne. We give it in its actual size.

[4] As late as the seventh century there existed, near Langres. a *pagus Chamaciorum*
(Guérard. *Divisions territoriales de la Gaule*)

"the arch-pirate."[1] The praetorian prefect, Asclepiodotus, having collected a fleet off the mouth of the Seine, crossed unseen one foggy day, and landed in the southern part of the island. To increase the determination of his soldiers, the Roman burned his vessels. Allectus was awaiting in the Isle of Wight the attack of Constantius, who had another fleet at Boulogne. Rendered anxious by the descent of the prefect, he hastened in disorder to meet him, was defeated and killed; and when Constantius arrived on the coast of Kent, the population, happy to be rid of these Emperors, who for ten years had isolated them from the rest of the Empire, welcomed him as a savior (296).

ALLECTUS.[2]

The city of London was already the chief market of Britain, and the Barbarian auxiliaries of Allectus had hastened thither in order to pillage. A part of the Caesar's fleet, astray in the fog, had entered the Thames; carried by the tide, these vessels arrived before the city in season to save it, — a service which the inhabitants recognized with gratitude.[3]

Maximian had quitted Milan, his usual residence, and had come to exhibit to the Barbarians, in the absence of Constantius, the imperial purple, lest they might be inclined to take advantage of the departure of the troops and fall upon Gaul. When the expedition was ended, the Augustus set out for Africa, while the Caesar returned to keep in his turn the guard over the Rhine. This vigilance could not be for a moment slackened, for the Alemanni never resisted the temptation to make a raid into the Gallic provinces. In 301 they crossed the Rhine, the Ill, and the Vosges mountains, and very nearly captured Constantius himself near Langres. He had been wounded, and was saved only by being drawn up with ropes to the top of the rampart.[4] Some troops were in the neighborhood, who, hastening up, chased away these marauders; Eutropius represents them as an immense army, speaking of sixty thousand killed and an enormous number of prisoners. Eusebius reduces the number of the slain to six thousand, which is still large. The captives were given up, under the title of colonists or *Læti*, to the Lingones and Treveri owning land.

[1] . . . *Archipiratam satelles occidit* (*Pan. vet.* v. 12).
[2] Allectus, crowned with laurel.
[3] *Ibid.* v. 17.
[4] Eutropius, ix. 23.

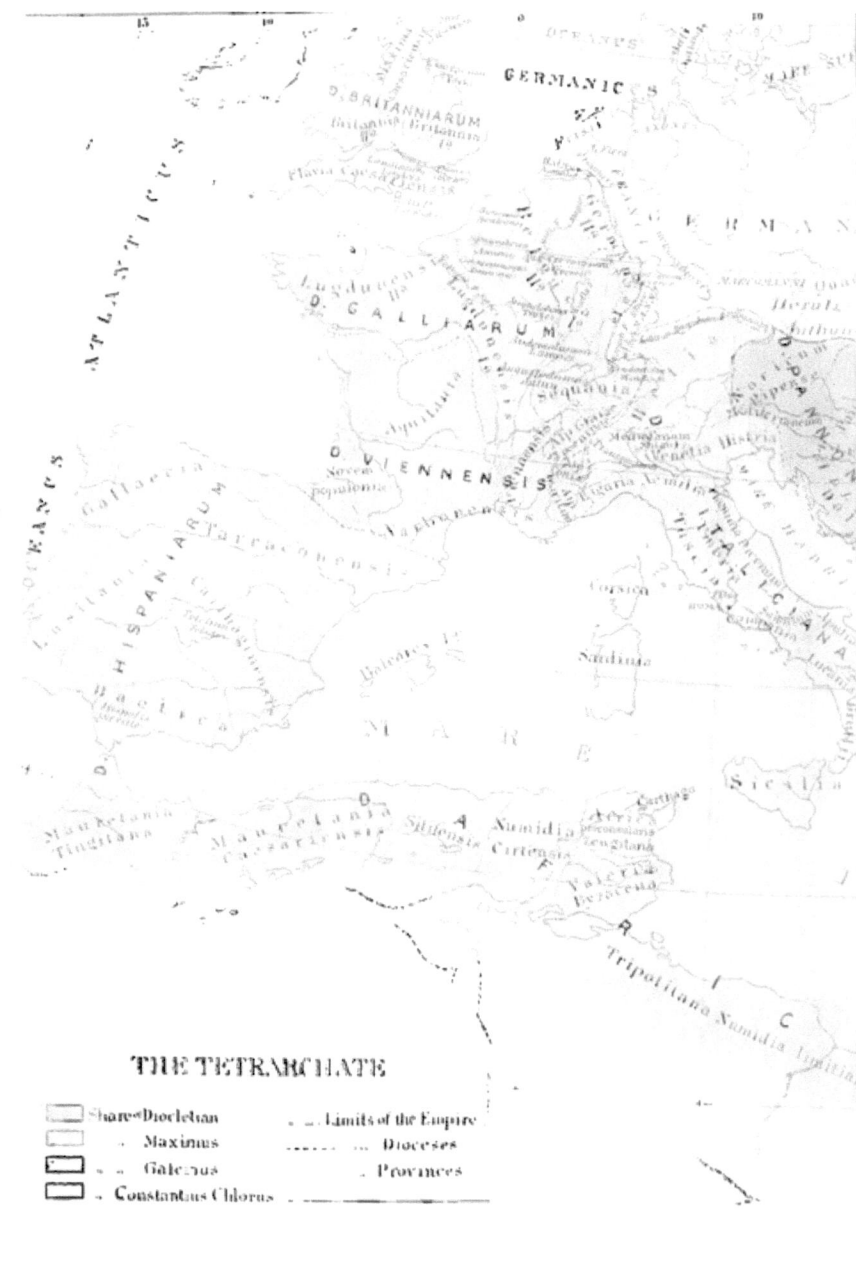

THE TETRARCHATE

Share of Diocletian	.... Limits of the Empire
" " Maximus	.... " Dioceses
" " Galerius	" Provinces
" " Constantius Chlorus	

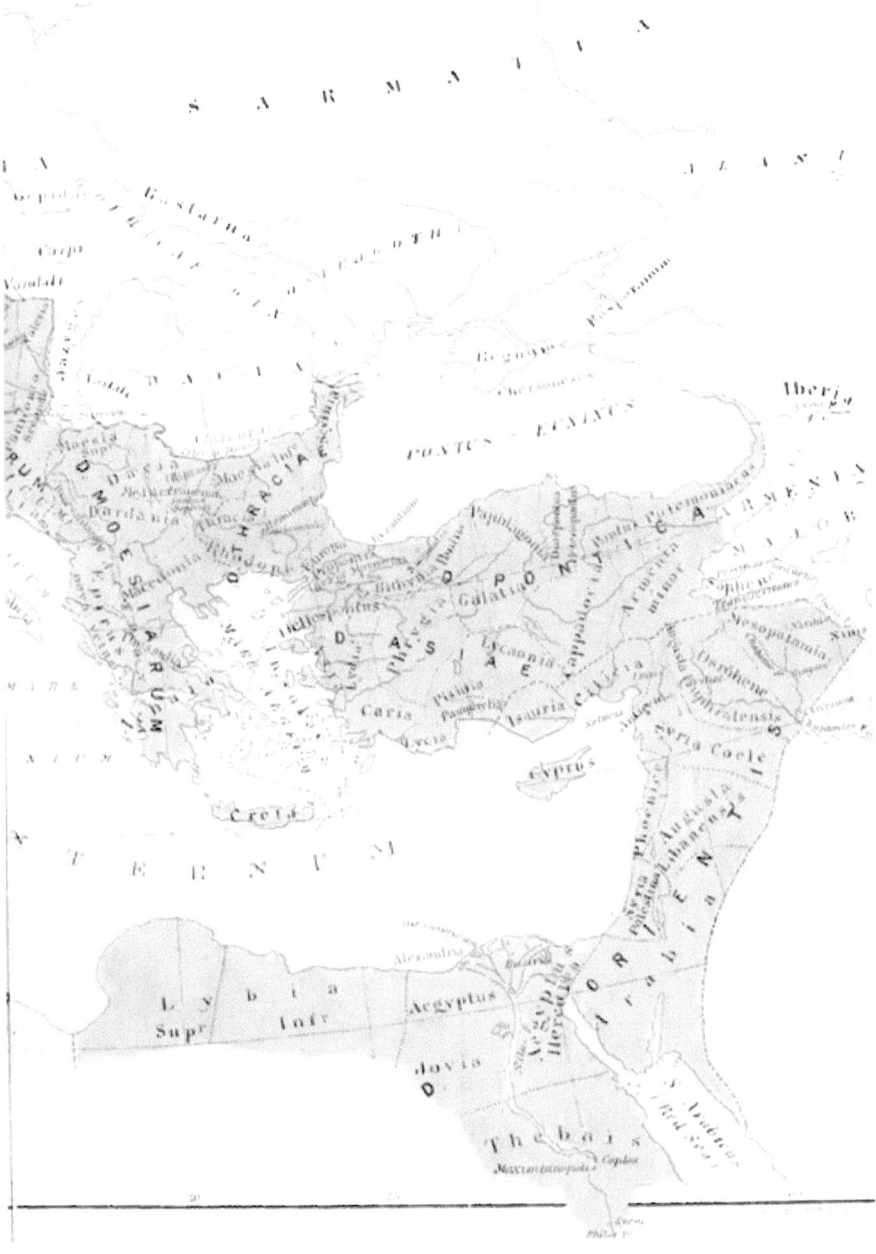

They thus occupied, with the consent of the Empire, the left bank of the Rhine, where, except in the cities, they caused the German race and speech to predominate.[1]   Eumenes saw some of them come as far as Trèves and even Autun, " accompanied by their wives and children, sad or desperate, and wildly shaking their chains ; but by degrees they grew milder, and cultivated the soil which they once ravaged, or, at the call of the generals, eagerly resumed their weapons, bent to the centurion's vine-stock, and were willing to fight and die for those who had torn them from the paternal forests."

This Eumenes, whose works we have, was the friend and secretary of Constantius; aiming to rival Cicero, he wrote panegyrics, where rhetoric and hyperbole have more place than eloquence and truth.   Some interesting details, however, are found in his writings concerning the schools of Autun.   Constantius raised this city from its ruins.   He rebuilt its baths, temples, and the aqueduct which brought abundant water ; he also strove to reconstruct the city in its intellectual relations, restoring life and distinction to its schools, whither formerly the Gallic youth flocked in crowds, and he wrote to Eumenes, putting him in charge of these schools, a letter which does him great honor : " Our Gauls deserve from us that we should take care of their children ; and what better could we offer them than knowledge, the only thing that fortune can neither give nor take away ?   Accordingly, we have determined to place you at the head of these schools, to which we desire to restore all their former distinction.   You will there direct the mind of youth towards the study of better living.   Do not fear that in accepting you will derogate from the honors you have already acquired.   That you may understand that our esteem for you is proportioned to your merits, your salary will be 600,000 sesterces, paid by the state."[2]

---

[1] The *Notitia dignitatum* (ii. 119-122) indicates an extensive distribution of the Laeti through Gaul, and only there.   These Laeti, who have given rise to so many discussions, did not belong to any one German tribe ; they were either captives whom the Empire established upon deserted territory, or German adventurers who had solicited lands in return for military service.   Guérard says in the *Polyptique d'Irminon* (i. 254) : " I have no doubt that the name *Laeti* had the signification of *auxilia* in the language of the nations of Germany.   The word *lid* or *led* has preserved this meaning in the most ancient monuments of the northern languages."

[2] *Pan. vet.* iv. 14.   In 376, at Trèves, the professor of eloquence (*rhetor*) received thirty rations (*triginta annonas*), the *grammaticus Latinus* twenty, the *grammaticus Graecus* twelve, *si qui dignus reperiri potuerit* (*Code Theod.* xiii. 3, 11).

We must place it to the credit of this Emperor that, in the days of the Roman decline, he had a taste for noble pursuits, and bestowed liberal recompense upon those who kept alive the last embers of the sacred fire, now so nearly extinct.

Eumenes was worthy of his master: he employed his 600,000 sesterces in the reconstruction of the schools, and they were opened with great public ceremonial. The governor of the province presided at the festival, and Eumenes made his finest oration. Words of sincere emotion are found in this address, and even of eloquence, when he exclaims, for example, pointing out to the governor's notice the distant ruins of the gymnasium which is about to be rebuilt: "You have seen on the walls of these porticos the earth represented with its nations, its cities and rivers, with its continents that the ocean enwraps like a girdle, that it separates from one another, or that it cleaves with its impetuous waves. In the presence of these pictures we shall explain the world, and relate the history of our invincible princes. When the messengers of victory come to tell us that our Emperors are visiting arid Libya, or Persia with the twin rivers, or the shores of the Nile or of the Rhine, we shall say to the youth gathered about us: 'Do you see this region? This is Egypt, chastised by Diocletian, and now reposing after its tumults. Here is Carthage and Africa, where Maximian exterminated the revolted Moors. This land is Batavia; this island Britain, with its gloomy forests, rearing its rough head above the waves: these Constantius holds under his powerful hand. Yonder, Galerius treads under foot the bows and quivers of the Persians.' It is a pleasure to study a representation of the world where there is nothing which does not belong to ourselves." [1] We have been accustomed to believe that our own age invented "object lessons:" but the Romans already had the idea two thousand years ago. [2]

The expedition into Africa of which Eumenes speaks took

[1] *Pro restaurandis scholis,* 20.

[2] *Ibid.* 20: . . . *Quae manifestius oculis discernuntur quae difficilius percipiuntur auditu.* Horace had already said the same thing in his *Ars Poetica,* 180: Varro (*De Re rust.*) speaks of a picture representing *in pariete pictam Italiam:* Propertius, iv. 3. 37: . . . *E tabula pictos ediscere mundos.* This was, says Florus, at the beginning of his history, a common usage; practised from the time of Alexander, adds Aelianus (*Hist. Var.* iii. 28), and Agrippa did but follow it. *Erat namque,* says Pliny (*Ep.* viii. 14), *antiquitus institutum, ut a majoribus natu non auribus modo, verum etiam oculis disceremus.*

place in 297. Five powerful Moorish nations had taken up arms.
"They were," say the writers of the time, "the most savage of
the African races." Like the tribes of the Sahara, always ready
for a raid upon the Algerine oases, these Moors had often burned
the farms of the African colonists. One of Diocletian's lieutenants
had already several times encountered them.[1] In 293 they recommenced their incursions, and threw the whole province into a state
of uneasiness, of which a usurper, Julian (?) by name, took advantage
to assume the purple in Carthage. This usurpation rendered the
situation so serious that the Augustus of the Western provinces
felt it necessary to show himself in Africa. After defeats, concerning which we have no details, Julian died by his own hand ;
the conquered Moors were pursued into the most inaccessible
retreats in the Atlas ; and the captives which were made were
transported into other provinces. To stifle the last embers of this
fire, for a moment formidable, Maximian remained in Africa till
the middle of the year 298.

These successes of the Caesar and the Augustus of the Western
provinces were matched by those of Galerius upon the middle
Danube, which river he had in charge. The Iazyges were
defeated, and a part of the nation of the Carpae transported into
Pannonia (295).

Some years later, in 299, the Sarmatians and the Bastarnae
were also constrained to emigrate to the right bank of the Danube.[2]
This system, begun in the first days of the Empire, was still
pursued ; Constantine, Valens, and Theodosius in turn continued
it ; and the frontier provinces were thus peopled with secret
enemies, who would begin by driving out the Roman civilization,
and afterwards open the gates to other invaders. The Emperors
believed their power eternal ; they expected to have time to Roman-
ize these foreign colonists. On the contrary, from the Scheldt to
the Save, the Barbarians Germanized the zone of colonization that
was given up to them, and peopled with Slavs the peninsula of
the Balkans.

Diocletian had remained during these years in Pannonia.

---

[1] *Bulletin de correspondance africaine*, January, 1882, p. 16.

[2] *Ingentes captivorum copias in Romanis finibus locaverunt* (Eutrop. ix. 25). Even the body-guard of the Emperors was formed of Barbarians (Lactantius, *De Morte pers.* 38).

Moesia, and Thrace, visiting the defences of the Danube,[1] inspiring salutary fear among the Barbarians who bordered its left bank, and, notwithstanding this prolonged stay on the extreme frontier, remaining, in a sense, present at all points of the Empire by the attention he gave to its wants. A multitude of rescripts dated from these regions show his legislative activity.[2] Under the powerful influence of this great ruler the Empire revived, security was restored to the provinces, and for this vast body, including all the civilized life of the world, it was enough to bring back prosperity that a strong hand kept the Barbarians at bay and the soldiers submissive.

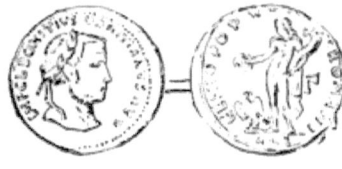

COIN OF ACHILLEUS.[3]

There was one country, however, in which prosperity did not again revive, — turbulent Egypt. In the capital of that country seethed an immense population of men of all races, conditions, and faiths, and under that burning sun men readily became hot-headed. Worshippers of Serapis, of Jehovah, or of Jesus, sceptics and *illuminati*, philosophers in search of the absolute, and neophytes who believed they had found it, all detested and despised one another. Hatred brought about riots, and riots became revolt. As soon as one man had struck, all came to blows; the streets were full of dead bodies, and in the harbor the sea was red with blood. "There is not a Christian," says the Bishop, Dionysius, "who is not involved on one side or the other." On Easter Day the church stood empty, for all men were at the barricades. The murders of which the Bishop speaks were in the reign of Gallienus; but the spirit of revolt still possessed the great city. We have seen Aurelian and Probus obliged to visit Alexandria to overthrow usurpers, and

---

[1] Idacius places at this time the construction of the strongholds in the country of the Sarmatians on the left bank of the Danube, and inscriptions mention the reconstruction, by Diocletian and Maximian, of cities in Switzerland, Africa, etc. The oration of Eumenes *Pro restaurandis scholis* testifies to the immense works at that time going on for the fortification of the frontiers along the Rhine, the Danube, and the Euphrates. From the *Notitia* have been counted 103 strongholds or fortified positions in the Eastern Empire.

[2] Letter from Dionysius, bishop of Alexandria, quoted by Eusebius, vii. 21.

[3] Bronze coin of Domitius Domitianus Achilleus. IMP. CL. DOMITIVS DOMITIANVS AVG., surrounding a wreathed head of the usurper. On the reverse: GENIO POPVLI ROMANI ALE, around the Genius of the Roman people.

under the reign of Diocletian, Achilleus even ventured to assume the purple there.[1]

This rebellion was a disaster for Rome, for it hindered the provisioning of the city; but it was not a peril to the Empire, since out of Egypt could come no dangerous enemy. The Emperors, no longer residing in their ancient capital, did not hear the starving cries of its populace, who demanded indeed *panem et circenses*, but made no riots. The insurrection breaking out in Alexandria did not therefore draw them away from more important duties upon the northern frontier. That region being pacified, Diocletian set out for Egypt, arriving there in the middle of the year 295. Alexandria resisted all his efforts for eight months, and he only entered the city after having cut the aqueducts which brought the water of the Canopic branch of the Nile. To end these perpetual revolts, which were a dangerous example, he gave the city up to a military execution; it was sacked, and blood flowed in torrents. Coptos and Busiris shared the same fate.[2] The country was then reorganized. Eutropius, who lived nearly a century later, says that this reorganization, of which he does not give the particulars, still remained in force in his time.[3] Like Augustus, Diocletian respected the Egyptian religion; but in that land of prodigies and credulity books of occult science were everywhere in circulation, and these the Emperor caused to be seized and burned.[4] He did another service to Egypt by protecting the country against the Blemmyes, who plundered caravans coming from ports of the Red Sea, and infested the Thebaïd with their brigandage. Instead of wasting his time and strength in tracking them in their deserts, he called in the little garrisons scattered through lower Nubia, between the

[1] Eutrop. ix. 22; Aur. Victor, *Caes.* 39. On the authority of a medal, Tillemont represents this Achilleus as reigning six years. But Diocletian was not the man to allow an insurrection to exist for so long a time if it could possibly be suppressed, and Eckhel (iv. 96) declares this medal false.

[2] Malalas (xii. 309) relates one of those stories so dear to the Oriental mind: Diocletian had given orders to kill until the blood should come to his horse's knees; but the horse having stumbled over a corpse, got up with his knees bloody. It was a sign sent by the gods; the Emperor comprehended it, and stopped the massacre.

[3] ix. 23: . . . *Ordinavit provide multa . . . quae ad nostram aetatem manent.*

[4] "Egypt was the headquarters of the occult sciences, to which the Chaldaeans seem to have added nothing except horoscopy and prophecy, founded on an examination of the skies" (Révillout, *Revue égyptol.* i. 147). Diocletian prohibited throughout the Empire divination by astrological diagrams, *ars mathematica damnabilis est et interdicta omnino* (*Code Just.* ix. 18, 2).

First and Second Cataracts, where they were too feeble to hinder anything. It was a movement of withdrawal; but the Empire in concentrating made itself stronger. A numerous garrison occupied the Island of Philae and intrenched themselves strongly there; another was posted on an inner line at Maximianopolis, which had been built on the ruins of Coptos. A wall, connected with the

SACRED EGYPTIAN BARQUE CARRYING A SHRINE.[1]

defences of the island, barred the whole valley, and remains of this wall are still to be seen. Not to neglect any means of making this frontier secure, he negotiated with the Blemmyes, who for an annual subsidy agreed no longer to molest Egyptian commerce. The agreement was consecrated by religious ceremonies in the temple of Isis. The Blemmyes were fervent worshippers of the Egyptian goddess; they claimed free access to her temple, and the renewal of the old law which authorized their priests[2] to

[1] Perrot's *Ancient Art.*
[2] Letronne, *Mémoires pour l'histoire du christianisme en Égypte*, etc., pp. 74 et seq.

come annually to the island and carry away her image, to keep
it for a certain time in their country. In an inscription which appears to be of the time of the Antonines we read: "Upon the Nile I have seen the rapid vessels bringing back the sacred temples from the land of the Ethiopians." The "temple" was a coffer, usually gilded, containing a statuette of Isis. Diocletian would never have consented to let a Latin divinity make excursions after this fashion. But the Roman pontifex maximus did not concern himself with regard to the adventures of Isis; and since the Blemmyes attached importance to these pilgrimages, he deemed it wise to permit them.

Diocletian had written his name in blood on the walls of Alexandria; but he reorganized there a method of relief for the poor.[1]

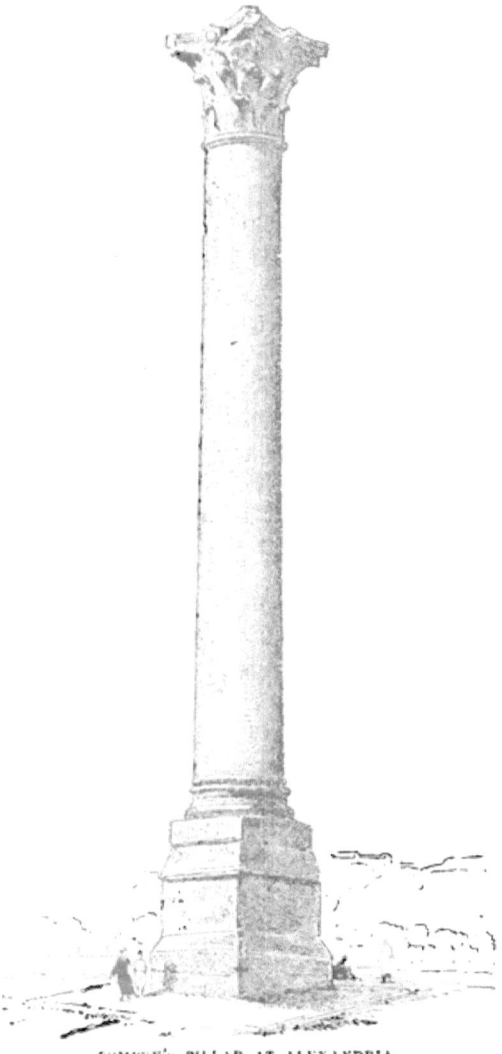

POMPEY'S PILLAR AT ALEXANDRIA.

and the fickle-minded city saw without displeasure the prefect

---

[1] It had already long existed there: see p. 220. Procopius (*Historia Arcana*, chap. xxvi.) speaks of 2,000,000 *modimni*, equal to 12,000,000 *modii*, dispensed at this time. (Cf. *Chron. of Alexandria, ad ann.* 302.)

Pompeius erect a column surmounted with the statue of Diocletian, with an inscription in honor of "the invincible Emperor." The statue has disappeared, and the column, still standing near the harbor, does not even bear the name of Diocletian, "the tutelary Genius of Alexandria;" it has long been believed a monument of him who was defeated at Pharsalia, and is called to this day "Pompey's Pillar."[1]

In 294 Narses, second son of the peace-loving Bahram, had assumed in Ctesiphon the diadem of Persia. He was a warlike king, who occupied himself in re-awakening the martial ardor of his people. Diocletian was at the time in the interior of Egypt, and Galerius in Pannonia: and the Persian judged it a favorable moment to attack Armenia, whence he drove out Tiridates, and at the beginning of the year 296 crossed the Tigris with a numerous army. Narses remembered the prosperity of Sapor, and he hoped to emulate, even to excel it, and to maintain it for a longer time.[2] Warned by the blow struck in Armenia, Diocletian had already called into Syria the Caesar of the Oriental provinces, and himself advanced towards Palestine, — but slowly, as suited a monarch whose calm majesty was never disturbed by impetuous movements.

Did Galerius know how and why Crassus had perished? Without being unjust to him, we may doubt if he did; the defeat of Valerian, however, was recent enough to be clearly in his mind, but he took no warning from it. He crossed the Euphrates and led his legions into that plain of Carrhae where the sand but scantily concealed so many Roman bones. The scenes of former times were repeated; his cavalry could not resist the shock of the cataphracti, and his heavy infantry, overcome by heat and by thirst, blinded by the dust in the midst of the rapid squadrons sweeping around it, experienced the fate of the legionaries of Crassus. It is said that Tiridates escaped only by swimming across the Euphrates, weighed down as he was with his armor. Galerius also escaped with his life and the shattered remnant of his army. Just outside Antioch he met Diocletian, who received him with a severe countenance, and refused to let him enter the imperial chariot. Then was seen the spectacle of the haughty Caesar, clad in his purple

---

[1] *C. I. G.* No. 4684.
[2] *Ad occupandum Orientem magnis copiis inhiabat* (Lactantius, *De Morte pers.* 9).

mantle, and with shame upon his brow, walking on foot for the space of a mile before the chariot of the angry Augustus.[1]

Diocletian rapidly collected the troops from the camps on the Danube, enrolled Barbarians in the army, especially Goths,[2] and re-formed a Syrian army, which seems to have been very strongly constituted. He divided it into two corps: with one he took up a position on the Euphrates, to defend the fords in case of need:

A CATAPHRACTUS. FROM TRAJAN'S COLUMN.

he put Galerius at the head of the other, tracing out for him the plan of a campaign, in which the military experience of the former lieutenant of Probus is clearly shown. He directed the Caesar to take, in the favorable season, the route formerly followed by Antony across the Armenian mountains, and gave him for a guide in this country the expelled king Tiridates. At their approach the people received them gladly; provisions and information came in abundantly to the camp: the legions had all the advantages which the complicity of the inhabitants gives to an invading army. The

<hr />

[1] Amm. Marcellinus, xiv. 11.　　　　[2] Jordanes, 21.

Persians came to meet them on this unfavorable battle-ground;
and filled with confidence by reason of their recent victory, kept
so careless a watch that Galerius with two horsemen, in reconnoitring
the position, was able to penetrate their very camp. By a vigorous night attack he created a panic among them, and made
great slaughter. Narses, who was wounded, escaped with the

greatest difficulty; but his wives and children
were captured, together with the treasure heaped
up in the royal tents (297). Since Alexander's
victory at Issus, six centuries before, the Oriental
barbaric world had suffered no such disaster.

COIN OF NARSES.[1]

At the news of this brilliant success Diocletian entered Mesopotamia and joined Galerius
at Nisibis. The Caesar was eager to repeat

Alexander's expedition. For the Macedonian conqueror it had not
been temerity when he hurled the mass of his army upon the empire of Darius and plunged into the remote East as far as the banks
of the Indus, for he had nothing to fear from the nations he left
behind him. But the Romans, who had to guard, on the west and
south and north, an immense frontier line always threatened, were
not in a position to imitate this dangerous enterprise. Diocletian
calmed the too-impetuous ardor of Galerius, and displayed towards
the captives that had been taken a consideration not at all usual at
that time. When Narses, won by this conduct, made overtures of
peace, Diocletian received them cordially. The first condition
claimed by the Romans was, however, rejected.[2] They wished the
Persians to agree to have all their commerce with the Empire pass
through Nisibis, — doubtless in order to simplify the service of the
imperial custom-house, and to concentrate the relations between the
two countries at a single point easily to be watched.[3] Narses

---

[1] Silver coin of Narses, son of Bahram II. Bust of the prince and a legend signifying
"the worshipper of Ormuzd, the excellent Narses, king, celestial germ of the gods."

[2] In the *Excerpta de legationibus*, edit. of Bonn, p. 134, are to be found curious details in
respect to these negotiations, preserved to us by Peter Patricius. He lived in the time of
Justinian, but was able to examine the archives. (Cf. *Fragm. Histor. Graecor.* iv. 188.)

[3] These questions of import dues had so great a financial and political importance for the
Empire that a schedule of duties, recently found at Palmyra (De Vogüé, session of the *Acad.
des inscr.* of June 1, 1883), shows the Romans as early as the reign of Tiberius interposing
in that city for the drawing up of a tariff of which they doubtless shared with the Palmyrenes the products. (Cf. *Code Just.* iv. 61, 13.) The Roman sway having crossed the

refused to agree to this, and the project was abandoned; but he admitted the Roman possession of northern Mesopotamia, whose limit on the south seemed to admit of being marked by the fortified city of Circesium, near the confluence of the Chaboras with the Euphrates, and by Singara, at the base of a mountain in an arid region, which rendered an attack difficult, and relief difficult also. Nineveh, on the Tigris, where for two centuries a Roman colony had maintained itself in some unknown way,[1] marks perhaps the eastern extremity of this line. In the upper valley of the Tigris the Persian king relinquished five Armenian provinces which had been conquered by Sapor I., and now, in the hands of Rome, would protect a part of Armenia and Asia Minor against the Persians.[2] Tiridates recovered his kingdom, increased by a part of Media Atropatene, and the Iberian chiefs in the basin of the Kour relinquished their allegiance to Persia and accepted the supremacy of Rome (297). This treaty was a brilliant success, worth far more than the recapture by Augustus of the standards of Crassus, for it gave the Empire as allies the nations living near the Caspian and the Caucasus, while Roman garrisons were established in the mountainous region on the north of Mesopotamia, who could arrest on its advance or defeat by a flank movement any force seeking to invade Asia Minor and Syria. The victory of Galerius and the statesmanship of Diocletian bestowed upon Roman Asia a peace that numerous fortresses, built along the

Euphrates, Diocletian desired to have Ni-ibis occupy the position that Palmyra had held, — that of being the desert mart between the two empires.

[1] Nineveh was still a great city in the time of Amm. Marcellinus (xviii. 6), and this author calls it the capital of Adiabene. Its inhabitants, like the Greeks of Seleucia, had doubtless a sort of municipal independence, which permitted them to incline towards whichever of the two empires seemed for the moment the more formidable. The Persians traversed it freely in 359.

[2] Uncertainty exists respecting the names of these five provinces, which Peter Patricius and Amm. Marcellinus (xxv. 7) give differently. — Zabdicene, Corduene, Arsacene, Intelene, and Sophene, according to the former; Zabdicene, Corduene, Arsacene, Moxoene, and Rehimene, according to the latter. We are not able even to assign to them all a well-determined geographical position. It is enough to know that they are all north of Nineveh, in the upper basin of the Tigris and on its eastern shore, in the Kurdistan of modern times. During the reign of Julian, Corduene had for governor a Persian satrap of Roman name, Jovianus, a man secretly in sympathy with Rome (Amm. Marcellinus, xviii. 6). The occupation of Corduene by the Persians was merely *de facto*, — doubtless acquired in the reign of Constantius; for this province was expressly ceded by Jovian in the treaty of 363.

eastern frontier, maintained for forty years.[1]   The Augustus had
well deserved the honor of a triumph: the Senate decreed it to
him, but he waited six years before celebrating it at Rome.

III. — Administrative Reorganization and Legislation.

It is in fable only that Minerva springs full armed from the
brain of Jupiter.   In history, political creations are prepared by
the travail of ages, and only such are lasting.

More than one Emperor before Diocletian
had felt the necessity of taking a colleague,
of dividing the great administrations, even of
sharing the Empire itself,[2] and enfeebling the
praetorians; more than one had allowed himself to be called lord or god,[3] and the coins of
Trajan and of Antoninus Pius represent them
with the radiate crown.   The coins of Trajan
as yet surround with the sacred nimbus, which
was later assumed by the Christian Emperors, only the head of
the fabulous bird which in Egypt was believed to spring from its
own ashes; but those of Antoninus give him that symbol of immortality.   The nations were displeased neither at these titles nor
these crowns, for the established religion made it a duty for them
to adore the Emperor living, and they were accustomed to erect
temples to their dead Emperors.

BRONZE OF ANTO-
NINUS.[4]

---

[1] Malalas says that the line of fortresses constructed by Diocletian extended from Egypt
to Persia.   See also Suidas, s. v. ἐσχατά, and Amm. Marcellinus, xxiii. 5.

[2] Vespasian had set the example of these divisions of provinces.   In the time of Caracalla
and Geta a division of the imperial authority had been under consideration.   See Vol. V. p.
157, and p. 75 of the present volume.

[3] Caligula had assumed to be both; Commodus had caused himself to be called god: . . .
ἐκαλεῖτο καὶ θεός (Zonaras, xii. 5).   The decurions of Barcelona declared themselves devoti
numini majestatique Claudii Gothici (Orelli, No. 1,026).   The same words were used in respect
to Aurelian by one of the legions (ibid. No. 1,024).   Medals of Aurelian and of Carus, struck
during their lifetime, gave them the titles of deus and dominus (Eckhel, vii. 508–9).

[4] Large bronze of Antoninus, representing him with his head crowned with rays and a
nimbus.   See W. Madden, The Numismatic Chronicle, xviii. 9 (1878).   A cameo represents
Severus also with the radiate crown, and Gallienus wore it: . . . Radiatus saepe processit
(Hist. Aug. Gall. 16), and Aurelian did the same.

A century and a half before Diocletian, Hadrian had made his council the principal machinery of government; and Caracalla and Gratian had separated the civil functions from the military in not permitting the presence of a senator in the army.[1] The offices of *comes, corrector,* and *dux* were very ancient; in the third century A. D. we find the *magister militum*; and the praetorian prefect had long been intrusted with the administration of justice and finance. The system of grants of land made to the soldiers, with the condition of military service, was an old republican institution,

COINS OF TRAJAN, REPRESENTING, ON THE REVERSE, THE PHOENIX CROWNED WITH THE NIMBUS.

— the *colonia,* preserved by Augustus, possibly regulated by Alexander Severus; and two of the dangers which were to end by destroying the Empire, — namely, the Germanization of the frontier provinces and of the army, — had begun with Augustus. Caesar had Germans in his army in Gaul, and Tacitus shows around the first Emperors and in the auxiliary corps of the legions foreigners of every race.[2]

A pride in titles was extremely ancient at Rome; we have seen the rigorous classification made by Augustus. From the first days of the Empire it was required to salute the senators as *clarissimi;* the knights of noble family were *illustres,* and under Marcus Aurelius the *eminentissimi* and the *perfectissimi* had privileges which lasted for three generations. A *procurator* under Commodus is called *egregius.* The *procurators* of Severus all bore this title; and from the third century, or even earlier, there was a sort of hereditary succession for the *curiales.* The nomenclature for the hierarchy was already formed.[3]

---

[1] Lampridius says of Alexander Severus (24): *Provincias legatorias praesidiales plurimas fecit.* Borghesi (*OEuvres,* iii. 377; v. 397 and 405) thinks that from this time forward the *praeses* had the civil administration, the *dux* the military command.

[2] Tac., *Ann.* i. 7; *Hist.* i. 46.

[3] *Dico Marco placuit eminentissimorum quidem nec non etiam perf. virorum usque ad pronepotes liberos plebeiorum poenis vel quaestionibus non subjici.* A dishonorable action (*violati pudoris macula*) arrested, however, the transmission of this privilege, which Ulpian recognizes,

Language, manners, and the exigencies of defence had prepared the separation of the Roman world into two empires. Asia had repeatedly had governors who were invested with full powers, — Agrippa and C. Caesar under Augustus, Germanicus under Tiberius, Corbulo under Nero; and Marcus Aurelius, Valerian, and Carus had relinquished to a colleague half of the provinces.

The Conscript Fathers had long since ceased to have any share in the government, and all authority had been vested in the imperial officials. The revival of the Senate in the time of the Gordians and of Probus had been but the last flicker of energy in a body whence life was departing: all things were now done in the offices of the sacred palace,[1] for the reason that there was the only force which could set in motion the vast machine. Finally, the industrial corporations and the agricultural colonization had made the beginning of a profound change in the world of labor.

Diocletian therefore did not create in all its parts a new political and social edifice; in reality he accomplished nothing more than a great administrative reform. But the republican exterior so carefully assumed by Augustus, preserved by many of the succeeding Emperors, and restored again by Carus, was thrown off: nothing now concealed the master, *el rey netto*, and the autocratic republic of Augustus appeared in its final aspect, — that of an Oriental monarchy.[2]

We have already spoken of the most important of the measures of Diocletian, — the establishment of the tetrarchy. To prevent revolutions, by making the regular succession to the Empire dependent upon the choice of the living Emperor; to defeat the intrigues of the ambitious and the riots of the soldiery, by dividing the commands, the armies, and the public treasure, — such had been his theoretic conception. To carry out this theory he decided that the Empire, divided equally, should have two Augusti (one being superior to the other) and two Caesars, who, subordinate to the

decurionibus et plebeiorum (*Code*, ix. 41; cf. C. I. L. vol. i. No. 1,085, and vol. vi. No. 1,603). The application of these exaggerated epithets went very low. In an inscription of the time of Alexander Severus an iron mine is called *splendidissimus* (*Rev. épigr. du midi de la France*, No. 257).

[1] Hirschfeld, *Römisch. Verwaltungsgeschichte*. We have seen, in the reign of Hadrian and in chap. xcv. sect. 3, the beginning of the slow evolution which transformed the monarchy of Augustus into an autocratic and Oriental despotism.

[2] Eutropius (ix. 26) says: *Imperio Romano regiae consuetudinis formam magis quam Romanae libertatis invexit.*

Augusti during the lifetime of the latter, should be their legitimate heirs. This form of government was something new, since Diocletian made a rule of what had hitherto been only a temporary expedient, and since, instead of Emperors reigning together in Rome — where their action, not being divided, might prove conflicting — each Augustus and each Caesar had permanently his share of provinces to govern and Barbarians to hold in check.

After the division of the Empire and the imperial power, came that of the provinces.[1] The Republic had not greatly changed the frontiers of the nations: its domain had been divided only into fourteen governments; at the accession of Hadrian there were forty-five. This increase was due to the conquests of Augustus, Claudius, and Trajan, but especially to the dismemberment of the early provinces. Since the time of Vespasian, the Emperors had been aware that commands extending over regions as vast as kingdoms gave rise to ambitious desires and dangerous attempts. More than any one of his predecessors, Diocletian had been aware of this peril; and as he had divided the Empire, in order the better to defend it, so he increased the number of provincial divisions in order to rule it more successfully. At the time of his accession there were fifty-seven provinces; during his reign the number was increased to ninety-six, forming thirty-seven new governments.[2] — which justifies the words of Lactantius, *provinciae in frusta*

---

[1] Aur. Victor, 40; Lactantius, *De Morte pers.* chap. vii.: . . . *Provinciae in frusta concisae, multi praesides et plura officia singulis regionibus ac paene jam civitatibus incubare, item rationales multi et vicarii praefectorum.* In Egypt were created the provinces Aegyptus Jovia and Aegyptus Herculia; in Moesia and in Pannonia the provinces Margensis (in honor of the victory gained by Diocletian at Margum) and Valeria (named from the Emperor's daughter); in Britain, Flavia Caesariensis (in honor of Constantius Chlorus); and many others in Asia Minor.

[2] The *Notitia dignitatum*, prepared about the year 400, gives 120 provinces; a list of 386 (?) comprises only 113; another, of 369 (?), gives 104. The list given by Mommsen in the *Proceedings of the Academy of Berlin* for 1862, p. 489, from a manuscript of Verona, probably dates from the year 297. It enumerates ninety-six provinces, distributed in twelve districts, as follows: 1, the East (comprising Egypt, Syria, and Mesopotamia); 2, Pontus (the northern and eastern portions of Asia Minor); 3, Asia (the western part of Asia Minor, with the islands); 4, Thrace (between the Rhodope, the lower Danube, and the sea); 5, Moesia (between the middle Danube and Thrace); 6, Pannonia (the western part of Illyricum); 7, Italy; 8, Africa; 9, Spain (with Mauretania Tingitana); 10, Viennensis (Narbonensis and Aquitania; later, the district of the Seven Provinces); 11, Gaul; 12, Britain. The memoir in which Emil Kuhn (1877) disputes the value of this document has, it is true, been justly combated by Czwalina (1881), but there still remain doubts in respect to certain provinces in the list of Verona, their formation appearing to date from the second half of the fourth century. See C. Julian, *De la Réforme provinciale attribuée à Dioclétien* (*Revue hist.* vol. xix. 2d part, pp. 331 *et seq.*).

concise, but does not justify the fault-finding spirit which dictated them, since the measure was excellent. Diocletian grouped these ninety-six provinces into twelve *dioceses*, or districts governed by *vicarii*, or vicegerents who had a surveillance over the consuls, *correctores*[1] and presidents or judges sent into the provinces. Two or three countries, by reason of their ancient renown, — Carthaginian Africa, Greece, and Asia, — were governed by proconsuls, who were amenable directly to the Emperor.[2] Thus we find, at the head, the Augusti; below them, the Caesars; lower yet, the vicarii; and lastly, the presidents. This was a political structure which seemed to be capable of resisting attacks from without, and suppressing disturbances from within. For more safety, the military order was rigorously separated from the civil, and the governors of provinces, whose promotion depended upon their services, were reduced to juridical and administrative functions.

Originally the provinces had been divided between the Senate and the Emperor; we have seen what the claims of the Conscript Fathers were in this matter as late as the reigns of Tacitus and Probus. In the new organization all the provinces were dependent upon the Emperor; and the extent of many of them being reduced, the care exercised by the governors was more thorough, justice more prompt, matters were examined at closer range, and decisions reached more quickly.[3] Severe regulations established the respon-

---

[1] The words *diocesis* and *corrector* were not new. The *diocesis* was originally a financial or juridical subdivision of the province (Or.-Henzen, No. 6,498; Mommsen, *Inser. Neap.* No. 1,433). Diocletian, on the contrary, united several provinces to form a *diocesis*. Under Caracalla we find an *electus ad corrigendum statum Italiae*. The *juridici* of Marcus Aurelius became *correctores*; under Aurelian, Tetricus was *corrector Lucaniae*. (Cf. E. Desjardins, *Revue archéol.*, 1873, 2d part, p. 67.) It has already been remarked that each supreme magistrate had his corps of subordinates (*officium*), which did not change with their chief: . . . *Officiales perpetui sunt* (Paulus, *Sent.* ii. 1, 5; cf. *Code Théod.* xi. 30, 59). They kept the official books, and could remind the judge of the statute in case he had forgotten it (*Code Théod.* xi. 10, 15).

[2] Böcking, *Not. dign.* i. 167, and ii. 118. Macer had said, as early as the time of Alexander Severus (*Dig. i*, i. 18, 1): *Proconsulis nomen generale est coque et proconsules et legati Caesaris et omnes provinciis praesides . . . praesides appellantur.* In the fourth century the name of *judices* prevailed, — a natural change, since the suppression of the formulary method of procedure greatly enhanced the judicial functions of the presidents. The Antonines had given currency to the idea that the principal function of a governor was to enunciate the law. The *juridici* of Italy date from Marcus Aurelius, and under Hadrian and Antoninus there had been these officers in the provinces.

[3] The ordinary procedure in a civil matter, the *jure ordinario agere*, that the Republic and the Early Empire had practised, had given place gradually to the *cognitio extra ordinem*. An

sibility of these officers. "He bound them fast," says Aurelius Victor, "by the most just laws."[1]

An inscription of the time of Diocletian — that of Caelius Saturninus — proves that the essentially Roman custom was still observed of causing the public servants to fill the most diverse offices, and of giving them but a short time in each. Saturninus held twenty, from the office of advocate of the treasury to that of praetorian prefect, — all of the civil order; by which we see that the rule established by Augustus, and maintained as late as the time of Severus and the Gordians, requiring service in the cavalry, was now no longer observed.[2] An absolute ruler likes to take his servants from every station, even the lowest. These functionaries, not being eminent by birth, consoled themselves with the pomp of titles: humble offices had become sacred magistracies, *stipendia cognitionum sacrarum aut palatii magisteria*.[3] The sepa-

---

ordinance of 294 authorizes the presidents to appoint judges only when they themselves were absolutely prevented by other duties from fulfilling this office. The *judices pedanei*, being appointed, pronounced sentence independently of the president, who had cognizance of these affairs only upon appeal of the parties (*Code Just.* iii. 3, 2). To prevent these governors from acting in any instance without due deliberation, Diocletian forbade their revoking sentences once rendered in criminal cases, so that their negligence might become known to the Emperor if an appeal brought the case before him (*Ibid.* ix. 47, 15). Every Roman magistrate had his council, composed of men whom he called together to aid him with their advice. This duty was an onerous one; it took time and caused expense and exposed to ill-will. Diocletian forbade the presidents to compel any man's services as *assessor*; they were to be allured to this office *spe praemiorum atque honorificentia* (*Code*, i. 51, i).

[1] *Officia, cincta legibus aequissimis* (*Caes.* 39).

[2] L. Fabius Cilo Septiminus, who was consul under Commodus and Severus (C. I. L. Nos. 1,408–1,410), also filled twenty different offices; but in his case the rule of military service was observed, as it was also for the father-in-law of Gordian III., Timesitheus, who made his entrance upon public life as prefect of an auxiliary cohort (*Antiquités de la ville de Lyon*, p. 162, edit. of 1857).

[3] Eumenes, *Pro rest. scholis*, 5, and C. I. L. vol. vi. No. 1,704. We give the *cursus honorum* of Septimius and of Saturninus, who, with a century between, both arrived at the highest positions, the one by services rendered in all kinds of civil and military offices, the other without ever leaving the civil career. The two inscriptions, therefore, well indicate the difference in the times.

Inscription of Septimius (C. I. L. vol. vi. No. 1,408, and Wilmanns, Nos. 1,292–1,292 b): 1. *Decemvir slitibus*. 2. *Tribun. milit. leg. XI Claudiae*. 3. *Quaest. prov. Cretae et Cyren*. 4. *Tribun. pleb*. 5. *Leg. pro praet. prov. Narbon*. 6. *Praet. urban*. 7. *Sodalis Hadrianal*. 8. *Leg. Aug. leg. XVI Flav. Firmae*. 9. *Proconsul. prov. Narbon*. 10. *Praef. aerarii militaris*. 11. *Cos. (suff. anno 195)*. 12. *Leg. Augg. pr. pr. prov. Galat*. 13. *Propositus vexillationibus Perinthi pergentibus*. 14. *Leg. pr. pr. provinc. Ponti et Bithyn*. 15. *Dux vexillat. per Italiam*. 16. *Leg. pr. pr. provinc. Pannon. sup*. 17. *Cur. Miniciae (porticus), R. P. Nicomediensium, Interamnatium, Nartium item Graeciscanorum*. 18. *Praefectus Urbi*. 19. *Cos. II (anno 204)*.

Inscription of C. Caelius Saturninus (C. I. L. vol. vi. No. 1,705): 1. *Fisci advocatus per Italiam*. 2. *Sexagenarius studiorum adjutor*. 3. *Sexagenarius a consiliis sacris*. 4. *Duc. varro*

ration between the civil and military functions, which had begun long before this time, was so rigorously kept up by Diocletian that service in the army, already prohibited to the nobility of the Empire,[1] was now denied to the municipal aristocracy also. He closed the legions against the decurions, their sons, and all those persons who by their fortune were eligible to municipal offices.[2] The army was recruited even among the Barbarians, and there was an end to the military spirit among this people who by it had achieved such great things.

We shall later show in its entirety the so-called "divine hierarchy:" but we must first speak of an important innovation,— the formation of an Asiatic court crowding that dwelling which Nerva and Trajan had called "the public palace." Diocletian was an admirer of the Oriental world, its royal customs pleased him, and he copied its stately ceremonial. He replaced by vestments of silk and gold the military tunic over which his predecessors had merely thrown a scarlet mantle; upon his forehead he wore the royal diadem which Aurelian had already assumed, and his purple slippers were studded with precious stones. To the imperator, whom all men, soldiers and citizens, might freely salute, succeeded the king-god, hidden in mysterious shadow, in the depths of a palace whose approaches were guarded by a crowd of eunuchs and officers. Whoever obtained from the *magister officiorum* an imperial audience, was led thither by a master of ceremonies and introduced by the *admissionales invitatores.* Crossing the threshold guarded by thirty mutes, he fell prostrate and adored "the sacred countenance," scarcely daring to lift his eyes to this motionless and dreadful majesty.[3] Those even to whom their rank gave daily admittance were subjected to this servile ceremonial.[4]

a consiliis (sacris). 5. Magister libellorum. 6. Magister studiorum. 7. Vicarius a consiliis sacris. 8. Magister censuum. 9. Rationalis vicarius per Gallias. 10. Rationalis privatae. 11. Vicarius summae rationum. 12. Praefectus annonae Urbis. 13. Examinator per Italiam. 14. Vicarius praefecturae praetorio bis, in urbe Roma et per Mysias. 15. Judex sacrarum cognitionum. 16. Vicarius praefecturae Urbis. 17. Comes domini nostri Constantini Victoris Augusti. 18. Alle tos postea senatus inter consulares. 19. Praefectus praetorio.

[1] See p. 194.

[2] . . . Omnibus in fraudem civilium munerum (Code Just. xii. 34, 2).

[3] Amm. Marcellinus, xv. 5, sect. 8: *Admissionum magistrum;* Boeking, Not. dign. i. 237, and ii. 305. The *magister officiorum* was the supreme magistrate of the palace, and had an extensive jurisdiction over civil and military officers. His duties explain his insignia.

[4] . . . Quibus adstum vestri dabant ordines dignitatis; et . . . admissis qui sacros vultus

All became sacred, the palace of the Emperor as well as his person, his words, and his acts. Never before in our European world had man so much encroached upon the honors due to divinity.

It was not for the gratification of a puerile vanity that Diocletian placed himself outside the pale of common life and condemned himself to this wearisome routine. The man who had said that the best monarch, the most prudent, the wisest, always is in danger of being sold by his courtiers,[1] did not undervalue the advantages to be derived from a free communication between the sovereign and the subject. But he believed that there would be fewer revolutions in the state when there should be more respect for the ruler; that imperial majesty would be more imposing in the twilight where he proposed to keep it; that servility in words and attitudes would guarantee in the interests of public tranquillity a servility in men's minds; that, finally, obedience would be better secured by a pomp of ceremonies and the severe forms of authority. This would have been a well-founded expectation in the case of an old dynasty, the object of public homage, or of a clergy speaking in the name of Heaven; but it was a mistake in the case of one asking from official etiquette a power that historic circumstances did not give him. Diocletian, rising from so low to so high a condition, had experience enough to know what these outside shows were worth, what a burden this sumptuous court, copied by the other Augustus and by the Caesars, would impose upon the treasury, what a deleterious effect it would exercise on the already effeminate minds of men in a time which demanded all possible effort to make them more virile. But the servility of the Asiatic races and of an Empire in its decline made him believe in the happy effects of this stately ceremonial.

Diocletian abandoned the fiction of a delegation of authority by the people to the Emperor. He had been unwilling to hold anything from the old sources of power, — the citizens, the Senate, the army; and from the authority given him by his generals he constructed a sort of divine right which he communicated freely

---

adoratui erant (Pan. iii 11). See Eutrop., ix. 26. The title of *dominus* is not, however, found on the coins of Diocletian (Eckhel, viii. 11), but he allowed it to be given him: *Dominum dici passus*, says Aur. Victor (*Caes. 39*), *parentem egit.*

[1] Vopiscus, *Aur.* 43.

to his colleague and to the successors chosen by himself alone.
The sovereignty was again displaced. From the forum and the
curia it had passed into the camps; now it was held within the
palace.[1] The court of Diocletian was an importation from the Asiatic
world of customs which certain European dynasties afterwards inherited. It created that factitious social condition in which the mind
grows fine and acute, and politeness and elegance give the most
charming exterior, but in which manners too often become corrupt
and characters degraded, and life is made up of flatteries, of secret
treasons, and of mendicancy. Under Diocletian none of these evils
appeared, for the reason that he imposed upon his courtiers a respect
for the law as well as for himself; but after him were opened " those
voracious mouths "[2] whereby Constantine suffered his people to be
preyed upon, and the splendors of Constantinople ruined the finances
of the Empire, as later the magnificent follies of the old Bourbon
monarchy exhausted the resources of France.

In presence of these innovations the ancient things languished
or died. Rome ceased to be the capital of the world; nothing
more came to it, and all things deserted it, — important public business, gay and animated life, barrack riots, palace tragedies. To
the eye the stage remained very nearly as Augustus had constructed
it. If there were no longer Emperors on the Palatine, there were
still the consuls and praetors in their curule chairs, the senators under
their laticlaves, — an assembly of the dead, in a city now entering
upon its new *rôle*, that of the great museum of the world.

There was, indeed, no place for Oriental kings in a city filled
with memories of the senatorial Republic and the Early Empire.
The liberty of speech, the habits of familiarity with their rulers
that the people had kept, would have been grave infractions of
the etiquette of the new court. At the time of the conference
of Milan, " Rome," says the Panegyrist, with his customary bad
taste, " Rome looked from her hill-tops, endeavoring, to catch a
glimpse of her Emperors in the distance."[3]   But she saw nothing

---

[1] The author of the *Actio gratiarum Julia* says that the comitia of Rome were now in the
breast of the Emperor: . . . *in sacri pectoris comitia* (*Pan. vet.* xi. 15), — an awkward imitation
of the words of Plautus in *Epidicus*, i. 2, which are at least witty: *Jam senatum consecuba in
corde consiliorum.*

[2] Amm. Marcellinus, xvi. 8.

[3] . . *E speculis suarum montium prospicere conata* (*Pan. vet.* iii. 12).

coming.   The Augusti remained occupied with the affairs of the
Empire. and. paying no attention to Rome, returned to protect
the frontiers.

Diocletian had received the purple in Nicomedeia from the hands
of his fellow-soldiers; he kept it without asking from the Senate
a confirmation of his titles.   Incessantly he made laws. — we have
twelve hundred of his rescripts, — and not one of them was prepared
by the assembly which had been the great council of the Empire.
Up to this time the Senate had appeared to make the consular
elections: it was a pure formality. but precious. nevertheless, to
an easily gratified vanity.   Diocletian now took the appointment of
the consuls into his own hands.[1]   Thus to drop the veil which hid
the nothingness of the Senate's authority, was a public insult: the
Conscript Fathers were justly incensed: there followed imprudent
words. possibly conspiracies, certainly executions.   Diocletian did
not pay these senile ebullitions the honor to concern himself personally with them; he gave the matter in charge to Maximian. —
well fitted for such a duty.[2]

The praetorian prefect, the man once called "the king's sword."
remained a person of importance: but he ceased to be dangerous.
His military authority was almost suppressed by the formation

---

[1] A consular diptych, that of Flavius Felix. "a very illustrious man. *comes* and *magister*
of the two military services. patrician and *consul ordinarius*." who was consul of the West in
428, was long preserved entire in the abbey of Saint Junien de Limoges.   There were
originally two panels of this diptych, one of which was brought in 1808 to the Cabinet of
Medals in Paris.   The other is lost. but we know it from the publications of Mabillon.
Annales ordinis Benedictini: of Banduri, *Imperium orientale:* of Gori, *Thesaurus veterum
diptychorum,* i. 120.   Ch. Lenormant has also reproduced it in the *Trésor de numism. et de
glyptique.*   The consular diptychs were double tablets of ivory which the consuls distributed
to the senators on taking office.   Justinianus, consul of the East in 521, inscribed upon his
diptych: —

> *Munera parva quidem pretio, sed honoribus alma,*
> *Patribus ista meis offero consul ego.*

Here the use of the consular diptychs is perfectly indicated.   A law of the *Theodosian Code,*
made in 384 under Valentinian II. and Theodosius. grants to the consuls exclusively the right
of distributing these ivory diptychs: *Exceptis consulibus ordinariis nulli prorsus alteri diptycha
ex ebore dandi facultas sit.*   See Chabouillet, *Revue des Sociétés savantes.* 5th series, vol. vi. 1873.

In this diptych the consul is represented as standing in his place in the theatre, holding
the long consular sceptre, surmounted by a globe, which bears the busts of the reigning Emperors. Valentinian III. and Theodosius II.   The inscription is as follows: FL[avii] FELICIS
V[iri] C[larissimi] COM[itis] AC MAG[istri].   There remains only one more ancient
diptych, that of Probus, consul in 406, under Honorius.

[2] Lactantius, *De Morte pers.* 8: . . . *Non decrant locupletissimi senatores qui suburnatis
indiciis affectasse imperium dicerentur* (Aur. Victor, 39).

of four distinct armies; by the regular and no longer accidental appointment of *magistri militum*, who left the prefect only the care of the commissariat and the pay;[1] lastly, by the suppression of the corps of *frumentarii*, which had given him absolute power over the lives and fortunes of the principal men of the provinces. In the Early Empire it had not been considered wise to multiply the administrative *personnel*; and yet many functionaries were necessary for the conduct of public affairs, and particularly for the maintenance of public order, which, necessary in every civilized country, is pre-eminently so in a monarchical country. The army fulfilled this duty. From the first days of the Empire it had furnished officers to watch over the interests of Rome in the free cities (for instance, Byzantium), or among turbulent allies like the Batavi and the Moors; later it furnished soldiers and centurions who were retained at Rome, *frumentarii*, under the authority of the praetorian prefect. After being trained for their new trade, they were sent into the provinces to see and hear, and afterwards tell what they had ascertained. By their reports the *frumentarii* often gave cause for accusations even against the governors of provinces.[2] Hence their odious reputation, and the joy caused by their suppression. With his new officials, Diocletian had no longer need of this vast system of espionage which had given the praetorian prefects so formidable a weapon.[3] He attached so much importance to having it known that all could rely upon the justice of the Emperor that, in the

---

[1] Under Constantine, who made them exclusively civil functionaries, there were four praetorian prefects: the opinion of Zosimus (ii. 32) seems most correct, that there were but two under Diocletian, as there were but two Augusti. The prefect Asclepiodotus, who aided Constantius against Allectus, was probably Maximian's praetorian prefect, and still held the early military position attached to this office. As to the *magistri*, we read of them from time to time during the third century; thus Aurelian, under Valerian and Claudius, held the *militiae magisterium*, either for command or inspection of camps and fortresses (*Hist. Aug., Aur.* 9, 11, and 15). A function like this was too useful for Diocletian not to have made it a permanent position (Lactantius, *De Morte pers.* 7). What the duties were, we do not know; it was doubtless a great service of inspection and command, which received from Constantine its definite form when he instituted two *magistri militum*, one for the infantry, the other for the cavalry.

[2] M. L. Renier has thus explained the character of the *frumentarii*, contrary to the opinion which represented them as officers employed in the commissariat. We know that centurions were employed in mines and quarries as superintendents of the works. With the Romans the army was useful for all purposes.

[3] Constantine re-established this police service, intrusting it to *agentes in rebus*.

rescript entitled. "Concerning those who, through fear of the judge, have not dared to appeal," he says: "If thou hast not appealed from the sentence pronounced against thee, it is because thou hast accepted it ; for in our sacred court thou hadst nothing to fear."[1]

As for the praetorians, their number was gradually diminished by sending malecontents into the legions ; and the haughty band which had made and unmade so many Emperors, fell without resistance to the condition of a guard of city watch, as this Senate, which had governed the world, was reduced to being only the municipal council of Rome. And thus the two ancient powers, so long enemies, perished together. The strength of the urban cohorts, who were under the command of the prefect of the city, was also reduced.[2]

The Augusti substituted for their body-guard of praetorians two battalions levied in the Illyrian provinces. These soldiers took the names of the Emperors, being called the Jovian and the Herculean, and, proud of being fellow-countrymen of their masters, they exhibited towards them absolute fidelity.[3]

The Dalmatian who cared so little about the people whom his predecessors had courted, desired, however, to have the Romans see in their own city a monument of his ostentation ; he caused to be built on the Viminal, with disdainful magnificence, baths more extensive than those of Titus and of Caracalla.[4]

[1] *Codex Just.* vii. 67, 1.

[2] *Inminuto praetoriarum cohortium atque in armis vulgi numero* (Aur. Victor, Caes. 39 ; Lactantius, *De Morte pers.* 15). After his victory over Maxentius, Constantine suppressed the praetorians, whose name thenceforward is lost to history. From the middle of the third century the Emperors, always absent from Rome, and always distrustful of the praetorians, had given themselves a private guard, composed of two corps, infantry and cavalry, who were called *domestici* and *protectores*.

[3] Zosimus, iii. 30. In respect to what may be called the line, Diocletian doubtless began that dismemberment of the legions which Constantine systematically continued. In the time of Hyginus the legion was still composed of six thousand men ; but Diocletian, having constructed many castles and fortresses along the line of the frontiers, wished, no doubt, to have them guarded by small bodies of troops, which should have, nevertheless, their complement both of men and munitions. For this service the legion was too numerous, and it became necessary to reduce it. From his reign on, the word *schola* takes the signification of " a detachment of soldiers," — a sense in which we find it both in the *Code* and in Amm. Marcellinus. It would seem that Hyginus wrote his book *De Munitionibus castrorum* in the beginning of the third century ; it is therefore useless to us for the period of the tetrarchy. The treatise of Vegetius, *Epitome rei militaris*, composed between 384 and 395, does not distinguish dates, and hence throws no light upon the military organization of Diocletian. Later we shall see that of Constantine.

[4] Many other buildings were erected by Diocletian at Rome, at Antioch (Malalas, xii.

Rome was now but an ordinary city, Italy but a province. Up to this time she had been required to furnish only the provisions necessary for the palace and for the troops stationed in the capital or in the peninsula (*Italia annonaria*). Diocletian subjected her to the land-tax, which since the time of Augustus she had never paid. He thus effaced a privilege offensive to the rest of the Empire rather than created any considerable financial advantage, for the tax was moderate at first. The country adjacent to Rome, as far as a hundred miles from the walls (*urbicaria regio*), remained exempt from the contributions to which the rest of annonary Italy was subjected.[1]

The *consilium*, already reconstructed by Hadrian, became the *consistorium sacrum*, — a sort of council of state, composed of the principal persons of the Empire, and filling in the administration the place vacated by the Senate. It deliberated in the presence of the Emperor upon subjects which he laid before it;[2] it assisted him in the exercise of his judicial functions; and a part or all of the members accompanied him on his journeys and formed part of his court at Nicomedeia, Antioch, and Sirmium. Finally, we see that he made a reform in the general maintenance of order throughout the Empire.

We mention, in passing, the completion of the judicial evolution which had been going on since the beginning of the Empire, — the *cognitio extra ordinem*, substituted for the formulary procedure; in criminal cases the *inquisitio*, or information, formerly the part of the accuser, now made officially by the magistrate; in civil cases the twofold prosecution, first before the praetor (*in jure*), and then before the judge (*in judicio*), replaced by the single suit before the judge, a state functionary.[3] The judicial system of the Republic,

306), at Nicomedeia, etc. (Cf. Orelli, Nos. 1,047, 1,052, 1,054, 1,055, 1,056, etc., and Lactantius, *De Mort. pers.* 7.) An inscription very recently discovered, shows an African city, which the rebels had destroyed, rebuilt by Diocletian and Maximian.

[1] Aur. Victor, 39. Cf. Lactantius, *De Morte pers.* 23.

[2] *Iupp. Imed. et Maxim.*, A.L., *in consistoria dixerunt* (*Cod.*, ix. 47, 12). The members of the council received as salary 60,000, 100,000, and 200,000 sesterces, as we know from the inscription of Saturninus.

[3] The praetor had the *jurisdictio*; that is to say, the right to grant or refuse an action. The action being allowed, he named judges, who were specially appointed for each case. These judges had the *cognitio*, or first inquiry, and could be readily challenged and set aside. When they were not selected exclusively from one of the great political bodies (as they were in the last century of the Republic), citizens possessed guarantees against the interested

RUINS OF THE BATHS OF DIOCLETIAN.

which Augustus had preserved, was entirely unsuited to the new imperial monarchy. Formerly the magistrate did not intervene in the case except by the *judicis datio*; henceforth he was to concern himself with it at every stage; and the judges being, as public functionaries, the delegates of the Emperor, the sovereign might revise their sentences, either directly or by the *vice sacra judicantes*, making in his name a second trial, whose decisions he would accept or reverse. All civil and criminal justice thus came to be in the Emperor's own hands; and thence it followed that when the venality of the last century of the Republic re-appeared in the Later Empire, justice, as well as the administration, was polluted by it, the two being then blended.[1]

The municipal law of Caesar had ordered for Italy a quinquennial census. To accomplish this for the entire Empire was difficult; accordingly, in the time of Ulpian it took place only every ten years. The minute description that Ulpian has left us of it proves what scrupulous care the Romans employed in making an equitable apportionment of the taxes.[2] At the expiration of each decennial period a new valuation of land was made, on the declaration of the owners, subject to correction by the *censitor*. Lactantius speaks of this necessary revision in terms of alarm which have misled later writers. It has been thought that Lactantius revealed outrageous exactions, begun by Diocletian and continued by Galerius;[3] when in reality this measure was nothing more than one of the most ancient customs of the imperial administration. Diocletian, who multiplied offices and lined all the frontiers with defensive works, must have been obliged to create means for so

sentences of magistrates and against arbitrary action on the part of government. The law of Diocletian, which is of the year 294, is found in the *Code of Justinian*, iii. 3, 2.

[1] In respect to this change, see above, p. 386, note 2, and Puchta, *Instit.* vol. ii. p. 264, sect. 182; Walter, sect. 743; Bethmann-Hollweg, iii. 164; and Cuq, *Le Magister sacrarum cognitionum*, or chief of the department where was made the preliminary investigation of matters submitted to the Emperor. The right of appeal to the sovereign had since the time of Augustus modified the judicial organization of the Republic. The reorganization of the imperial council by Hadrian, who made it into a supreme court of judicature, had prepared the way for the reform accomplished by Diocletian. The Emperor was at that time the source of all justice.

[2] *Digest*, l. 15, 4.

[3] *Agri glebatim metiebantur; vites et arbores numerabantur; animalia omnis generis scribantur; hominum capita notabantur* (*De Morte pers.* 23). The *Theodosian Code* (ix. 42, 7) shows the regularity of the work which was done in the time of Augustus and before him: ... *Quod spatium et quod sit ruris ingenium; quid aut cultum sit aut colatur; quid in vineis, olivis, aratoriis, pascuis, silvis fieri inventum.*

many expenses. Taxes certainly were increased; perhaps it was he who made general the tax of twelve and a half per cent formerly levied on articles of luxury [1] alone; and if he abolished the tax of the twentieth on inheritances and on enfranchisements, of which we find no trace after his time,[2] he increased that of one per cent upon sales, which is later mentioned as a very heavy burden.[3] But the re-establishment of order and industry prevented the weight of public expenses from being very much felt; Aurelius Victor has already shown us that under Diocletian they were easily borne.

A document recently discovered attributes to this Emperor a curious simplification in the administration of the finances.[4]

Like Augustus, he divided the lands into various categories, — vineyards, olive-yards (two classes), corn-lands (three classes), and grass-lands, which were taxed in proportion to their supposed productiveness. To render the collection more easy, he formed a taxable unit, *jugum* or *caput*, including lands of different character and unequal extent, which having, taken together, the same value, 100,000 sesterces or 1,000 aurei ($3,000), owed the state an equal sum.[5] Thus five *jugera* of vineyards, or twenty *jugera* of arable land of the first quality, made a *caput*. Forty *jugera* of the second quality, or sixty of the third, 225 olive-trees in full bearing, or 450 mountain olive-trees (*in monte*) were required to constitute a like taxable unit. The *jugum* or the *caput* was therefore not a mathematical, but a taxable unit.[6] Every financial

---

[1] *Code Just.* iv. 61, 7: . . . *Octavas* more solito *constitutas*, under Gratian. We have seen Diocletian much occupied during the negotiations with Persia by the question of the *portorium*. The enormous duties paid at Palmyra (above, p. 380, note 3) show that the tax of 12½ per cent could not have been a *maximum* established only in certain places.

[2] An inscription of Gruter does indeed place, under Valens, a *procurator XX hered.*; but this inscription is doubly suspicious, both by the manner in which it is composed, and from the writer, Panvinio, who gives it. Orelli (i. 59) says of him: *Dubia omnino haud rara ejus est fides.*

[3] Cassiodorus, *Variarum*, iv. 19.

[4] The *Syrisches Rechtsbuch*, published by Bruns in 1880.

[5] *Nov. Major.* vii. 16; *Nov. Valent.* iii. 5, sect. 1; Cassiodorus, *Variarum*, ii. 37. The taxable unit had not everywhere the same name, nor, perhaps, the same extent. In Africa it was the *centuria*; in Italy the *millena*; and it is said in the *Theodosian Code* (xi. 20, 6): . . . *Sive qua alio nomine nuncupentur.*

[6] Mommsen, *ap.* Hermes, iii. 150, and Marquardt, ii. 219. Every proprietor declared personally to the imperial officer (*censitor*), — in the presence of the other tax-payers, who were interested in his declaration (*professio*) being truthful, — the amount of his fortune, as is done

district comprised a certain number of them, and this number determined the amount due from the whole district. According to the needs of the government, the sum of the whole tax was raised or lowered (*indicebat*, whence *indiction*), as in the modern world percentages are added or taken off. When government consented to make a reduction in the case of a proprietor or of a city, the number of *capita* were diminished which were ascribed to the city or the man in the registers of the census.[1] Hence the request inspired by the classic souvenir of the labors of Hercules: "Regard us as Geryones, and the tribute, the monster; that I may live, cut off three heads."[2]

The sum imposed by the state upon the financial district was made known to the decurions of the city, who apportioned the tax among the *possessores*, collected it, and gave over to the agents of the treasury the sum demanded by the Emperor. If there was any deficit, it was made good from the property of the decurions; that is to say, they were held responsible for the tax.[3] Citizens are always so held, since deficits can be made up only by them; but among the moderns it is the entire mass of tax-payers who make the sum complete. Under the Empire it was a particular class, and the responsibility at last proved fatal to it.

Notwithstanding these precautions, the taxes did not always

in England in the case of the income-tax. *Omnia ipse, qui defert, æstimet* (*Digest.* l. 15, 4). If his statement were doubted, he might be required to prove it, and a false declaration was punished by confiscation. This was the law (*Codex Theod.* xi. 2, 2) in the case of senators, and doubtless it applied equally to those of lower rank. The census, originally quinquennial, later decennial, appears to have been made, after 312, at intervals of fifteen years, which gave origin to the method of reckoning time by *indictions*.

[1] Thus the territory of Autun contained 32,000 *jugera*, which Constantine reduced to 25,000 (*Pan. vet.* viii. 11). Julian diminished in Gaul the tax for each *caput* from 15 to 7 aurei (Amm. Marcellinus, xvi. 5, 14). The *Theodosian Code* (xi. 20, 6) speaks of *capita relevata vel adaerata levius*. The basis of the *caput* served even in the matter of furnishing supplies by the *possessores*: in Thrace, twenty *capita*; in Scythia and Mœsia, thirty; in Egypt, in the East, in Asia, and Pontus, thirty-three (?) collectively are required to furnish a military garment (*Hist. Aug., Gordian III.* 28, i. and *Theodosian Code*, vii. 6, 3).

[2] *Geryones nos esse puta monstrumque tributum :*
   Hæc capita, ut vivam, tu mihi tolle tria.
                    SID. APOLLIN., *Carm.* xiii. 19.

[3] . . . *Decaproti et icosaproti . . . pro omnibus defunctorum fiscalia detrimenta resarciunt* (*Digest*, l. 4, i. sect. 1; 3, sect. 10; 18, sect. 26). The latter law (18, sections 1-30) should be read in all its details in order to understand the extent of the *munera civilia*. The lists of the apportionment were preserved in the *tabularium* of each city by the *tabularii civitatum* (*Theodosian Code*, xi. 28, 3); several of these are in existence; for example, that of the Volceii, in the country of the Lucanians, for the year 323 (Mommsen, *Inscr. Neap.* No. 216).

come in readily, for the reason that, the Romans obtaining their principal public revenue from real estate, crushing burdens were laid upon it. Accordingly, there were insolvent *possessores*, ruined *curiales*,[1] proprietors who, when about to sell their land, had kept back the payment of the arrears with which the property was

LABORS OF HERCULES.[2]

burdened, and thus escaped paying it, — a dead loss to the treasury, since they possessed nothing else with which to answer for their debt.[3] Thus arrears accumulated (*reliqua*), for recovery of which the advocate of the treasury instituted proceedings, usually upon information given by a *delator*, whose trade was encouraged

[1] The *curiales* were doubly responsible, first, towards the state, as members of the committee of ten or of twenty (*decemprimi, decaproti, icosaproti*), or simply as *curiales* required to collect the tax (Papinian, in the *Digest*, l. i. 17, sect. 7); second, towards the city as magistrates (Ulpian in the *Digest*, l. 2, 2, sect. 8). In both cases their fortunes were at stake; and it so often happened that the *curiales* became impoverished in the public service that a law was made rendering the city responsible, in such cases, for their support (*Digest*, l. 2, 8).

[2] Bas-relief from a sarcophagus of the Borghesi Villa. Under the principal design is represented the chase of the leopard, the wild boar, and the wild bull. Upon another side of the same sarcophagus appear other exploits of Hercules and similar hunting-scenes. In Vol. V. facing p. 566, is represented another sarcophagus, a so-called cinerary urn, having bas-reliefs of the same kind.

[3] Constantine renewed in 319 (*Theodosian Code*, xi. 3, 1) the prohibition long ago made against bargains of this kind (*Digest*, l. 15, 5).

RUINS OF THE BATHS OF DIOCLETIAN. ENTRANCE TO THE CHURCH OF S. MARIA DEI ANGELI

by a premium of a fourth part of the sums recovered (*quadra-plator*). From time to time policy dictated to the Emperor the re-linquishment of these arrears. This was done by Domitian, Trajan, Hadrian, Antoninus, Marcus Aurelius, and Aurelian, and later by Constantine.[1] There is no mention in any document of a like measure adopted by Diocletian; but the relief granted by Constantine in 310 embraces only the *reliqua* of the five years preceding,[2] — which gives ground to suppose that his great predecessor had left none.

SMALL TRADES: A CUTLER'S SHOP. FROM A BAS-RELIEF.

Diocletian confirmed all the privileges which had been accorded in preceding reigns to the decurions,[3] and also the authority of the municipal laws, which the governors were required to respect;[4] he even exempted from the capitation tax the artisans in cities (*plebs urbana*) for the small landed possessions they might hold in the country.[5] But anxious, like his predecessors, to secure the

FIELD-LABORERS SURROUNDING A PLOUGHSHARE.[6]

performance of all public duties in the cities, he took care not to let the *possessores* withdraw from municipal duties,[7] while making

---

[1] Hadrian remitted about $10,000,000. [2] *Paneg. ret.* viii. 13.

[3] *Codex Theod.* ix. 41, 11, and 47, 12; x. 31, 4, and 42, 3.

[4] *Ibid.* xiii. 49, 1; xi. 29, 4.

[5] *Ibid.* xiii. 10, 2. The words of this rescript, addressed to the presidents of Lycia and Pamphylia, *sicut in orientalibus provinciis observatur*, show that the immunity granted by Diocletian had been abolished in the provinces of Galerius (Lactantius, 23). In 313 Constantine and Licinius re-established it throughout the entire Empire.

[6] Engraved stone; Caylus, vol. v. pl. 83, 6.

[7] *Codex Theod.* x. 41, 6–10.

the obligation of the *munera personalia* cease for them at the age of fifty-five.[1] That he never accorded exemption from the capitation tax to the rural population, was due to the fact that this favor would have been profitable only to the great landowners, who were responsible to the treasury for their coloni;[2] the peasants therefore remained subject to the capitation, to the *annona*, and to the compulsory labor and the furnishing of extra supplies. But the ordinance *Ne rusticani, ad ullum obsequium devocentur,*[3] protected them against all other dues or taxes; and when the cities made an attempt to throw off upon the country the superindictions, under pretence that they were tributes *extra ordinem*, he established distinctly that these were to be paid by the *possessores*.[5] Finally, by another ordinance he declared that the colonist who had fulfilled the terms of his contract should not be held responsible for the debts of his landlord.[6] We have seen the formation of a new social condition, — that of the colonist; we now see another division made among the inhabitants of the Empire, — the *urbani*,

LIBRARY OF THE LATER EMPIRE.[4]

CHANGER OR VERIFIER OF MONEY.
FROM A PAINTED GLASS.

---

[1] *Codex Theod.* 49, 3.   The exemption was valid only *si inopia civium non est* (*ibid.* 2).

[2] *Ibid.* XI. i. 4.

[3] *Ibid.* xi. 54, 1; an ordinance undated, but signed with the names of Diocletian and Maximian   [4] From Garrucci, *Storia dell' arte crist.*

[5] *Ibid.* x. 41, 10: . . . *Quandoquidem ea patrimonii munera esse constet.*

[6] *Ibid.* iv. 10, 3, *anno* 286.

exempt from capitation; the *rusticani*, who pay it.   These divisions announce the approach of the mediæval period.— the time, that is to say, of inequality and rural distress.

In abolishing the capitation-tax for the *plebs urbana*, Diocletian favored the lesser industries. He attempted to assist legitimate traffic by two other measures, the one excellent, the other bad, — a monetary reform which Constantine was later to complete, and the establishment of a maximum price for articles of daily use.   We have seen what evils were caused by the monetary crisis of the second half of the third century. With the idea that to give to a piece of metal any desired value, it sufficed to engrave the Emperor's name upon it, the Roman government had ended by putting in circulation gold pieces and silver pieces which contained neither gold nor silver. But when the buyer offered to a dealer, in exchange for what the latter had to sell, a piece of copper coated with tin, it was natural that the trader should require, before parting with his merchandise, a large amount of this copper, whatever might be the designation which the authorities had attached to the piece. Very high prices resulted, therefore, from the depreciation of the currency, and the whole state was disturbed by a false economic idea. Diocletian quickly saw the cause of this evil; but he thought he could remedy it by an act of supreme power. " All men know." he says in the preface to his edict. " that articles of traffic and objects of daily use have attained exorbitant prices, four or' eight times their true value, or even more than that; so that, through the avarice of monopolists, the provisioning of our armies becomes impossible. We have therefore determined to fix, not the price of these articles, which would be unjust, but the amount which in each case they will not be allowed to exceed."   Many fragments of this edict remain to us; the following are some of the items: —

Rye (per bushel)	$1.50
Oats ,,	0.82
Common wine (per quart)	0.20
,, oil ,,	0.30
Pork (per lb.)	0.20
Beef ,,	0.20
Mutton and goat's flesh (per lb.)	0.13
Lard, first quality	0.26

A pair of chickens	$0.72
„ ducks	0.48
A hare	1.78
A rabbit	2.48
Oysters (a hundred)	1.20
Eggs „	1.20
Field-laborer's wages (and food) a day	0.30
Mason or carpenter's wages (and food) a day	0.60
House-painter's „ „ „	0.89
Decorative painter's „ „ „	1.78
Shepherd's „ „ „	0.24
Barber's „ (per person)	0. 2½
Reading-master's „ (per month, one pupil)	0.60
Arithmetic „ „ „ „	0.90
Writing „ „ „ „	0.60
Grammar „ „ „ „	2.40
To the rhetorician or sophist „ „	2.98
„ lawyer for an inquiry	2.40
„ lawyer for obtaining a judgment	11.92
„ bath attendant (per bather)	0. 2½
Nailless shoes of muleteer or peasant	1.43
Horse's bridle, with bit	1.20
An oilskin	1.20
Hire of an oilskin (per day)	0. 2½
Pack-saddle for a mule or camel	4.16
„ „ an ass	2.98
Woman's boxwood comb	17.0

" As a whole, these prices differ but little from city prices in our own time; the dearness of common wine is perhaps the thing most noteworthy, the more so since wine was abundant in all the provinces of the Empire, — possibly it paid to the treasury a high tax, comprised in the duty on sales." [1]

We have no right to reproach Diocletian severely for the economic fault he committed, for fifteen centuries later the Convention in France again established by law a maximum of prices. The event showed the Emperor that no human will could prevail in matters like these against the force of circumstances. The dealers, required to sell at a lower price than they had paid, concealed their commodities; scarcity increased; street-brawls followed, in which blood was shed; and it became necessary to let the law drop into disuse.[2]

[1] Waddington, *Édit de Dioclétien, établissant le maximum dans l'empire romain*, p. 6.
[2] Lactantius, 7. The edict *De Pretiis* is of the year 301.

But that which the edict could not effect by order, the monetary reform, which took place between 296 and 301, slowly effected. Diocletian coined *argentei*, of which ninety-six were made to the pound, their weight averaging 3.40 gr.,[1] and *aurei* sixty to the pound, weighing therefore 5.42 gr., which gave them an intrinsic value of about $3.41;[2] lastly, *denarii* of copper, or *folles*, worth $\frac{1}{7\frac{1}{5}3}$th of an *aureus*, or about a cent and a quarter.[3] This last figure is unfortunately uncertain;[5] it is therefore proper

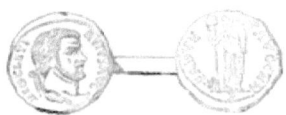

MEDIUM BRONZE.[4]

to exercise discretion in respect to the view we have just given,

MEDIUM BRONZE.[6]

wherein values are stated on the scale of the worth of the copper *denarius*. But if this list does not give veritable prices, it is at least interesting, as it shows relative values existing between different commodities and in the remuneration of services. As to the effect produced by the monetary

[1] They were called *milliarii* (μιλιαργήσιον), because it took a thousand of them to equal in value a pound of gold, — which shows us that at this time silver was to gold as 1 to 14.

[2] We have seen that Julius Caesar made 40 *aurei* from the pound of bullion; Constantine made 72, each weighing 4.55 gr. This piece, called *solidus*, was not again changed until the fall of the Byzantine Empire. An ordinance of the year 367 gave 72 *aurei* to the pound; one of the year 325 (*Codex Theod.* xii. 7, 1) says there shall be 7 *solidi* to the ounce of gold, or 84 to the pound (*uncia* = $\frac{1}{12}$ of the *libra*); but it was long ago proposed to read in this text *sex* instead of *septem*. A kilogram of pure gold being worth to-day $442.06, a Roman pound of 327 grammes of gold represents about $211.20, which gives the *solidus* an intrinsic value of a little over $2.88. Like the *aureus*, the *solidus* always bore the effigy of the reigning emperor; and this usage still lasts. Procopius (*Bell. Goth.* iii. 33) says that a piece of gold bearing any other than the Emperor's head would not be received in trade, nor even have currency among the Barbarians.

[3] In reckoning, the *follis*, or purse, represented 125 *milliarii*, or two purses were equivalent to the ancient *sestertium* (1,000 sesterces). Throughout the Levant men still compute by purses, and the purse is equal to $22.08.

[4] DIOCLETIANVS AVG., laurelled head. F[elix] ADVENT[us] AVGG. XX.; Africa holding a standard and an elephant's tusk.

[5] Mommsen reckons the *follis* equal to two cents, while Waddington considers it as little over one cent. By weight and chemical analysis we are able to determine exactly what quantity of pure metal is found in a coin, and what is the present value of the metal. But it is almost impossible for us to know its relative value in antiquity; that is to say, what debt could be paid, or what merchandise purchased, with such a coin. Another thing disturbs our calculations, the interest in those days was twelve per cent, sometimes in business twenty-four per cent; the rate at which in prosperous times the banker Jucundus of Pompeii lent money.

[6] IMP. C. DIOCLETIANVS P. F. AVG., laurelled head. On the reverse: GENIO POPVLI ROMANI ALE; Genius of the Roman people.

reform, it was inevitable; as the circulation of good money increased, prices fell back to their natural level.

ARGENTEUS.[1]

We have already called attention to the legislative activity of Diocletian. The *Codes* have preserved twelve hundred of his rescripts. Most of these are administrative ordinances, established to regulate the movements of the great machine which he had set at work. Those which concern civil legislation are often merely the repetition of earlier provisions; but to revive good measures and to restore legal force to them, is a merit in itself. In these acts elevated sentiments bear sway, and that spirit of justice which marked the decisions of the Antonines. Diocletian will not allow the child to refuse support to those who gave him life;

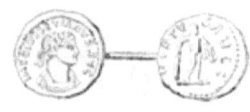

COIN OF DIOCLETIAN.

the son to be called to testify against the father, the slave against his master, brother against brother, a ward against his guardian. A father complained that his son had plotted against him. " You have the right to demand justice," the Emperor said, "if the sentiments that you ought to feel for your son do not restrain you;"[2] and he declares that a son can neither be sold nor given in pledge by his father.[3]

He repeats that the tenant (*colonus*) is not liable for the debts of his landlord,[4] and charges the judges to remind advocates of the law,[5] and even to supply what may be lacking in the pleas, *si quid minus fuerit dictum*.

Like Ulpian, he disapproved of the use of torture, and would have the judge resort to this means of obtaining the truth only after everything else had been tried;[6] and though he calls mathematics applied to astrology a damnable art, he declared geometers useful servants of the state.[7] His justice was alike for all; he repulsed the solicitations made to his superior authority by those who sought to free themselves from a legal obligation. " We are

---

[1] *Argenteus* of Diocletian, marked with the legal number XCVI. within a wreath.

[2] *Codex Just.* viii. 47, 5; *ibid.* iv. 20, 6; *ibid.* ix. 1, 13; *ibid.* ix. 1, 17: *Iniquum et longe a seculi nostri beatitudine esse credimus*; *ibid.* ix. 1, 14.

[3] *Ibid.* iv. 43, 1 and 2.   [4] *Ibid.* iv. 10.

[5] *Ibid.* ii. 11, 4, under the heading: *Ut quae desunt advocatis paritum judex suppleat*.

[6] *Ibid.* ix. 41, 8: *Hac ratione universi provinciales nostri fructum ingenitae nobis benevolentiae consequuntur*.

[7] *Ibid.* ix. 18, 2.

not accustomed," he wrote, "to grant one man an advantage which
may be harmful to others." [1] And on another occasion: "An
imperial rescript cannot undo that which has been done according
to the law." [2]

Under this Emperor, who had spent so large a part of his life
in camps, the soldier was not allowed to urge his claims with arrogance. To unreasonable demands made from the army, Diocletian
answered: "This is not befitting the gravity of the soldier." [3] On
soldiers claiming the right to retain as slaves Roman citizens who
had fallen into the hands of the enemy, and whom they had recaptured: "The captives," Diocletian wrote, "will be restored to all
their former rights; for they have not been taken, but recovered.
Our soldiers are not their masters, they are their defenders." [4]

The preambles to his edicts are highly moral. One reproaches
men with their avarice; another recalls to mind that it is the
gods who have given Rome her prosperity, and that they will
preserve it only so long as the Romans lead a virtuous and devout
life. [5] These are but commonplaces, in which the most profligate
rulers have sometimes taken delight; but nothing comes to us against
this Emperor's personal morals, and we know by his laws that
he sought to check profligacy. [6]

There remain many edicts issued by Diocletian for the protection
of person and property, to prevent frauds in trade, to guard the
unwary, the minor, the slave, even the debtor, whom he would not
have kept in servitude. [7] — in a word, to regulate all things throughout his vast empire according to justice and humanity. [8]

It was to be feared that the division of the Empire might
destroy the unity of legislation and of jurisprudence. To facilitate
the work of the tribunals, Diocletian caused a compilation of the
imperial laws to be prepared by one of his jurisconsults. [9] The

[1] *Codex Just.* viii. 19, 4.

[2] *Ibid.* v. 3, 9. See p. 386, note 3, the precautions taken by him to increase the guaran-
ties of justice.

[3] *Ibid.* iv. 52, 4.   [4] *Ibid.* viii. 51, 12.

[5] *Codex Greg.* v. *De Nuptiis.*

[6] *Codex Just.* iii. 28, 19; viii. 51, 7; and the numerous fragments of book ix. 9, 19–28.

[7] *Ibid.* iv. 10, 12: *Ob aes alienum servire liberos creditoribus, jura compelli non patiuntur.*

[8] Naudet, *Les Changements dans l'administration de l'empire*, pp. 365–371.

[9] The *Gregorian Code* was followed by the *Code of Hermogenianus*: both of them have
come down to us in a merely fragmentary condition. The most ancient ordinance given in the

Gregorian Code begins, it is believed, with an ordinance of Hadrian; it is also with this Emperor, his precursor in great administrative reforms, that Diocletian caused the *Augustan History* to begin.[1] He desired to place before the eyes of his subjects the political and constitutional life of the Empire during the last two centuries; and this idea had at once the grandeur and the utility which characterize all the acts of his government, — one alone excepted, whose gloomy history it remains for us to relate.

Lactantius reproaches the founder of the tetrarchy with his buildings,[2] — but Trajan and Hadrian also erected a great number; with the ostentation of his court, — a display really useless, which he made the mistake of believing necessary; finally, with the expense required for the maintenance of four courts, and the increase of the administrative staff.[3] But the well-being of a state is not measured by the taxes that it pays. Very small taxes are heavy in ill-governed countries, and heavy ones are light to a prosperous people. Now, in Diocletian's lifetime his expenditures had already caused much security,[4] and they would have occasioned more if his system had endured; for, all productive forces developing themselves in the midst of peace, the Empire would have seen the return of the prosperity which characterized the age of the

former is of the year 196; the most recent of 296 (?). But as it served as a basis to the *Code of Justinian*, which was a collection of the imperial ordinances since the time of Hadrian, it has been thought the ordinances contained in the *Gregorian Code* began with that Emperor. The *Codex Hermogenianus* contains, in the *Corpus juris* of Haenel, only the ordinances of Diocletian and Maximian. The *Theodosian Code*, prepared in the reign of Theodosius II., who ordered a collection of all the edicts and ordinances which had been in force since the accession of Constantine, was published in 438. Cf. Hugo, *Hist. du droit rom.* ii. 295.

[1] Of the six compilers of the *Augustan History*, three wrote in the reign of Diocletian, — Vulcatius Gallicanus, Trebellius Pollio, and Spartianus; the other three, Flavius Vopiscus, Aelius Lampridius, and Julius Capitolinus, were also contemporaries of Diocletian, but do not appear to have published their works until some time in the reign of Constantine. These writers are entirely destitute of ability; but without them we should know almost nothing of the period extending from 117 to 284. We therefore owe gratitude to Diocletian, who stimulated this twofold work of codification and of history.

[2] In sect. 7, *De Mort. pers.*, written about the year 313. Diocletian, it is true, erected palaces and basilicas, baths and porticos; but he also repaired the fortifications of the frontiers and rebuilt many ruined cities. See on this subject, *passim*, Preuss, *Kaiser Diocletian*, pp. 117-120, gives the long list of his public works.

[3] This increase of taxation was, according to Aurelius Victor, easily endured: . . . *Pensionibus inductis hic nova quae sane illorum temporum modestia tolerabilis, in perniciem processit* (*Caes.* 39).

[4] *Cultura duplicatur . . . ubi silvae fuere, jam seges est* (*Pan. vet.* iii. 15).

Antonines. It was great during the twenty years of this Emperor's reign; contemporaries attest this, even Lactantius, who extols "the supreme felicity of this period," and the Bishop of Caesarea, who exclaims: "How flourishing was the Empire at that time! Its power increased daily, and it enjoyed an unbroken peace." [1]

"Peace!" This word sums up the whole. Diocletian was able to secure it; and it might have been preserved by his successors, if, remaining faithful to his system, they had, after the example of the first four rulers, formed, "as it were, a chorus gathered around the leader who regulated the movement and the measure." [2]

---

[1] *Tamdiu summa felicitate regnavit, quamdiu manus suas justorum sanguine non inquinaret* (Lactant., *De Morte pers.* 9; Euseb., *Hist. eccl.* viii. 13; see also many passages of Aur. Victor, *Caes.* 39). Burckhardt (*Die Zeit Constantins*) discusses the passionate accusations of Lactantius, and refutes them all; he concludes thus (p. 64): *Ueberhaupt möchte seine Regierung, Alles in Allem genommen, eine der besten und wohlwollendsten gewesen sein, welche das Reich je gehabt hat. Sobald man den Blick frei hält von dem schrecklichen Bilde der Christenverfolgung und von den Entstellungen und Uebertreibungen bei Lactantius, so nehmen die Züge des grossen Fürsten einem ganz andern Ausdruck an.*

[2] "Diocletian," says Julian in the *Caesars*, "presents himself at the banquet of the gods, accompanied by the two Maximians and Constantius, my ancestor. Although they hold each other by the hand, they do not come forward in line; they make, as it were, a choir surrounding Diocletian. They would precede him as his guards; but he prevents them, because he desires to attribute to himself no honor above his colleagues. . . . After these four, who together formed so beautiful a harmony . . ."

CHAPTER C.

THE ERA OF THE MARTYRS (303-311 A. D.).

I. — THE EDICTS OF PERSECUTION (303).

THE persecution which, beginning under Diocletian, continued for six years after his time, was a terrible one. It has been attributed to the enmity of an old woman,[1] to the cruelty of Galerius, and to the enfeebled mind of an Emperor advanced in years. It was, on the contrary, a well-planned measure of government, a campaign conducted with remarkable ability; but also it was the application of a policy doubly evil, since it shed blood unjustly and did not attain its end. Diocletian, who believed it necessary, must be held fully responsible for it.

This Dalmatian, the son of a slave, was worthy of the old Roman stock; he was a man of authority and of cool determination, who decided only after mature reflection, and whose faith in the old cult had not been shaken by the religious novelties brought from the East. He persecuted the Christians for the reason that he believed them dangerous to the established religion, to military discipline, and to social order. At the beginning of an edict against the Manichaeans, he says the same that, nine centuries later, the Roman Catholic Church said, in other words, against the Albigensian Manichaeans: "The gods have determined what is just and true; the best men have, by counsel and action, demonstrated and firmly established this. It is not, therefore, permitted to go counter to this divine and human wisdom, and to assume that a new religion may be better than the old; it is the greatest of crimes to wish to change the institutions of our ancestors."[2] These are the views of the high pontiff of Rome. The Emperor,

---

[1] The mother of Galerius, a zealous pagan, whom Lactantius calls: . . . *Deorum montium cultrix.*

[2] Preamble to the edict *De Maleficiis et Manichaeis (Gregor. Cod.* xiv. 4). These were the views of enthusiastic pagans and short-sighted statesmen. The idea that the prosperity of the

the statesman, did not at first conform his conduct at all to them. He had respected the edict of Gallienus favoring the churches, and had suffered the Christians to make their way everywhere into the army, into the court. Eusebius names many who were living near the Emperors and on terms of friendship with them, and made proselytes even in the very family of Diocletian, whose wife and daughter seem to have been gained over to the faith; and he writes: "It is difficult to tell in what high esteem our doctrine is held, and how great is the liberty which we enjoy. The Emperors have made many of the believers governors of provinces without requiring them to sacrifice to the gods. They have permitted their officers publicly, and accompanied by their wives, their children, and their slaves, to fulfil the duties of religion even in the imperial presence. The bishops are honored, and churches have been built in all the cities." [1]

Mazarin said of the French Protestants of his time: "This little flock browses upon pernicious weeds, but it does not go astray." At this epoch of his reign Diocletian had the same opinion in respect to the Christians. A singular phrase in an edict of 311 aids us to understand this involuntary respect for the Crucified. Galerius, in granting peace to the Christians, says: "Our indulgence lays you under obligation to pray to your God for our health and for the prosperity of the Empire." Galerius manifestly believed that Jesus was a divinity, and that, like Apollo or Jupiter, he could do men good or harm. With the doctrine of the δαίμονες, all was explained. In that time of philosophic and religious confusion, pagans and Christians believed in *daimons*: the evil spirits

Empire depended upon an assiduous worship of the gods, was in the mind of the Emperor and in the minds of many of his subjects. Vopiscus (*In Caro*, 9) promises Galerius and Diocletian the most brilliant triumphs, *si a nostris non desecatur penitissus numinum favor*.

[1] *Hist. eccl.* viii. 6: "Dorotheus and Gorgonus, raised to high office, were loved by the Emperors as if they had been their own children." Lucian, chief of the eunuchs, had relations with the Bishop of Alexandria, Theonas, who wrote thus to him: *Quanto . . . ipsis Christianis, velut fidelioribus, vitam et corpus suum curandum credidit* (*Diocletianus*), *tanto decet vos sollicitiores esse . . . ut per id plurimum Christi nomen glorificetur*. In the same letter Theonas speaks of the peace *per bonum principem ecclesiis concessa* (Routh, *Reliq. sacr.* iii. 439). This letter, the passage of Eusebius which has just been quoted, and the whole history of the reign of Diocletian, prevent us from agreeing in the opinion held by various Roman Catholic writers that there was an official persecution in the early years of this Emperor. I say "official," because there may have been isolated condemnations pronounced for assumed crimes against the civil law. In respect to Christians who were called "the Emperor's friends," see Le Blant, *Suppl. aux Actes de Ruinart*, p. 76.

were the opponents' gods; the good, those whom the individual himself adored, and miracles, attributed to either class, were readily accepted by all. Diocletian certainly held this opinion, and continued to hold it so long as toleration did not seem to be dangerous.

To prevent revolutions, to render alike hopeless the intrigues of ambitious men and insurrections among the soldiery, and by a policy of intimidation to repress all hostile designs from without, — such had been the object of his reign; and up to this time all had yielded to his prudence and his arms. But within the Empire a grave difficulty remained, which was increasing every day. For forty years the Christians had enjoyed freedom of worship, and their confidence had increased with their numbers. They might be heard passionately accusing the whole human race of having lived in mental darkness, except in one remote corner of the world. Nothing had as yet impaired the Roman idea of the family; domestic worship was still performed on the hearthstone of the parental abode or at the ancestral tombs, and now men heard a doctrine taught which condemned these beloved dead to eternal flames. At a time when the state, accepted as a divine existence, claimed the right to rule men's consciences as well as their outward acts, the Christians were in revolt against the gods, and nearly so against the Emperors. "Who are you?" Galerius said to them. "A turbulent Jewish sect, which has denied the God of its fathers, and then attacked the gods of the Empire; which has made laws for itself according to its own caprice, and gathers in seditious assemblies." [1] And, in truth, they formed in the midst of the sickly and disordered pagan world a state full of life and hope; for this new republic had what the old had long since ceased to possess, — its popular assemblies, its elections, its leaders chosen by common consent, and, in its councils, that representative system whose force the Empire had never fitly recognized. Upon whatever point in the provinces the Emperors turned their eyes, they beheld communities of men at once enthusiastic and disciplined, docile

---

[1] These are the terms of the edict of 311. Euseb., *Hist. eccl.* viii. 17, and Lactantius, 34 : *Valeriaous . . . jus a leges reser s et publicam disciplinam, Romanorum cuncta corrigere atque id providere, et etiam Christiani, qui parentum suorum reliquerant sectam, ad bonas mentes reducent.*

at the voice of their pastors, sometimes rebellious against that of
the magistrates, leading a different life and actuated by another
spirit from that of their fellow-citizens, strangers in the midst of
their native country, indifferent to her and to her fate. Certainly
it was a peril for the pagan state and for the social order which
the state represented. In the administrative and in the official
world there were many who regretted that the misfortunes of the
time, the captivity of Valerian, the weakness of his son, had not
permitted the extirpation from the social body of this hostile ele-
ment which undermined it; and certain incidents seemed to justify
this feeling on the part of those blind adherents of a perishing
past.

Eusebius speaks of a great agitation of the churches about this
time. Was it a revival of the old Montanist spirit? Were some
hot-headed disciples of Tertullian[1] declaring that the camp-life was
incompatible with the Christian life? This we do not know. The
soldiers were not volunteers, the service was obligatory; and once
enlisted, the soldier must remain in the camps for many long years.
The tedium of barrack-life gave men time for conscientious scruples,
and many of them came to regard it as impiety to serve idolatrous
rulers, and as sacrilege to share in national festivals which the
army celebrated with military pomp. It is probable that in the
army the Christians lived separately, forming *conciliabula* which
excited suspicion; that in the cities secret visits to Christian communities were detected which had the air of being intrigues leading
to plots. The *Acts* of St. Victor give this last motive as the
cause of that martyr's condemnation.

The Bishop of Caesarea was the contemporary of the events
which he relates, and his testimony is to be received when he has
no interest in altering the fact. His own words authorize us to
believe that there were in the army excesses of zeal, and for the
sake of religion violations of the military law; that Christians
refused to be enrolled, which was desertion; that they refused to perform certain duties commanded them, which was a disobedience; or to
fulfil certain obligations resting upon every soldier as such, like

[1] See the *De Corona mili.* of Tertullian, and what he says in chap. xi.: *Credibusne
humanum sacramentum divino superduci licet?* "Does any one think that the pledge to the
Emperor stands higher than the pledge to God?"

the carrying of particular standards, etc. The *Acts* of individual
martyrs confirm this interpretation.

At Theveste, a citizen who, by the amount of his land-tax,
was bound to furnish a soldier, brings to the proconsul his son
Maximilian, whom the recruiting officer had accepted for military
duty. Upon the order to place himself under the measure, that
his height might be marked, Maximilian replies that, being a
Christian, he cannot be a soldier. The magistrate pays no attention to this, but orders him to be measured; then directs the
cord to be put round his neck upon which is suspended the leaden
tablet bearing his description. "I shall break it," Maximilian exclaims; "I will never wear anything but the token of my only
master, Jesus Christ." The proconsul explains to him that he can,
as so many others have done, freely fulfil all his religious duties
in the army; but the Montanist persists, and is put to death for the
refusal of the military oath. The sentence makes no reference to
the Christian faith.[1] A little later, in this same Africa where Tertullian had lauded desertion from the army and had urged to
martyrdom,[2] at Tingis, on one occasion when the garrison celebrated Maximian's birthday, the centurion Marcellus threw down at
the feet of the soldiers his vine-stock, his military belt, and his
weapons, saying: "I will no longer serve your Emperors, and I
despise their gods of wood and stone." Instead of silently taking
advantage of what the government at that time allowed, — liberty
of conscience, or even his dismissal from the army, — he insulted,
in the midst of a solemn ceremony, both the state religion and
the Emperors; this was a public provocation which could not be
tolerated, and he was put to death.[3] The law commanded this
punishment, and Marcellus had sought it.

At last the government began to notice these acts of disorder.
Both for its own sake and the sake of the Empire, it needed to
be sure of its troops; and this it could not be with soldiers who
put any limit to their obedience. The army was subjected to

---

[1] Extract from the official acts: *Ut a notariis exceptum . . . in sacro comitatu Christiani sunt et militant* (Ruinart, *Acta sincera*, p. 299). This took place in the year 295
or 296.

[2] See above, chap. xvi. Tertullian says, in the *D. Fuga*, 9: *Spiritus omnes paene ad
martyrium accessos.*

[3] *Acta sincera*, p. 302. The date is uncertain; it may have been 298.

examination, and those who declared their presence under the standards incompatible with their religious faith were discharged.

"Many," says Eusebius,[1] "left the service. A general having given his soldiers the choice of renouncing their religion or their military grade, they preferred to confess the name of Jesus and part with their worldly advantages."

This consideration for soldiers who refused to submit to the common rule was not habitual with the Romans.[2] Galerius was indignant at it; he saw in it — and rightly — the loss of discipline; and he proposed to employ against all Christians the means of intimidation employed against those in the army.

Although Diocletian had shown in Egypt that he did not hesitate in shedding blood when it was a question of chastising rebels, he hesitated to strike those who were not so. He hoped that an execution now and then, in virtue of military law, would suffice to repress everywhere the extremes of religious zeal. But now civil society, in its turn, becomes unsettled, and the great administrative instrument of the Empire, the municipal system, begins to work badly and threatens to become useless. The Christian is no more willing to be a citizen than to be a soldier.[3] He refuses the office of duumvir, even of decurion, because of the pagan observances these offices impose; he divides or distributes his property that he may no longer possess the twenty-five *jugera* which condemn him to the curia, and the Christian Emperors later were compelled to take severe measures against those "who had rather serve the Church than the Senate;"[4] and such is the penury of the *honestiores* that Diocletian permits the duties of the decurionate to be imposed upon freedmen, and even upon persons who have been branded as infamous.[5]

---

[1] *Hist. eccl.* viii. 1, 4. The measure was general, — *datis ad propositos litteris*, says Lactantius (*De Morte pers.* 10); and he adds: *Nec amplius quidquam contra legos, sed respondens Dei fecit.*

[2] The edict was not formally obeyed everywhere. The *Acts* of SS. Julius, Nieander, and Marcian, show soldiers put to death for having refused to burn the usual grain of incense upon the altar, on receiving the largess given by Galerius on occasion of the tenth anniversary of his accession. Generals accustomed to punish severely all disobedience had felt themselves, in condemning these soldiers, to be acting in accordance with military law.

[3] "Public affairs are not our affairs" (*Nec ulla magis res aliena quam publica.* — Tertullian, *Apol.* 38).

[4] *Curiales qui ecclesiis malunt servire quam curiis* (*Codex Theod.* xii. 104, 115).

[5] *Infames personae . . . curialium vel civilium munerum vacationem non habent* (*Codex Theod.* x. 56 and 57).

At this time, also, between philosophers and Christians, and between differing sects, disputes are beginning or going on, and the air is full of clamor. From Persia comes a new religion, — that of the Manichaeans. Containing elements derived from the doctrines of Zoroaster and from those of Jesus, it disturbs men's minds in the border provinces of the two Empires, and, as usual, the magistrates accuse its followers of a thousand crimes which Saint Epiphanes repeats, turning against these sectaries the same accusation of scandalous rites which had so long been made against the Christians.[1] In Egypt, Meletius makes a schism;[2] Hierax begins another. In Africa the language interchanged among the bishops at the Council of Cirta (305) shows the violence of some of these men of peace, and announces that of the Donatists, who a few years later were to cover the province with blood and ruins. Porphyry, or a Neo-Platonist of his school, composes at this time his treatise against the Christians, which doctors and bishops combat with angry refutations.[3] A famous rhetorician, Arnobius, attacks the Church, which later he will defend, and a great functionary of the Empire, Hierocles, vicar of the district of Bithynia, mingles in the fray. The latter publishes his *Philalethes*,[4] "the Friend of Truth," setting over against the miracles of Jesus those of Apollonius of Tyana, — "who, however," he says, "was not made a god for that." And it is not questions of dogma

---

[1] Before becoming an orthodox Christian, Saint Augustine had been for nine years a Manichaean, — which leads us to believe there could be no immorality in this cult. The ordinance of Diocletian says: . . . *De Persica adversaria nobis qvate . . . multa facinora committere, populos quietos turbare* (*Codex Greg.* xiv. 4), — the chiefs of the sect shall be burned, with their books; the adherents belonging to the lower classes decapitated; the *honestiores* sent to the mines. The date of the receipt is uncertain.

[2] "Separating himself from Peter, his metropolitan, and the other bishops, he published calumnies against them" (Fleury, *Hist. eccl.* viii. 24 [about 304]).

[3] Lactantius mentions a philosopher who, in 303, wrote at Nicomedeia three books against the Christians. It has been maintained that this philosopher could not be Porphyry, because the author of the *Divinae institutiones* (v. 2) speaks of his disorderly life. But Lactantius never hesitates to calumniate his adversaries, and we know from Saint Augustine (*Cic. Dei*, x. 52) that at the time of the persecution Porphyry was still living. It is at least established by the words of Lactantius that a philosopher wrote at Nicomedeia against the Christians at the time when Diocletian's edict was promulgated, and this suffices for our statement. Some critics place the composition of Porphyry's book between the years 290 and 300. Saint Methodius wrote against it a poem of ten thousand lines (Saint Jerome, *De Viris ill.* 83). Eusebius also refuted it.

[4] *Ausus est libros suos nefarios ac Dei hostes φιλαληθεῖς inscribere* (Lactantius, *Div. inst.* v. 2; cf. what remains to us of the treatise of Eusebius against Hierocles).

which are in dispute; to such the people would not care to listen.
Porphyry, with murderous accusation, shows the plague ravaging
cities, and Aesculapius failing to drive it away, because he himself has fled far from the abominations of the Christian faith.[1]
To the strifes of doctors corresponds that of the crowd. Some
exclaim that the gods of Olympus are evil spirits, and assume to
themselves the power of driving them out; others dread this
satanic power, and imagine that the sign of the cross will hinder
sacrifices from being completed.[2] No man has seen the gods flee
away, or the flame upon the altar go out, at a Christian's gesture;
but the pagan world believes the Christians capable of every
crime, and reviles them while it waits for permission to drag
them into the arena.

The Christians fight among themselves also. "The liberty
which we enjoyed," says Eusebius, "had caused the relaxation
of discipline. The war began among ourselves by violent language, — bishops against bishops, people against people. When the
evil had reached its height, Divine Justice raised its arm to punish
us. The believers who followed the profession of arms were the
first to be persecuted. After this warning from the Lord, instead
of seeking to propitiate him, we added crimes to crimes; our
pastors, despising the divine rules, disputed bitterly with each
other, and strove for the highest rank. Then, according to the
word of Jeremiah, the Lord from heaven overthrew the glory
of Israel."[3]

It was in the East that religious animosities were the most

---

[1] Euseb., *Praep. Ev.* v. 1; Lactantius, *Div. inst.* iv. 27.

[2] Lactantius, *De Morte pers.* 10; *Cum adstaretur immolanti imposuerunt frontibus suis immor-
tale signum, quo facto fugatis daemonibus, sacra turbata sunt.* Prudentius also relates that the
sacrifices of Julian were disturbed by the presence of a Christian.

[3] *Hist. eccl.* viii. 1. These deplorable quarrels continued throughout the persecution.
Eusebius breaks off in his account of the martyrs in Palestine to say again : "I will not speak
of the ambition of some men, of their rash and unlawful laying-on of hands, of the differences
and disputes of the martyrs themselves, of the divisions by which they tore the members yet
remaining to the Church." See Tillemont, *Mém. eccl.* v. 98, 100, and 103, in respect to the
disorders at Rome; the canons of the Council of Elvira for those which it was necessary to
repress in Spain; the act of the scandals later abominable, of the African *circumcellions*; the
wretched intrigues attributed by Saint Athanasius to the Eusebians; the denunciations sent in
to Constantine in 325 by the bishops against several of their brethren (Rufinus, i. 2), etc.; and
we shall be convinced that along with great virtues the Christian communities had many
weaknesses, — which is very human, — and that it will not do always to accept the Church of
the legends as the real Church of history.

bitter, and from February, 299, to the beginning of the year 302 Diocletian resided there almost constantly.[1] When in the autumn of this latter year he returned to Nicomedeia, his mind was made

COIN OF
NICOMEDIA.[2]

up to put an end to these agitations and bring back tranquillity into civil society, as he had brought it back into the legions and into the provinces. Galerius had long been of this opinion. But what means should be adopted? During the entire winter the two rulers discussed this terrible question. Lactantius asserts that Diocletian would have been content with prohibiting the army and the palace to the Christians, — that is to say, military and administrative duties; that, finally, he laid the matter before his council, and that they coincided with the opinion of Galerius. The measures with which it is supposed Diocletian would have been satisfied, would not have been more severe than those which excluded from public office and the liberal professions the Protestants of France up to the time of the Revolution, and the Roman Catholics in England to our own time. But the obstinate con-

DIDYMAEAN
APOLLO.[3]

servatives of the day made every effort to force the Augustus into the most sanguinary road. The contradictory feelings of the statesman and the pagan which fought within him threw this strong soul into an uncertainty, whence he sought escape by asking advice of Heaven. He decided that the question should be laid before the oracle of the Didymaean Apollo at Miletus.[4] Apollo could have no indulgence for those who ruined his priests and blasphemed his name; he replied that the enemies of the gods must be destroyed. The Christians therefore appeared to be condemned both by human and divine wisdom.

If we may believe Lactantius, Galerius proposed to have those who refused to sacrifice burned alive. Diocletian hoped to effect

[1] So we infer from the date of many rescripts (Mommsen, Z. etc. p. 414).

[2] NIKOMHΔEΩN ΔIC NEΩKOPΩN. Love fleeing from a kneeling Psyche (reverse of a bronze of Maximus).

[3] Didymaean Apollo, on a coin of Miletus. MIΛYMEYC MIΛECIΩN. The god standing, holding a bow and a small figure of a stag (reverse of a bronze of Claudius).

[4] Lactantius, De Morte pers. 11.

the suppression of the Church without bloodshed. The resolution
he was about to take was a very serious one, and he asked the
pontiffs to designate a propitious day for its execution. They
indicated the festival of the Terminalia (23d February, 303) as
the day on which the accursed sect should be brought to an end.
At daybreak the praetorian prefect, accompanied by *duces*, tribunes,
and soldiers, presented himself before the church in Nicomedeia,
forced an entrance, seized the sacred objects, and committed them
to the flames. He would have set fire to the buildings; but Dio-

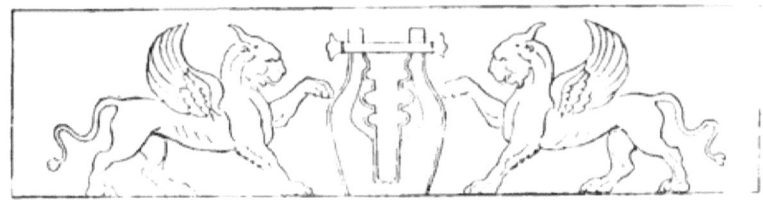

BAS-RELIEF FROM THE TEMPLE OF THE DIDYMAEAN APOLLO AT MILETUS.[1]

cletian, who from the roof of his palace surveyed what was done,
fearing lest the flames might spread to the adjacent buildings,
ordered the temple to be demolished. On the following day
appeared the first edict of persecution: the Christian churches were
to be destroyed, the religious books burned, and the sacred places
and cemeteries confiscated.[2] Those who refused to sacrifice were
to be branded with infamy, of whatever rank they were, declared
incapable of filling any public office, and in case of condemnation
for any crime, subjected to the penalties denounced against the
humiliores.[3] All judicial proceedings would be authorized against
them, while they could institute none against others;[4] their
assemblies were prohibited; he who was already placed by his
condition among the *humiliores* was made a slave of the treasury.[5]

[1] Texier, *Descr. de l'Asie Mineure*, pl. 140, fig. 2.
[2] De Rossi, *Roma sotteran.* vol. ii. pp. viii and 378. Constantine, in his turn, ordered the
books of Porphyry to be burned.
[3] See Vol. VIII., Appendix.
[4] To leave to the Christians no way of eluding the law, *arae in secretariis et pro tribunali
positae, ut litigatores prius sacrificarent* (Lactantius, 15).
[5] Euseb., *Mart. de Pal.* 1, and the *Actes* of Saint Theodosius of Ancyra (Bollandists,
May 18).

and the Christian slave could never be enfranchised. This first edict did not go so far as that issued by Valerian,—it did not order the death of the Christians; but it made of them a people of pariahs. Measures nearly similar to these were adopted upon the revocation of the Edict of Nantes, —a double iniquity, which was the consequence, and has remained the condemnation, of established religions.

MUTILATED STATUE.[1]

Violence calls forth violence. Diocletian would have been glad to escape shedding blood; but it was to flow in torrents. An indignant Christian tore down the edict and destroyed it with loud reproaches against the Augustus and the Caesar. "These are their bulletins of victory over the Goths and Sarmatians!" he cried ironically. To pluck down an imperial edict was a crime of high treason, and the man was burned on a fire of charcoal.[2] Soon after this a fire broke out in the palace, and a fortnight later a second fire occurred near the rooms occupied by the Emperor. It is difficult to impute all this to chance. Lactantius accuses Galerius of it, and says that the latter then threw the blame upon the Christians, in order to exasperate Diocletian. Eusebius makes Constantine relate to the Fathers, at the Council of Nicaea, that he had seen a thunderbolt, the instrument of divine justice, fall upon the palace and set it on fire.[3] But the Constantine of Eusebius often saw, between heaven and

---

[1] Mutilated statue found in the ruins of the temple of the Didymaean Apollo (Texier, *Ibid.* fig. 3).

[2] *Legitimo coctus*, says Lactantius; that is, burned according to the established rules (*De Morte pers.* 14). It is remarkable that the first edict was not promulgated in Syria till fifty days later, and in Africa after four months. With his habitual prudence, Diocletian waited to see the effects of the blow he had struck at Nicomedeia.

[3] *Orat. ad S. Cœt.* xxv. According to this passage, the damage done by the fire must have been very considerable.

PRINCIPAL FAÇADE OF THE TEMPLE OF MINERVA AT THEVESTE (MODERN TEBESSA).

earth, things that no other man ever witnessed. It was more natural to accuse the Christians, and the life of the Emperors appeared threatened by an extensive conspiracy. If they were not at all threatened in this way, they at least had reason to dread the revenge of individuals, for the Christians were now so numerous that there were to be found among them, besides resigned victims,

FRAGMENTS OF THE ENTABLATURE OF THE TEMPLE OF THE DIDYMAEAN APOLLO.[1]

others who would by no means submit quietly to injustice. Galerius was no longer safe in Nicomedeia, and he quitted the city. Left alone in the palace, Diocletian, who also believed himself surrounded by assassins, ordered a severe search to be made, and all who were suspected of being adherents to the new faith to be required to sacrifice. The Emperor's wife and daughter — though with reluctance, it is believed — set the example; others followed. But there were slaves, freedmen, and eunuchs who refused; and this refusal appeared to convict them as authors or accomplices in the recent crime, and they were cruelly put to death. The investigation was pursued outside of the palace, and suspicion produced culprits; the Bishop of Nicomedeia was beheaded, and many persons of humble condition were burned or thrown into the sea.

[1] See in Vol. III. p. 713, the bases of the columns of this temple, and in Vol. V. p. 365, a view of its ruins. (From the Louvre.)

At Nicomedeia the Christians suffered as incendiaries; in the provinces they were punished as rebels. It appears, at least, that to the exasperation caused at certain points by the destruction of the churches, may be attributed two insurrections, — disturbances unknown in twenty years, — which broke out, one at Antioch, the other in the Melitene, on the upper Euphrates. Nothing is known of the latter, which might have become dangerous, owing to the neighborhood of Armenia, where Christianity, preached by Saint Gregory Illuminator, was at that time making great progress.[1] As to the revolt in Syria, Libanius represents it, eighty years later, as a foolish freak of the soldiers.[2] But the leader of these soldiers had assumed the purple, and the magistrates of Antioch and of Seleucia, with many of the inhabitants, were put to death. If the Christians had not been in some way concerned in these movements, Eusebius would not have mentioned them, — especially he would not have indicated them as the cause which determined Diocletian to issue a new and more severe edict.[3] The rigor of the repression proves the importance of the revolt. In the eyes of the Emperor it had been an attempt to transfer the Empire to the Christians; and this attempt was not at all rash, since that which failed to be accomplished in 303 was undertaken with success eight years later. In the last year of the persecution the governor of Palestine, hearing a martyr speak of the Heavenly Jerusalem, formed the idea that the Christians proposed to build a city and fortify themselves in it against the Romans. This governor is ridiculous, but his apprehension was not so: for he naturally believed that the persecuted, whose ardor to meet death he could not understand, would seize any method of escaping from persecution.

A century earlier they aspired to heaven only; but their strength increasing with their numbers, they began to concern themselves with the affairs of earth. With his usual sagacity, Diocletian took note of the change which in the minds of many was

---

[1] Simeon Metaphrastes relates the story of the thirty-three Christians martyred at Melitene; but Tillemont (*Mém. eccl.* v. 171) does not believe that these *Acts* are trustworthy. If they have historic foundation, we must still see in them, according to their own details, an execution for refusal of military service, and for blows and wounds inflicted on the recruiting officers.

[2] *Disc.* xiv.   [3] Euseb., *Mart. de Pal.* ii.

at this time going on, — unconsciously to themselves, it is true, but revealed to him by the fire in the palace and the two revolts breaking out amidst the profound calm of the Empire. For twenty years this Emperor, who placed the interests of order above every other consideration, had constrained his gods and their priests to toleration; from the moment when he believed the public peace in danger he sought to save it by energetic measures, and yet, if possible, to avoid bloodshed. He bethought himself of an old law of the Empire which permitted him to punish, without leaving them the resource of an appeal, those who were regarded as *seditionum concitatores vel duces factionum*;[1] and against the insurrection, or the preaching that he dreaded, he took the clergy as hostages: his second edict ordered the arrest of all bishops, priests, and deacons who should refuse to deliver up the Holy Scriptures. By demolishing the churches he prevented the Christians from holding their assemblies and celebrating their religious rites; by depriving these communities of their pastors, he hoped that, left without direction or discipline, these societies would dissolve or would cease to be dangerous; lastly, by the destruction of their sacred books he expected to put a stop to teaching, and by all these methods, to extinguish the faith.[2] In the moral condition of the world these measures could not but remain powerless: the future belonged to Christianity, and against it two Emperors will waste their strength.

The two edicts of the year 303 did not mention the death-penalty; Diocletian had not thought it needful to go to this extreme.[3] The Christians, at that time numbering several millions, could not all be punished; but the Emperor hoped to intimidate all, to cause apostasies among the leaders, and easily bring back the frightened crowd into the temples of the gods. The *Acts* of

---

[1] *Digest.* XLIX. i. 16.

[2] An edict of Constantine (Euseb., *Life of Const.* ii. 30-34) gives liberty to Christians detained in islands, quarries, or mines; restores their property to those who, without being *curiales* by birth, had been *addicti curiae*, which had placed their fortune at the disposal of the municipal administrations; and gives back their grades, or the *honesta missio*, to officers and soldiers who had been expelled from the army, their honors to those who had been branded with infamy, their condition of free-born to those who had been made slaves, etc. This edict completes our knowledge of the penalties pronounced against the Christians.

[3] See the *Acts* of Saint Hilary (Bollandists, March 16): . . . *Ut ipso tormentato, universi ejus corrigantur exemplo* (Le Blant, *op. cit.* p. 42).

Saint Romanus, though mingled with legend, prove that Galerius himself dared not pronounce a death-sentence. He was present at Antioch when Romanus was condemned to be burned alive, — less, perhaps, on account of his noble persistence in confessing his faith, than for words which his judge considered acts of treason; for example, these: "Christ alone is my king." The authorities dared not proceed to execution without the order of Galerius, and the Caesar did not give the order.[1] At Carthage the same hesitation was manifested, not in torturing, but in taking life. The proconsul permits Saint Saturninus to proclaim his faith openly, and makes this no ground of accusation, but inquires of him whether he has taken part in assemblies contrary to the imperial law, and whether he has kept books of magic.[2] The saint replies in language which is still the Church's teaching: "First of all we must obey God." The Christians refused, therefore, to submit to the laws of exterior order. That these laws were bad, no man doubts; but the revolt against them was none the less a revolt against the established government; and still the proconsul, after having put the accused to the torture, in the hope of obtaining from them a word which will permit him to set them free, sends them to the public prison, and there he leaves them.[3] On the subject of these *Acts* we shall remark further that the magistrate carefully separates the question of religion from that of public order. When the brethren cry out to him: "We are Christians!" he replies: "That is not what I ask you;" and the sole question that he puts to them is this: "Have you been at the assembly?" or "Have you in your possession forbidden books?"[4] These gatherings having been prohibited by the sovereign power, fell under the action of the old laws against secret societies; and the *Evangels* which propagated the faith, and the *Passiones* which stimulated

---

[1] Euseb., *Mort. de Palest.*, 2. The same happened in the case of Alpheus and Zaccheus: Ναυατος ζαικεω Ιατρος (*ibid.* 1). Procopius, being called upon to burn incense in honor of the four rulers, replies with a line of Homer: "It is not good to have so many masters; we desire but one." The judge considers these words an insult to the Emperors and a revolt against the government, and orders the punishment of treason (Euseb., *ibid.*). Many of the judges attempted to transform the prosecutions against the Christians into political prosecutions.

[2] Ruinart, *Acta sinc.* p. 387; *Acta SS. Saturnini, Dativi*, etc., sect. 12.

[3] Bollandists, February 11, sections 7 and 16.

[4] Ruinart, *Acta sinc.* p. 367.

SPALATO (FROM THE VOYAGE IN DALMATIE OF CASSAS).

it, seemed to the pagans to have the character of books of magic, which were proscribed.[1]

The imprisonment of the priests did not, however, produce the expected effect; a third edict ordered the setting at liberty of those who would sacrifice, and the constraining of the rest by all possible means to abandon their faith.[2] The government could legally prohibit assemblies which it believed dangerous, and require of its functionaries that they should sacrifice to the gods of the Empire; but it had not the right to impose this obligation upon all Christians. Drawn on by the fatal development of a false idea, the intelligent but severe man who ruled at Nicomedeia was about to make his reign, until then peaceful and renowned, the era of the martyrs.

MARBLE HEAD.[3]

As is the case in all times of persecution, there were governors who, averse to violence, closed their eyes, or contented themselves with an apparent submission. The Bishop of Carthage, Mensurius, had left only a few heretical treatises in his church: these the proconsul seized; and when he was informed where the sacred books were concealed, he refused to make search for them. Nor were all the churches demolished; several of them were only closed, and some even were allowed to remain open.[4]

In other places much ingenuity was used in finding ways for

---

[1] Prudentius (*Perist.* i. 75) says that many of the *Acta* of the martyrs were at that time destroyed. We have seen Diocletian in Egypt burn books of occult science.

[2] Euseb., *Hist. eccl.* viii. 6.

[3] Marble head found in the ruins of the palace of Diocletian at Nicomedeia. This antique head, now lost, was drawn by Peyssonnel at the time of his journey in 1745. The unpublished MS. of this journey is in the library of the Institute of France, whence we have taken the above sketch.

[4] Tillemont, *Mém. eccl.* v. 29, 37, etc.

the Christians to satisfy the law against their own consent. " A man," says Eusebius, " being dragged to the altar and constrained to touch the abominable viands, was set free as if he had willingly sacrificed. Another had held out his hand towards the box containing incense, but had taken none from it; and the pagans cried out that he had sacrificed to the gods. The former, half dead from the blows he had received, was cast in with the renegades; the latter vainly protested that he had not done what was required of him; they stopped his mouth by force, so eager were these wretches to have it believed that they had succeeded in their attempts." [1] Elsewhere the judge said to the Christian: " Sacrifice to whom you will, even to your own God;" [2] and to make those present believe that a Christian had yielded, drinking the wine of libations, there was offered him water in a red glass.[3] " I have seen," Lactantius further says, " governors boasting that they had never pronounced a single death-sentence, and proud of having conquered the Christians." [4] It was not that persecution always offended their consciences: for their reputation of skill, one apostasy was worth more than ten condemnations. The Donatus to whom Lactantius dedicated his book *De Morte persecutorum*, was nine times put to the torture, never in a manner to be fatal, but always with cruelty enough to make recantation probable. In many *Acta* we even read of money offered and honors promised in return for an abjuration.[5]

When, on occasion of the festivals which celebrated the twentieth year of his reign, Diocletian, according to custom, proclaimed an amnesty,[6] the prison-doors, opened for all ordinary convicts, remained closed upon the Christians. He had put the clergy in confinement through fear of an insurrection; and as he still retained that fear, he still held his prisoners. By the two first edicts the Christians had been degraded from civil honors,

---

[1] Euseb., *Mart. de Pal.* 1. However, in certain places there existed a strong antipathy: not only did men crowd the scene of execution as a spectacle, but they also pillaged the goods of the prisoners and fugitives (*Actes de S. Théodule d'Ancyre*, Bollandists, May 18).

[2] Bollandists, March 3 and July 14.

[3] Derenbourg *Hist. de la Palestine*, p. 422.

[4] *Div. instit.* v. 11.

[5] Léop. Delisle, *Note sur un manuscrit de Prudence*, p. 6. Cf. Edm. le Blant, supplement to the *Actes* of Ruinart, p. 35.

[6] Euseb., *Mart. de Pal.* 2. This is the *abolitio generalis* of the *Code Just.* ix. 43.

deprived of the protection of the laws, and declared criminals if they did not surrender their sacred writings, or if they continued to hold their meetings.[1] The third had directed the employment of all means to obtain retractations, — without authorizing, however, in the first phase of the persecution, the extreme penalty. There were executions for offences regarded as crimes against the common law, — insults to the gods, to the Emperors, secret assem-

FRAGMENT OF A GLASS DISK.[2]

blies, or forbidden meetings ; and as it was not possible that a severe policy like this should be everywhere conducted with moderation, privations and tortures had caused many captives to perish in prison. Many, also, under the weight of moral and physical sufferings, had yielded to weakness. The *lapsi* who sacrificed, the *traditores* who gave up the sacred books, the timid who concealed their faith,[3] had been numerous, and became, after

---

[1] Euplius, a deacon, was beheaded at Catana, Aug. 12, 304, for having, contrary to the edicts, called together the Christian community ; likewise Philip of Heraclea in Thrace, the martyrs of Abitina in Africa, Saint Saturninus, etc.

[2] Fragment of a glass disk representing the commemoration of the twentieth year of Diocletian's reign (*Bulletin de la commission archéologique de Rome*, tenth year, No. 3, pl. xx. July to September, 1882).

[3] The canons of the Council of Elvira, held in 305, show that many believers had concealed their faith, had filled the offices of duumvir, flamen, and sacrificer, had given money for pagan festivals, for spectacles, and games ; the Council even allows them, if they fear to be denounced by their slaves, to keep idols in their houses, on condition of paying them no worship, etc. This is not contradictory to what has been said above of the decline of the municipal system, through the unwillingness of Christians to accept office. The penances imposed by the Council of Elvira are evidently addressed to certain rich men who have tampered with their consciences in order to preserve their wealth ; and these compromises occur in all ages of the world. The heresy of the Donatists began in 311, when Donatus attacked the election to the see of Carthage of Cæcilianus, who had been ordained by a bishop *traditor*.

the persecution had ceased, a subject of violent dissensions in
the Church. At Antioch, a great city already half Christianized,
Romanus was the only person left in prison.[1]

It seemed, then, that one more blow would suffice to destroy
this Church whose pillars were tottering, and to bring back the
whole Empire to the old faith. This was the opinion of Maximian
and Galerius; and when, in 304, Diocletian's long and serious illness left them masters of the government, they revived in all its
original vigor the last edict of Valerian. The *Acta* of Saint Sabinus,
of which the authenticity is doubtful,[2] relate that when Maximian
was present at the games of the circus at Rome, all the people
cried out, "Let the Christians die!" and that the Emperor
caused it to be proposed to the Senate by the praetorian or urban
prefect that a decree should be prepared condemning the Christians
to sacrifice or die.[3] This is improbable on the face of it; as thus
to relinquish to the Senate an act of legislation so important, is
contrary to all that the history of the time teaches us. We
should therefore reject this decree, mentioned in *Acta* of doubtful
authenticity, were it not that Eusebius speaks of imperial letters
ordering all men to be present at the sacrifices and take part in
them.[4] Maximian must therefore have written these letters, or
Galerius must have caused them to be signed by the second
Augustus in a moment of excitement, and the crime of Christian-
izing was again inscribed in the laws. Then war, unchained by
the three wild beasts, as Lactantius says, raged with fury.

The persecution was destined to last eight years. What part in
this tragic history belongs to Diocletian? We have seen his repugnance to extreme measures. The Christians made no mistake in
identifying their enemy; it is Galerius whom they have pursued
with their maledictions. We must remember also that the just
horror inspired by these cruelties has deceived the world in respect
to the number of victims. Palestine was full of Christians; but in
the year 304 only ten perished, of whom six came of their own
accord to the executioner.[5] Italy and Spain had few; at least,

---

[1] Môros, says Eusebius (*Mart. de Pal.* 2).

[2] Tillemont, *Mém. eccl.* v. 41 and 603.   [3] *Ap.* Surius, December 31.

[4] Euseb., *Mart. de Pal.* 3.

[5] During the eight years that the persecution lasted, Eusebius, who was on the spot and
has written the history of it, enumerates, in Palestine, only eighty martyrs. From this number

in those countries the *Acta* are rare, and mostly of doubtful
authenticity,[1] and we read that Roman believers wishing to obtain
relics, went at that time to seek them in the East. Illyricum,
too near the Barbarians to possess great cities given up, like Antioch and Alexandria, to theological quarrels, occupied itself first
of all with its mundane safety. It had few bishoprics, and the
martyrs assigned to it are few in number; one only became popular, Saint Irenaeus of Sirmium.[2] In Britain and in Gaul, Constantius Chlorus contented himself with destroying a few churches:
"He did not destroy the temple built up to God in the hearts of
the faithful."[3] In Egypt and in the Oriental provinces the
martyrs put to death, and still more the confessors sent to the
mines after cruel tortures, were very numerous.[4] One thing,
however, is singular, — in the chapter in which Eusebius relates
the glorious deaths of the "pastors of the Church," during all the
years of persecution, he names only nine bishops.[5] But the imperial government knew them all; they were the heads of the
Churches, and according to the system of Diocletian the head was
to be struck; but we have seen that he did not wish to strike
mortal blows.

It does not seem even that the administration made search after
the Christians (*inquisitio*); otherwise it would have been necessary to
employ one part of the population of the Empire in exterminating the
other. Moreover the search was needless, for most accounts speak

Gibbon estimates that there may have been, throughout the entire Empire, two thousand
martyrs in the eight years, a vast and sad number, certainly, since one single victim would
have been too many; but every estimate must be uncertain.

[1] Tillemont, *Mém. eccl.* v. 11, 58, 74, etc. The most celebrated of the Spanish martyrs of
that time was Saint Vincent, whose *Acta* are a legend filled with miracles. The famous inscriptions of Clunia are ranged by Hübner (*C. I. L.* vol. ii. No. 253) among the apocrypha,
and are in their right place.

[2] Bollandists, March 25. For the *Passio SS. IV coronatorum* (Gurius, November 8),
see Hauziecker, *Zur Christ-necrj.* p. 262, and De Rossi, *Bull. d'archéol. crist.*, sections 3 and 4,
No. 11.

[3] Lactantius, *De Morte pers.* 15. Eusebius (*Life of Const.* i. 15) maintains even, very
mistakenly, that mass was celebrated in his palace at Treves.

[4] Cedrenus (*Hist.* p. 467) mentions an edict ordering the right eye of condemned Christians to be plucked out. We cannot tell whether this was an official order, or a practice of
certain judges. Eusebius often speaks of this punishment and of the burning of one of the
tendons of the foot in the case of Christians sent to the mines by Maximin.

[5] *Hist. eccl.* viii. 13. Sixteen had already occupied in succession the see of Alexandria;
only the last one died by martyrdom, in 311.

of the Christians giving themselves up. This one overthrows an altar of the gods; that one burns a temple of Cybele; another goes straight up to the governor who is offering a sacrifice, and plucks the incense from his hands; another insults him by word and act. "They were," says Saint Augustine, "arrows of God shot by the saints at the faces of the oppressors." [1] Then there was seen something like an epidemic of religious suicides. Contrary to the Church's teaching, which disapproves of men by voluntary acts of imprudence or provocation rushing to meet their martyrdom, the *Acta* show a multitude of Christians eager to exchange their mortal life for the blessedness promised by the Scriptures.[2] And we must also say, with a bishop of the time,[3] among these saints of the eleventh hour were found — a thing less strange than it appears — men who speculated upon torture, hoping, doubtless, that it would not be carried to the fatal point; some overwhelmed with debts, to finish gloriously a worthless life; others, to live in prison on the charity of the Christian community; still others, incapable of a high spirituality, to gain salvation by a last effort of bodily endurance. But, on the other hand, how many admirable instances of devotion, and stoical deaths! As we read some of the answers

[1] Saint Augustine, *In Psalm. XXXIX.* sect. 16 ; Euseb., *Mart. de Pal.* 4 and 5 ; λόγοις τε καὶ ἔργοις. Cf. Bollandists, February 7, Saint Theodore of Amasia.

> *Martyr . . .*
> *Infremuit usque tyranni oculos*
> *Sponte jacit.*
> PRUDENTIUS, *Peristeph.* iii. Saint Eulal. 126-128.

Cf. Le Blant, *Supplément aux Actes de Ruinart*, p. 33.

[2] Like the three Cilician martyrs, Tarachus, Probus, and Andronicus (Tillemont, *Mém. eccl.* v. 285), and a crowd of others. Sulpicius Severus (*Hist. sacra*, ii. 46) says: "They ran to these glorious combats, seeking for death more eagerly than now cupidity seeks for bishoprics." On the question of voluntary martyrdom, and on the means employed, on the other hand, to urge to his death a brother disinclined to it, see p. 68.

[3] See the letter of Mensurius, bishop of Carthage (*ap.* Saint Augustine, ix. 568), who was anxious that those who voluntarily provoked punishment should not be reckoned as martyrs : . . *Quidam fuciosuci et fisci debitores qui occasione persecutionis, vel carcere velint onerosa multis debitis esse, vel poenare se putarent, et quasi abluere facinora sua, vel certe ad quiere pecuniae et in custodia deceni pasci de obsequio Christianorum.* Thus did the Peregrinus of Lucian. There is also mention in the *Acta* of Saint Theodoret (*ap.* Ruinart) of debtors seeking death to escape the severity of the treasury or of their creditors. Cf. Le Blant, *Suppl. aux Actes de Ruinart*, pp. 10 *et seq.* The fate of insolvent debtors was so cruel that Constantine was obliged to moderate it, but long after him, even, Valentinian I. put to death insolvent debtors to the public treasury (Amm. Marcellinus, xxvii. 7). I have mentioned (p. 253, note 5) the banquets and the intoxicating liquors by which the courage of certain irresolute martyrs was stimulated.

given at the trial, we seem to hear the songs of a virginal purity already far above the level of earth.[1]

Political history does not record all the acts of courage in a battle, and of the soldiers who die for their country she preserves only the memory of their victory. Neither is it within her province to relate those triumphant deaths which have been the strength and are the honor of the Church. This duty belongs to religious history, which must determine what deeds are to be remembered, — a long and difficult work, begun centuries ago, and not yet ended. We refer the reader, therefore, to the hagiographers for the story of those heroic and horrible scenes where human wickedness exerted itself to discover new methods of causing the flesh to cry out, and where the victims suffered for the noblest of causes, — liberty of conscience. Like the sufferers by persecution, Diocletian also was to endure his pain: this man, so sagacious, who near the close of his reign thus lost his wisdom, was to behold from the retirement of his palace at Salona the death of his gods and the triumph of the Christ.[2]

II. — ABDICATION AND DEATH OF DIOCLETIAN (305-313).

AT the close of the year 303 the two Augusti were approaching the twentieth year of their reign, and they had taken together at the altar of the gods a pledge to mark this anniversary by a deed which has been imitated but once, at which posterity is amazed, and which, in the interests of the Roman world, it would have been better not to do. In the spring of 303 Diocletian quitted Nicomedeia and travelled slowly through Thrace and the Danubian provinces towards Italy. He had at last decided to visit that Rome which he had never seen since his accession, and to celebrate at one and the same time the festival of the *Sacra Vicennalia*

---

[1] For instance, that of Saint Theodora of Alexandria.

[2] The Christians followed him in later ages with their maledictions, as was their right; and so far as the persecution was concerned, it was justice. An historian of this Emperor, Casagrandi (*Diocleziano*, p. 308, No. 1) has even put this question: *Quale è stata la mano che dalle storie di Ammiano e Zosimo strappava le pagini dedicate a Diocleziano? Chi ha distrutta la vita che di lui scrisse il suo segretario Eustenio?*

and the triumph which the Senate had long before decreed to the
two Emperors.[1] But as he did not love an unwholesome popularity,
and was not of the number who stoop to obtain or to keep power,
he proposed to make but an official and brief visit to the old
capital of the world. On the twentieth of November he entered
the city with Maximian in a chariot drawn by four elephants,
as a memorial of his Asiatic victories. Behind him were borne
figures representing the Persian king whom he had conquered,
and the wives and children of Narses captured in his camp, all
arrayed in purple robes embroidered with pearls; and after these
the trophies recalling victories gained over the nations adjacent to
the frontiers. According to the custom on these anniversaries, he
granted an amnesty which opened the prison doors to all, the
Christians excepted, and gave largesses in all the great cities.
The people of Rome had their large share in this, — a *congiarium*
of 310,000,000 denarii, or 1,500 denarii apiece, if the population
still numbered 200,000.[2] Games and combats of animals were the
necessary accompaniment of these ceremonies; Diocletian gave
some, but they were lacking in magnificence. In the hunts, few
animals were killed; in the amphitheatre, few gladiators. The
people cried out against the niggardliness of the Emperor; they
murmured still more when they heard reported this saying of
Diocletian's, which made parsimony the rule: "In presence of the
censor there should be moderation." At bottom this captious
crowd displeased the ruler, who cared much more for the needs
of the Empire than for those of the populace of Rome;[3] content

---

[1] M. Lépaulle, a learned numismatist, in his *Note sur l'Atelier monétaire de Lyon*, 1883,
announces, from three denarii in his collection, found in 1880, a fact which is nowhere
mentioned; namely, the celebration of the Secular Games by Diocletian about fifty years later
than those of the Emperor Philip. The authority of the coins is great, but the silence of
historians on this important fact is very singular, especially of Zosimus, who speaks at great
length of the Secular Games, and knows nothing of those of Diocletian, although in speaking
of them he mentions this Emperor.

[2] It is more probable that this sum of 310,000,000 denarii (Mommsen, *op. cit.* p. 618)
represents the entire amount granted by Diocletian to the great cities of the Empire. — πᾶσῃ τῇ
Ῥωμαίων πολιτείᾳ, says Malalas (*Chron.* xii. 305, *ad ann.* 302). The *Alexandrian Chronicle*
mentions also (p. 515) for this same year a distribution in Alexandria of *panis castrensis*.
The triumph of Diocletian was not, as it has been said to be, the last triumph ever witnessed in Rome. Constantius celebrated one in 357, and Honorius another, after the victory
of Stilicho over Alaric.

[3] *Cum libertatem populi Romani ferre non poterat* (Lactantius, 17).

with having flung them gold, he scorned to take pains to amuse them. This disdain of his is comprehensible when we read what Ammianus Marcellinus has to say of the frivolity of these men, wholly absorbed in their sanguinary amusements, or shaking the folds of their togas to display their long-fringed sleeves and their tunics, in whose texture were interwoven various forms of animals.[1]

The senators were treated with no greater consideration. The ceremony of the installation of the consuls was approaching. It was for the Senate and the city a festival in which the Emperors formerly shared; but Diocletian did not attend it. On the 18th of December[2] he left Rome, which had not been able to detain him for an entire month, and visited Ravenna, there taking possession for the ninth time of the consular office (304). This triumph and these festivals, which had now brought to men's minds all the successes

MEDIUM BRONZE.[3]

of his reign, were a matter of policy with the skilled statesman. About to seek, in the remote palace which he had so carefully made ready for himself, that which contemporaries have called the "repose of the Augusti" (*quies Augustorum*),[4] — which, however, was for him really the carrying out of a deep design, — he had chosen not to retire from the world until he had given this brilliant manifestation which was to immortalize his fame.

From Ravenna he went to Aquileia and Istria, and probably as far as Salona, to make sure that all things were ready for his reception,[5] and then returned to Nicomedeia in the middle of 304. From this city is dated one of his last rescripts, — on the 28th of August of that year.

Diocletian had been seriously indisposed during this journey. But he was not yet sixty years old, he had a robust constitution,

---

[1] x.v. 6.

[2] Lactantius, 17. It is probable that before leaving Rome he caused Maximian to renew in the temple of Jupiter Capitolinus the engagement to abdicate at the same time with himself (*Pan. vet.* vii. 15).

[3] The Repose of the Augusti. QVIES AVGG.

[4] *Pan. vet.* xi. 11, and Eckhel, viii. 14.

[5] Conjecture authorized by the words of Lactantius, 17: *Per circuitum ripae Istricae Nicomediam venit.* Diocletian, in feeble health and habituated to Eastern climates, was likely in January, 304, to avoid the valley of the Danube, through which certain authorities represent him as passing, — a region subject to cold so extreme that the mighty river is sometimes frozen.

and, with his habitual tenacity of purpose, he returned to the city
where he had assumed the purple, and where he proposed to lay it
off. His illness increased during the winter; all the gods, assailed
with prayers for the recovery of him who had protected them,
remained deaf to these supplications. On the 15th of December
he had a fainting fit; the palace was in tears, and a rumor of his
death spread through the city. When this report was contradicted,
many refused to believe that he was still alive, thinking that it
was designed to conceal the truth until Galerius should arrive,
lest there might be an outbreak among the soldiery. The Emperor
did not appear again in public until the kalends of March. "He
could scarcely be recognized," says Lactantius, "so greatly had he
changed; though he had regained his health, he had lost his
reason, and never again recovered it for more than a few moments
at a time."[1] But Lactantius, his enemy, takes pleasure in showing the persecutor of the Christians deprived of his dignity as a
man by the Divine Justice, of his imperial crown by the Caesar
whom he had himself made, and the entire edifice he had so
laboriously erected falling into ruins over his head. The historian
has seen in the secret apartments of the palace Diocletian groan-
ing, with tear-stained face; he has heard the rude language and
threats of Galerius, and the humble answers of the old Emperor, — a
rhetorical embellishment which certain writers have accepted for
historic fact.[2] This abdication, which Galerius is supposed to have
extorted from a feeble and irresolute old man, was one of the conditions of existence of the new political system, which reserved
power for the prime of manhood. This Diocletian himself had
affirmed on the day when he ordered the sons of the Caesars to be
only additional soldiers in the imperial army; and the keenest
joy that this valiant mind could have anticipated for his latter

---

[1] Lactantius, 17 : *Demens enim factus est, ita ut certis horis insaniret, certis resipisceret.*

[2] To render this scene less improbable, Lactantius had shown Galerius since the year 297
inflated with pride on account of his victory over Narses, and exclaiming : *Quousque Caesar ?*
"How long must I remain Caesar?" The skilful rhetorician is mindful of the rule of his art,
that great effects must be prepared for long in advance. But he refutes himself when he says
later, in chap. XXXI., that Galerius was determined also to abdicate after his *Vicennalia*, showing that abdication after twenty years of rule was to be regarded as the principle of the new
government. Aurelius Victor knows nothing of any enfeeblement of Diocletian ; "He renounced the cares of government," says this author, "being in full vigor of body and mind
(*cunctanter curam reipublicae abjecit*)."

days must have been to behold his great institution subsisting without him. He had succeeded in preventing military usurpations by giving himself colleagues who acknowledged his supreme authority. But to secure in the future the peaceable transmission of the supreme power, he had resolved to limit his exercise of it to a period of twenty years, in order by his own example to lay an obligation of unselfishness upon future Augusti, and also to calm the impatience of new Caesars by showing them that the hour of sovereignty would come for them also. Thus was to be made secure the system which had been the great work of his life: succession according to merit taking the place of the principle of heredity or the accident of military favor. We have two decisive proofs that such was really his intention, — the care given for nine years to the construction of his palace at Salona, in a remote corner of the world, far from all public life and business ; and the abdication which he had long before compelled the ambitious Maximian to promise. Upon a coin struck on occasion of the abdication, these words are to be read : "To the

GOLD COIN.[1]

victorious Fates." For the pagans, fatality was the supreme will of Jupiter, "Master of Destiny," and human wisdom was an inspiration from the god. The resolution of the two Emperors was therefore to be attributed to Jupiter himself, *Fatis Victricibus* ;[2] and in retiring they obeyed the divine will.

When, in the month of December, 303, Diocletian had celebrated at Rome his *Vicennalia,* he was in his twentieth year of imperial power ; and the year was not completed until the 17th September, 304. The time that he had fixed for his abdication had in fact come ; but he waited some months longer, to allow Maximian to enter upon the twentieth year since the date of the latter's appointment as Caesar. By this delay Diocletian attained the period at which he could rightfully claim from his colleague the fulfilment of the latter's promise.

The Empire at this time was in the enjoyment of a profound peace, which to the imperial ear was not disturbed by the far-off

<hr />

[1] Victorious Destiny, FATIS VICTRICIBUS (reverse of a gold coin of Diocletian).

[2] Eckhel, viii. 6. An inscription found at Carlsburg (C. I. L. vol. iii. No. 1060) calls Jupiter *divinarum humanarumque rerum rector fatorumque arbiter.* (Cf. Pausanias, v. 15, in respect to Jupiter μοιραγέτης.)

cries of martyred Christians.   In the interior, no disorder; from without, no threat of danger.   In presence of this well-ordered government and of these securely guarded frontiers, ambitious men held their peace and the Barbarians remained in an attitude of respect and fear.   Nothing, therefore, prevented Diocletian from making the experiment, so formidable in an absolute monarchy, of the transmission of the supreme authority.

SEVERUS II.[1]

Three miles distant from Nicomedeia, upon a low hill overlooking the city, stood a column surmounted by a statue of Jupiter.   It was on this spot that Diocletian had given to Galerius the purple of the Caesars.   Hither the old Emperor caused his throne to be brought, and came to sit upon it for the last time.   The nobility of the Empire, the officers of the palace, and the representatives of all the legions having been assembled in their order around him, he rose and announced his resolution.   His strength, he said, was decreasing, and, after so many labors, repose was needful to him; he gave back to the god whose image glittered above his head that which the god had given him, and he now transmitted the Empire to the Caesars, whose places would thenceforward be filled by the experienced generals Severus and Maximin Daza.   The latter, a nephew of Galerius, was present.   Diocletian summoned him, and taking off his own purple mantle, laid it upon the young man's shoulders.   On the same day, May 1st, 305,

MAXIMIN DAZA.[2]

Severus was proclaimed Caesar at Milan by Maximian, and Diocletian, "now Diocles again," says Lactantius, quitted Nicomedeia to seek the seclusion of his palace at Salona.[3]

It was a grand and beautiful scene.   This Emperor, who — not like Charles V., in the decline of his power, but in full prosperity, and as yet far short of the limit of his life — resigns the imperial

[1] SEVERVS AVGVSTVS.   (Gold coin.)

[2] Laurelled MAXIMINVS P. F. AVG.   (Gold coin.)

[3] . . . *Et iterum Diocles factus* (Lactantius, 19).   This remark of Lactantius is not more truthful, however, than many other things that he says.   Diocles, on the contrary, remained Diocletian, with possession of all imperial honors.   Coins struck after the abdication represent him as crowned, and have the legend: *Domino nostro Diocletiano, beatissimo seniori Augusto.* On others is the following: *Aeterno Augusto,* or *Providentia deorum, quies augusta.*   Maximian withdrew into Lucania.

power that he may thus give solemn sanction to a political system, was a man of distinguished ability. "After him," says an old
historian, "the decline of the Empire began, and by degrees
Barbarism gained upon it." [1]

On the shore of one of those beautiful bays with which the
Adriatic indents the Dalmatian coast, where the calm water is
protected by islands from the angry waves of the open sea, now
stands the town of Spalato,[2] which was once almost completely
occupied by the palace of Diocletian. On one side is the sea,
with its changing aspects; on the other, wooded hills, vineyards,
and villages: and the air is always mild and fresh, except in
the burning heats of summer. In this favored scene Diocletian
had erected the sumptuous edifice wherein he proposed to end his
life near the spot where it began. The vast structure covered a
surface of more than eight acres. Its exterior wall, defended at
the four corners by huge quadrangular towers, gave admittance,
under fortified gateways known as the Gates of Gold, of Iron, of
Brass, and of the Sea, to four streets bordered by colonnades of
red granite. The old soldier had designed his palace after the
likeness of his Empire: seen from without, it was a camp and a
fortress. But the interior told of its imperial occupant, — baths,
a forum, halls of reception and council, barracks for the guard,
and two temples for his favorite divinities, Aesculapius (?) and
Jupiter (?) The latter temple, octagonal without and circular within,
with arches resting on the columns instead of the architrave placed
directly upon capitals, was a prelude to the Byzantine architecture.[3]
A thick wall, rising from the sea, supported an open gallery five
hundred and ninety feet in length, the roof resting on fifty columns:

---

[1] Zosimus, ii. 7: . . . βαρβαρωθεισα (ἡ Ῥωμαίων ἀρχή).

[2] Spalato, corruption of *Saloniae palatium*. The stone, almost as beautiful as marble, of
which the palace was built, was obtained from the quarries of Tragorium. Much porphyry
also and Egyptian granite were employed in the edifice.

[3] M. A. Choisy, the learned author of *L'Art de bâtir chez les Byzantins*, says very well,
p. 152: "It has been customary to date the Byzantine architecture from the fourth century.
According to the accredited opinion, Justinian was its originator, and Saint Sophia its first
example. In fact, no style of architecture ever comes into existence thus at a fixed date and
with a masterpiece as its first work." The author mentions, as examples of the beginnings
of Byzantine art in the Empire, two tanks at Constantinople, constructed in the time of
Constantine, the palace of Spalato, etc.: and he very justly finds its origin in Assyria.
"Byzantine art," he says, "existed from the Roman epoch beside the official architecture, and
waited only the decline of classic traditions to make itself conspicuous."

an incomparable *loggia*, whence the view extended beyond the islands
over the open sea, at that time crowded with vessels. By great
underground passages opening on this side, supplies were brought
into the palace and quietly distributed. In the neighborhood was
a hunting park; but where was the famous garden which Diocletian
cultivated with his own hands, and from which he wrote to
Maximian, when the latter besought him to resume the purple: "If
you could see the fine vegetables that I raise here, you would

INTERIOR VIEW OF THE TEMPLE OF JUPITER AT SALONA, FROM THE ATLAS OF CASSAS.

never speak to me again of such wearisome tasks"? The place is
unknown to us; but the answer lives in history, and men weary
of public life delight to quote it.

This dwelling was not that of a philosopher; but Diocletian
was not inclined to philosophize. He had done a political action
which implies uncommon grandeur of soul; and the sacrifice
being made, it pleased him to preserve as a private individual all
the magnificence of imperial station. The Temple of Jupiter,

so called, received the daylight only through the door of entrance,
and it is a very small building: scholars have been disposed to
think that it was a tomb. At the summit of power Diocletian had
prepared a stately shelter for his old age: it is quite probable
that while in retirement he constructed for his last home a
sumptuous tomb.[1]

The Emperor passed eight years at Salona, respected by those
whose fortune he had made. An inscription of the year 305 calls
him "the father of the Emperors." When his baths were inau-
gurated at Rome, his name was left to the colossal
edifice:[2] and on coins of this period he is called
"the eldest of the Augusti" (_Augustus senior_).[3]
Galerius consulted him in respect to the elevation
of Licinius, and in 310 Eumenes extolled in the
presence of Constantine the great Emperor whom

VALERIA
AUGUSTA.[4]

the new masters of the world revered.[5] But Diocletian saw the
ambitions that he had restrained break out anew: civil wars and
murders of Emperors succeed one another; Christianity obtain a
legal recognition; his wife, the Empress Prisca, and his daughter
Valeria, the widow of Galerius, despoiled of their possessions
and confined in a place of exile.[6] These blows, falling upon the
Emperor, the husband, and the father, were not enough to satisfy the enmity of the Christians. They depicted him as steeped
in insults and trembling for his life. Constantine throws down
his statues, has his name effaced from the public edifices,[7] and

---

[1] For a temple, the edifice is remarkably small, — 42½ feet in diameter, 69 in height. The
columns are but 23 feet high, but are surmounted with a heavy entablature and a second order
of pillars 11½ feet in height. On the other hand, tombs were never placed so near dwellings;
but Diocletian perhaps was desirous to place his own within the fortifications of his palace.
Lanza places the tomb in the Temple of Aesculapius.

[2] C. I. L. vol. vi. No. 1,130: . . . _Seniores Augusti patres imperatorum et Caesarum._

[3] Eckhel, viii. 14.

[4] VALERIA AVGVSTA, daughter of Diocletian and wife of Galerius. (Gold coin.)

[5] _Divinum illum virum . . . quem vestra tantorum principum colunt obsequia privatum.
. . . multo jugo fultus imperio et vestro tegitur latus umbraculo_ (_Pan. vet._ vii. 15).

[6] The two Empresses were decapitated, by order of Licinius, early in the year 315, and
their bodies thrown into the sea. A son of Galerius, Candidianus, whom Valeria had brought
up tenderly, was at the same time put to death.

[7] _Statuae revellebantur_ (Lactantius, 42). Constantine, he says, caused to be destroyed
the paintings in which the two Augusti are represented together, overthrew those of their
images where the statue of Diocletian formed a group with Maximian's, and effaced the inscriptions which were common to the two. This posthumous proscription was addressed to Maximian, whom Constantine had caused to be murdered. As for the mutilation of the inscriptions

writes him menacing letters:[1] Maximin makes no reply when
Diocletian begs, with humble messages, that his daughter be restored
to him; and the last days of this mighty monarch are so sad that
he poisons himself, or dies by voluntary starvation. The wrath
and indignation of the Christians against their persecutor require
that his punishment should begin in this present world. Since no
man killed him, it must needs be that he kill himself in the midst
of all the anguish of despair; thus justice would be done.

DIOCLETIAN.[2]

The scene is dramatic, and the legend that it
embodies lives yet; but Eusebius, a contemporary
and an enemy, and Eutropius, an indifferent person,
have no knowledge of this sad story. The latter
represents him as growing old in honored tranquillity; the former tells of a long illness which,
in the end, carried him off.[3]

In an ordinance published a few days before the death of Diocletian, Constantine still calls him, "Our lord and father;"[4] and,
lastly, he permits the Senate to decree him apotheosis, although
the ex-Emperor at Salona was no more than a private individual.[5]
The senators of Rome, protectors of the established religion, took
pleasure in protesting against the victory of the Christians by
causing their persecutor to be enrolled among the gods. But the
act could not be done without consent of the reigning Emperor;
it was therefore by the will of Constantine that Diocletian was apotheosized;[6]   upon earth honors to his memory

peculiar to Diocletian (L. Renier, *Inscr. d'Alg.* 108; C. I. L. vol. ii. No. 1,439; and Wilmanns, 769A, No. 1,050), we must see in this an act of rage on the part of the Christian populations, avenging themselves upon their persecutor, rather than the execution of an order from
government.

[1] Constantine is said to have endeavored to compel him to attend the conference at Milan
in 313, and, on the old man's refusal, to have written a letter which decided him to take his
own life; the Senate is said to have condemned him to death, etc. (Cf. Tillemont, *Hist. des
empereurs,* iv. 54.)

[2] D[omino] N[ostro] DIOCLETIANO BEATISSIMO SENIORI AVG[usto]. The
reverse: PROVIDENTIA DEORVM QVIES AVG. (Medium bronze.)

[3] *Praeclara otia sennit* (Eutrop., ix. 28; Euseb., *Hist. eccl.* viii. 17).

[4] *Codex Theod.* xiii. 10, 2; edict of the kalends of June, 313. Diocletian, not being
called *divus,* was still living at that date. It may be inferred from Lactantius (*De Mort. pers.*
35–45) that he died before Maximin (July, 313); consequently a few days after the date of
the edict.

[5] *Contigit ei ut, quum privatus obiisset, inter Divos referretur* (Eutrop., ix. 28).

[6] Under the Christian Emperors the word *divus* was retained to designate the dead

RUINS OF SELEUCIA (LÉON DELABORDE, VOYAGE EN ASIE MINEURE, PLATE 72).

were not lacking: his tomb remained always covered with the imperial mantle.[1]

The conqueror of Actium gave the Empire its first form; namely, absolute power, concealed under a republican exterior, with liberal institutions in the cities and provinces. Diocletian undertook to abolish whatever remained of the government of the Caesars, in order to establish in its stead a skilfully organized monarchy whose agents should be everywhere present. The union which had not been made between low and high by means of free institutions, was to be made between high and low by administrative links throughout the whole Empire, and they proved strong enough to keep a portion of it standing for ten centuries. We have seen how much ancient material was employed in the construction of the new edifice; it is always so. In public affairs the successful innovators are those who organize well, rather than those who invent; for the present, in order to stand securely, must begin by resting upon the past.

Emperor. The reign of Diocletian has given rise to many discussions, into which it would be out of place to enter here; they will be found in various special works, of which some are excellent: Hunzicker, in the *Untersuch. zur rom. Kaisergesch.* of Max Büdinger, ii 115-281 (1866); Preuss, *Kaiser Diocletian*, 1869; Casagrandi, *Diocleziano*, 1876; Mason, *The Persecution of Diocletian*, 1876; Corra, *L' Abdicazione di Diocl.*, 1877; Morosi, *L' Italia dell' imp. Diocl.*, 1880; Burckhardt, *Die Zeit Constantins des Grossen*, 1880. For a part of the chronology of this reign there is a learned paper by Mommsen, *Ueber die Zeitfolge der Verordnungen Diocletians*, which we have already had occasion to quote.

[1] Amm. Marcellinus relates (xvi. 8) that a certain Danus was, under Constantius, accused of treason for having taken away from Diocletian's tomb a purple covering (*velamen purpureum*).

TEMPLE OF ROME. BRONZE COIN.

FOURTEENTH PERIOD.

THE CHRISTIAN EMPIRE: CONSTANTINE TO THEODOSIUS
(306–395 A. D.).

CHAPTER CI.

CONSTANTINE, MAXENTIUS, AND LICINIUS (306—324).

I. — SIX EMPERORS AT ONE TIME.

WHILE Diocletian was on his way to Dalmatia, the four new masters of the Empire — the two Augusti, Constantius and Galerius, and the two Caesars, Severus and Maximinus — took possession of the imperial power, under the conditions prescribed to each by the founder of the tetrarchy. The system, therefore, seemed to be firmly established. It had, however, only an outward show of permanence: in order to subsist, it needed at its head a man whose supreme authority would be respectfully accepted, and whose firmness would keep each in his appointed place. Which of the four rulers will be able to fill the place of the recluse of Salona?

Will it be Constantius Chlorus? He is the senior Augustus, but he has no desire to wield an authority too heavy for his feeble hands; instead of going to Milan or Rome, he chooses to remain at Trèves, thus abandoning to Severus the central post. What cares Constantius — who has already one foot in the grave, and will be dead in a few months — for power? Will it be Galerius? This Emperor deserves a better reputation than he has had;[1]

---

[1] Eutropius (x. 2) says that he was *pede moratus*; and the author of the *Epit.* 40: . . . *inculta agrestique justitia.*

CONSTANTINVSCAES

CONSTANTINE CAESAR. STATUE FOUND IN THE BATHS OF
CONSTANTINE AT ROME.

he is an active man, a good soldier, and his twelve years of command give him authority. Trusting to his military talents, Diocletian, in dividing the Empire, has given him a very important share. Maximinus receives only Egypt and Syria, Severus only Italy and Africa; so that from the Taurus to the Alps, Galerius commands the richest provinces, the most warlike populations, and will have more gold and more troops than his colleagues. To him evidently was intrusted the duty of maintaining that wise balance which could be preserved only by incessant vigilance. But he is not far-sighted. Instead of the sagacity which discerns approaching danger, and the firmness which dispels it, he

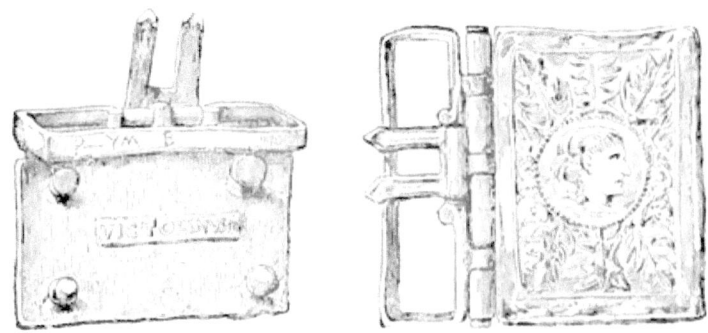

GOLD BUCKLE WITH THE HEAD OF CONSTANTIUS CHLORUS (?) [1]

will manifest anger only; and he will be able to baffle neither the ambition of Constantine, which Diocletian had suspected and held in check, nor that of Maxentius, whose father had been compelled by the great Augustus to keep his unruly son at a distance; and two barrack-revolutions will shortly renew all the public misfortunes.

Diocletian had left in the palace of Nicomedeia the son of Constantius, a young man thirty-one years of age,[2] skilful in all

---

[1] The father of Constantine, or perhaps Constantine himself, on a hinged clasp of gold. The inscription in relief on the reverse of the clasp was made with a stamp; it doubtless is the name of the owner: VICTORINVS (*Cabinet de France*, No. 2,689).

[2] Flavius Valerius Aurelius Constantinus, born in 273 or the following year. All his successors in the fourth century, Maximus alone excepted, took his gentile name, Flavius. See the *Tituli domus imperatoriae* of Wilmanns.

manly exercises, brave, and handsome.[1] To these exterior advantages, which delight the crowd and the soldiery, he united a keen and crafty mind, unscrupulous in the matter of useful lies or what he judged to be necessary murders, even were the victim a child; but, also, a ready perception of the best means to serve his ambition, the talent to use them well, and that resolute will which neutralizes contrary influences. As a general, famous for rapid combinations, he will preserve as a ruler the prudent reserve taught to him by the twelve years he spent as hostage at an Asiatic court.[2]

This son of an Augustus had enjoyed hitherto only the honors of the military tribuneship; and now while Constantius was master of the West, he remained the suspected guest of his father's secret enemy. Constantius called his son to him by letters, constantly more and more urgent. Diocletian, no doubt, had received similar letters and had made no reply to them, being unwilling to encourage hopes of hereditary succession, — an idea diametrically opposed to his elective system, and to the conception formed by the Romans of their Republican magistracies, and even of the imperial office, for which there had always been the semblance of an election. Galerius, less prudent, yielded to the solicitations of Constantine; he gave the young man leave to depart, and furnished him with the authorization necessary in order to employ the public post. This time again Lactantius relates what he has seen, or believes that he has seen, in the mind of Galerius, — the Emperor's regrets at having yielded, his determination to retract his promise on the morrow, or to gain time that he may send to Severus an order to arrest the fugitive as he is crossing the Alps. It was late in the afternoon, says Lactantius; the Emperor advised Constantine, as he gave him the authorization, not to make use of it until the next day, — hoping to find meanwhile some excuse

---

[1] He is said to have killed a Sarmatian warrior in single combat, and to have destroyed a monstrous lion. This lion is without doubt the ancestor of the one which Pepin the Short vanquished. Legend shows us Constantine as an invincible hero, and Galerius as a cruel tyrant, who, to rid himself of a future rival, exposed his colleague's son to dangers of all kinds. *In insidiis saepe juvenem apposuerat, . . . feris illum objecerat* (Lactant., *De Morte pers.* 24). For the personal description of Constantine, cf. Eusebius, *Life of Constantine*, i. 19. The historian saw him in Palestine with Diocletian.

[2] See p. 366.

for preventing the journey, or at least the opportunity to despatch a warning to Severus. But as soon as Galerius had fallen asleep after supper, Constantine made his escape; and lest he should be pursued, seized and carried off all the horses from the first stations of the imperial post.[1] Galerius slept till noon of the following day. On awakening, he sends for Constantine, learns that the latter has gone, and orders couriers to be sent out in all haste to recall him. But Constantine is already far on his journey; the post-stables are empty; and the Emperor "cannot refrain from tears."

Lactantius enjoys these pictures, which are made according to the rules of the schools. But I confess to incredulity as to the Emperor's tears. I have no confidence in this flight which might so easily have been prevented, in this hope that Severus would close the Alpine passes, after Galerius had left open the gates of Nicomedeia. And how heavy the Emperor's sleep in this night which must have been one of so much anxiety! But the rhetorician had need of these fifteen or twenty hours to place Constantine beyond pursuit, and of this dramatic narrative to secure to his hero the favor always gained by the innocent captive who breaks his chains. Constantine's history thus at a thousand points skirts the domain of legend, because it was necessary to transfigure the ruler by whose agency Christianity triumphed. Lactantius has not observed that in making Constantine a rebel, he places to his account the consequences of this usurpation. The noble but impracticable system of Diocletian was, in fact, about to perish; civil war to return; with it murders and destruction, and for the Empire a period of anarchy which lasted eighteen years.

The eloquence of those times was so entirely regardless of truth that another rhetorician — and a pagan, in this case — says of the journey: "They were not the horses of the public post which brought the prince from the ends of the world, but it was a celestial chariot, drawn by divine steeds."[2]

Constantine joined his father at Boulogne, and went with him into Britain. "He did not go," says Eumenius, "to seek

---

[1] In later accounts Constantine is represented as having hamstrung the horses that he left behind him (Zosimus, ii. 8).

[2] *Pan. vet.* vii. 7.

trophies of victory in the sacred island, nearer to heaven than lands situated in the midst of the continents; he had heard divine voices calling him to the extremities of the world. Before

DIVO CONSTANTIO AVG.[2]

taking his place among the celestial powers, he desired to contemplate Oceanus, the father of the gods, and in those regions to see a day almost without night."[1] The Augustas of the Western provinces had not the heated imagination of the rhetorician. Instead of a pilgrimage to the Fortunate Isles, he had destined for his son an expedition which would give him an opportunity to make the acquaintance of the troops; successes easily gained served as a pretext for largesses which completed the conquest of the soldiers' hearts. When Constantius died, a few days later, in the city of Eboracum (York), July 25, 306, the legions proclaimed his son Augustus.[3] Crocus, a king of the Alemanni, who was in command of the auxiliary corps, distinguished himself by the ardor of his zeal for the new Emperor.[4]

In assuming the title of Augustus, Constantine had gone too fast and too far. From the moment when Galerius had authorized his departure, the latter had certainly foreseen, and accepted in advance, the inevitable results which the health of Constantius Chlorus gave ground for expecting. There was reason to fear that on the death of the Western Augustus some ambitious man would draw away the legions of these remote provinces, as Carausius had done twenty years earlier. To be in a position to thwart all designs of usurpation, Constantine had been sent to his

---

[1] *Pan. vet.* vii. 8.

[2] Laurelled head of Constantius Chlorus, on a medium bronze.

[3] The Senate placed Constantius among the *divi*, — *Divo Constantio Aug.* (Eckhel, viii. 32). Eumenius (*Pan. vet.* vii. 8) and Eusebius (*Hist. eccles.* viii. 13) speak of this *consecratio.* The sons of his second marriage were as yet children, the eldest being only thirteen years of age. In preparing the way for the accession of Constantine, the Augustus of the Gauls hoped to secure the throne in his own family, and give a protector to his other children, who were not yet of an age to defend themselves. Constantius was the author of a law, important in its results, declaring that donations were not valid unless they had been declared in the curia (*si actis insertæ non essent*). It was also necessary that wills should be inscribed there. In 397 Honorius speaks of this as an ancient usage (*Codex.* vi. 23, 18, and *Codex Theod.* iii. 51). The curia thus became, in civil matters, an office of registration, and as such it survived the invasion.

[4] *Epit.* 41.

father with promises, but without the imperial title, that the constitution should not be violated, there being as yet no vacancy among the Emperors. Instead of awaiting his elevation by legal procedure to the rank of Caesar, Constantine took advantage of a military tumult; and the soldiers, delighted to resume the lucrative part of king-makers, promptly bestowed upon him the desired title.

According to custom, Constantine sent to the Emperor his image crowned with laurel, and he reported the event to Galerius in modest terms, deploring the impatience of the soldiers, which had made it impossible for him to await the recognition of his rights by the legal head of the Empire.[1] Lactantius asserts that Galerius was at first disposed to throw into the fire the image, the letter, and the messenger; he calmed himself, however, accepted the apology, but conceded to the favored candidate of the British legions only the title of Caesar, and the fourth place among the Emperors.[2] Severus was raised to the second place, with the title of Augustus; Maximinus remained in the third, as first Caesar. In this situation Constantine showed that he knew how to mitigate boldness by prudence; he accepted the position assigned him. He would, in fact, have declared himself a rebel, had he kept the title the soldiery had given him, and he would have drawn upon himself the forces of all the other Emperors, as happened the year after to Maxentius.

The tetrarchy, for a moment imperilled, seemed to be again firmly established. But why should the son of Maximian, the son-in-law of Galerius,[3] be more unselfish than the son of Constantius? After his father's abdication, Maxentius had retired to a villa in the neighborhood of Rome. In the great city much silent displeasure was fermenting: the Senate, without political authority, the praetorians, without military importance, the people, without amusements or largesses, detested the Emperors, who lived far away from them. A circumstance increased the exasperation. — Galerius ordered a new census, a sort of revision of the government register, designed to render taxation more equal, by bringing into their place as tax-payers those who had

---

[1] Such, at least, is the theory maintained by Eumenius (*Pan. vet.* vii. 8).

[2] Lactant., *De Morte pers.* 25.   [3] *Bull. épigr. de la Gaule*, i. 108.

escaped from it, as the *plebs urbana* lately exempted from the capitation-tax, or those who had never been in it, as the Italians, for five hundred years free from the land-tax. Diocletian had annulled this latter privilege, and it may have been for the execution of this decree that Galerius ordered returns of persons and estates not only in Italy, but throughout the Empire, and even in Rome itself.[1] The mistress-city of the world fallen to the condition of a stipendiary, — what a disgrace! Riot breaks out against this insolent Dacian who dares subject to tribute the heirs of Augustus and of Trajan. People and praetorians unite, and seal their alliance with the blood of Abellius, the prefect of the city. But they need a leader. Maxentius, whose hand and whose wealth were in this riot, is proclaimed Emperor (Oct. 28, 306). He calls his father Maximian to come to him, and the latter, less wise than Diocletian, leaves his retreat: he again assumes the purple, amid the acclamations of the Senate and the people, and Rome has six Emperors. This number was to be quickly reduced, for it was a revolt, changing the established order, to the detriment of the legitimate rulers.

Severus was an Illyrian, a soldier of fortune, as all the Emperors for the last forty years had been, but a man not made for such a dangerous post, to which he should never have ascended, since he knew not how to defend himself in it. He had not as yet had time to gain the confidence of the troops and make sure of their fidelity. Galerius despatched him to Rome to overthrow the usurper. Rashly entering the narrow peninsula, without having made preparation for safe retreat in case of disaster, he arrived before the ancient city with troops already gained over to the general who had long been their leader. The defection began with a corps of Mauretanian soldiers, whom Maximian had not long before brought back from Africa. The praetorian prefect Annulinus persuaded the rest, and Severus fled, almost alone, to Ravenna, where he was at once besieged. The place was strong, and, with the Adriatic fleet, Severus remained master of the sea, and con-

---

[1] Lactantius (*D. Morte pers.* 23) describes with ludicrous terror the operation of the *censitores*, which was very simple, habitual, and in the interest of all, tax-payers and government alike, with the sole exception of the *plebs urbana*, from whom Galerius withdrew the exemption from the capitation-tax accorded by Diocletian.

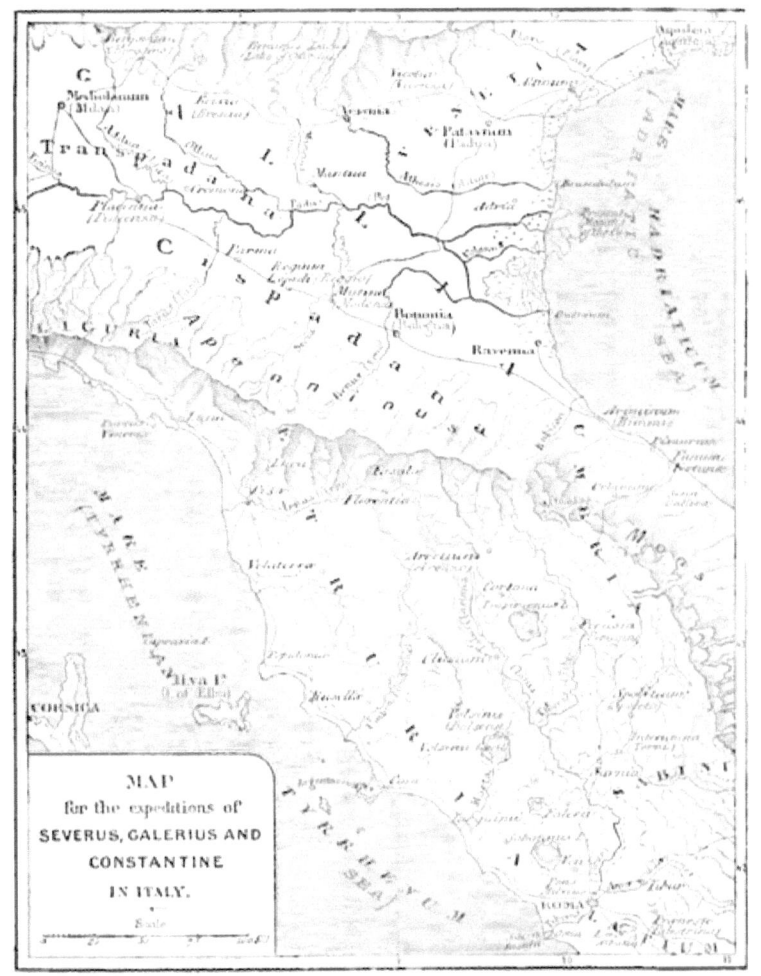

MAP
for the expeditions of
SEVERUS, GALERIUS AND
CONSTANTINE
IN ITALY.

Scale

sequently at liberty to go to meet the reinforcements which Galerius would not fail to send him. But, his mind distracted by these sudden disasters, he believed himself surrounded by traitors, and listening to the crafty proposals of Maximian, he surrendered,

laying down the purple which less than two years before the latter had bestowed upon him (February or March, 307). He expected to be honorably treated. Being carried captive to Rome, and imprisoned in a villa on the Appian Way, he there received the order to relieve his conquerors of their last anxiety; the choice was left him of the manner of his death. He had his veins opened, and went to share the tomb of Gallienus, another assassinated Emperor. His son, Severianus, also met a violent death a few years later. These murders of Emperors, following one another almost uninterruptedly during a half century,

THE EMPEROR MAXIMIAN.

makes us appreciate in contrast the tranquil grandeur of the reign of Diocletian.

Maxentius remained master of Italy, but Galerius was preparing to avenge Severus and dethrone his daughter's husband. What would now be the conduct of the sovereign of the Gallic provinces? Maximian came to ask this question of Constantine. He crossed the Alps to meet him, and proposed an alliance, offering

¹ Colossal statue of Greek marble; this has the original antique head (Palazzo Odescalchi. — Clarac, pl. 946, No. 2,525).

the hand of his daughter, the beautiful Fausta, and the title of Augustus. Constantine accepted both, and the marriage was celebrated at Arles, "the Gallic Rome,"[1] with great magnificence; in return he promised his friendship. He was very decided in giving nothing more, and in awaiting further developments. Events followed each other rapidly. Galerius, entering Italy with the Illyrian legions, advanced undisturbed as far as Narnia, sixty miles from Rome. At his approach the cities had closed their gates, the country population had escaped to the hills, and of the entire region he possessed only the space covered by his camp. To Italy Maxentius was the national ruler, while the Augustus of the Oriental provinces appeared to them a stranger, an enemy. To advance, in the midst of universal disaffection, as far as the great city, which by a solid wall Aurelian had protected against assault, was a rash act, whose peril the old soldier clearly discerned. He had not the material for a siege, — neither the provisions nor the

DIOCLETIAN.[2]

engines; and he also asked himself what Constantine was intending to do. A Gallic army coming across the Alps could easily shut him up in the peninsula; he dared not advance farther, and after a vain attempt at negotiations he retreated upon Illyricum, ravaging Italy as a barbaric chief might have done.

The Empire had fallen back into extreme confusion. To restore order, Galerius had recourse to the wisdom of Diocletian; he invited the old Emperor to meet him at Carnuntum — a fortified

---

[1] Ausonius, Clar. Urb. vii. They had already been betrothed, with the consent of Constantius, if we may believe a passage of Julian (Disc. i. 6). A panegyrist relates that in a picture exhibited in the palace of Aquileia, Fausta, puella divina decore venustatis, was represented offering to the young Constantine a helmet of gold glittering with diamonds (Pan. vet. vi. 6). Diocletian opposed this marriage, which would have caused too many hopes to spring up. When it took place, in 307, Constantine found himself the brother-in-law of his mother-in-law, his father having married an elder daughter of Maximian. Constantine already had, by a concubine, a son, Crispus (Zosimus, ii. 20; Zonaras, xiii. 2). See p. 366, note 1. The title of Augustus seems to have been assumed by Constantine, March 31, 307.

[2] Coin of Diocletian struck after his abdication. D. N. DIOCLETIANO FELICISSIMO SEN. AVG. On the obverse, a laurelled head of Diocletian. On the reverse, PROVIDENTIA DEORVM QVIES AVGG. Two women standing, one with the right hand raised, the other holding a branch and a sceptre. (Medium bronze.)

position whither the legions had been summoned, probably by some menacing attitude of the German tribes. Maximian, driven out of Rome by his son, whom he had sought to depose by instigating the praetorians against Maxentius, hastened to this rendezvous of the Emperors. An old comrade in arms of Galerius, — like himself the son of a peasant, but reported to be a descendant of the Emperor Philip, — Licinius, was already there. The discussions at this imperial council have not been preserved to us. We may, perhaps, attribute to Diocletian the double idea of accepting what had taken place, by leaving the provinces to the usurper, and at the same time protesting against the usurpation by giving Licinius the title of Augustus, with the government of the Empire and the second rank in the Empire (Nov. 11, 307).[1]

The Caesar of Syria and Egypt, Maximin, was exasperated at seeing a man who was neither Caesar nor akin to the imperial family obtain the precedence over himself. At the beginning of the year 308 he caused himself to be proclaimed Augustus by his troops, notwithstanding the decided opposition of Galerius, who, compelled to allow his nephew to remain in possession of that title, could not refuse it to Constantine. There were therefore four Augusti legally recognized as such throughout the Empire; a fifth, Maxentius, was so in Italy only; and the sixth, Maximian, wandered up and down, with his imperial purple and his restless ambition, without money, without an army, without provinces. To obtain all that he needed, he conspired against his son-in-law, set in circulation a rumor of the latter's death on an expedition

---

[1] It will be remembered that Galerius allowed Constantine only the title of Caesar. The edict of 311, in the text of Eusebius (*Hist. eccles.* viii. 17), gives the second rank to Constantine, and neither Maximin nor Maxentius is named in it; this part of the text was arranged, therefore, to give Constantine the precedence over Licinius. Lactantius asserts that in 312 the Senate gave the first rank to Constantine. It is possible that after his victory over Maxentius, Constantine caused a senatus-consultum to this effect to be issued. By itself, the Senate did and could do nothing; but it was easy for a conqueror to set this old machine at work for a moment, and in the transcription of the edict of 311, Eusebius followed the order most favorable to his hero. In respect to the omission of the names of Maximin and Maxentius, Tillemont (*Hist. des Empereurs*, iv. 116) believes there is an error of the copyists. It is more probable that in giving the edict of toleration, which Lactantius declares to have been issued in the names of all the Emperors (*communi titulo*), Eusebius purposely omitted the name of him who six months after violated it, and also of him who was conquered at the Milvian Bridge. Official documents were not, in those days, papers scrupulously transcribed.

against the Franks, and seizing the military chest, which had been
left in Arles, incited to insurrection the troops in Narbonensis.
On news of this, Constantine hastened to the scene of action with
the greatest promptness; he showed himself to the soldiery, who at
once returned to their allegiance; and Maximian, who had taken
refuge at Marseilles, was given up to him (308). The latter lived
for some time at the court of his son-in-law, deprived of the
imperial honors, and impatient at his humble position. Did he
betray a secret displeasure, from which Constantine freed himself by
a sentence of death, or shall we accept the tragic story which is
told by Lactantius, — from whom nothing seems hid, who sees in
the darkness, and hears what is whispered in imperial ears?
Listen to his story. Maximian frames new plots: in a secret interview with his daughter, he essays by prayers and caresses to
persuade her to betray her husband; he promises her one more
worthy of her, and asks her only to leave open the door of the
room where the Emperor sleeps, and to remove the guards who
usually are stationed before it. Fausta relates all to Constantine.
The latter perceives, in his father-in-law's words, a plan of
murder, and to take the criminal in the act, he orders a eunuch
to take his place for the night in the imperial couch. In the
darkness Maximian arises and makes his way to the spot. All

things seem propitious to his designs: the
guards are few or remote. To those who
meet him, he says that an important
revelation has just been made him in a
dream, and he is hastening to tell it to
his son-in-law. He enters the imperial
bedroom, stabs the eunuch, and, rejoicing
in his crime (*gloriabundus*), comes out exclaiming, "The Emperor is dead!" But
Constantine appears with his guards; he
points to the dead body, while the assassin

TOMB OF MAXIMIAN.[1]

stands silent and dismayed; he permits the latter to choose what
death he shall die; and the old Emperor strangles himself: "*Nodum
informis leti trabe nectit ab alta.*"[2]

----

[1] Tomb of Maximian upon a coin of Maxentius (from Parker's *Forum Romanorum*).

[2] Lactant. *op. cit.* 30, quoting Vergil. *Aen.* xii. 603.

The restless spirit and misguided ambition of Maximian had thrown him into intrigues attested by the two plots, — at Rome against his son, at Arles against his son-in-law;[1] But the story of his last moments is very strange, and seems to have been copied from some Arab tale. We shall probably not be far from the truth if we believe that this narrative was devised to conceal the odiousness of the murder of an old man who, abandoned by all the world, was in no way to be feared, and whose age and long services ought to have been respected by the husband of his daughter (310).[2]

No man has ever killed his successor: and it is with institutions as with men, those which are of the future always triumph over those which belong to the past. Galerius, not having been able to destroy Christianity, confessed himself conquered by putting a stop to the persecution, which, always a bad thing, was besides useless unless it were general. But Constantius and his

son had promised the Gallic provinces exemption from it; Maxentius did not continue it in the provinces of Italy and Africa;[3] and only Maximin, in Syria and Egypt, still ordered the execution of Christians. On April 30, 311, Galerius

MAXIMIAN.[4]

MAXENTIUS.[5]

issued an edict, in which he said: "For the general welfare of our subjects and for the preservation of our authority we had resolved to re-establish the discipline of our ancestors. We desired to bring

---

[1] Zosimus, ii. 11, and *Pan. vet.* xii. 14 and 15.

[2] Eusebius, in his *Life of Constantine,* avoids all mention of this murder; and in his *Ecclesiastical History,* contents himself with saying that, according to a prophecy, Maximian strangled himself. Eumenius (*Pan. vet.* vii. 20) also speaks of suicide. This was the official version: . . . *Nec se dignum vita judicavit, cum per te locatus ut vixerat.* Aur. Victor (*Caes.* 40) says, *jure interivit,* and the author of the *Epitome,* that Constantine caused him to be strangled (*fractis laqueo cervicibus*). While Maxentius was alive, it was for the interest of Constantine to have it believed that Maximian died by suicide, which permitted the apotheosis of this somewhat unworthy personage, to whom an inscription (*Bull. épigr. de la Gaule,* i. 108) and coins (Eckhel, viii. 27) give the title of *divus.* After the battle of the Milvian Bridge, Constantine caused his father-in-law's monuments to be thrown down, and his name defaced from the milestones (Euseb., *Hist. eccl.* viii. 13, and *Revue archéol.,* July, 1883, p. 39 *et seq.*). The *Epitome* represents him as only sixty years of age.

[3] Euseb., *Hist. eccl.* viii. 14.

[4] DIVO MAXIMIANO SEN[iori] FORT[issimo] IMP[eratori]. Laurelled head, on small bronze coin. (Cohen, No. 323, and Eckhel, viii. 27).

[5] MAXENTIVS P. F. AVG. (Gold coin.)

back to a better mind the Christians, who had the temerity and the presumption to oppose the established rites of religion. . . . These persons have been exposed to great dangers, and many of them have suffered death. Since they persist in their folly, our benevolence towards our subjects is such that we now permit them to hold their ordinary assemblies. This indulgence will oblige them to pray to their god on our behalf." Thus ended the era of the martyrs. But the wild beast that is in the human heart did not die with the gods who had so savagely defended themselves. The men yesterday persecuted will to-morrow be themselves the persecutors, and religious animosities will shed a thousand times more blood than has up to this time been poured forth.

A month later Galerius, attacked with a frightful disease — which Eusebius and Lactantius describe with complacency, died at Nicomedeia, before attaining that twentieth year of Empire which, faithful to the order established by Diocletian, he intended to signalize by his abdication.[1]

II. — Defeat and Death of Maxentius and of Maximin Daza (311–313).

Two Emperors have now disappeared from the scene: four remain. But this is no longer the tetrarchy of Diocletian: all bear the title of Augustus, and there is no subordination among them. The Empire is torn into four hostile kingdoms, — into five, even; for Alexander, the governor of Africa, was proclaimed Augustus by the army, and recognized by the cities which had refused to receive the images of Maxentius (308). The Barbarians not having yet recovered from the salutary alarm caused them by Diocletian, the new Emperors were at liberty to turn their strength against each other, and for twelve years the provinces were the scene of civil wars.

THE USURPER ALEXANDER.[2]

Hostilities were on the point of being declared between Licinius and Maximin Daza in respect to the inheritance of Galerius; but

[1] Lactant., De Mort. pers. 20.   [2] Bronze coin.

an agreement accepted by the former left to the latter the whole of Asia, the Bosphorus separating the two Empires. War, averted in the East, broke out, however, almost immediately in the West.

The Frankish youth, disgusted with peace, had fallen upon Gaul; Constantine easily defeated these adventurers, and exposed to wild beasts in the amphitheatre of Trèves his prisoners, among them the two chiefs. This execution caused the formation of a league of many Frankish and Alemannic tribes: an impetuous attack of the Romans soon broke this fragile tie. All the dis-

RUINS OF THE AMPHITHEATRE AT TRÈVES.

tricts occupied by the Bructeri were given up to devastation, the villages were burned, the cattle driven away, and the captives sold or thrown to the beasts, — cruelties which did not seem to promise one neophyte to the Church, any more than did the Frankish games, — a purely pagan solemnity instituted by Constantine in memory of his successes, and for a long time maintained.[1] The reorganization of the flotilla of the Rhine, and the construction of a permanent bridge over the river, announced to the Barbarians that Constantine was determined to have free entrance into their

1 *Ludorum celebrationes deorum festa sunt* (Lactant., *Inst. div.* vi. 20).

country.[1] In the interior of the provinces his administration was able and useful; the Christians were not interfered with, and in 310 he worthily celebrated his *quinquennalia* by remitting to the populations under his sway the *reliqua* due on the taxes since his accession. Eumenius had represented to him that the land no longer gave back what it cost, and that the farmers were everywhere abandoning their profitless industry; and at the entreaty of the Aeduan orator the Emperor reduced from 32,000 to 25,000 the taxable units, *capita*, of the territory of Autun,[2]—which was equivalent to reducing the land-tax nearly one fourth. He must have done the same in other cities, for the success obtained by Eumenius could not have failed to stimulate the efforts of rhetoricians, from the schools of which this orator was the director. At Trèves he rebuilt the walls, constructed a circus, basilicas, a forum, a praetorium,—monumental gifts which gratified the population and gave them employment, and must have been supplemented by financial gifts.

In Italy, on the contrary, Maxentius appears to have followed in the footsteps of the worst of the Roman tyrants. The man whom Constantine overthrew is accused by the victor's courtiers of every vice,—profligacy, violence, and cruelty; and we have no reason to doubt them, since the pagan authors, Zosimus, Eutropius, and Victor condemn him, and Julian excludes him from the banquet of the Caesars.[4] He repressed with great harshness the revolt in Africa; Alexander was put to death (311); Carthage and Cirta were sacked, the country given up to pillage, many citizens executed, and many more deprived of their possessions. At Rome, a saturnalia of crime,—noble matrons dishonored, senators plundered,[5] sometimes put to death on charge of treason, that their

[1] It is believed that this bridge, built near Cologne, lasted till the reign of the Emperor Otho I. (Wietersheim, *Völkerwanderung*, iii. 175). Remains of piles are seen in the bed of the Rhine, opposite Mayence; but it is a matter of doubt whether these were the work of the Romans or of Charlemagne.

[2] *Pan. vet.* viii. 10.   See p. 396.

[3] *Ibid.* viii. 22.

[4] Zosimus (ii. 15) says of Maxentius: μετὰ πάσης ὠμότητός τε καὶ ἀσελγείας. However, Lampridius, in promising Constantine to write the history of Licinius, Severus, Alexander (the African usurper), and Maxentius, says that he will do *ita ut nihil eorum virtute derogatur* (*Heliog.* 35).

[5] Aur. Vict. (*Caes.* 40) seems to attribute to Maxentius the establishment of the *follis senatorius,*—a tax paid by the senators outside of their land-tax, which was regulated by

entire fortune might be confiscated; but to the soldiers the utmost
license, even to the degree that once they were suffered to attack
the populace.[1] Accordingly, secret solicitations soon came from
Italy to Constantine, who, on his part, had personal wrongs to
avenge.[2]

After the murder of Maximian, Maxentius had affected great
zeal for his father's memory; he had thrown down the statues of
Constantine, and concluded an alliance with the Egyptian Augustus;[3] whereupon the Gallic Emperor made alliance with Licinius,
giving the latter in marriage Constantia, his sister. Finally,
Maxentius was making great preparations for war, gathering a
powerful army, with the avowed purpose of subjugating Gaul and
Illyria; he is said to have had 200,000 men, and Constantine
half that number. These figures are, however, extremely large; the
Roman armies were not usually so numerous.[4] After providing
for the defence of the Rhine and of Britain, Constantine crossed
Mont Cenis[5] with 25,000 men, consisting of veterans and Barbarian
auxiliaries. This army contained a small number of Christians,
who in the son of Constantius recognized a future protector, and
many pagans whose only religion was victory; a chief who had
hitherto been fortunate could rely upon their devotion. Con-

Constantine. The Emperor, as a member of the Senate, paid also the *follis senatorius*. But
this was a foolish affectation of senatorial equality; in reality he paid nothing, since what he
paid, he paid to himself.

[1] Euseb., *Hist. eccl.* viii. 14; *Pan. vet.* ix. 4 and 14: . . . *Ut praetorianos caedem vulgi
quondam meruerit* (Aur. Vict., *Caes.* 40). According to Zosimus (ii. 13), while a fire was
destroying the Temple of Fortune, the populace murdered a soldier because he scoffed loudly
at the burning goddess. His comrades, to avenge him, attacked the citizens, of whom a great
number perished, and "they would have destroyed the city if Maxentius had not checked
their fury."

[2] Eusebius congratulates Constantine on having brought on this war (*Life of Constant.*
i. 26), and Eutropius lets it be understood that he instigated it: . . . *Bellum civile commovit*
(x. 4).

[3] Medals attest the union of these two Augusti, called by Eusebius (*Hist. eccl.* viii. 14)
brothers in wickedness.

[4] Zosimus, ii. 15. The author of the Ninth Panegyric (sect. 3) who, to fill his office well,
was bound to represent the Italian army as formidable, and that of the Gallic Emperor as com-
paratively small, gives Maxentius *centum millia hominum*, and Constantine *vix quarta parte*.
"Thou hadst," he says, "fewer soldiers than Alexander led against the Persians" (*Ibid.* 5).
Alexander's army consisted of 30,000 foot, and 4,500 horse.

[5] The highway from Lyons into Italy led over Mont Cenis. Constantine, arriving from the
North, must have taken this route; thence he could fall upon Susa and Turin. He would not
have chosen the road over the Cottian Alps — which some writers believe him to have taken —
unless his army had come from Southern Gaul.

stantine had given them booty; he had also given them what men call "glory;" and occasionally he said manly words, which went to

CONSTANTINE.[2]

the hearts of the warriors. To him is due that legal provision which permits the soldier, dying on a campaign, to make his will "in any way possible, were it on the field of battle, by writing his wishes with his blood (*literis sanguine suo rutilantibus*), on his buckler and the scabbard of his sword, or on the sand with the point of his weapon."[1] The officers did not share in the confidence of their leader; they dreaded the war, remembering the two unsuccessful expeditions of Severus and Galerius: moreover, the responses of the

aruspices had been unfavorable.[3]   But Constantine intended to conduct this expedition better than his predecessors had done theirs:

[1] *Cod. t.*, xi. 21, 15, *anno* 334.   The words are Constantine's; but the right to make such a will had been established by the early Emperors, for the text is preceded by these words: *Sicut facts ratioadous licuit.*

[2] Agate bust, 24 centim. in height, with base of silver-gilt, 17 centim. (*Cabinet de France*, No. 287.)   The workmanship of this curious object fixes its date in the fourth century.   Before the Revolution of 1789, it adorned the tip of the *bâton* of the choir-leader of the Sainte-Chapelle, and was in turn considered as a representation of Saint Louis, Titus, and Valentinian III.   More recently it has been believed to represent Constantine the Great.   (Cf. Chabouillet, *Catal. général, etc.*, p. 55.)

[3] *Contra haruspicum monita* (*Pan. Const.*).

he was sure of his troops, and the sympathy that he knew existed towards him in Italy promised assistance which had been denied to the two Augusti.

Susa was captured by a surprise; a cavalry engagement gave him Turin and Milan; and another, near Brescia, made him master of the entire Lombard plain. The second gate of Italy, that which opened the road to Illyria by way of the Julian Alps, was better guarded. Maxentius had feared an attack from Licinius; and judging it would be more formidable than the attempt made by Constantine, he had sent troops into Venetia with his praetorian prefect, the brave Pompeianus, who took up a position at Verona. The Adige, a deep and rapid stream, protected this place; but Constantine crossed it by a sudden advance, and surrounded the city. Before all the avenues were closed, Pompeianus effected his escape; he gathered all the troops scattered through the province, and returned to offer battle. He was defeated and slain; Verona, Aquileia, and Modena opened their gates.[1] In a few days there was not an enemy left in the valley of the Po, and thence Constantine could give assistance to Licinius, or call the latter to his aid. His army, rendered confident by success, refreshed and well fed in these luxuriant regions, was ready to follow him anywhere. With extreme military sagacity, he had not yielded to the temptation to advance straight upon Rome as soon as the road to the city was open to him; he gave himself, in the northern part of the peninsula, a solid base of operations, as fifteen centuries later Bonaparte did when he advanced from Montenotte to Verona, writing to the Directory that the conquest of Italy must be made in the valleys of the Po and the Adige.

During this victorious march Maxentius remained in Rome, consulting the Sibylline Books, which replied, with the habitual prudence of oracles, that the enemy of Rome would certainly perish. Deceived by the failure of the two preceding invasions, he believed that the Roman Campagna would be the tomb of the Gallic army, as it had been of the Illyrian army, and that his own troops, covered by the Tiber, resting upon the wall of Aurelian, and fed by fertile provinces, would receive the shock in an impregnable

---

[1] *Pan. vet.* x. 19–27.

position. But by going to meet his adversary he turned all these
advantages against himself. He threw a bridge of boats across
the Tiber adjacent to the Milvian Bridge, then went across to offer
battle with the river at his back, and for his retreat only two
narrow issues. A hot charge from the Gallic cavalry threw terror
into these improvised legions, and the greatest confusion followed;
all ran to the bridges and crowded upon them. The stone bridge

RUINS OF THE CIRCUS OF MAXENTIUS.

was only as wide as a Roman highway, and was almost instantly
blocked; the wooden bridge gave way and precipitated all who
were upon it into the water. Maxentius among them, whom the
weight of his armor or the grasp of drowning soldiers carried
down (Oct. 28, 312). Common language is not enough for Eusebius
to relate the success of Constantine; he needs the burning words
of Moses against the Egyptian Pharaoh: "Thou didst blow with
thy wind, the sea covered them; they sank as lead in the mighty

waters. . . . And Miriam answered [the women], Sing ye to the Lord, for he hath triumphed gloriously ; the horse and his rider hath he thrown into the sea."

The conqueror made a triumphal entrance into Rome ; behind his chariot, as a trophy, was borne the ghastly head of Maxentius, and after the ceremony it was sent into Africa, to be there exhibited.[1] In the action the praetorians alone had fought bravely ; it was their own cause that they defended. Constantine disbanded this seditious guard, dismantled its barracks, which were a fortress, and sent the survivors into the legions of the Rhine. The friends and councillors of Maxentius and the son who remained to him were put to death.[2] But Constantine apprehended his duties as a ruler too clearly to allow the civil war to continue after these executions, or to suffer private individuals to have their victims, as he had had his. A law put a stop to the lodging of information,[3] — always so promptly furnished when upon great political changes it is desired to transfer to new men the fortunes and honors possessed by the defeated party.

For the people Constantine instituted the games and largesses which always ended Roman tragedies ; in the Senate he spoke modestly of his services, promised the Conscript Fathers to hear their counsels with deference and to restore to them their old prerogatives. These prerogatives were, as a matter of fact, forever gone ; but the Senate, flattered that the Emperor should recognize its existence, made use of an ancient right, recovered for the moment, to assign Constantine the first rank among the Augusti, to vote him a triumphal arch, — for whose decoration an arch of

---

[1] . . . Sequebatur hunc comitatum suum tyranni ipsius teterrimum caput (Pan. vet. x. 31).

[2] Zosimus, ii. 17, and Pan. vet. x. 6: . . . Sed stas persequeris. Constituta enim et in perpetuum Roma fundata est, manibus qui statum ejus labefactare potuerunt, cum stirpe debitis, Romulus, the eldest son of Maxentius, whom he had made Caesar and twice consul, perished before his father (Eckhel, viii. 59, and the inscription, Divo Romulo nobilissimo viro, bis consuli).

[3] A law of 313 against informers makes mention of an earlier law which is lost. That of 313 was confirmed by two others, dated 319 and 355 (Cod. Theod. x. 1, 2, and 3). The development of the judicial system, especially the appointment of agents of the treasury having it for their official duty to protect the rights of the state, rendered the informer now a useless personage, although he had once been indispensable, — at a time when neither Greek nor Roman states had what we call "departments." We shall see, however, that in 325 Constantine himself instigated informers.

Trajan was despoiled, — and to inscribe his name upon a temple and a basilica built by Maxentius.[1] He summoned to the curia a great number of provincials,[2] and he created or regulated the *follis senatorius*, — a tax at once real and personal, since the senators paid both for their dignity and for their landed property. This double measure doubtless displeased them; but at heart Constantine was no more disposed than Diocletian had been to seek the favor of these former masters of the Empire.

TOMB OF THE ELDEST SON OF MAXENTIUS.[5]

In the administration there was no change made: most of the officials of Maxentius were retained in their positions, his praetorian prefect even received the most important government in the Western Empire, that of Africa, with the duty of there effacing the traces of the civil war. Cirta, rebuilt, received the conqueror's name, which it keeps to this day, — Constantine. Every Emperor owed Rome some architectural work: Constantine

---

[1] This arch of Trajan has disappeared. The bas-reliefs taken from it are on the upper part of Constantine's arch. See, later, the arch of Constantine, and also the bas-reliefs and statues that decorate it. The basilica begun by Maxentius was an edifice of colossal proportions, long believed to be a temple of Peace built by Vespasian.

[2] *Pan. vet.* x. 35.   [5] On the Appian Way. (Restoration after Canina.)

repaired at his own expense the Aqua Virgo,[1] and doubtless began on the Quirinal the Thermae that bear his name.

He remained but two months in Rome, and thence went to Milan; he there met Licinius, and he would have been glad to persuade Diocletian to come thither also.   At Milan he issued the famous edict of which we shall speak later.   To keep the narrative more distinct, we shall first follow the sequence of political events until the unity of the Empire is re-established; after which we shall be more at liberty to examine in its successive phases the great revolution which was about to take place under the direction of the man who had become the sole master of the world.

From year to year the number of the Emperors had been reduced.   Maximian, Galerius, Maxentius, and Diocletian have disappeared.   Three still remain. — Constantine, Licinius, and Maximin Daza.   Maximin, a sincere pagan like his uncle Galerius, and always surrounded by priests, magicians, and charlatans who called themselves prophets, had continued intermittently the persecution.   He fought against the Church in two ways,[2] — by sentences of condemnation, and by the endeavor to give to paganism, by means of an organization modelled after that of the Christian Church, the discipline which it had always lacked.   In each city he strengthened the authority of the priest appointed to superintend the public worship of the gods, and also that of the supreme pontiff, who had under his jurisdiction all the provincial clergy.[3]   For the purpose of securing great respect for his pontiffs, he chose them from

[1] Aur., *Vict. Caes.* 44. — The mosaic represented on the preceding page was found in 1876 in the village of Oued Atmenia, on the road from Constantine to Sétif, and was published by the archæological society of the former city.   In Vol. VI. p. 150 is given a fragment representing a Numidian horse.   (See *Mém. de la Soc. arch. de Constantine*, vol. xix.)

[2] He favored riots against over-zealous Christians in the cities, and condemned them to the mines.   See the reply of Maximin to the request of the inhabitants of Tyre, begging him to free their city from the Christians (Euseb., *Hist. eccl.* ix. 7).   Eusebius speaks of deathpenalties inflicted; Lactantius (*De Morte pers.* 36) mentions only mutilations: . . . *Oculi eruos Dei eruit, debilitari jussit.   Itaque confessoribus effodiebantur oculi, amputabantur manus, pedes detruncabantur, nares et auriculæ desecabantur.*   But these mutilations may frequently have caused the death of the persons suffering them.   Maximin's morals are depicted in the same colors as those of Galerius and Maxentius, and as, later, those of Licinius, notwithstanding his advanced age, after he became Constantine's adversary.   Lactantius (*ibid.* 38) goes so far as to impute to Licinius the prohibition of all marriage without his permission in each case, *ut ipse in omnibus nuptiis præ gustator esset.*

[3] Euseb., *Hist. eccl.* viii. 14, and ix. 4; Lactant., *ibid.* 36.

among persons of the highest consideration, and gave them an authority almost equal to that of the provincial governors. His disputes with Licinius, whom he had compelled to relinquish the whole of Asia Minor, and the relations that he had formed with Maxentius, rendered him the enemy of the two Augusti of the West. In 313, while Licinius was still with Constantine at Milan, he believed the occasion favorable for taking his adversary

THE TRIUMPH OF LICINIUS.[1]

unawares by an invasion. A numerous army, secretly collected beyond the Taurus, rapidly traversed the Asiatic peninsula and crossed the Straits; in a few days this force captured the stronghold of Byzantium, and after this, Heraclea, and penetrated as far as the neighborhood of Hadrianople. Here Licinius awaited him. The latter's troops were inferior in number; but the skilful old general had collected them from those garrisons on the

[1] Cameo in the *Cabinet de France*, No. 255. Licinius, standing in the triumphal quadriga, holds in one hand a javelin, and in the other the globe, symbol of sovereignty. The horses of the quadriga tread under foot vanquished adversaries. Two winged Victories hold the reins of the horses, the one on the right carrying a trophy, that on the left a standard on which are the "images" of the two Emperors. The two figures, each presenting a globe to the Emperor, represent the sun and moon (sardonyx of three layers, 55 mill. by 70). The rarity of iconographic cameos of the fourth century gives special importance to this one, on which a paper has been published by M. Chabouillet, *Rev. archéol.* ix. year.

Danube where the neighborhood of the Barbarians had kept courage and discipline alive. He easily defeated the Syrian legions, without need of the miracles which Lactantius narrates (May 1, 313). Maximin fled as far as Tarsus, in Cilicia, where he died.[1] His wife was thrown into the Orontes; his children — a boy of eight and a girl of seven — and his principal officers were murdered. The conqueror, who has been represented as protected by angels at the battle of Hadrianople, was no more clement than was the brother-in-law of Maxentius at Rome after the apparition of the miraculous cross. A few months later Licinius put to death a son of Galerius, the wife and daughter of Diocletian, and the young Severianus, who paid by a premature death for his father's sad honor of wearing for less than two years the imperial purple. At this time Constantine, after some successes over the Franks, continued to send his captives into the amphitheatre for the amusement of the people of Trèves. Notwithstanding celestial visions and marvellous dreams, these men were destitute of heart, and their faith, if any they had, was without influence upon their conduct.[2] Their cruelty was universally commended; in referring to all these murders, the Christian preceptor of a son of Constantine utters a cry of triumph.[3] The inspiration of the gentle Galilean teacher was replaced by that of the implacable Jehovah of the Mosaic law.

III. — DEATH OF LICINIUS; CONSTANTINE SOLE EMPEROR.

THE Empire had now only two masters; but this was one too many. War, in fact, soon broke out between these two ambitious men. Under pretext of a conspiracy formed against him by his brother-in-law Bassianus, Constantine caused the latter to be put

[1] The account of his death, as given by Lactantius, resembles that of the death of Galerius. Both deserved to come to a bad end, by reason of their cruelty towards the Christians; but it is impossible to accept as historic facts the legends which, by repetition, have lost even the dramatic interest which the narrators sought to give them. Eusebius (*Hist. eccl.* ix. 8) mentions an Armenian war of Maximin, of which we know nothing.

[2] Malalas (xii. 314) speaks of the massacre of two thousand inhabitants of Antioch in the circus of that city by order of Licinius, in revenge for sarcasms current there in respect to himself ( ).

[3] *Bestias malas delevit Dominus et erasit de terra. Celebremus igitur triumphum Dei cum exsultatione* (Lactant., *De Morte pers.* 52-53).

to death, and then required of Licinius the exile of Senecio, a brother of the supposed criminal, who was also a relative of the Augustus of the East:[1] in reality he desired part of the spoils of Maximin Daza. Licinius refused. This Emperor was a brave soldier and a skilful general, — a friend of the lower classes, says an old writer (but we are not told in what way he befriended them); on the other hand, an enemy to the courtiers and eunuchs, whom he called rats gnawing at the palace; a good administrator of the public finances, — a virtue which would lead us to pardon his contempt for the lawyers, whom he treated as a public pest,[2] had he not been cruel, like all who in those days had the power of life and death.

Without declaring war, Constantine crossed the Alps at the head of twenty thousand men. On the 8th of October, 314, the two armies met near Cibalis, in Pannonia, between the Save and the Drave. The battle was long and desperate. Licinius fell back, half conquered, but saved enough men to enable him to fight a second time in Thrace, in the plains of Mardia. Constantine's victory was even less decisive; he was far from his provinces, in a hostile country, and opposed to an adversary whom two heavy blows had not crushed, and who fortified himself as he retreated. Constantine decided to negotiate. Licinius had appointed as Caesar, Valens, one of his generals; this was a new claimant to be dealt with, and Constantine refused to recognize him. To render negotiations possible, Licinius ordered the death of the new Caesar, and then accepted terms which left him in Europe only Thrace and the shores of the Euxine, — that is to say, the gates of Asia, which was now his sole domain; but in the East he preserved all the inheritance left by Maximin.[3]

The two brothers-in-law, being thus reconciled, agreed that their respective sons should be made Caesars. Constantine gave this title to Crispus, who, now approaching maturity, was already a

---

[1] According to the anonymous fragment which Valesius attaches to his edition of Ammianus Marcellinus, a plot was formed against Constantine by Bassianus, whom he had appointed Caesar, and by Licinius. This story is extremely vague, and it does not seem probable that Constantine, having a son Crispus now fourteen or fifteen years of age, would have prepared a rival for him by giving Bassianus the title of Caesar.

[2] *Epit.* 41; Aur. Vict., *Caes.* 41.

[3] Zosimus, ii. 19; Peter Patricius, *Fragm. hist. graecorum,* iv. 189.

CONSTANTINE AUGUSTUS. STATUE FOUND IN THE BATHS OF
CONSTANTINE AT ROME.

useful auxiliary;[1] while Licinianus. a child not two years old. would in all probability witness the death of his aged father before himself emerging from childhood (March. 317). The conditions were not equal in the case of the two Augusti. and it was to preserve this disparity that Constantine had forbidden Licinius to retain in Valens a second in command capable of being to him a protector.

The numerous family borne by Fausta to Constantine had also increased the ambition of her husband. Within eight years she had given birth to three sons. — the younger Constantine. Constantius, and Constans.[2] For these new-comers it was necessary to provide; and their father had the design of eventually giving them the provinces of his colleague. He must have intended this from a very early period: for after the year 319 the names of Licinius and his son are omitted from the consular Fasti. Two years before the final rupture the official orators at the Western court no longer dared to speak of the second Augustus; and the fact that Constantine received a Persian embassy gives us reason to believe that in anticipation of the struggle he had sought allies among the natural enemies of the Eastern Emperor.[3] He strove to gain others by a declamatory edict. very favorable to the public debtors, which he addressed to all the cities subject to him (*ad populum*), and by an amnesty which opened all prisons. except in case of poisoners. adulterers. and homicides. in whose behalf no one was interested. These edicts. speedily made known beyond his frontiers, must have gained him partisans in the provinces belonging to Licinius. But the humanity that he manifested was a legitimate war-measure against his adversary.[4]

[1] Tillemont (iv. 17) represents him as born about 309; Ducange (*Fam. byz.* p. 46) in 296.

[2] The younger Constantine was made Caesar when only four years old, that the son of Fausta might be equal in dignity to the son of Minervina (Zosim., ii. 20).

[3] In his description of the solemnity of March 7, 321, Nazarius, who gives the most brilliant picture of the Empire. makes no allusion to the Augustus of the Eastern provinces. It is also he who mentions the Persian embassy.

[4] *Codex Theod.* xi. 7, 3, anno 320. This edict forbids the use of torture and of too harsh imprisonment in the case of the public debtors. *Securi transeant*, he said; and any who are so foolish that they do not escape. let them be kept under arrest in an open and convenient place; their property alone shall answer for them. It has been shown (p. 128, note 3) to what distress the severity of the Government had been able to reduce the public debtors, and later, these persons were put to death by Valentinian I. (Amm. Marcellin. xxvii. 7). The pretext for the second edict. which is dated Oct. 30, 322, just as hostilities were breaking out, was the birth (?) of a son to Crispus (*ibid.* ix. 38, 1).

As Maxentius has been represented as entirely in the wrong, in order to save Constantine from the reproach of ambition, so Licinius has been accused of bringing about a war which it was on all accounts for his interest to avoid. Already twice defeated, and having left only a third of the provinces and the poorest troops of the Empire, he would have been guilty of extreme folly in provoking his formidable colleague. Constantine, on the contrary, who owed Italy and Africa to one successful war, and Greece and Illyricum to another, had an ardent desire to re-establish, to his own advantage and to that of his race, the unity of the Empire.[1] He had the skill — which has been more than once exhibited since his time — of throwing upon his adversary the blame of the rupture and of making himself appear to be the defender of the oppressed.

There were many churches established throughout the East. Did Constantine despatch secret emissaries to them? He had no need of doing so in order to make the eyes and hopes of the Christians turn towards him. His consideration for them, and the letters he addressed to the bishops, said plainly enough where they were to find their protector. It is possible that he encouraged an active preaching of the gospel in the states of the Oriental Augustus, although the scanty documents of the period do not permit us to assert this. We do not go beyond legitimate probabilities, however, in asserting that the bishops of Asia desired the triumph of the real author of the edict of Milan. This, Eusebius does not attempt to conceal: "Licinius believed that in our churches we prayed only for Constantine; and truly we were the friends of the great Emperor, beloved of God."[2] These words explain why Licinius banished certain Christians from his presence, why he prohibited the episcopal synods, where he feared that political affairs should be mingled with religion, and the too numerous assemblies of the devout in the cities. He did not prohibit these assemblies, he said; outside the gates he authorized them, — in the open country,

---

[1] Eutropius (x. 13) and Zosimus (ii. 18) impute the rupture to Constantine.   To Eusebius, of course (*Life of Const.* i. 50), Licinius appears the sole offender.

[2] *Life of Constantine*, i. 56, and *Hist. eccl.* x. 8.   He forgets that, a few chapters earlier, he had extolled the services rendered to religion by Licinius, "the most religious Emperor, the preacher of peace and piety," and that the Christians asserted that at the first battle of Hadrianople this Emperor had received the aid of Heaven.

"where the air is purer for a crowd than within narrow walls."[1] He thought, in reality, that a mob was less likely to gather in the fields, and could be more surely repressed there. These precautions make it evident that he was seriously alarmed.

Licinius, one of the signers of the edict of Milan, was never a zealous pagan. After his victory over Maximin he had put to death in Antioch the priest of Jupiter and the more violent persecutors of the new religion. Certain of the Christians (who were, it is true, considered heretics) remained about him (as Eusebius, bishop of Nicomedeia), and the measures that he either took or recommended,[2] — the separation of the men and women in the churches, and the religious instruction of the latter, no longer by the clergy, but by deaconesses set apart for that duty, — do not represent him as a great enemy of religion. At most, we may infer that he still believed in the old accusations current among the heathen in respect to the assemblies of the neophytes.[3] The inclinations, real or supposed, of his clergy drove him to acts of severity which justly exasperated the orthodox believers and provoked resistance, to which authority responded with the terrible laws wherewith it was armed. Churches were again closed or destroyed; confiscations and sentences of exile pronounced; persons of free birth reduced to slavery, others sent to the mines, and possibly a few bishops put to death.[4] However, only individuals were at this time struck, and there was no general declaration against Christian believers; accordingly, the ecclesiastical authors do not indicate a persecution in the reign of Licinius.[5]

In the history of this period we walk amid darkness, so much has religious passion veiled or distorted the facts: the works which it has left us are like those palimpsests whose visible writing hides a text more important, but very difficult to read. A few lines by

---

[1] Euseb., *Life of Constantine*, i. 55. Maximin had also forbidden assemblages in the cemeteries.

[2] *Ibid.*

[3] Eusebius (*Hist. eccl.* ix. 5) shows that these accusations still continued.

[4] Eusebius (*ibid.* x. 8) names not one, he mentions no special fact; and while implying that there was at that time a violent persecution, he ends by saying that the tyrant would have decreed a violent persecution if he had not been overthrown.

[5] Sulpicius Severus in his *Historia sacra*: *Sed et inter persecutiones non computatur.* The eleventh canon of the Council of Nicæa speaks of Christians who, under Licinius, had apostasized "without constraint, without loss of their goods, and without peril."

Theodoret,[1] for example. authorize a conjecture which may be the truth. "Constantine." he says. "later accused Eusebius. bishop of Nicomedeia. of having been the soul of the war between the two Augusti."[2]   Arianism. which. simplifying the Christian dogma.

threw a bridge across between the old religion and the new. was already making great progress in the East.   This Eusebius. a zealous partisan of Arius. may have instigated the Emperor. in whose confidence he was. to be severe towards the too-zealous adversaries of the doctrine which he himself defended : so that we can see in the severity of Licinius the results of a struggle between two

VICTORIA GOTHICA.[3]

Christian sects.   Thus would be explained the local disturbances that the other Eusebius. bishop of Caesarea. relates.   Committed in violation of the edict of Milan. they gave Constantine a legitimate pretext to appear as the defender of the great law which had proclaimed religious liberty to all.

Since the late war with Licinius. Constantine had been able to keep his troops in fighting order and to secure to them victory and plunder. — a double guarantee of their fidelity.   In Gaul Crispus had become habituated to the soldier's trade by easy campaigns against the Alemanni and the Franks. who seemed to relieve one another in the duty of keeping the Rhenish legions

SMALL BRONZE.[4]

in a state of incessant activity (320).   On the shores of the Danube. Constantine repulsed an incursion of the Sarmatians. whom he pursued along the left bank of the river ;[5] and the Goths who ventured into Moesia and Thrace met the same fate.   From these two expeditions Constantine had brought back captives. who, according to custom. were dispersed among the cities as slaves and colonists, or

[1] *Hist. eccl.* i. 19.

[2] *Hic et exploratores oculos in me mittebat et tantum non armatae militiae operam navabat caranus (ibid.),* and Constantine's letter to the Nicomedeians against Eusebius.

[3] Bronze medal struck in memory of the success of Constantine against the Goths.   A helmeted Rome receives the wreath which a Victory offers her.

[4] Coin of Constantine struck in memory of victories over the Sarmatians.   SARMATIA DEVICTA.   Victory holding a trophy.

[5] Eckhel. viii. 75.

enrolled among the imperial troops.[1]   These easy campaigns were
excellent preludes to more serious combats.   At the same time the
Emperor constructed a fleet of two hundred galleys, he improved
the port of Thessalonica, and numerous troops were collected in
the neighborhood of that city.

To these preparations corresponded those made by Licinius ; if we
may accept the
statements of Zos-
imus, nearly three
hundred thousand
men encountered
one another in the
plain of Hadrian-
ople.   The two
armies were sepa-
rated by the River
Hebrus. A skil-
ful manœuvre of
Constantine,
which escaped the

MAP FOR THE WAR BETWEEN LICINIUS AND CONSTANTINE.

vigilance of his adversary, secured to him again a complete victory.
He had bravely shared in the actual dangers of the field ; after having made excellent arrangements for the battle, he had fought
among his troops and had been wounded (July 3, 323).   Licinius,
with the remains of his army, shut himself up in Byzantium, to
bar against his rival the passage from Europe into Asia.   His three
hundred and fifty galleys, supreme in the Hellespont, secured his
supplies and hindered those of the enemy, which for the most
part must arrive by sea.[2]

The Euxine, pouring its waters into the Mediterranean through
a narrow channel, forms in the Hellespont a rapid current, which
in certain weathers it is difficult to stem, becoming more navigable
when the south wind drives back into the Dardanelles the waters
of the Aegaean Sea.   The admiral of Licinius had this current in
his favor ; but he did not know how to profit by it.   In a first

[1] Zosimus, ii. 21.   The two adversaries had each in his army Gothic auxiliaries.   This
was already a long-established custom.

[2] Constantine so fully depended upon his convoys for provisions that he had assembled
as many as two hundred freighters.

engagement between the two fleets the losses were equal ; but the
following day a south wind blew, and Crispus, in command of
Constantine's fleet, advanced his galleys to the attack, and the
enemy lost a hundred and thirty vessels. Constantine, now secure
in respect to his convoys, went on to press the siege of Byzantium,
and the victorious fleet of Crispus drew near the Golden Horn.
Before the blockade was completed. Licinius escaped into Asia.
He named Martinianus, his *magister officiorum*,[1] either Caesar or
Augustus,[2] rapidly reorganized his army, and extended it along
the coast from Chalcedon to Lampsacus to guard the landings.
But Constantine, master of the sea, could find a landing some-
where. His fleet carried the troops to the foot of the heights of
Chrysopolis (Scutari), where they at once threw up intrenchments ;
in this way the line of defence projected by Licinius was turned.
The latter broke camp, and attempted by a resolute attack to drive
his enemy into the sea ; but he was repulsed, and fled to Nicomedeia.

Having neither soldiers nor resources, the valiant old man
could do nothing else than lay down the purple at the feet of

the harsh and inexorable conqueror (Sept. 23, 323).
Constantine had promised his sister, the wife of Li-
cinius, that he would spare the life of the discrowned
Emperor, and accordingly banished him to Thessa-
lonica. But a man who had been twelve years
Emperor, caused anxiety, even though a captive ; and

MARTINIANUS.[3]

the Oriental method of finding a relief
from this anxiety in destroying him
who caused it, was not displeasing to
the all-powerful master of the Roman
world. Notwithstanding the pledge to
Constantia, an order of death was sent

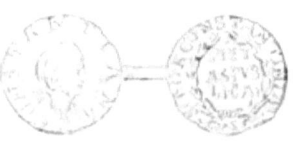

COIN OF CONSTANTIA.[4]

to Licinius (324).[5] Martinianus had been murdered the day after
the defeat. According to the custom of the time, the servants and

---

[1] This functionary had the superintendence of all audiences with the Emperor, and
exercised extensive jurisdiction over both civil and military officers.

[2] Some very rare coins give him the title of Augustus (*Comptes rendus de l'Acad. des
inscr. et belles-lettres*, November, 1879).

[3] D. N. M. MARTINIANO | P. F. AVG. (Small bronze.)

[4] CONSTANTIA and the bust of the wife of Licinius. On the reverse : SOROR CON-
STANTINI AVG. In a wreath, PIETAS PVBLICA ; below, CONS. (Small bronze.)

[5] *Contra religionem sacramenti occisus est* (Eutropius, x. 6).

friends of Licinius shared the fate of the conquered Emperor. Even his acts were annulled; and the reaction lasted nearly two years. When Constantine put a stop to it by the rescript of July 8, 326,[1] there was nothing left in the East which could recall the rule of him whom the conqueror entitled "a tyrant." What perturbations in social life must have been caused by these measures of political revenge! Unhappily, more or less seriously, they continue in all times.

This war has been represented as the decisive struggle between two religions. Eusebius represents Licinius as saying to his soldiers before the battle: "Look upon our gods and those of our fathers: our enemy has forsaken them to follow one whom we know not. We shall see this day whether he or we be in the wrong, and victory shall decide whom we are to worship. Our gods, who are many, against his who is alone, will assuredly give us the victory." History does not find in these events the character which the bishop gives us. This war was, like preceding wars, one of ambition; but it had the results of a religious war, because the vanquished party had been supported by the pagans and heretics. When Constantine saw the orthodox bishops of the East welcome him as their savior, and the crowd of those whose beliefs are determined by the success of a cause pass over to the new faith, he found himself more than ever confirmed in the belief that the future belonged to the Christian Church, and that political wisdom counselled him to throw in his lot with her. This he did; but with sagacious precautions which we shall now examine.

---

[1] *Codex Theod.* XV. 14, 3: "That which the tyrant decided conformably to the laws, shall remain in force."

[2] SOLI INVICTO AETERNO AVG. Constantine, with radiate head, standing in a quadriga, crowned by a Victory who holds a palm. Beneath, S. M. T. (Reverse of a gold coin.)

CONSTANTINE, WITH RADIATE HEAD,
CROWNED BY A VICTORY.[2]

CHAPTER CII.

THE RELIGIOUS POLICY OF CONSTANTINE.

I. — THE MIRACULOUS VISION; THE LABARUM; THE WORSHIP OF THE SUN.

IT was upon the way to Rome, during the march to meet Maxentius, in 312, that, according to Eusebius, the conversion of Constantine took place. In his *Ecclesiastical History*, published fourteen years after the battle of the Milvian Bridge, Eusebius makes no mention of the apparition which later he describes in his *Life of Constantine*. But this latter is a pious, and not an historical work. The author declares that he proposes to make known to posterity neither the wars and victories of the Emperor, nor his laws and labors for the good of his subjects:[1] he will relate only

---

[1] I. 11. He speaks in the same way in his *Ecclesiastical History* (viii. 2) and in his book upon the Martyrs of Palestine (12); accordingly Socrates, who continues the work of Eusebius, declares that he has obtained no material for the history of the Church from the *Life of Constantine*. Eusebius even dared to maintain, in his *Præparatio Evangelica* (xii. 31), the monstrous doctrine of useful falsehoods; and he employs them largely. Constantine, as a special favor, diminishes by one fourth the land-tax of Autun (*Pan. vet.* viii. 11); the historian represents him as extending this favor to the entire Empire, — which would have been the ruin of the imperial finances (*Life of Const.* iv. 2). The Emperor closes or destroys some heathen temples: Eusebius asserts that they were all destroyed. Constantine refuses to heretics the immunities which he had granted to the orthodox believers (*Codex Theod.* xvi. 5, 1); his historian declares that all heresies are destroyed (*Life of Const.* iii. 66), while he himself was the leader of the most lasting of them all. To hear Eusebius, we should believe that Constantine subjugated the whole world, from the North to the South (*ibid.* i. 8); whereas he added not one foot of ground to the territory of the Empire. And so on indefinitely. The historian's courage is of the same rank with his impartiality and his intelligence. In the *Ecclesiastical History*, composed before the death of Crispus, he speaks with enthusiasm of this unfortunate prince. In the *Life of Constantine*, prepared during the reign of the son of Fausta, he does not mention the name of the elder brother. The monk Zonaras is equally reluctant to write a word of blame; on this topic the pen drops from his hand, and he cries: "No, I can say nothing which may impair the fame of this divine man" (*Ann.* xiii. 4). Gelasius of Cyzicus fabricates a speech of Constantine before the Council of Nicæa. I have great doubt in respect to this Emperor's strange letter to Arius, and also the discussions which Sozomenus reports between the bishops and philosophers at the Council of Nicæa, and the

his pious acts: and as the hagiographers have their minds strained towards the supernatural, instead of narrating to us the skilful military measures of his hero, he represents him as specially concerned in defeating the diabolical machinations of Maxentius. The process of reasoning which he assigns to the Emperor, and believes to be most Christian, is in reality very shrewd. "Constantine," he says, "was well aware that to defeat these magical incantations, some other aid than the sword of his soldiers was needful, and he was seeking among all the gods that one who should give him the strongest support. Then the thought came into his mind that his predecessors had put their trust in a multitude of gods, and had most of them perished miserably. His father only, who had never shared this error, had had a glorious life and a prosperous end.[1] The Emperor now felt that these useless gods were an imposture, and began to call upon the God of Constantius, praying him to extend help and reveal himself to the suppliant; whereupon a sign appeared in the sky. If any one else had related this miracle," the historian adds, "it would not be credible. But long after, the Emperor himself told it to me, and confirmed by an oath the truth of what he said. Marching at the head of his troops, he saw above the setting sun a luminous cross, with these words: Ἐν τούτῳ νίκα, 'By this conquer.' The following night the Christ of God

---

justitium which he asserts that Constantine established on Friday, in honor of the cross. Laws even are fabricated, like the too-famous constitution De confirmando judicio episcoparum (Const. Sismondi, No. 1). Roman Catholic writers acknowledge this. "In the collections relative to the Council of Nicaea," says the Duc de Broglie (L'Église et l'Empire romain au quatrième siècle, vol. i. 2d part, p. 65), "there are a great many canons and decrees manifestly fictitious; it is a deluge of forgeries." The confusion was increased by rivalries of sects, each inventing documents to support its claims. Thus Theophanes, in his Chronicle, accused the Arians of having fabricated the constitutions said to have been addressed by Constantine to Pope Melchiades (Tillemont, Hist. des Emp. iv. 11). It appears from the pretended donation of Constantine, from the legend of his baptism at Rome, from so many acts of martyrs which cannot be admitted, and from the fictitious Decretals, that this usage continued for a long time. The learned Abbé de Meissas says in one of his papers on the evangelization of the Gauls: "The ninth century was preëminently the age of falsehood." We may say the same of many others, — the Council of Tyre in 335 is famous by its "living dead man" (τὸν ζῶντα νεκρόν, Gregory Nazianzen, Eulogium of Athanasius, 15). Athanasius asserts that letters were fabricated there, purporting to be written by him; and he says to Constantine in his Apologia: "These skilful forgers have more than once imitated the writing of your own royal hands."

[1] Eusebius, "the double-tongued" (διγλώσσου δόξαν ἐκτήσατο, Socrates, i. 25) was so well pleased with the reflections assigned by him to Constantine at this crisis that he attributes the converse process of reasoning to Licinius, in the address which he represents him as delivering before the battle of Hadrianople (Life of Const. ii. 5, 6).

appeared to him with the same cross, and ordered him to make a standard in the likeness of it." [1]

There is a sad lack of dignity in this oath by which the Emperor attests to a subject the imperial veracity; and the story, made public after Constantine's death by a courtier-bishop desirous to prove that he had been admitted to intimate familiarity with the Emperor, is in itself extremely improbable. If, however, we remember the promise given by Constantine to his sister to spare the life of Licinius, whom, shortly after, he put to death, we shall perhaps be disposed to accuse the bishop of nothing more than a simple-minded credulity. But Eusebius makes too free use of visions, venturing even to say that God often appeared to Constantine; that he revealed the future to him, and after the battle of the Milvian Bridge designated to the Emperor which of the friends and kindred of Maxentius should be put to death.[2] To suspect Eusebius of a pious fraud is not a thing which would have greatly angered him, and in the days in which he lived no one would have blamed him for it. Constantine does likewise; it is by the order of God (*Deo jubente*), he says, that he founded Constantinople.[3] Heads of states and heads of religions have long governed the world by announcing their own ideas as divine inspirations, and presenting them to the nations as an order from heaven. Historic criticism, which believes in the permanency of natural law, and says, with Seneca, that God obeys the order that he has established (*semel jussit, semper paret*), no longer discusses the question of miracles. But it is easy to understand how a legend may have quickly formed on the subject of such an event as the transformation of the pagan into the Christian Empire. The contrary would have been surprising; for it is also a law of history that at certain epochs the human mind proceeds in this

---

[1] Eusebius, *Life of Constantine*, i. 28, 30. According to Eusebius and Socrates (i. 2) the soldiers also saw the miraculous cross. In that case the famous vision would have had witnesses enough to render unnecessary the Emperor's story and his testimony by oath to the reality of the miracle. The historians of the period are often singularly deficient in imagination. Saint Cyrillus (*ap.* Baronius, *anno* 353, note 26), Philostorgius (iii. 26), Socrates (ii. 28), Sozomenus (iv. 5), and, following them, Nicephorus (ix. 32), repeat this legend of Eusebius in the case of Constantius II, at the moment when he was about to engage with Magnentius, a cross appears in the sky.

[2] *Life of Const.* i. 47; ii. 12, 14, etc.

[3] *Code Theod.* xiii. 5, 7.

way, because the belief in the marvellous, which is in the depths
of the soul of man, comes out in those times with an irresistibly
expansive power. Even in the eyes of the pagans the victory
over Maxentius was a divine act, since they believed that the
god Constantius guided the army of his son (*divinas expeditiones*);[1]
it was even more natural that the Christians should recognize in
this divine leader the Christ whom they adored. Emerging from
their prisons, and amazed to find themselves received with tolerance
and consideration, the Christians saw in the conduct of Constantine the effect of divine intervention. From the very beginning,
the legend assumed various forms. Instead of the vision clear in
the sunlight, Lactantius speaks of a dream in which the Emperor
received the command to place the cross upon the soldiers'
shields.[2]

In the case of an ambitious man who was never a visionary,
apparitions and dreams are subjects of history. The motives are
too evident which have caused such things to be believed by those
interested. It is different in respect to the *labarum;* for this
standard, borne in battle at the Emperor's side, may be regarded
as the symbol of the Constantinian policy.

The Christians saw the cross everywhere, — in the trophies
and standards of the legions, even upon the human face, where
the line of the eyes and of the nose designed for them that instrument of the death-penalty employed especially for slaves; and it
is to their honor that they have made from an object of infamy
the symbol of salvation.[3] But this sign, and even a character

[1] *Ducebat Constantius pater . . . qui divinas expeditiones jam dicus agitabat* (Pan.
ct. x. 14.)

[2] *De Morte pers.* 44.

[3] Saint Justin, *Apol.* i. 55; Tertull., *Apol.* 16; *Victorias adoratis, cum in tropaeis cruces
inhstina sint tropaeorum;* and, still better, Minucius Felix, in chap. xxix. of the *Octavius,* who
concludes a long enumeration of pagan objects resembling a cross, with these words: *Ita signo
crucis aut ratio innititur aut vestra religio formatur.* At the same time the representation of a
cross is very rare in the catacombs, and appears by stealth, concealed under some other symbol,
such as an anchor, a lateen-yard, a man praying with arms outstretched, "the bird flying
straight up to heaven and extending the cross of its wings, with a sound which seems a
prayer" (Tertull., *De orat.* 39). It is very seldom that the cross appears without disguise on
any monument before the time of Constantine; the Chevalier Rossi has seen it but once
(*Roma sotter.* vol. ii pl. 48), and Minucius Felix says (*Oct.* xxix.): *Cruces non colimus.* But
the cross, or symbols resembling this figure, even what we have called the monogram,
were of very common use in pagan antiquity. "Must we not believe," says the Abbé
Martigny, "that the early Christians formed the idea of appropriating also, and even of

resembling that which later was the monogram of the Christ, was in use long before our era on parchments, on coins which had

preferring the ⚹, a very common sign in ancient times, which, being also employed by the pagans, had the advantage, while offering to the believer the first letters of the name of Christ, of satisfying that need of secrecy which was one of the most salient characteristics of the primitive Church " (*Dict. des ant. chrét.* p. 478). The whole design of Munter's book, *Sinnbilder und Kunstvorstellung der alten Christen,* is the development of this idea.

The *crux ansata* (Fig. 2) of the Pharaohs and of the Egyptian gods is seen upon Christian monuments in the Thebaid and in Nubia (paper by Letronne in the *Mém. de l'Acad. des inser.* vol. xvi. new series), and on Persian and Cypriote monuments (the Duc de Luynes, *Numismatique des satrapies et de la Phénicie sous les rois achéménides,* pl. i. Nos. 3 and 4; pl. viii. Nos. 2, 13, and 17 ; *Num. et inser. cypriotes,* pl. i. Nos. 5, 6, 7, etc., passim).

The Greeks had this monogram in their running hand ; it served also as a mark on the tetradrachms of Athens and on certain coins of the Ptolemies (Eckhel, viii. 89) ; it is found

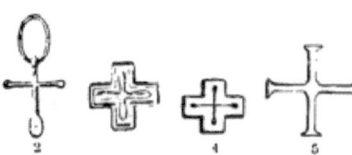

also on a coin of Decius, the great persecutor of the Christians : EΠI ΣTP AΦΦIANOY BA-XPATOY, where the X and the P are united (Munter, p. 33). In this case it is only an abbreviation, but elsewhere it has a religious signification. A Christian inscription published by Egger (*Mém. d'hist. anc. et de philol.* p. 427), begins with a chrisma and ends with a tau (T), which, according to Tertullian, represents the cross, and was to the Gentiles a symbol of salvation. Similar signs, and others giving the image of the Christian cross more perfectly, have been found in ancient Assyria, where they had a double signification, both astronomical

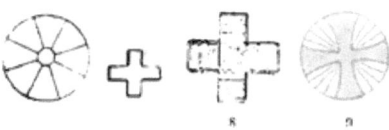

and religious. Thus we frequently see on Babylonian cylinders figures resembling the equilateral cross (3 and 4), sometimes accompanied by the Sun and Moon. Marking, as they do, the four cardinal points, these figures naturally served to express the idea of the horizon, of the infinite in space and time,

and, passing from the natural to the ideal meaning, the idea of God. Another, the cuneiform cross (5), is the figure of the god Anou, personification of the sky (Rawlinson, *Inser. of Western Asia,* vol. ii. pl. 48), which is itself represented by the cross with eight rays inscribed in a circle (6). These are the eight regions of the Sun and the Sky, — a figure much used on astrological tablets, and of which there are many specimens in the Museum of the Louvre. This symbol appears on two monoliths representing the king Asshurnazirpal (about 884 B. C.) and his grandson Samsival. The same sign, which is found on an image of Sennacherib in the British Museum (Fr. Lenormant, *Hist. anc. de l'Orient,* p. 364) was also placed on the standards of the Assyrian army. (Note by Ménant.) On a Theban tomb, Aramaean soldiers have, suspended to a necklet, either the equilateral cross (7), or a cross (8 resembling those worn in the same way by the priests and monks of the Roman Catholic Church. In Chaldean texts recently brought home by M. de Sarzec, this cross, with three rays in each branch (9), signifies that which has eternal duration. (Note by Oppert.)

* Coin of Trajan Decius, struck at Maeonia in Lydia, and having the monogram ⚹. (Bronze.)

extensive circulation,[1] on military standards[2] and religious monuments. The *gamma*[3]-cross, which means benediction and good augury, was placed by the Hindoos in their most ancient temples and on the images of Buddha, by the Gauls on their tombs, and we find it in the Roman catacombs on the vestments of priests represented there.

Under the form of the ansate cross, which exactly reproduces the *chrisma*, it signifies salvation, eternal life, and was in the hands of the Egyptian divinities the essential attribute of their power. When Theodosius destroyed the Serapeum of Alexandria, the Christians were astonished to find a great number of these crosses engraved on the stone.[4] They are found upon coins of the Achaemenides and on Assyrian monuments, where the four-armed cross inscribed in a circle is the symbol of "the invincible God," the Sun, which darts its beams in every direction.[5] In the third century of the Christian era the Persians placed this cross upon their standards, and the king signed his messages with the title "Brother of the Sun."[6] A thousand years before that time the Assyrian kings Samsivul and Asshurnazirpal had worn suspended around their necks, as

[1] On those, for example, of the Syrian king Alexander Bala, and of the Bactrian Hermaeus. We even find almost the complete form of the *labarum* on coins of the Indo-Scythian kings. (See W. Madden, *The Numismatic chron.* xvii. 293.)

[2] Eckhel, viii. 88. See in the works of Longpérier (ii. 250), two standards from Trajan's Column. Vegetius (ii. 13) says that the cohorts were divided into centuries, each having its *cædium*, or military ensign, on which was a figure. (See Vol. V. p. 86, and Vol. VI. p. 230, two *cecilia*.) The soldiers therefore were accustomed to see on their standards the figure X, which is the first part of the monogram.

[3] So called because it can be represented by four *gammas*, Γ, crossed. This figure has been found among the Scandinavians (Worsae, *Les Temps préhist. du Nord*). The six-rayed circle of the Gallic helmets (Vol. III. p. 249) was a representation of the Sun or of the Divinity, as was the wheel which the city of Rome bears on a coin of Hadrian commemorating the ninth centenary of the foundation of Rome (Vol. V. p. 351), and that of Jupiter found at Landouzy-la-Ville (*Rev. arch.*, Jan., 1881).

[4] "The pagans explained," says Socrates (*Hist. eccl.* v. 17), "that these crosses signified the future life." Cf. Raoul Rochette, *Mémoire sur la croix ansée*, vol. xvi. 2d part, pp. 237 *et seqq.* of the *Mém. de l'Acad. des inscr.*

[5] Zahn, *Constantin und die Kirche*, p. 14; Burckhardt, *Die Zeit Constantins*, p. 350. The plastic symbol of the Assyrians represents the Sun by a disk in which is inscribed a cross, sometimes with rays between the arms.

[6] Tertull., *Apol.* 15, and Amm. Marcell., xvii. 5. See in Layard's *Worship of Mithras* (pl. x. No. 11) a hemispheroid of agate, with a crescent above it and a six-branched star, representing the Sun. Artaxerxes bore one of these figures upon his tiara (see p. 133).

bishops of the Christian Church do now, the equilateral cross, a symbol of the divinity.[1]

Ideas and their symbols travel as men do, and with them.[2] When the West was invaded by the Oriental cults and those Chaldaean diviners who made their way everywhere, many beliefs and symbols of these old religions penetrated the Roman world, where the symbol of the Sun must have been as well known as the solar cult was popular. Roman horsemen on Trajan's Column bear upon their bucklers an eight-rayed star, which to them was perhaps an ornament merely, but for the Assyrians a representation of the Sun:[3] on the reverse of a coin of Gallienus, Apollo held a sceptre surmounted by a cross. The pagans, therefore, were extremely familiar with the cross in its different forms, as the symbol of victory or of divine power, especially as a representation of the

ASSHUR-NAZIRPAL, KING OF ASSYRIA (884 B. C.).[4]

[1] According to Oppert (*Études assyr.* p. 166), the name of this cross is *labar*, — a word whose significance will later be explained.

[2] What journeys, for instance, have our popular tales made, — the lightest and most fragile of things; many of them have come to us from India.

[3] *Œuvres* of Longpérier, i. 170. See also, p. 111, a coin of Elagabalus, "Priest of the Sun," with a star.

[4] Monolith found at Nimrud, at the entrance of the N. W. Palace (British Museum).

SAMSIVUL, ASSYRIAN KING, SON OF SHALMANESER, 824 B.C. (BRITISH MUSEUM).

Sun. — at that time their great divinity; and Constantine incurred no risk of a military tumult when he utilized the double meaning of the symbol in placing upon his own helmet and on the weapons of his soldiers the cross which both pagans and Christians could accept without conscientious scruples.[1]

APOLLO.[2]

The word *labarum* is neither Greek nor Latin, but Chaldaean, being derived from *labar*, which in the Assyrian language means "duration, eternity." While taking from the Orientals the name of his new standard, Constantine very naturally took from them also the symbol of their god, whom we shall soon see he had himself long worshipped. Paganism, therefore, furnished the principal elements of the *labarum*, and even its name.[3]

According to Eusebius, who saw this standard in the last years of the reign, it was a spear with a transverse bar attached to it, from which hung a purple cloth adorned with precious stones, having the heads of Constantine and his two sons embroidered on it in gold, and above it a gold wreath surrounding the monogram. To the Christian soldier the bar represented the arms of the Cross;[4] to the pagan it was a part of the construction of the standard, which, as usual, bore the Emperor's head and the customary gold wreath. The old

---

[1] The Church historians very naturally saw in this confusion — which pleased the Emperor, because it existed also in his own mind, and because it served his policy — a means of Christian propaganda ingeniously devised by him. "He put the cross upon the *labarum*," says Sozomenus (*Hist. eccl.* i. 4), "so that the soldiers, accustomed to venerate the military standard, should come by insensible degrees to venerate the Christ, whose symbol they had before their eyes, and that thus, forgetting their idols, they should come to honor the true God."

[2] Apollo holding a sceptre surmounted by a cross. Reverse of a coin of Gallienus. Mr. Lewis, of Corpus Christi College, Cambridge, the owner of this coin, which is unique, has had the kindness to send me a galvanoplastic reproduction of it.

[3] Oppert, *Études assyr.* p. 160, and *Exp'd. en Mésopotamie,* ii. 293. It is probable that the word *labarum* was in use from the time of Constantine; but this is not certain, for Eusebius never employs it, and it is found, I believe, for the first time in the writings of any author, seventy years later in Sozomenus (i. 4). Ducange, in his *Glossarium,* derives it from a German word *lap,* a piece of cloth, — which is not probable.

[4] Tertullian (*Apol.* 16) a century earlier, tells us what Christians thought in looking at the standards: "The images you attach to them, the drapery with which you adorn them, are the decoration of the cross." Stockbauer (*Kunstgeschichte des Kreuzes,* p. 99) says: "The *labarum* of Constantine, as Eusebius describes it, was . . . nothing new: it was only a *vexillum,* which the Romans had long used, and Constantine had seen numberless times on the ancient monuments." The only difference, he adds, was the monogram inscribed in the wreath; and we have explained that this monogram offended no one, since it very probably had its simplest form, X, which was the figure borne by the *vexillum* of one of the legions.

cohorts regarded the eagles of the legions as their divine protectors (*numina legionis*), and kept them in a sanctuary[1] in the camp: the new will regard this *labarum* — called by a name mysterious to them, and supposed to be magical — as a fetich endowed with peculiar virtues: it was believed that he who bore it was never wounded in battle.[2]

At what period was the faith in the miraculous standard established?[3] The ecclesiastical writers consider the famous vision to have preceded the battle of the Milvian Bridge (312). But this war was entirely political, and had not the religious character which has been ascribed to it. Eusebius, who in his *Life of Constantine* represents Maxentius as the great enemy whose downfall should rejoice the hearts of all Christians, forgets that in his *Ecclesiastical History* he has represented that Emperor as almost a believer.[4] In making war upon Maxentius, Constantine attacked a rival whose possessions he coveted; it was not the execution of divine vengeance against the persecutor of the Christians, since Maxentius had never persecuted them,[5] and Constantine was himself at that very time a pagan. On the eve of his expedition against Rome, the orator Eumenius reminded him of the temples he had restored and the sacrifices he had performed;[6] on his entrance into

THE LABARUM.

---

[1] Herod., iv. 4. The place where the eagles were deposited became a sacred asylum (Tac., *Ann.* i. 36). Eusebius makes an oratory of that in which the *labarum* was placed. During the Republic, the standards were kept, in time of peace, in the *ærarium*, which was regarded also as a consecrated place.

[2] Eusebius, *Life of Const.* i. 31 and 70. Tertullian (*Apol.* 16) says of the respect of the legions for their standards: *Religio tota castrensis signa veneratur, signa jurat, signa omnibus diis praeponit.* The pagan temples also had their banners, *signa templorum* (*Hist. Aug. in Gall.* 8), to which certain peculiar virtues were attributed. These old beliefs prepared the way for faith in the *labarum*.

[3] The book of Eusebius contains not a single date; he places the construction of the *labarum* in the time of the expedition against Maxentius, but gives it its marvellous effects only in the war against Licinius.

[4] *Hist. eccl.* viii. 14.

[5] Eusebius, *Hist. eccl.* viii. 14; Tillemont, *Mém. eccl.* v. 73-100, 103, and 120.

[6] ... *Diis immortalibus fere quae ... cueras* (*Pan. vet.* vii. 21). *Augustissima illa*

Autun, some days earlier, there had been brought out to meet him and do him honor the statues of all the gods.[1] Also he attached his signature without repugnance, in 311, to the edict of Galerius, which contained severe language towards the Christians. The toleration which this edict proclaimed agreed with Constantine's policy, and the pagan formulas contained in it did not contradict his belief. One of his coins, of the year 307, bears the pagan legend: *Genio Cæsaris.*

However, as often occurs, the legend handed down by Eusebius and Lactantius must have had an historic foundation. The Christians unconsciously were becoming a political party, and their favor was a matter of concern to the Emperor. Under one form or another, he often sought to win their good will without offending the pagan majority of his subjects by a conspicuous acceptance of the faith lately an object of condemnation.

GENIO CÆSARIS.[2]

The affection of the early Christians for symbolism is well known; and by many figures borrowed from pagan customs they revealed their faith to the adepts, while concealing it from the profane. The sign that Constantine had given to his soldiers gave offence to no one, and yet sufficed, so long as he was obliged to practise a certain reserve, to make known his secret intentions to those interested.

Constantine was above all a statesman; he regarded religion as a means of government; and many rulers, among the greatest who have reigned, have thought likewise. As a private individual, it is probable that he would have concerned himself but little with the religious questions of his time; as an emperor, he carefully examined both sides. One party, lukewarm in its faith, doubtful as to its gods, having but little confidence in their power, is a great flock which follows the old ways because it has followed them. The other, an ardent and well-organized minority, breaking out for itself, in spite of all obstacles, a new path, and marking that path with its own blood, has proved amid tortures its inde-

---

delubra tantis donariis honestatis ut jam cetera non quærant. Jam omnia te vocare ad se templa videantur, præcipue Apollo (ibid.). . . . Et templa pulcherrimæ tuæ liberalitate reparentur. . . . Circa tua, Constantine, vestigia urbes et templa consurgant (ibid. 22).

[1] In the year 311. *Omnium deorum simulacra protulimus* (Pan. vet. viii. 8).

[2] Genius having a modius on his head, and holding a patera and a cornucopia. (Medium bronze.) Reverse of a coin of Constantine.

structible force; and its attention appears so fixed upon heaven that it seems likely to give no cause of anxiety to the masters of this world who may hereafter share its faith. The former are those half-hearted adherents with whom a ruler loses the battle; the latter, those believers who insure his victory. But many who no longer held to paganism by mental ties, held to it still by customs, and took pleasure in its ceremonial; so that if the members of the two societies had been counted, there would probably have been twenty times as many in the old as in the new; the number, therefore, on one side balanced the zeal on the other. Moreover, the edict which under Diocletian had expelled the Christians from the legions and from public office not having been repealed, the army and the administration remained pagan. Eight years after this, in 320, Constantine was still saluted in the camps, by officers and soldiers, with the old pagan cry: "Augustus, may the gods preserve thee!"[1]

A situation like this called for extreme prudence, and hindered the Emperor from prematurely taking sides with either of the two adversaries, although he doubtless early became aware that on the religious question the imperial government would be obliged to change its policy. During his long residence in the East he had observed the strong organization of the churches; he had seen the enthusiasm of the Christians in the presence of death, and the pity which began to spread among heathen populations for the innocent victims. His father's toleration, the failure of the late measures against Christianity, and lastly, the position taken by his personal opponents, Galerius and Maximin, at the head of the pagan party, — all had counselled him, from the time of his accession, to pursue a favorable course towards these persecuted believers whom so many Emperors had vainly tried to conquer.

For two hundred years the moral history of the world had been that of the persevering efforts of philosophy to bring together those ideas of the divinity which were local and individual expressions of the religious sentiments; and these conceptions had been so thoroughly blended and fused that from this rich mass of precious ore had been formed by degrees the statue of the one God, already visible to many. The local deities had lost their personality and

---

[1] Codex Theod. vii. 20, 2. Julian's army was almost entirely pagan (Julian, Letters, 3, 8).

assumed a general character.   They were now only the diverse
manifestation of that Supreme God whom Constantine suffered his
official orators to invoke in his presence. and to whom the pagan
Hierocles subjected all the lower powers.
"But this great God is ours," the Christians
replied to him. "and it is his worship which
you forbid."[1]   The more prudent. through fear
of falling back into polytheism. gave him no
name ; they vaguely called him "the Divinity"
(*Divinitas*).[2]   Hadrian. not even venturing to
designate him thus. had built temples to stand
empty of any image whatever. and only to be
filled by the religious thought.   Others. having need of a god whom they could see and
touch, called him Serapis or Mithra.[3] Apollo
or the Sun ; Mercury. the modest servant of
the gods and of commerce. became "the very
sacred, august, and great Preserver of the
world."[4]   Those whose piety sought violent
emotions went to Mithra. "the invincible hero
who drives away the darkness."   By the mysterious ceremonies of his cult, by the baptism of blood and the long hierarchy of his

MITHRA.[5]

believers,[6] he attracted the soldiers : in the camps of the Danube

---

[1] See Vol. VI. p. 491 *et seqq.* the progress of ideas towards divine unity in the midst of
pagan society.

[2] Or the *rerum arbiter deus qui spectat nos ex alto* ; or Force, *illa vis, illa majestas fandi et
nefandi discriminatrix quae omnia meritorum momenta perpendit, librat, examinat . . .* (*Pan. vet.*
x. 6 and 7).   Eumenius speaks in the same way in the *Pan. vet.* viii. 10 : *. . . Divina illa mens
quae totum mundum nunc gubernat . . . quidquid cogitavit illico facit.*

[3] Mithra, "the daily sky." is identified with *Sol,* whose name is also borne by Serapis
(Orelli, No. 1,892). Macrobius (*Saturn.* i. 17-23) sees in all the gods only personifications of
solar virtues : *diversae virtutes Solis nomina diis dederunt, et omnes deos referri ad Solem.* See
in the *C. I. L.* vol. vi. Nos. 713-756. and in the *Additamenta* (*ibid.* Nos. 3,722-3,728) the
numerous inscriptions referring to the worship of Mithra.

[4] Orelli-Henzen. Nos. 1,061 and 1,108. Doubts exist in regard to the authenticity of one
at least of these two inscriptions ; but according to Saint Justin the pagans called Mercury
"the Divine Reason," and Ammianus Marcellinus, *mundi velocior sensus.* He was very popular with the Gauls : Caesar regarded him as one of their great gods (*Bell. Gall.* xii. 16).
The Arverni honored him particularly. and the Treasure of Bernay. now in the *Cabinet de
France,* was originally in one of his temples.

[5] Roman statuette of bronze (*Cabinet de France,* No. 2,950).

[6] Wilmanns, No. 131. See in Vol. IV. p 185. the bas-relief of Mithra. with the solar char-

and the Rhine are found numerous traces of their worship of Mithra. Apollo, a purified representation of Mithra,[1] was the god

THE SUN.[5]

of the wind, the author of being and of thought.[2] The Christians did not regard all his oracles as false; they believed that a priestess of Apollo, the Erythraean Sibyl, had announced the coming of Christ.[3] Of all the gods of the Graeco-Roman Olympus, he alone, notwithstanding the increasing scepticism, could not be renounced or called useless, since he was the same with the Sun, whom Aurelian called " the unquestionable god " (*deus certus*).[4] The radiant heavenly body which gives warmth, light, and life, whereby all live, without which all die, had been, under various names, the great divinity of the third century, and

---

iot in the upper part. The worship of this divinity was very widely spread in Gaul. An inscription found at Eauze in 1881 (*Revue épigr. du Midi*, No. 277) shows it established in that city, as also in Lyons, Narbo, and many other cities. The baptism of the worshippers of Mithra was to them like a new birth, and they had religious repasts, fastings, and ascetic practices. Their priests made the sign of the cross on the forehead of the initiated, consecrating them " to fight with Mithra in the struggle between light and darkness." There were seven of these initiations (Saint Jerome, *Letter* 107).

[1] Mithra was the same as Apollo. Antiochus, king of Commagene, constructed for himself on the summit of Nemroud-Dagh (6,500 feet high) a magnificent tomb, where he placed the statue of Apollo-Mithra (*Rev. arch.*, July, 1883, p. 57).

[2] Plutarch, *On the Decay of Oracles*, 7 and 42.

[3] Eusebius, *Disc. of Const. to the Nicaean Fathers*, 18, and Lactantius, *Inst. div.* iv. 19, 48.

[4] *Aug. Hist., Aur.* 11. Apollo had been the favorite god of Augustus. Cf. Boissier, *La Religion romaine d'Auguste aux Antonins*, ii. 417. We have seen that Diocletian consulted the oracle of Apollo before deciding on the persecution of the Christians.

[5] The Sun represented as a youth, crowned with rays. Base of a candelabrum

was more than ever that of the fourth. The Constantinian family had chosen the Sun as their divine protector. Claudius II., the head of this house, Aurelian, whose mother was a priestess of the Sun, and Constantius Chlorus, had specially adored this divinity. The orator Eumenius, addressing himself to Constantine, in 310, on occasion of a great solemnity, reminded him of his hereditary god, *Apollinem tuum*.[1] Many of the coins of this Emperor bear on the reverse the legend, *Soli invicto*. Some, belonging to the period when Constantine was in alliance with Licinius, add these words: *Comiti Augustorum*, " to the counsellor, the comrade, of the Augusti."[2] Others represent Constantine himself with

MERCURY.[3]

solar[4] attributes, the head surrounded by rays; and in one of his *Orations*, Julian represents Jupiter saying to Apollo: " O my son, why did you not strike with your keen dart this mortal who has dared to desert your worship?" After Constantine had

consecrated to Mithra (second century A. D.). Museum of the Louvre (Frœhner, *op. cit.* No. 124).

[1] Apollo was also one of the chief divinities of Roman Gaul; cf. Héron de Villefosse, *Les Antiquités d'Entrains*, 1879.

[2] Eckhel, vii. 74. This legend is on a coin of the Caesar Crispus, which belongs, therefore, between 317 and 326.

[3] Engraved stone from the *Cabinet de France* (17 millim. by 14). No. 1,604 of the Catalogue. This pleasing intaglio of Roman work represents the god of travel and commerce, wearing the winged *petasus* and standing before an altar on which is placed a *pedum*, or travelling staff. At the side of the altar a column, perhaps a milestone, is surmounted by a globe, and the branch of a tree is attached to it.

[4] Cohen (vol. vi. p. 108, No. 109). With the radiate crown, and the legend *Soli invicto æterno Aug.* This confusion existed in the minds of so many that we even find in Eusebius (*Life of Const.* i. 43) an involuntary allusion to *Sol invictus* when the historian compares Constantine to the rising sun which sheds light over all the earth.

become avowedly Christian he still preserved respect for the god of his fathers (θεὸν πατρῶν); he never allowed the statues of Apollo

to be insulted; he placed several of them in Constantinople, and caused a bronze figure of the god to be brought from Ilium which he placed on a porphyry column, adding a radiate crown to the figure's head. These images were to him at that time objects of art, preserved, like the Jupiter of Dodona and the Muses of Helicon, for the adornment of his capital. But it seems to me that we may also discern in this selection a feeling of respect for the divinity whose protection he had implored as a boy and in his early campaigns.

THE SUN.[1]

In those days of religious confusion we must not expect to find the well-defined conceptions which our complete mental freedom gives us. Many pagans believed that the

THE SUN.[2]

Christians' God was the Sun.[3] Constantine seems to have held this view; and we have reason to believe that for many years he identified the Sun and the Christ,—his paternal divinity with him whose image Alexander Severus had placed in his lararium, and whose divine power Galerius, in the edict of 311, had lately acknowledged.

THE SUN.[4]

To Saint John, Jesus Christ is the Light of the World which shall illuminate Jerusalem,[5] as to Eusebius, Gregory of Nyssa, and Saint Augustine, he is the Sun of Righteousness which enlightens the human race. Accordingly, the apostle's thought was embodied upon a Christian monument by giving the Christ the radiate crown which belongs to Apollo.[6] Christian inscriptions apply to the first

---

[1] SOL INVICTO COMITI. Radiate head of the Sun on a small bronze of Constantine.

[2] SOLI INVICTO. The Sun, with radiate crown, in a mantle, standing, raising the right hand and holding a globe. (Reverse of a small bronze of Constantine.)

[3] . . . Alia Solem credunt Deum nostrum (Tertull., Apol. 16).

[4] SOLI COMITI AVG. The Sun, with radiate crown, standing, presenting to Constantine a globe surmounted by a Victory; between them a captive; underneath, S. M. T. (Reverse of a gold coin.)

[5] Saint John, viii. 12, ἐγώ εἰμι τὸ φῶς τοῦ κόσμου. Ibid. ix. 5; xii. 46; Isaiah, lx. 1-3. Saint Cyprian says of Jesus Christ: Est lux et dies (Opera, p. 208, edit. of 1625); sol verus et dies verus (pp. 157 and 215).

[6] Garrucci, Vetro, ecc., pl. I, 713. In Julian's theology (Εἰς τὸν βασιλέα ῾Ήλιον) the Sun, the visible image of the invisible god, in certain respects resembles the λόγος of Plato, and God the Son, of Christian theology.

day of the week, "the Lord's day," the name of the Sun's day;[1] and the habit of the early Fathers of comparing the coming of the Christ to the rising of the sun authorized the Church to fix as the date of the nativity the day on which it had been customary to celebrate in the temples the *natalis invicti Solis* (December 25).[2] After so many sanguinary encounters, Christians and pagans at last met as friends, — the latter uniting their many

RADIATE SUN.[3]

divinities into the one supreme God of whom philosophy had taught; the Christians also forming with their three Divine Persons one God, whose name and whose title to the adoration of all men, *divinitas*, the Emperor constantly recalled.

Constantine favored in every way this reconciliation, which political sagacity counselled him to encourage. The division of the months into weeks, and of the weeks into days, each one consecrated to some divinity, is an Oriental usage which gained ground among the Romans under the influence of the Alexandrian astrology.[4] In the time of Tertullian the pagans honored Saturn's day (Saturday), and the Chris-

THE CHRIST.[5]

tians, Sunday (the day of the Sun).[6] In ancient representations of the tutelary divinities of the week the Sun holds only the second place, and Saturn the first. On a vase, on the contrary, belonging to the middle of the fourth century, the Sun is first, and for the reason that in the interval the pagan *dies Solis* had be-

---

[1] HMEPA HΛΙΟΥ (Le Blant, *Inscr. christ. de la Gaule*, i. 355).

[2] Munter, *Sinnbilder und Kunstvorst. der alten Christen*, p. 75.

[3] Reverse of a coin of Trajan (gold and silver), with the legend PARTHICO PM. TR. P. COS. VI. P. P. SPQR.

[4] See, in the *Gazette archéol.* of 1877, p. 31, a learned paper by M. de Witte on *Les Divinités des sept jours de la semaine*. This author believes that the custom was introduced at Rome at the time when Caesar reformed the calendar. The figures will be found in the *Topographia Helvetica* of Mathieu Merian, p. 54 or 58, according to the edition.

[5] The Christ with radiate crown. From a painted glass by Garucci.

[6] *Apol.* 16.

come identified with the Christian *dies dominica*. The days of the week being thus consecrated, each to its particular divinity, the

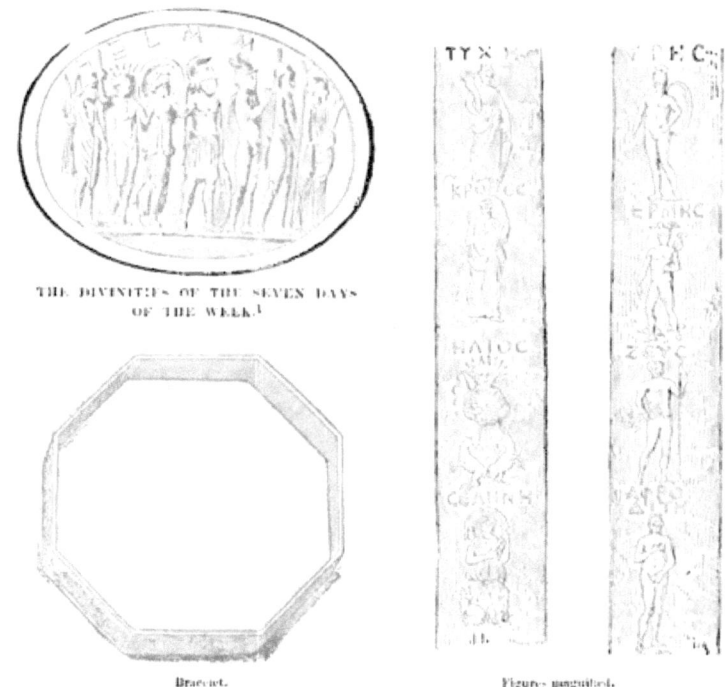

THE DIVINITIES OF THE SEVEN DAYS OF THE WEEK.[1]

Bracelet.   Figures magnified.

DIVINITIES OF THE SEVEN DAYS OF THE WEEK, ON A GOLD BRACELET FOUND IN SYRIA.[2]

devout had a prayer for each one of these deities; and since the growing popularity of the solar cult, the *dies Solis* was marked

[1] Engraved stone in the collection of Mr. Maxwell Somerville. The gods which preside over the days of the week, walking to the right, have over their heads inscribed the initial letter of each one's name (Saturnus, Elios, Luna or Diana, Mars, Mercury, Jupiter, and Venus). Saturn is veiled like a priest, the Sun has the radiate crown, Diana has the curved veil above her head, Mars is armed and helmeted, Mercury wears the winged cap, Jupiter holds the sceptre, and Venus the apple.

[2] This little bracelet is only two and a third inches in diameter, and the engraved figures are but two fifths of an inch. The careless workmanship marks the period as near the close of the third or the beginning of the fourth century. On the eight faces of the octagon are engraved the seven gods or goddesses of the week, and Fortune, TYXH, which opens the series. She holds in the right hand a cornucopia, and rests the left hand upon a rudder. Saturn, KPONOC, comes next in order. He is clad in a long garment, and with the left hand holds a scarf which is floating above his head. The third place is occupied by the Sun,

by devotional exercises in honor of Apollo.[1] Constantine availed
himself of this practice doubly to consecrate the dominical day.
A law of the year 321 ordered tribunals, shops, and workshops
to be closed on the day of the Sun,[2] and he sent to the legions, to
be recited upon that day, a form of prayer which
could have been employed by a worshipper of Mithra,
of Serapis, or of Apollo, quite as well as by a Christian believer.[3] This was the official sanction of the
old custom of addressing a prayer to the rising sun.[4]
In determining what days should be regarded as

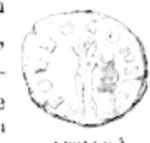

APOLLO.[5]

holy, and in the composition of a prayer for national use, Constantine exercised one of the rights belonging to him as pontifex
maximus; and it caused no surprise that he should do this. The
new decrees gave satisfaction to the Church, who on Sunday celebrated the resurrection of the Lord, and no less were satisfactory
to her adversaries, who in this *justitium*, instituted apparently in
honor of Apollo, beheld an act of homage to their great divinity.
A law of the year 315 perhaps belongs in this category of measures
which each party believed to have been adopted in its interests.
It forbade the branding of criminals in the face, "not to disfigure
that which is made in the image of the celestial beauty."[6] These

HλIOC, radiate, and standing in a chariot with two horses. He holds in the right hand a whip,
and in the left a globe. The Moon, CEAHNII, is the fourth figure. She wears a double tunic,
a double crescent is on her head, and a veil, puffed out by the wind; she holds a lighted torch
in her right hand. After the Moon comes Mars, APHC, naked, helmeted, carrying his
buckler. The sixth figure is Mercury, also naked, with wings on his feet and on his cap, and
holding a money-bag and the caduceus. The seventh is Jupiter, ZEYC, bearded, armed with
the thunderbolt, and leaning on a long sceptre. The series ends with Venus, — a nude figure
in the pose of the Venus de' Medici. Cf. *Gazette archéol.* 1877, pl. 8, and pp. 83–84.

[1] *Codex Theod.* ii. 8, 1 : . . . *Dero Solis veneratione sui celebrem.*

[2] *Codex Just.* iii. 12, 3. Two exceptions were made. — it was permitted on Sunday to
continue agricultural labors, and it was lawful to enfranchise a slave or to emancipate a son
(*Codex Theod.* ii. 8, 1). In some cases even the Emperor authorized the holding of markets
(Orelli, No. 508).

[3] Eusebius, *Life of Constantine*, iv. 19, 20.

[4] *Plerique restena affectatione aliquando et caeli dia adorandi, ad Solis ortum labia vibratis*
(Tertull. *Apol.* 16). This was an old custom; on the morning of the battle of Cremona, in 69,
a whole legion adored the rising sun. (Vol. V. p. 87).

[5] APOLLO CONSER. The god, standing, his right hand on his head, the left on his
lyre, placed on a column. (Reverse of a coin of the Emperor Gallienus.)

[6] *Codex Theod.* ix. 40, 2. Though it was forbidden to brand the face, it remained
customary to brand upon the hands or legs (*ibid.*, anno 315). Moreover, this law, like so
many others, was not observed: Constantius II. ordered the bishops who were condemned to
the mines to be branded on the forehead (Saint Hilary, *Contra Const. Imper.* chap. xi.). In

words remind us of the language of Scripture, and the Christian influence is evident; but Apollo was also the ideal type of human
beauty, and where the Christians saw a reference to Jehovah, what
prevented the pagans from seeing a reference to the son of
Latona?

It has been usual to place the conversion of Constantine in
the year 312. At the same time, during his stay in Rome in
that year he neither did nor said anything which indicates a
change in his convictions.[1] It has been thought that after his
victory he did not perform the customary sacrifices at the Capitol.
To fail to do this would have been a conspicuous apostasy in the
midst of an entirely pagan city. We know, on the contrary, that
his triumphal entry gave occasion for the usual solemnities, and
that he was present at the gladiatorial combats, and also at the
sacred games[2] to which the statues of the gods were carried, —
always guests at these festivals, which were an essential part of
the pagan cult;[3] and when we see him filling up the Senate by
calling into it many provincials,[4] we are justified in saying that
most of them — probably all of them — were adherents of the old
faith, since until the reign of Theodosius the curia remained the
stronghold of the last of the gods. Rome, with its hundred and
fifty-two temples and its eighty-three shrines, was still full of the
splendors of paganism, while those of Christian Rome had scarcely as
yet begun to appear;[5] to Saint Jerome the Capitoline city remained,

---

[1] Constantine condemned to the punishment of the cross (*ibid.* 8, 1); later, he abolished
this punishment (Aur. Vict., *Caes.* 4, and Sozomenus, i. 9). This plainly was a concession
to the Church, and not an amelioration of the penal laws, which he rendered more severe.

[1] The edict of Milan, promulgated some months later, makes a vague allusion to a rescript,
probably issued in Rome in 312, the character of which it has never been possible clearly to
define. Ecclesiastical writers regard it as a proof of the zeal of Constantine for the new religion; it may have been only a measure designed to secure the execution of the edict of Galerius. Since the year 311 toleration had again become one of the principles of the imperial
government; and, more than ever before, the conqueror of Maxentius was determined to make
it the rule of his conduct.

[2] . . . *Homeres de luis munerum sacrarumque ludorum . . . te ipsum spectare potuerunt . . .*
(*Pan. vet.* ix. 19). In 357 Constantius, then at Rome, set apart the sums necessary for the
pagan ceremonies (Symmachus, *Letters,* x. 54), and these ceremonies were not abolished
until the reign of Gratian.

[3] *Idololatria ludorum omnium mater,* says Saint Cyprian and Lactantius (*Inst. div.* vi. 20).

[4] *Pan. vet.* x. 35; *Ut senatus . . . ex totius urbis flore constaret.*

[5] Lists prepared in the second half of the fourth century mention an immense number
of temples, and not one church. Certainly there were churches at this time, but they were
passed over in silence. These temples, with their extensive possessions and revenues, were

as late as the end of the fourth century, "the sink of all superstitions."

Eusebius asserts that a statue holding the *labarum* was erected in honor of Constantine after his victory.[1] The ecclesiastical his-

THE AQUEDUCT OF AQUA VIRGO.   FROM CANINA.

torian has been misled by some obscure words of a panegyrist.— which, however, unquestionably refer to the erection of a statue by the Senate and Italy in the Emperor's honor. According to pagan usage, he was represented with some divine attribute,[2] which

the property of the pagan priesthood, who could not have been deprived of them without a special law, which was not made until the time of Gratian (*Codex Theod.* xvi. 10, 20).   The enlightened class was long hostile towards the Christian religion; and even among Christians themselves, those who preserved a taste for literature sadly compared the rude style of the New Testament with the elegance of Cicero and Vergil. Saint Augustine does not conceal this, and Saint Jerome feels the same regret.

[1] *Life of Const.* i. 40; *Hastam in modum crucis.* It has been shown how in the *labarum*, at once an old and a new standard, each man, pagan or Christian, could see that which suited himself.

[2] . . . *Merito tibi . . . senatus signum dei dedit et pmda ante Italia scutum et coronam.*

Eusebius reconstructs into a Christian symbol.   But doubt is impossible when, after this passage, we hear the orator invoke the divine soul spread through the material universe which the Stoics had made their God.[1]

About this time,[2] in memory of the German victories of the Emperor, the dux Senecio, one of his relatives, consecrated a temple to the divinity of Constantine, *numini ejus*, — a formula which may still be read in the inscription engraved to commemorate his restoration of the Aqua Virgo, and on many other monuments.[3] We cannot wonder, therefore, that the arch of triumph consecrated at Rome in 315 bears pagan sacrifices, and neither the *labarum* nor the cross.   Two words of the inscription, however, *instinctu divinitatis*, have been thought to be a veiled confession of the Christian faith.[4]   The word *divinitas*, scarcely known to Latin antiquity, was at this time on the lips of many, since it corresponded to the unconscious travail of souls which were quietly abandoning the

cuncta aurea dedicarunt . . . Debitum divinitati et simulacrum aureum et virtuti scutum et corona picturi. Quamobrem, te, summe rerum sator (Pan. vet. ix. 25-6).

[1] "O thou, sovereign master of the world, who hast deigned to bear as many names as there are human languages, hear my prayer!   We know not how thou desirest to be called; whether, as force and divine soul diffused through the material universe, thou minglest thyself with all the elements and givest motion to the world without any impulse from without, or whether, a power above the heavens, thou contemplatest from that high citadel the world which thou hast made. — I supplicate thee, preserve this prince forever!" (*Pan. vet.* x. 26.)   This is what was said, in Constantine's presence, by an official orator in 313.

[2] Certainly after the death of Galerius, in 311, since that Emperor is not named in the inscription (Or.-Henzen, No. 5,579).

[3] *Comptes-rendus de l'Acad. des inscr.*, 1882, p. 12, and L. Renier, *Inscr. d'Alg.* Nos. 3,286, 3,355, etc.

[4] *C. I. L.* vol. vi. No. 1,139.   The cast taken by M. Léon Renier, which is in the Sorbonne, gives no ground for the supposition of certain scholars that the inscription originally bore the words *nutu Jovis O. M.*, and that these words were effaced and the present phrase, *instinctu divinitatis*, substituted.   The arch commemorated the tenth year of Constantine's reign. — 315.   The inscription, engraved in letters of gold on the triumphal arch which was erected in front of the Constantinian Basilica, and was destroyed by Bramante in building St. Peter's, is as follows: —

Quod duce te mundus surrexit in astra triumphans.
Hanc Constantinus victor tibi condidit aulam.

Muratori does not believe this inscription to be of Constantine's time, and neither Orelli nor Henzen includes it in the *monumenta historica* of this Emperor.   Inscriptions in letters of gold are found only in mosaics of the sixth century, and what we have said of the religious policy of Constantine leads to the conclusion that this inscription is of much later date than his reign.   Eusebius, who outlived the Emperor three years, and who speaks at considerable length of the arch of triumph which is still standing, would not have failed to mention that of the Vatican basilica, had it been erected in his time.   The inscription, in fact, seems only to recall the memory of Constantine.

old gods without expressly renouncing them, and were on the way
towards the God of the Christian faith, without as yet proclaiming his indivisible sovereignty.   Six years later, in the festival
which celebrated the fifteenth year of Constantine's imperial power,
the pagan author of the Tenth Panegyric compares the Emperor
to Mars and to the Dioscuri ; he asserts that it was by the celestial inspiration of the god Constantius, *divini instinctu*, that his
son had defeated both Maxentius and the Franks.   Thus within
four years of the Council of Nicaea the official orators were remind-
ing Constantine of the apotheosis of his father[1] and of the assistance of that higher Power whom Cicero, Seneca, and Plutarch
worshipped, and whose name recurs constantly in the words and
in the legal institutions of the Emperor, — in the prayer that he
prepared for his soldiers, and in the long rescript which, after the
defeat of Licinius, obliterated the effects of the late persecution.
The God whom he thus took pleasure in invoking was not so
much the Christ as it was the Divinity, whoever he may be, who
is enthroned in the highest heaven: *quidquid illud est divinum
ac caeleste numen.*[2]   These words are in the edict of Milan, in the
message of Licinius to the governor of Bithynia, even in letters
of Constantine to the bishops.   It is not without intention that he
repeats them thus persistently.[3]   He would willingly have united
all the nations subject to his sway in one faith, whose forms might
vary, while its substance should be the worship of the one God;
and he believed that when this revolution was accomplished, the
administration of the Empire would become more easy, the public
peace would be more secure.[4]   This same thought prevented him

---

[1] He himself, referring in his laws to the acts of his predecessors, calls these Emperors
gods, *divorum retro principum* (*Codex Theod.* xiii. 3, 3). But we have already remarked on
the meaning attached in the fourth century to the word *divus.*

[2] Eusebius, *Hist. eccl.* x. 5: ὅ τι ποτέ ἐστι θειότης καὶ οὐράνιον πρᾶγματος.   M. Egger,
whom I have consulted in respect to this very singular phrase, has kindly given me his opinion,
as follows: " It is extremely incorrect   It is conjectured that this language may express the
idea of a vague pietism which reconciled itself alike to Christianity and to philosophy and the
other cults. . . ." Cf. Lactant., *De Morte pers.* 48; *Divinitatis reverentia.*   In a law published
a month after the Council of Nicaea, we find these words: *Ita mihi summa divinitas et propitia
sit* (*Codex Theod.* ix. 1, 4).

[3] He says again, in an ordinance of 355: *Quam divinitatis affectu confidimus* (*Constit. Sismondi,* No. 4).   *Caeleste numen, coel. praesidium, divinum numen,* are words constantly used
by Marcellinus (xix. 1, 6, 11; xx. 6, etc.).

[4] Eusebius, *Life of Const.* ii. 65.

from celebrating the Secular Games, which certain calculations caused to fall in the year 313. This was the greatest of all the Roman festivals, but also the most pagan; and all Italy was invited to attend it. It would have stimulated to the highest degree those passions which Constantine specially endeavored to tranquillize. As there had never been any certain date for this solemnity, the public did not observe this voluntary forgetfulness. Only a few pagans lamented secretly that from day to day respect for the old Roman customs was growing less.[1] But Constantine was well satisfied to have avoided an occasion for disturbance.

II. The Edict of Milan, and its Results.

But why fix a date for the conversion of this Emperor? Chronology sees no importance in this matter. It was not, in fact, a case of a sudden resolve, like that of Henry IV. of France when he exclaimed, "Paris is well worth a mass!" but of slow modifications taking place, in the course of years, in a mind at once circumspect and confused, much more occupied with events than with theology, where the religious conscience to the end was never free from uncertainties. Two pagan authors, Libanius and Zosimus, represent Constantine as going over to Christianity,—the former after the defeat of Licinius (323), the latter after the death of Crispus (326); but the historians of the Church set this date back fourteen years. We have just demonstrated that as late as the year 313 nothing testifies to the Christian faith of the Emperor. In that year appeared the edict of Milan,—the grandest legislative act that sovereign ever promulgated; for fifteen centuries were to pass before the world would again hear similar language.[2] But this was not a Christian act. It proclaims the equality of all cults; it grants complete liberty for religious observances; and it bears the signature of two Emperors who assume the pagan title of pontifex maximus, all of whose rights they preserve. The moment is unique in history; for then seemed to

---

[1] *Adeo in dies cura minima Romae urbis* (Aur. Vict., *Caes.* 28; Zosimus, ii. 7).
[2] See above, p. 464.

TRIUMPHAL ARCH OF CONSTANTINE.

perish that established religion which, undergoing the fate of all human institutions, had become a useless and odious instrument, after having for centuries secured the prosperity of Rome. But it was only a momentary flash of good sense across the political heavens; no later than the year 325 an established religion was to re-appear, and with it its necessary companion, Intolerance, which under the successors of Constantine let loose again new persecutions.[1]

Dating from the edict of Milan, the Catholic Church attempts to prove the piety of Constantine by testimony[2] most of which is true, but does not give the whole truth, since it shows but one face of this policy, which, without hypocrisy or falsehood, and solely in the interests of the public peace, had two aspects, — one towards the Christians, the other towards the pagans. The latter remains somewhat obscure, because of the scarcity of documents of pagan origin. These documents suffice, however, to render the Constantine of history a greater man than he of the Church: for instead of the imprudent zeal of a neophyte, we see the patient wisdom of a ruler, — a man occupied above all things in fulfilling his royal task and compelling the partisans of the old and of the new faith to live in peace, when, if left to themselves, they would have fallen upon each other in deadly strife.[3]

The Emperor very early had about him Christians who would keep him informed as to what went on in the churches and among the heretical sects. One of these counsellors, the Arian Strategus, whom on account of his eloquence Constantine surnamed Musonianus, was appointed to keep watch over the Manichaeans and other sectaries.[4] But there were pagans also at the imperial court. Philosophers were received there, and the Emperor took pleasure in causing them to discuss with the clergy, — occasions which, according to the ecclesiastical writers,

---

[1] It did, in fact, re-appear in 315; for in that year Constantine renewed the edicts of Vespasian and of Severus against those who embraced Judaism (*Codex Theod.* xvi. 8, 1).

[2] Eusebius, Theodoret, Sozomenus, Philostorgos, Rufinus, Socrates, and the modern writers who have followed them.

[3] Baronius (*Ann. eccl.* iii. 91) says that many bishops, returning into their dioceses after the edict of Milan, broke the idols, overthrew the altars, and even destroyed temples.

[4] Amm. Marcell., xv. 13: *Constantinus cum limatius superstitionum quaereret sectas, manichaeorum et similium. . . .*

always turned to the confusion of the heathen and gave opportunity
for miracles.   Thus Alexander, the bishop of Byzantium, matched
against a rude antagonist, said: "In the name of Christ I forbid
thee to speak;" and the other on the spot became dumb. "This
miracle," says Sozomenus. "is greater than that of the Chaldaean
who cut the stone with his word."[1]   The philosopher Nicagoras of
Athens, who in Egypt testified, in an inscription engraved upon a
tomb, his gratitude towards the Emperor,[2] must have been of the
number of pagans made welcome at the imperial court.   We know
that Constantine was for a long time much attached to Sopater
the Neo-Platonist. — whose death, however, he finally ordered when
the episcopal influence gained the ascendency over him.   "The
Emperor put Sopater to death," says Suidas, "in order to show
that in religion he now no longer had anything in common with
the pagans by whom formerly he had been always surrounded."[3]
However, until the last years of his reign the Emperor had them near
him; and we shall find them at the court of all the Christian
Emperors, even Theodosius: it was a matter of imperial tradition
and of political necessity.   One of the authors of the *Augustan
History*, a zealous pagan, dedicates his work to Constantine.[4]
The Emperor exchanged letters with Optatianus, a foolish poet
from whom the Venerable Bede refuses to quote, considering him
too pagan; and about the year 331 Constantine employed as teacher
of eloquence for one of his sons the rhetorician Arborius, the uncle
of Ausonius, and, like him, a pagan, — or, like him, indifferent as
to either religion.[5]

The republican Senate and the Emperors had had secretaries
for the Greek language, even for the Arabic language, — doubtless

[1] Sozomenus, *Hist. eccl.* i. 18.

[2] Boeckh, *C. I. G.* No. 4,770.

[3] *Sub verbo Sopater.* He was killed between 330 and 337. According to Eunapius (*Lives of the Sophists*, s. v. Aedesius) he was accused of having chained the winds and hindered the frumentary ships from arriving at Constantinople. He must have fallen under the application of the law against magicians; see later. Mention is also made of another pagan philosopher, Canonaris, who is said to have been put to death. Cf. the Anonymous of Banduri, *Ant. Const.* p. 38, in the *Imperium orientale* of the learned Benedictine.

[4] Capitolinus, *Gord.* I. and *Maximini duo*, I. Tatius Cyrillus, whom Constantine employed to translate historical works from Greek into Latin, must also have been a pagan (*ibid.*).

[5] The elegy of Arborius. *Ad Nympham nimis cultam*, is entirely pagan (*Ap* Wernsdorf. *Poetae lat. min.*).

also for other tongues;[1] Constantine was obliged to have them for the affairs of the Christians and of the pagans, each secretary addressing his correspondents in their own language. As early as the year 313 the bishop Hosius was employed in the correspondence with the African churches.[2] Thus we are enabled to account for despatches of contradictory import, which merely corresponded with the twofold interests which it was the duty of the government to protect. In 314, in order to persuade the African bishops to put an end to the violent schism of the Donatists which was distracting the province, the imperial chancery despatched to them a letter wherein were contained some very Christian sentences[3]

BRONZE COIN.[5]

which it was politic and suitable for Constantine to address to the powerful Church of Africa. But, a few months earlier, he had authorized the pagans of that province to institute, in honor of the Flavian family, priesthoods which were still in existence eighty years later,[4] and he had given to all the pagans of the Empire a signal gratification by permitting the Roman Senate to decree the apotheosis of Diocletian.

[1] See Vol. VI. p. 224 ; Foucart, *Schantse. inédits*, p. 7, and *Bull. de corresp. hellén.*, 1882. p. 369.

[2] Euseb., *Hist. eccl.* x. 6. Later the Donatists accused Hosius of having prejudiced the Emperor against them, and Saint Augustine says that, acting on the bishop's advice, Constantine exiled them. Hosius was intrusted with an imperial letter to Alexandria in the case of a dispute between the patriarch and Arius, his disobedient deacon. At the Council of Nicaea he sat at Constantine's right hand; we might call him the minister of the Christian cult.

[3] . . . *Meum judicium postulant qui ipsi judicium Christi expecto* (Optatus of Milevi, *Gesta purgat. Caeciliani*, p. 25). See also (p. 22) the close of the letter to the proconsul Ablavius also De Rossi, *Bull. di arch. crist.*, July, 1865, p. 49. It is not without some hesitation that I quote the text of Optatus. He wrote long after the events with which we are concerned, for he died near the close of the fourth century; and he is not accurate, for he makes no mention of the Council of Arles, and attributes to the Council of Rome acts which do not belong to it. The seventh book of his treatise *De Schismate* is generally rejected. It is well known that documents entirely spurious were often given as authentic. The imperial letter quoted by Optatus appears to me of extremely doubtful authenticity, and the same doubt is felt by the Duc de Broglie (vol. i. p. 290, note 1), — at least it must be admitted, if the letter is genuine, that the Emperor's Christian secretary causes him to employ in 314 language which at that date he could not have used. At that time he was not accustomed to speak of Christ, but always of " the Divinity," or " the supreme God."

[4] *Tum* (after the death of Maxentius and the subjugation of Africa) *per Africam sacerdotium decretum Flaviae genti* (Aur. Victor, *Caes.* 18). A consul of the year 350 was still pontiff of the Flavian cult (Orelli, No. 3,672).

[5] Coin of Aegae, in Cilicia. Hexastyle temple, in which are Aesculapius and Telesphorus. (Reverse of a bronze of Philip.)

When the defeat of Licinius had subjected to Constantine the Oriental provinces, he annulled there the effects of the recent persecution by an edict, preceded by a letter in which some bishop's hand can plainly be recognized. But although his pref-

ROMAN BRIDGE NEAR APHACA.[1]

erences at this time were certainly in favor of the new religion, he contented himself with exhorting his pagan subjects to venerate the law of the Almighty God, without prescribing anything against them. In another edict of the same year (324) he urged his subjects to maintain a spirit of mutual toleration, so that those

[1] Roman bridge near Aphaca, and falls of the River Adonis, now the *Nahr Ibrahim* (after a photograph by Dr. Lortet, v. 61).

RUINS OF THE TEMPLE OF APHACA (AFKA), AND VALLEY OF THE RIVER ADONIS (NAHR-IBRAHIM)

FROM A PHOTOGRAPH BY DR. LORTET.

who persevered in the pagan error might enjoy the same peace
and tranquillity with the Christian believers.[1] His acts corresponded with his words: long after the Council of Nicaea, in reply
to a petition from the pagan inhabitants of Hispellum, the pagan
secretary sent out a decree, in which it was directed, in reference to
a temple consecrated in that city to Constantine, that the worship
there offered "should not be contaminated by the frauds of
contagious superstition."[2] The contagion at this time threatening
these Umbrians was the Christian faith, and not paganism, which
was now dying. As often occurs in administrative acts, the
imperial rescript quoted back the language employed in the petition, and gave these belated zealots of paganism the protection
that they sought against the invasion of their mountains by a
new faith.

This double character of Constantine's government appears in
everything. At Antioch, at Nicomedeia, at Bethlehem, at the
Holy Sepulchre, he builds churches, "which rose like lilies, filling
the air with a divine perfume:"[3] and he closes at Heliopolis and
at Aphaca the temples of the Syrian Venus (which were said to
be the haunt of all vices), and later that of Aesculapius of Aegae,
—a divinity dangerous on account of his revelations, which placed
the person consulting him in communication with the invisible
world, whence priests and soothsayers could cause disturbing utter-
ances to proceed.[4] But at Constantinople he allows the pagan

---

[1] Eusebius, *Life of Constantine*, ii. 26-42 and 48-70.

[2] . . . *Ne aedis nostro nomini dedicata cujusquam contagiosae superstitionis fraudibus
polluatur* (Orelli-Henzen, No. 5,580, and Wilmanns, No. 2,845). Hispellum was at the foot of
the Apennines, near the Flaminian Road, four miles from Foligno. In this document Crispus
is not named with the other children of Constantine, — which dates it as later than the
young man's death (326).

[3] Euseb., *Hist. eccl.* x. 4, and *Life of Const.* ii. 45. At Rome is shown his baptistery, —
in which he was never baptized, — and seven churches claim him as their builder, of which he
probably built but one, that of the Vatican, which gave place in the sixteenth century to St.
Peter's. It is said that when the Vatican basilica was removed, tiles, bricks, and coins
bearing Constantine's name were discovered. Later are given the ancient designs which have
been preserved (Ciampini, *De Sacris aedificiis a Constant. Magno constructis*, chap. iv.
pp. 28-41).

[4] Euseb., *Life of Const.* 55, 56. We must conclude that occurrences causing anxiety to
the government had taken place at Aegae, for there were throughout the Empire sanctuaries
of Aesculapius much more celebrated than that in Cilicia, and Eusebius mentions only the
destruction of the latter. His chap. iii. 54, which has as its title "Temples and Idols
everywhere destroyed," would lead to the belief in a universal destruction; whereas he
mentions (chap. lv.-lvi.) but three temples overthrown, — those of Aegae, Aphaca, and

SYRIAN VENUS, WEEPING FOR THE DEATH OF ADONIS.[3]

builds shrines to the Dioscuri, to the Mother of the Gods, and to Fortune,[4] so that the orator Themistius could assert that Jupiter

Heliopolis. That of Aphaca, which the historian represents as destroyed by the soldiers of Constantine, was standing in the time of Zosimus (i. 58). The temple of Daphne, near Antioch, was in Julian's time deserted, but not overthrown; and it was a bishop of the fifth or sixth century who put an end to the worship of Venus at Heliopolis (Tillemont, *Hist. des emp.* iv. 207). Julian (*Oration against Heracl.* 19) reproaches Constantine with having "despised the temples and despoiled them of the offerings made by the pious;" but he does not accuse the Emperor of having destroyed them, while he does thus accuse the sons of Constantine.

[1] Malalas, *Chronogr.* xiii. 324.

[2] *Codex Theod.* xvi. 10, 3.

[3] Statuette of white limestone found in Syria (Collection of the Duc de Luynes in the *Cabinet de France*). This Venus, in a reclining attitude, wrapped in her peplum, corresponds to the description of her given by Macrobius in his *Saturnalia* (i. 21): *Simulacra hujus deae in monte Libani fingitur capite obnupto, specie tristi, faciem manu laeva intra amictum sustinens; lacrymae visione conspicientium manare creduntur.* Aphrodite weeping for Adonis was in all the Syro-Phoenician religions the personification of the sadness of the Earth at the periodical departure of the Sun. This statuette is the object of a paper published by the *Gazette archéol.*, 1875, p. 97 *et seq.* and plate 26.

[4] Zosimus, ii. 32 . . . . τὸ τῶν Διοσκούρων ἱερόν . . . ποιησάμενος, etc. Zosimus employs, not the word ναός, which designates only the habitation of the God, but the word ἱερόν, which signifies besides the temple, the space of ground outside consecrated to the God. He therefore alludes to small buildings erected by Constantine. Lactantius (*Inst. div.* xi. 10) seems also to

was the protector of the two Romes.[1] In 312 Constantine had authorized the Senate to engrave his name upon a temple; twenty-two years later he permitted them to reconstruct the temple of Concord.[2] Temples were even dedicated to the Flavian family; and the rescript of 326, which forbade the beginning of new structures in any city where old ones remained still unfinished, made exception in the case of temples to the gods.[3]

The Emperor asks from Eusebius many copies of the Scriptures for the clergy of Constantinople; but Athens, which Libanius calls "the holy city, the common delight of gods and men," is loaded with imperial gifts. He accepts from her the title of strategus,[4] and he confirms the immunities granted by his predecessors to grammarians and professors, their wives and children.—a significant measure, for it was adopted at a time when we may be sure there were no professors, officially so called, who were Christians.[5]

---

allude to new temples built at this time (*templorum novorum dedicationes*). Moreover, the old divinities had already undergone so many metamorphoses that Castor and Pollux had very little in common with the valiant sons of Leda who had fought for Rome at Lake Regillus. Their attributes had become extremely numerous; and we shall not wonder at seeing them honored by Constantine if we remember that they were frequently placed on Christian tombs, as representing the resurrection and immortality. Cf. Maurice Albert, *Le Culte de Castor et de Pollux*, and later, a Sarcophagus of Arles.

[1] *Disc.* vi. *ad fin.* Eusebius (*Life of Constantine*, iii. 48), who represents the Emperor as the destroyer of all idolatry, naturally is unwilling to admit that a pagan was left in ancient Byzantium. Saint Augustine, it is true, says (*Civ. Dei*, v. 25) that Constantinople was *sine aliquo daemonum templo simulacroque*; this was perhaps the case in his time, but it was not, and could not have been, so in 330. Himerius the sophist (*Disc.* vii. 9) complains, indeed, that the pagans of that city were not allowed, under Constantius, to sacrifice to their gods. But we know that Julian, when he visited Constantinople, found the pagan sanctuaries open, and was "received with acclamations" in the temple of Fortune (*Letters*, 65).

[2] Aur. Victor, *Caes.* 40, and Orelli, No. 26: . . . *Et cultu splendidiore restituerunt.* The consul Faustus Paulinus (325) dedicates an altar to the invincible Hercules (Gruter, p. 47, 9), and Petronius Probianus erects one to Juno (*ibid.* p. 450, 1).

[3] . . . *Exceptis dumtaxat templorum aedificationibus* (*Codex Theod.* xv. 1, 3). A coin subsequent in date to the year 330 represents Fortune, or the Genius of the city of Constantinople, seated at the prow of a vessel and holding an oar; that is, the helm of state. Later, the image of this Genius would be only a mythological reminiscence; at the period where we now are, it shows that the Emperor still thought it unwise, in the last year of his reign, to change the custom in respect to the coinage. According to the *Chron. of Alexandria*, anno 330, Constantine caused an image of Fortune to be erected, and placed his own statue beside it, before which, on certain days, religious acts were to be performed.

[4] Julian, *Pan.* i. 8; ". . . All his life he honored this city with praises and benefits."

[5] *Codex*, x. 52, 6, anno 321. Lactantius was a pagan at the time when he was appointed to teach rhetoric in Nicomedia. See *ibid.* 8, anno 363, a curious rescript of Valentinian against those who unwarrantably assumed the *habitum philosophiae*. It recognized a right to immunities only in the case of those *a probatissimis approbati*.

In Palestine religious rivalry made a quarrel between a Christian village, Majuma, and Gaza, the pagan city to which it appertained: the Emperor raised the village to the rank of a city,[1] and the public peace was maintained.

In those regions where dominant Christianity called for the closing of some pagan sanctuary, Constantine confiscated to the

COIN OF GAZA.[2]

imperial treasury all the precious metals contained in the temple, and even the brass from the doors and the roofs. This, Eusebius — taking his own wishes for reality — represents as occurring throughout the entire Empire; and he depicts the ancient gods deprived of their beards of gold or their silver eyes, shapeless and dishonored wrecks, flung out into the streets amid the jeers of the crowd.[3] But where

COIN OF ANTIOCH.[2]

the population was chiefly pagan these acts of pillage could be prevented. A decree of 320 forbids that cities should be deprived of the ornaments which belong to them.[4] Forty years later Antioch and Alexandria, almost holy cities to the Christians, had, the one its famous statue of the Daphnic Apollo, the other its great temple of Serapis.

Christians plundered certain temples of their wealth,[6] as, in the

[1] Eusebius, *Life of Const.* ii. 5.

[2] Two divinities standing in a distyle temple; between them the *mem*, or M., Phoenician initial of the name of Marna, the principal divinity of Gaza. (Reverse of a bronze of the Empress Plautilla, wife of Caracalla.)

[3] "Lieutenant of the King of Heaven, he pursued the vanquished and distributed their spoils among the soldiers of the victorious God. He took away the images of gold and silver, shapes of error, and sent throughout the provinces and cities men, who, going into the temples, despoiled the statues of their ornaments of precious metal and left to the pagans only the shapeless remains. The priests were obliged to hide these fragments in the most secret retreats" (Eusebius, *Eulogy upon Const.* 8). It is always the false theory of the suppression of paganism by Constantine. But we must admit local acts of violence, as in the case of the persecution of the Christians; for the *lex talionis* is common to the populace everywhere. Doubtless priests were insulted, and altars broken down. Under Julian, suits were instituted against certain Christians for the restoration of silver stolen from the temples. These are occurrences common to all times of reaction.

[4] *Non sua propriis ornamentis esse privandas existimet civitates* (*Codex Theod.* xv. 1, 1). As his share of the pillage, Constantine robbed Jupiter of his titles, bestowing them upon the God of the Christians: *Deus optimus maximus* (Euseb., *Life of Const.* ii. 55).

[5] GENIO ANTIOCHENI. The city of Antioch seated; at her feet a river (the Orontes) swimming. (Small bronze.) See the same type reproduced, Vol. V. p. 155, by a statue in the Vatican, and p. 64 of this volume upon an engraved stone from the *Cabinet de France.*

[6] Libanius (*Letter* 730) intercedes, in the reign of Julian, for a Christian accused of

time of persecutions, the pagans had plundered churches: this was a form of local disorder that the Empire was not able to prevent. But when they sought to destroy tombs, the attack was very serious upon the ideas and custom of the Roman world, where the family was based upon the double foundation of tombstone and hearthstone; and a law forbade the act of violence.[1]

Constantine abolished the penalties imposed on celibacy, and in so doing gave satisfaction both to the Christians and to many pagans;[2] but he maintained the advantages secured by the Papian-Poppaean Law to the fathers of many children, and he granted like advantages to the *navicularii* who brought to Constantinople the corn of the provinces.[3]

As the Twelve Tables, the republican Senate, Tiberius and Diocletian had done, and as the pontifex maximus, the guardian of the official rites of religion, was bound to do, Constantine proscribed private divination (319) and magical incantations, which were believed to have the power of life and death. But he preserved the public divination, which was practised according to the ancient customs and could be superintended and controlled;[4]

stealing the money destined for sacrifices. But he does not say that Constantine confiscated the revenues of the temples; he only reproaches him with having impoverished the gods (*Deor.* 27, vol. ii. p. 162, Reiske); and he adds: . . . τῆς κατὰ νόμους δὲ θεραπείας ἐκήρυξεν οὐδὲν τυ. Julian (*Orat. against Heracl.* 17) speaks also only of offerings stolen from the temples. It has already been stated that the government contributed to the expenses of pagan worship until the reign of Gratian.

[1] *Codex Theod.* ix. 17, 1 and 2, *annis* 349 and 349. An ordinance of 331 (*Ibid.* iii. 16, 1) admitted three cases in which the wife could obtain divorce, — when her husband was a homicide, a poisoner, *vel sepulcrorum dissolutorem*. The law of 319 recognizes the long-established jurisdiction of the Roman pontiffs in all questions concerning tombs.

[2] *Codex Theod.* vii. 16, *anno* 320.

[3] *Ibid.* xiii. 5, 7.

[4] *Ibid.* ix. 16, 1 and 2. Another law of 321 orders a consultation of the aruspices. . . . *retento more veteris observantiae*, when lightning had struck a palace or a public edifice, with the condition that the matter be at once reported to the Emperor; that is to say, to the pontifex maximus (*Ibid.* xvi. 10, 1). The occult sciences, harmful to the individual and to the state, were always regarded with disfavor, and justly, by the imperial government. (See Vol. V. p. 506, note 2.) Constantine did not put an end to these practices, for Amm. Marcellinus speaks of them repeatedly, — xiv. 7; xvii. 10; xxi. 1; xxviii. 1; and Constantius renewed these prohibitions in 357 (*Codex Theod.* x. 16, 1–5). To understand the history of the Empire, we must bear in mind that the laws often failed of execution, as is attested by their frequent repetition. We have Christian amulets designed to put the devil to flight (cf. *Bull. épigr. de la Gaule*, ii. 35), and papyri now in the libraries of Paris, Leyden, and London have preserved to us books of magical incantations which are nothing less than manuals of crime (Revillout, *Cours de langue démotique*, pp. 20–21). Diocletian burned some of these in Egypt (p. 375), and we have seen (pp. 417 and 423) that the Christian Scriptures were proscribed as such. Diocletian certainly did not confuse the Gospels with these abominable

and through indulgence towards innocent superstitions, in which possibly he had some faith himself, he even allowed the incantations which were believed to restore health, allay tempests, and secure the harvests against hail.[1]

He prohibited sacrifices in private houses,[2] because being, as he was, a man of order and authority, he wished to bring everything into clear view and under his regulation; but he authorized those made publicly upon the altars of the gods,[3] he respected

books; but though he did not so confuse them, many in the pagan world did, and in religious wars governments always make use of the passions of the crowd.

[1] *Codex Theod.* ix. 16, 3.

[2] *Ibid.* xvi. 10, 1. Eusebius (*Life of Const.* ii. 44–45) transforms, as we might expect, this special into a general prohibition. Constantius, or rather Constans, speaks in 341 (*ibid.* 2) of another law made by his father, dated 333, which has been lost, but is known to have repeated the prohibitions of the law of 321; and perhaps the meaning of this latter law should be also given to that of Constans; it was, moreover, only a threat, destitute of legal sanction. La Bastie (in the *Mém. de l'Acad. des inscr.* xv. 100) and the Duc de Broglie (*L'Église et l'Empire Romain au ive Siècle,* i. 405) adopt this interpretation. It will be remarked that the severe law of 341, which says: *Cesset superstitio, sacrificiorum aboleatur insania,* is subscribed by only one Emperor whose name is not certain, and bears no date of days and month, nor indication of the place where it was published. If it does belong to Constans, there is extant another law of this Emperor, addressed in 346 (?) to the prefect of Rome, ordering him not to suffer the temples outside of the walls of the city to fall into ruins . . . *Intactae incorruptaeque consistant* (*Codex Theod.* xvi. 10, 3). Countless facts and the rescripts of Constantine, the oration of Libanius in behalf of the temples, divers passages of Themistius and the author of the *Vetus orbis descriptio,* written in 347, prove the public observance of the pagan cult during the whole of the fourth century. Lactantius, in his *Instit. div.* (iii. 30) shows the power that paganism preserved in the time of Constantine; and the expressions of anger in the *De Errore profanarum religionum* of Firmicus, written in 346 or 347, as well as many incidents in the youth of Julian, attest that, under Constantine, this power had not as yet been much weakened. Until 375, the Emperors retained the title of pontifex maximus, and the curiales that of perpetual flamen (see p. 518 and note 1). The procession of Cybele still took place in Gaul in the time of Saint Martin, who hunted down so many pagan idols. At the time when the Christians put Hypatia to death, there were still so many pagans in Alexandria that Saint Cyril, the bishop of that city, thought it needful to publish a minute refutation of Julian's book against Christianity. Up to the middle of the fifth century the worship of Isis and Osiris was maintained at Philae, notwithstanding the edict of Theodosius which had abolished paganism sixty years before (Letronne, *Mém. de l'Acad. des Inscr.* x. 171–217). Paganism was not definitively extirpated from Egypt until in the seventh century by the Arabs (Revillout, *Cours de langue démotique,* p. 37). See in Beugnot, vol. i. pp. 277–315 and 364–395, a multitude of other proofs of the long persistence of paganism. It is a law of history that the past is only very slowly destroyed.

[3] *Qui etiam adhuc existimatis conducere, adite aras publicas atque delubra et consuetudinis vestrae celebrate solemnia* (*Codex Theod.* ix. 16, 2, anno 319). If we compare this language and that of the law just now mentioned with the vague and confused terms of the pretended edict addressed to the provincials (Eusebius, *Life of Const.* ii. 48–60) we shall perceive this latter document is a Eusebian paraphrase. At the same time, the imperial intention is so manifest in the government and in the laws that Eusebius is compelled to let it appear in his amplification in chap. lvi., where he represents the Emperor as saying that he is willing to have each man act according to his conscience.

SCENES OF GLADIATORIAL COMBATS: FROM A ROMAN MOSAIC
AT BOGNOR (SUSSEX, ENGLAND).

the ancient law which permitted religious assemblages,[1] and long
after his time temples were
still built: Constantius and
Theodosius in their reigns
found paganism in Rome
alive and vigorous.[2] The inscription mentioned on p. 499
attests that in the latter part
of Constantine's reign Tus-
cany and Umbria still had
their pagan festivals, their
public sacrifices, their games,[3]
presided over by an annu-
ally elected priest, and even
their combats of gladiators,
which a law of 325 had
sought to abolish,[4] which
Constantius found occurring

GLADIATOR RETIARIUS [6]

in 357,[5] and of the regular existence of which, at the end of the

[1] *Religionis causa coire non prohibetur* (*Dig.* lxviii. 22, 1; fragment of Marcianus, who lived in the reign of Caracalla).

[2] Orelli (No. 17), speaking of a temple of Remus built by a consul in the reign of a son of Constantine, says: *Vides Constantinianis quoque temporibus deorum templa passim vel exstructa fuisse vel restituta*; and, in fact, a certain number of them are found. A law of 365 forbids the judges to give to Christians the guardianship of temples, *custodiam* (*Codex Theod.* xvi. 1, 1); this guardianship was therefore a recognized public office, at times solicited by Christians. An inscription of Auranitis, of the year 320, shows that paganism at that date had confidence enough in the future to erect to its gods edifices of importance (Waddington, *Inscr. de Syrie*, No. 2.393). Nearly a century after this, Rutilius saw celebrated in the Tuscan plains the festival of Osiris (*Itin.* i. 373-6); and in the time of Saint Jerome a temple built on one of the highest summits of the Anti-Libanus was the object of a famous pilgrimage among the pagans (*Rec. archéol.*, 1883, p. 213).

[3] The Emperor himself in 306 and in 322 instituted, in commemoration of his victories, the Francic and Sarmatic Games, — festivals entirely pagan in their character; for, says Lactantius (*Inst. div.* vi. 20), *ludorum celebrationes deorum festa sunt*.

[4] *Codex Theod.* xv. 12, 1, and Eusebius, *Life of Const.* iv. 25. Many Emperors had regulated gladiatorial combats so as to render them less murderous. Augustus and Nerva, for instance, had prohibited the giving of games with the express condition that the encounter should end only on the death of one of the combatants. Cf. Vol. V. p. 321 and note 2.

[5] *Codex Theod.* xv. 12, 3. Libanius (vol. ii. p. 6, edit. Reiske) speaks of combats of gladiators, given by his uncle at Antioch, about the year 329. In 365 Valentinian forbade condemning a Christian to fight as gladiator (*Codex Theod.* ix. 40, 8). It appears therefore that these games still continued.

[6] From a mosaic discovered at Bignor, Sussex (see colored plate; Lysons, *Reliquiae Britannicae Romanae*, vol. iii. pl. v.). The engraving facing this page represents scenes of gladiatorial combats which are fragments of the same mosaic. The gladiators have wings, as

century. we still find proofs.[1]   In other provinces Constantine had
permitted Flavian priesthoods to be established : two years before his
death he promulgated a law in favor of curiales raised to the office
of flamen.[2]   And many were, like the Emperor, without hatred

VENUS.[3]   AESCULAPIUS.[4]

towards the old religion. which its latest transformation had brought
to the worship of the one God.   Christian tombs bear the words
dis manibus sacrum.[5] and we know Christians had solicited the

the Romans were accustomed to represent figures personating the genii of any profession.
See the bas-relief represented on p. 160 of this volume and the note explaining it. The lowest
group on the opposite page shows the preparation for the combat : in the middle we see the
actual engagement : above, the *retiarius* is borne to the ground, and his helmet, falling off,
reveals his face.   We have already (Vol. II. p. 376) represented a combat between the
retiarius and the *secutor*.

[1] *Codex Theod.* xv. 3: *Si quos e gladiatori ludo . . .* in the year 397.   It is evident from
this case that laws contrary to the habits of peoples could long remain a dead letter.

[2] *Post flaminii honorem et sacerdotii* (*Codex Theod.* xii. 1. 21).

[3] From an engraved gold ring brought from Syria. (Collection of the Duc de Luynes in
the *Cabinet de France*.)   The goddess, seated, wrapped in her peplum, in sign of mourning
by reason of the death of Adonis, gives us again the type of the Syrian Venus adored at
Aphaca, near the source of the river which took the name of the divine shepherd.

[4] Engraved stone in the *Cabinet de France* (cornelian, 32 millim by 15), No. 1,190 of
the Catalogue.

[5] *Revue archéol.*, July, 1881, p. 22, and Héron de Villefosse, *Inscr. de Thala et de Haidrah*,
pp. 9, 10.

office of flamen, since the Council of Elvira in 305 prohibited this to believers.

To protect the public peace. Constantine maintained between the two cults the equality that he had promised to them in 315. Corporations, legally recognized. were at liberty to enfranchise slaves; and the Christian communities, under the title of *collegia*. had long been accustomed to do this. He gave this custom the sanction of law,[1] so that the churches. as well as the sanctuaries of Apollo and of Bacchus, of Minerva and of Aesculapius. of Venus and of Serapis, had the power of enfranchisement.

The temples had immunity from the land-tax; they received legacies or donations, which could also be made to *collegia*;[2] and the right of asylum was recognized as belonging to temples. statues of the gods and of the Emperor. and even to the place where the eagles of the legions were planted. Constantine recognized the same privileges in the churches.[3]

---

[1] *Dig.* xl. 3. 1, rescript of Marcus Aurelius. Constantine (*Codex Just.* i. 13) himself calls the enfranchisement by the Church an old custom (*jamdudum placuit . . . anno* 316). Cf. *Codex Theod.* iv. 7, *anno* 321. It was even a Greek custom. Foucart and Wescher found on the walls of the temple of Delphi four hundred and thirty-five acts of enfranchisement. The passage of time constantly simplified more and more the formalities connected with this act; a book of law of the fifth century, *Syrisches Rechtsbuch*, edited by Bruns in 1880, mentions the *manumissio inter amicos*; and this usage must have been of earlier date than the book which mentions it.

[2] *Dig.* xxxiii. i. 20, sect. 1, and *Codex Just.* vi. 24, 8. (Cf. Vol. VI. p. 94.) The *senatus-consultum* given under Marcus Aurelius, and renewed by Diocletian in 290 (*Codex Just.* xi. 24, 8). prohibited the making of legacies to unauthorized corporations; but Paulus (*Dig.* xxxiv. 5, 20) declared valid those made individually to their members: hence the latter could accept in behalf of their corporations as trustees. To solicit and receive daily offerings, the temples had boxes set up, as later the churches had. Tertullian adds even: "Men pay for the privilege of entering a temple. and for the place they occupy within it: . . . paganism begs at the doors of wine-shops."

[3] *Codex Theod.* xvi. 2. 4, *anno* 321. By an ordinance whose date is unknown (*ibid.* xi. 1. 1. with Godefroy's commentary, iv. 6–8). Constantine is believed to have freed the churches from the land-tax. The persecution having but just ended, the churches possessed very little property. only their houses of worship and cemeteries. This is what the edict of Milan secured *corpori christianorum*, and Constantine could exempt it from taxation without seriously impairing the resources of the treasury. But the clergy assumed the right of sharing personally in the immunity accorded to the corporation. Constantius opposed this by many ordinances (*ibid.* xvi. 2. 15); and it is doubtful whether he maintained the exemption in the case of Church property, which increased daily. since Constantine had authorized the churches to receive legacies and donations. In 360 the Synod of Rimini having claimed this immunity, Constantius refused, *quod nostra rebitur dudum sanctio repulisse*. and granted only the renewal of the dispensation *a sordidis muneribus*. and in the case of those of the clergy who carried on some petty traffic, exemption from the tax paid by persons engaged in trade (*ibid.*). A little later, Saint Ambrose said, *Agri ecclesiae solvunt tributum*, in the discourse *De Basilicis non tradendis*. In

The pagan priests were exempt from certain municipal burdens,[1] and almost supported by the community.[2] He granted like advantages to Jewish and Christian priests,[3] but refused them to Manichaean heretics and Donatists, who, especially since the Council of Nicaea, were to him, as they were to the Church, rebels.[4]

If we regard the favors shown to the churches without remembering the identical privileges of the pagans, we are impressed with the ardent piety of Constantine. If we bring together all these privileges, we shall see in the Emperor's conduct a plan sagaciously followed out for the purpose of making the edict of Milan a reality. But he did not propose to have civil order disturbed, and the municipal burdens avoided, under pretext of religion. Many persons, to escape from them, became priests. By three laws, of which the last is posterior to the Council of Nicaea, he decreed that there should be no election of new priests except to fill places rendered vacant by death; he forbade the admission to orders of those who by their fortune were able to fill the *munera*; and if a decurion, the son of a decurion, or a *possessor* was among the clergy, he should be removed from his position and given back

respect to the right of asylum granted to the churches, there is extant no law of Constantine ; but there are laws of the years 386, 392, etc., which mention it as an ancient right (*Ibid.* ix. 44 and 45). The privileges resulted in so many abuses that a law of 398 restricted it (*Ibid.* ix. 45, 3). This law was in its turn repealed in 431 (*Ibid.* 4).

[1] *Lex Col. Gen.* art. 66, and *Codex Theod.* xvi. 5, 2, anno 337. The latter text applies to the *sacerdotale et flamines perpetuos.*

[2] Independently of their share of the sacrifices offered to the gods, and of the revenues appertaining to the temples where they officiated. (Cf. *Ball. de corresp. hellén.*, 1881, p. 219, and Marquardt, *Staatsverwaltung*, ii. 80.) Constantine placed the *cursus publicus* at the service of the bishops convoked to the councils of the Church ; later, they received the supplies given to public functionaries, *annonas* and *cellaria* (Sulpicius Severus, *Hist. sacra.* ii. 55). This right must have been given them early, for in the mind of Constantine the clergy were a new body of public functionaries, and in prescribing that the clergy should be chosen from among the poor, he says that the poor ought to live from the resources of the Church : *Pauperes ecclesiarum divitiis sustentari* (*Codex Theod.* xvi. 2, 6 ; cf. Sozomenus, v. 5). Theodoret (*Hist. eccl.* i. 10) places this concession of the *annona* to the clergy at a later date than the Council of Nicaea : in the Council of Alexandria (339) it is mentioned as an established usage. See in the *Codex Theod.* xvi. 2, 14, an ordinance of Constantius which, confirming the advantages given by Constantine to the clergy, extends the same to their wives and children (*mares et feminae*) who are *immunes a censibus . . . et muneribus.* The word *census* is used in this law to signify the tax which might have been exacted from those of the clergy who were engaged in trade or in keeping the *caupteria vel tabernas.*

[3] To the Christians, *Codex Theod.* xvi. 2, 1–2, annis 313 and 319 ; to the Jews, *Ibid.* xvi. 8, 2, and 4, annis 330 and 331.

[4] *Ibid.* xvi. 5, 1, anno 326.

to the public service.[1] This principle remained the rule with the
Christian Emperors. A century later Valentinian III. said: "The
priest who before entering holy orders has not fulfilled all his
municipal obligations, shall divide his property among his children
and keep only a part of it for himself. If he has neither children
nor other kindred, two thirds of his property shall go to the curia,
since he ought to be richer in faith than in worldly goods."[2]

Lastly, Constantine did not relinquish his title of pontifex
maximus, which placed him at the head of the pagan clergy;[3] and
to authorize his intervention in the government of the Church,
he called himself the bishop at a distance, the universal bishop, or,
according to the etymology of the word, the supervisor of religious
matters in the whole Empire:[4] and he was so by acknowledgment
of the clergy themselves. We shall see that the Donatists applied
to him for judges.

Neither were the pagans removed from public office, any more
than from the altars of their gods. Many inscriptions show them
during the reign of Constantine, and long after his time, occupying
high offices and priesthoods. A senator whom he had appointed
consul was priest of Vesta and member of the college of
pontiffs.[5]

To prove the happy influence which Christianity had over this
Emperor's mind, it has been customary to call attention to the
humane character of certain of his laws, — those, for example, which
forbid seizing, for debt to the public treasury, the oxen and agricultural implements of the husbandman, and those which prohibit
the separation of families of farm-laborers in the sale of portions
of an estate, or the exacting of special labor-dues in the time of

---

[1] *Codex Theod.* xvi. 2, 3, 5, and 6: . . . *Procul a corpore clericorum segregatos, curiae re-
stitui et civilibus obsequiis inservire.* Antoninus had acted in the same manner in limiting the
number of those who, as practising a liberal profession, were exempt from the *munera.*

[2] *Nov. Val.* III. tit. iii. *anno* 439: . . . *Fidei magis divitem quam facultatibus.*

[3] It took the bishops sixty-four years of effort to obtain the suppression of this strong-
lived title, to which they wished to give a successor themselves. Gratian relinquished it in 375
(Zosimus, iv. 36). This author relates that at the accession of each Emperor the college of
pontiffs officially presented him with the sacerdotal robe.

[4] Euseb., *Life of Const.* iv. 24, and i. 44: ἐγὼ δὲ τῶν ἐκτὸς ἱπὸ θεοῦ καθεσταμένος
ἱπίσκοπος ἂν εἵην. See La Bastie, *Du souverain pontificat des empereurs romains.*

[5] . . . *Adlectus inter consulares judicio dici Constantini* (Orelli, No. 1181). Cf. Symmachus, x. *letter* 53.

harvest. These were ancient regulations which he has only the merit of bringing into force again.[1]

The assistance which he attempted to give to poor families, in order to prevent their selling their children, must be mentioned to his honor.[2] But the endeavor was unsuccessful, we find,[3] for the exposure of these unfortunate beings continued; nor can we forget the great alimentary institution that was founded by Trajan and his successors, nor the restrictions which the legislation of the Antonines laid upon the father's right over his child. Constantine even rendered the condition of exposed children more severe. The Antonines had secured to them the liberty which was their birthright; Constantine withdrew this, making them the slaves of those who had taken them up, and deprived fathers of the right of recovering children whom they had abandoned,[4] at the same time restoring to them the liberty (which Diocletian had taken away) of selling their new-born infants (sanguinolenti).[5]

One measure is attributed to him, however, which would have been to his pagan subjects an outrage and a crying injustice. Our juridic collections contain a text, according to which Constantine, committing to the Church a portion of the public authority, is asserted to have given to the bishops the power of judges in their own dioceses. It is one of the pious frauds so common at that epoch. The clergy at this time possessed that jurisdiction which associations of all kinds are accustomed to bestow upon their superior officers.[6] As early as the first century Saint Paul had counselled the Corinthian Christians to submit their disputes to the elders of the Church. This usage, which was in conformity with the ancient Roman law giving an arbiter to litigants,

---

[1] See, in Vol. VI, pp. 1 and 325 et seq., the legislation of the Antonines and the ameliorations introduced into the condition of slaves. In respect to the law concerning instruments of agriculture, see Quintilian, vii. 8. Constantine (in the Codex Just. vi. 1, 4) fixes at 10 solidi the price of a slave ten years old; the ordinary slave (sine arte), 20; cum arte, 30; he who can be employed as a scribe, 50; or as a doctor, 60; the eunuch sine arte, 50; the eunuch artifex, 70. We have seen (p. 165) the reign of eunuchs at the imperial court commence under Gordian II.

[2] Codex Theod. xi. 27, 1-2, annis 315 and 322.

[3] Saint Basil, in his Homilia upon Avarice, complains that fathers still sell their children Cf. Zosimus, ii. 38, and Wallon, iii. 412.

[4] Codex Theod. v. 7, 1, anno 331.

[5] Ibid. v. 8, 1, anno 329, and Codex Just. iv. 43.

[6] Cf. Dig. xlvii. 22, 4.

continued, and had no need of legal sanction. The ordinance *De confirmando judicio episcoporum et testimonium unius episc. accepto ferri*,[1] which is arbitrarily dated 331 A. D., is inconsistent. — first. with the words of Christ, who disclaims judgment upon temporal matters;[2] second, with a law of the same year, which forbids citizens to refuse to serve as judges;[3] third, with another of 334. which forbids the judge in any case to decide upon evidence given by one man only, even were that one a member " of the illustrious order ;"[4] and it far exceeds the recognized privileges of the Church a century later, for we must look forward nearly eighty years, until 398 and 408, before we find rescripts legalizing episcopal sentences of arbitration in civil affairs.   Furthermore, writs of execution were not granted by the civil magistrate in case of such sentences, unless where both parties had agreed to accept the decision of the bishop.[5] All the legislation of the fourth century is inconsistent with this ordinance, which would have thrown into confusion the whole judicial organization of the Empire; and Constantine, so anxious to preserve the public peace, so long carefully holding the balance equal between the two great religious parties, could not have wished, and would not have been able, to subject his pagan subjects to episcopal jurisdiction.

---

[1] *Const. Sirmondi*, No. 1. It bears no dates, Godefroy rejects it, and the Duc de Broglie (*L'Église et l'Empire romain*, etc., vol. i. part 2, p. 266) agrees in this rejection.

[2] He refused to decide between two brothers in respect to the division of an inheritance. "Man, who made me a judge or a divider over you?" (*St. Luke* xii. 14).

[3] *Cod.* iii. 14. The *Const. Sirmondi* says: *Etiamsi alia pars refragatur*. Sozomenus, in the fifth century, speaks of a similar law (i. 9), but with this important condition : "If the two parties consent" (ἡν δοκιμωσι). This is the law of Honorius : *Episcopale judicium ratum sit omnibus qui se audiri a sacerdotibus elegerent* (*Code.* i. 4. 8. *anno* 408).

[4] *Codex Theod.* xi. 39, 3.

[5] The same advantage was granted in 398 to the Jews, who submitted their disputes to the arbitration of their patriarchs, *ex consensu partium* (*Codex Theod.* ii. 1. 10) : and these two laws were doubtless only the confirmation of earlier legal provisions. This jurisdiction was destined, before the close of the century, to become one of the chief occupations of the bishops (cf. Saint Augustine, *Confess.* vi. 8, in the case of Saint Ambrose, and *On the Hundred and Nineteenth Psalm*, in his own case), and the Church gave it still greater importance. The Councils of Carthage (397 and 398) forbade the clergy under pain of deposition to prosecute a suit before the civil magistrate, and the laity under pain of excommunication to seek redress from a judge who was not of the Christian faith. In the Middle Ages we find this ecclesiastical jurisdiction attempting to invade the whole province of civil jurisdiction.

III. — Coins of Constantine; Summary of his Religious Policy.

A STUDY of the Constantinian coins reveals plainly this desire not to sacrifice one party to the other. Hopes held out to either,

in government despatches, went no farther than to the persons addressed; but coins circulated everywhere, and there remain so many of them with the effigy of Jupiter, Mars, Victory, and especially of the Sun, even with the

MEDIUM BRONZE.[1]   MEDIUM BRONZE.[2]

legend, "To the Genius of the Roman People," or "of the Emperor," that the great numismatologist Eckhel regards the monetary history of this reign as altogether that of a pagan Emperor.[3] This opinion, however, is no longer tenable, since a certain number of Constantinian coins have been found with Christian devices, and others in which, on the same piece, the two cults are associated, — the legend *Marti patri conservatori*, for instance, with the cross.[4] The writers who certify to the Christian zeal of the Emperor from the year 312 refuse to acknowledge this confusion, so disastrous to their theory; impartial history sees in it a demonstration of that policy which was, fortunately, guided by circumstances rather than by principle or by religious conviction.

To conclude, when the Emperor built Constantinople, pagan rites were practised. The first earth was thrown up, in preparing to lay the wall, on the fourth of November, the day when the Sun entered the sign Sagittarius, in the intent that thus the city's fortifications should forever remain under the protection of the celestial archer. When the horoscope of the new city[5]

---

[1] Coin of Constantine bearing the legend: GENIO POPVLI ROMANI.

[2] Coin of Constantine bearing the legend: GENIO IMPERATORIS.

[3] Vol. viii. p. 88. The *Cabinet de France* alone contains 138 small bronzes with the legend *Soli invicto comiti*.

[4] See W. Madden, *The Numismatic Chronicle*, xxii. 212 et seq.

[5] Glycas, Βίβλος χρονική, part iv., edition of Bonn.

was drawn, the philosopher Sopater and a Roman hierophant performed the mystic ceremonies which were to insure its lasting prosperity.[1] In the foundations supporting the enormous column of

porphyry, of which a fragment still remains, was placed, it is said, a copy of the talisman of Rome, the Trojan Palladium,[2] and on its top a statue whose radiate head might be taken for

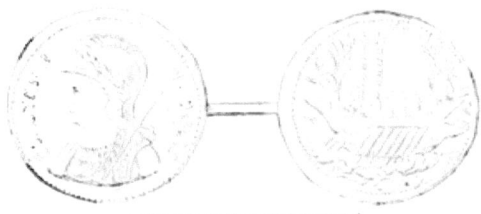

COIN OF CONSTANTINOPLE.[3]

that of Apollo or of the Emperor himself. According to a legend, Constantine concealed in this structure a piece of the true cross

GOLD COIN.[5]

which his mother, Saint Helena, had brought from Jerusalem. Accordingly, both pagans and Christians came to offer prayers and burn incense at the foot of this column,—the former to Apollo, the latter to Christ.[4] When they passed through the Forum of the Golden Milestone, the Christians made the sign of the cross before that emblem held in the hand of Saint Helena's statue, while towards those numerous images of divinities which stood there, the pagans made the gesture of silent adoration with which the ancient gods were content.

A statue holding an image of Fortune or of the Genius of the city was erected in the edifice where the senate assembled, as the statue of Victory presided over the deliberations of the Roman Senate.[6] Every year, on the anniversary of the founding of Con-

---

[1] Lydus, Περὶ μηνῶν, iv. 2. Πρωτάγατος ὁ ἱεροφάντης; Eunapius, *Life of Sopater*; Suidas, *ad loc. verbum*.

[2] *Chron. Pasch.* p. 528, edition of Bonn. The Anonymous of Banduri adds (p. 10) that αἱ ἑτέρα πολλὰ ἀγαλματομικά were placed there. Amm. Marcellinus relates (xvii. 4) that Constantine wished to have transported to Constantinople an Egyptian obelisk consecrated to the Sun, but that death prevented him.

[3] On the obverse the bust of the personified city and its name: CONSTANTINOPOLIS. On the reverse: VICTORIA AVG(usta) and a vessel carrying standards. (Bronze coin.)

[4] Socrates, i. 17; Philostorgius, ii. 18.

[5] The Empress Fl. Jul. Helena, mother of Constantine.

[6] According to the *Chron. Pasch. ad ann.* 330, p. 589, edition of Bonn, this was a statue of Constantine. But the Emperor could not with solemn ceremonial crown his own image every year; and Julian, in throwing this statue into the sewer, on account of the cross engraved on it (Banduri, p. 15), makes it certain that the figure did not represent Constantine.

stantinople, it was placed on a triumphal car and carried with great pomp to the Hippodrome;

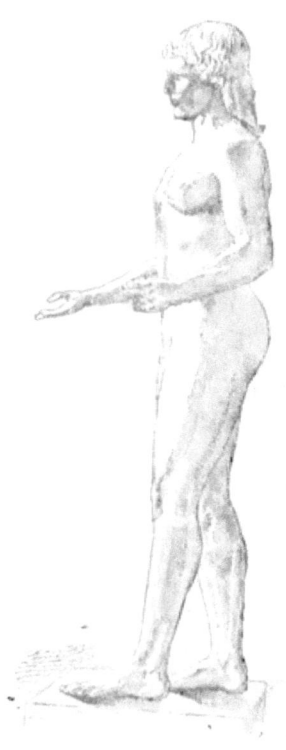

DIDYMALAN APOLLO.[2]

when the procession arrived at the Emperor's throne, he rose and saluted the statue, and placed a crown on its head. As it passed along the streets, all bowed before it and worshipped.[1] But this pagan ceremony was sanctified by a symbol. Constantine had caused a cross to be engraved on the forehead of this image; and Christian priests led the procession, chanting the *Kyrie eleison*, which a pagan without sacrilege could also repeat, as homage to the supreme God.

When Julian, after a public declaration of his pagan faith, approached Constantinople, the whole city, says Ammianus Marcellinus, went out rejoicing to meet him, and gave him a triumphal entry. The "apostate" could not have been thus welcome had there not remained a great multitude of pagans in this city which Constantine had sought to make the Christian capital of the Empire.

If it be thought that the considerations above presented show Constantine as too prudent a statesman, let the reader observe the triumphal arch erected by him in Rome in memory of the victory which decided his success. This is the principal edifice constructed during his reign, — certainly, at least, it is the only one now standing. For the history of art this arch is of great importance; for

[1]   εἰς Ἑῴαν τῆς πόλεως προσκυνεῖσθαι παρὰ πάντων. . . . (Banduri, *Ant. Const.* i. 9+; cf. *ibid.* pp. 3 and 13). According to Codinus, it was the statue of the Sun which carried this Fortune, ἡ τὸ Ὕλιον φορέμενον. Fortune and the Sun were the great divinities of the time. Many cities, notably Byzantium, had consecrated a temple to the former, Τύχαιον, before which the imperial edicts were read (*C. I. G.*, Nos. 2,024, 4,554). A quarter of Alexandria bore its name, the *Tychaeum*, as we learn from Julian's letter to the Alexandrians, which is addressed πρὸς δῆμον εὐρισκόμενα ἐν τῷ Τυχαίῳ.
[2]   Bronze statuette from the Museum of the Louvre.

BAS-RELIEFS AND STATUES FROM THE ARCH OF CONSTANTINE.

it has bas-reliefs of the Antonine epoch which by their elegance form a striking contrast with the rudeness of the Constantinian sculptures.[1] Upon this work of the first Christian Emperor

[1] The columns, entablatures, great bas-reliefs of the central passage under the small arches, and the Dacian prisoners surmounting the columns, were all taken from an arch of

religious history beholds pagan sacrifices, and not a sign of Christianity. This arch was too nearly connected with the fame of

Trajan which is no longer standing. The oval bas-reliefs represent scenes of hunting and of sacrifice. The square bas-reliefs represent,—one, a triumphal entry of Trajan into Rome, and the establishment of the Via Appia; the other, the alimentary institution of Trajan, and

Constantine for the Emperor to omit examining the plans made
for it, or to neglect their execution. That the *labarum* and the
cross are nowhere represented, while military standards of great
size are very conspicuously carved upon it, proves that he did
not wish, at this period, to exhibit Christian symbols in the midst of
Rome, still a pagan city, and destined long to remain so.

The religious policy of this Emperor may be summed up
briefly thus: he very early became aware that Christianity, in
its fundamental dogma, corresponded with his own belief in one
God; he recognized it as a force which must be employed in his
government; and he regarded the bishops as state officials in the
religious order, — a condition in which his successors long retained
them. On their side the bishops respected his supremacy and
submissively received his orders, even his sentences of arrest or
deposition. Fifty years later, Saint Optatus writes: "The Church
is contained within the State; above the Emperor there is none
but God."[1] Under the first Christian Emperor no man, except
perhaps Athanasius, dared to say: "We must obey God rather than
men."[2] But paganism was also a power, which Constantine was
unwilling to enlist against himself; we have seen that he destroyed
neither all its temples nor all its privileges.

After the defeat of Licinius (323) the Emperor was certainly
Christian as far as he could be so. He called the bishops to his
court, he always had some of them near him, and in the vestibule of
his palace "he set up before the view of all men," says Eusebius,
"the sign of salvation represented in a picture over his head; and
under his own and his children's feet, in encaustic painting, exhibited
a dragon wounded with a dart and cast into the depths of the sea,
denoting thereby the secret enemy of mankind thrust down into
the pit of destruction by that salutary trophy placed above his

that Emperor receiving a captive king. Of the fourth century are the two long belts under the
medallions which represent Constantine haranguing the people and distributing a *congiarium*.
These coarse bas-reliefs and the medals represented in the present volume, with the Triumph
of Constantine on a cameo (later), attest the decline of the arts at this epoch. The arch itself,
as a whole, is given above, facing p. 191.

[1] *De Schismate*, in book iii.

[2] Saint Peter (Acts v. 30) was the first to utter this sentiment, which has had, and still
has, consequences so important.

head."[1] But he never subjected himself to religious authority, and could not take part in religious solemnities, for the reason that he never received baptism. That he avoided till his last hour giving the Church this irrevocable adhesion, was due, not, as Eusebius says, to a hope of obtaining regeneration in the waters of the Jordan, but to an unwillingness to give his pagan subjects the right to say, "The Emperor is a Christian," until he had reached a time when this could no longer be a danger. Moreover, he even took pains to reassure them, by giving, at the very time when he made his long-delayed entrance into the Church, a pledge of his impartial justice towards all. In reply to a request of the provincial assembly of Africa, he dictated a rescript confirming the privileges of the perpetual flamens, and ordered, with unusual solemnity, this decree to be engraved on tablets of brass, "to the end that it might endure forever."[2] These two simultaneous acts, which gave security to each of the two great religious parties, give also the true character of Constantine's policy. Further, we should observe that he sought baptism from an Arian bishop, that another Arian was the depositary of his will, and that his opinions were so clearly understood that, in the Council of Milan (355), a bishop,

---

[1] *Life of Const.* iii. 3. It is a mistake to say, with Rapp (*Das Labarum und der Sonnencultus,* Bonn, 1866, p. 116), that Constantine put upon his coins only the cross, and not the monogram. See, p. 530, the coin bearing the legend *Gloria exercitus.*

[2] . . . *Ut perpetua observatione firmetur, legi hanc incisam æneis tabulis jussimus publicari. XII Kal. jan., Karthagini, anno 337 (Codex Theod.* xii. 5, 2). This law confirmed a similar ordinance of 335, which prohibited the municipalities from imposing on the flamens and on the *sacerdotes* the obligation to keep *mansiones* for the public service (*ibid.* xii. 1, 21). Constantine, in 358, issued orders regulating the election to the provincial priesthood of Africa (*ibid.* xii. 1, 46). In 395 Honorius recalled the *sacerdotales* who, under Theodosius, had deserted Carthage (*ibid.* xii. 145); in the ordinance of 412 (*ibid.* xvi. 5, 52), which enumerates the various social conditions, he again mentions the *sacerdotales* as holding the highest rank in the cities, before the chief magistrates and the decurions; and in 413 he speaks of those who, in that city, *munus sacerdotii transigerunt,* and of those who should give the people the usual games (*ibid.* 176). In the fifth century the conversion of one whom his birth placed among the nobles was considered as a desertion. Paulinus Nolanus, after his baptism, writes: "Where are now my friends and kindred? Where are they who once were my companions? They hide themselves from me like a river hurrying away; to them I am as a dead man" (*Ep.* xi. *Severo,* sect. 34). Victorinus Afer hesitates about receiving baptism, fearing the anger and contempt of the nobles (Saint Augustine, *Confess.* viii. 2). We know of what faith were Aur. Victor, Libanius, Themistius, Symmachus, and Rutilius, persons of distinction and meritorious authors, and we do not know the religious opinions of Ausonius; whence it is inferred that he had none. Even later than this there were illustrious pagans. Honorius erected, in Trajan's forum, a statue of Claudian, who closes not ingloriously the list of poets of the Pagan Muse.

Lucifer of Cagliari, reminded the assembly that Constantine " had distilled the poison of the Arian heresy." [1]   In his last moments, therefore, he maintained the faith which, in the interests of the public peace, he had always professed, — a belief in the *summa divinitas* of the philosophers and the Arians, which was that of the majority of the Eastern Christians.

Catholic writers have called Constantine "a vessel of mercy;" the Greeks have made him a saint equal in rank to the Apostles (*apostolis aequalis*); the Roman Senate apotheosized him, and for many years he was
worshipped by the soldiers.[2] He had priests
consecrated to his cult, games and festivals
instituted in his honor, as the *divi*, his

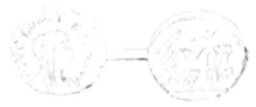

SMALL BRONZE.[3]

predecessors, had had; and his sons struck, "with the effigy of the god Constantine," medals on which the symbols of the two religions were peacefully blended.[4]

As Bonaparte sought to conciliate the Church and the Revo-
lution, so Constantine proposed to have the old and the new religions live peaceably side by side, — at the same time favoring the latter. He understood which way the world was moving, and aided its movement without precipitating it. It is to the honor of this Emperor that he made good his claim to the title assumed by him on his triumphal arch, *quietis custos*; and history, concerning itself only with human affairs, ought to give him the credit of having effected, without wars or punishments,[5] an inevi-

---

[1] *Pro. Athan. ad Const. imp.* p. 11. Socrates (i. 39) and Sozomenus (ii. 34) speak of this testament confided to an Arian. It concerned doubtless only his domestic affairs, the political question having been decided by the act of 335, of which we shall speak later.

[2] *Inter divos meruit referri* (Eutropius, x. 8). In his *First Panegyric* on Constantius, sect. 7, Julian says, in 355, "The soldiers continue to worship him as a god."

[3] Coin bearing the inscription DIVO CONSTANTINI AVG. Small bronze, represent ing on the reverse Constantine in a quadriga. He extends his hand to another hand reaching down to him from heaven (Cohen, No. 569).

[4] Cf. *Byzant. Fam.* p. 23, and Eusebius, *Life of Const.* iv. 69. Symmachus, in his famous *Letter* (x. 54), says that Constantine held both religions, pagan and Christian. On one of these medals he is represented with the nimbus (Eckhel, viii. 79, 502); on the other he appears with veiled head, that is to say, as pontifex maximus, with the legend, *Divo Const.*; on the reverse, a chariot drawn by four horses carries him to heaven. On another medal is the same legend, *Divo Const.*, and on the reverse a soldier carries a globe surmounted by the monogram (La Bastie, *Du souverain pontificat des empereurs romains*, pp. 523, et seq.).

[5] Except the two murders, mentioned p. 496.

table revolution. In all the series of the ages, none, king or people, share this glory with him.

We have sought to penetrate the deepest recesses of Constantine's mind, and have found there a policy of government rather than a religious conviction. Let us now observe this policy in his acts.

<hr/>

[1] Coin of Constantine bearing the *labarum* and the inscription GLORIA EXERCITUS. Two soldiers standing, holding a lance and leaning on their shields; in the centre the *labarum* with the monogram ✗. (Reverse of a small bronze of Constantine.)

COIN OF CONSTANTINE.[1]

CHAPTER CIII.

THE DONATISTS, ARIANISM, AND THE NICENE COUNCIL.

I. — THE NEW CHURCHES.

THE military history of Constantine has been brought down to the date of his victory over Licinius, and we have investigated his religious opinions and taken note of the precautions he employed to prevent his pagan subjects from believing that persecution was about to be turned against them. While he succeeded, however, in preserving peace in the State, he was not able to introduce it into the Church; and since these battles of beliefs were destined to have very serious results for the Empire, it becomes our duty to narrate them. The Council of Nicaea was shortly to inaugurate the reign, new to the Graeco-Roman world, of religion placed under the charge of a powerful sacerdotal body.

After his victory at the Milvian Bridge, Constantine had remained in Rome but a very short time; early in January, 313, we find him at Milan, where the marriage of his sister Constantia with Licinius was about to be celebrated. In the midst of these festivities the two Emperors proclaimed, in terms worthy of the great cause whose defenders they announced themselves to be, a complete liberty of conscience for Christians of all the churches, and pagans of every cult. "Religious liberty should not be denied," they said; "but it should be granted to every man to perform his duties towards God according to his own judgment," — words which should have been engraved in letters of gold on the palaces of kings and pontiffs. After this followed legitimate restitutions made to the Christians. Their cemeteries and churches, and the property held by them in common, were to be restored to them; and where there were honest holders to be indemnified, this was to be done at the public expense.[1]

The edict of Milan in its first part renewed the provisions of the edict of the year 311;[2] in its second it prescribed the measures needful to prevent the imperial promise from becoming a dead letter. The principle was not new, but the resolution to apply it honestly was so. To the toleration granted by Gallienus in 260, and by Galerius in 311, Constantine and Licinius added equality with the old religion. Henceforward Christianity will be not only tolerated,

BAS-RELIEF OF A SARCOPHAGUS.[3]

but officially recognized, and protected by the state as much as paganism is. Constantine did in fact more than to grant to the churches the restitution of their possessions, and to the individual Christians of their personal rights and honors; the proconsul Anulinus — sent into Africa with the head of Maxentius, that the province might no longer doubt that its former ruler was dead — carried to Caecilianus, the bishop of Carthage, an imperial ordinance recognizing in the new clergy all the immunities which had been enjoyed by the pagan priesthood.[4]

The edict of Galerius had been for the Christians a deliverance. The prisons had been thrown open, from mines and quarries the imprisoned Christians had come forth and made their way home-

---

[1] Lactant., De Morte pers. 48; Eusebius, Hist. eccl. x. 5.

[2] See p. 454.

[3] Bas-relief of a sarcophagus from the Museum of the Lateran, representing two churches of the fourth century.

[4] Eusebius, Hist. eccl. x. 7, and Codex Theod. xvi. 2, 1 and 2. See pp. 506-508.

ward, singing, as they went, hymns to the Lord. They exhibited to their brethren, who came to meet them along the road, the marks of the chains and tortures: men kissed their wounds and implored their blessing; and the hearts of the believers strengthened themselves in the faith, "since Satan might be again at some time unchained." With the edict of Milan the last fears

FAÇADE OF THE BASILICA OF CONSTANTINE.[1]

were dispelled; Christianity was legally recognized, the age of persecutions was ended, that of victory had begun. The Christian communities might now assemble in open day without fear of being pursued with threats or insults; gifts to the poor, or "the contributions to the Lord," became more abundant, and a more numerous crowd thronged the religious solemnities. Accordingly, it became necessary everywhere to build churches to receive the neophytes attracted to this belief — which now the Emperor himself protected — by the dogma of the resurrection of the body.

[1] Façade of the Basilica of Constantine which, in the sixteenth century, was destroyed to make room for St. Peter's at Rome. When in the sixteenth century the Vatican basilica was demolished to build St. Peter's, bricks were found, it is said, which bore the name of Constantine. That Emperor doubtless began the building of the church, whose interior is extremely ancient; but the façade had undergone numerous restorations, and cannot be dated from the Constantinian period.

which took away the dread of destruction, and by the promises of immortality, which gave the victory over death.

The new houses of prayer, or "houses of the Lord," οἶκος κυριακός, were constructed on the plan of the Roman basilicas, or on the enlarged model of the churches in the catacombs.[1] At

the back of the building, where the prætor's seat had been, the bishop now sat upon his throne, βῆμα or θρόνος, with the priests beside him; before him the eucharistic table and the table for the offerings, where the people deposited their gifts in money and their contributions of food for the support of the clergy and the poor of the congregation.[2] Then came the mass of the worshippers, the men on one side, the women on the other; behind them the catechumens, and outside the doors the penitents. The catechumens listened for two or three years to the instructions of the bishop and the reading of the epistle and the gospel by the deacons; but they were to go out of the church before the actual

THE CHRIST.[3]

service began, which hence was called the *missa*,[4] or the sending forth. At Eleusis only the initiated were present at the mysteries; so also only the baptized of Christ could commune with him. On the threshold of the sanctuary were the water and salt — which the priest had blessed as he mingled them — to "preserve from the attack of evil spirits" those who employ them, "driving out devils from their dwelling, sin from their hearts, disease from their bodies."

---

[1] Clement of Alexandria, *Strom.* iii. 18. In respect to the churches built in the time of Constantine, see in Eusebius, *Hist. eccl.* x. 2-4, the description of the Cathedral of Tyre, and in respect to the church of Bethlehem, De Vogue, *Les Églises de la terre sainte*.

[2] Saint Cyprian in the middle of the third century already calls the eucharistic table *altare Dei* (*Epist.* lxx. 1).

[3] Byzantine cameo in the *Cabinet de France* (light-colored amethyst, 26 millim. by 13). No. 258 of the Catalogue.

[4] In certain churches the catechumens were obliged to go out even before the reading of the gospel. The first Council of Orange, in 444, prohibited this usage (P. Le Brun, *Explication de la messe*), p. 214.

As a rule the baptistery — φωτιστήριον. or place of illumination[1] — was constructed outside of the church, as we still see it in St. John Lateran.

The temple, facing the east because it is from the east that light comes, is bare and sombre like the catacombs whence it is derived. Candles burn in it. — an illumination formerly indispensable in the subterranean darkness, now symbols of the divine light shed abroad in the hearts of men.[2] In these first days of her deliverance the Church has not the splendors that she will show later, when all the arts will unite to fill her with their magnificence. and to hold captive by sensuous enchantments those whose souls have been allured by the sweetness of the gospel words or terrified by the threats of hell. She has now no painted glass in the windows. no carving in the woodwork. no pictures on the walls.[3] even the

---

[1] See. p. 15, Saint Cyprian speaking of the new light which came down into his soul by the grace received at baptism.

[2] The candles were lighted when the gospel was to be read. in memory, says Saint Jerome, of this verse of the Psalms: "Thy word is a lamp unto my feet" (*Epist. adv. Vigilantium*). Candlemas Day, the commemoration of the presentation of Jesus in the Temple, was called the feast of the holy lights, and the paschal candle was a symbol of the resurrection. There was originally for this part of the Christian cult less symbolism and more pagan reminiscence. Candles burning in the daylight were a sign of royalty, of public rejoicing, or of piety. "At the festivals of the Minerva of Sais," says Themistius (*Disc.* iv. 49, ed. Hardouin). "Egypt was brilliant with illuminations: it is the feast of lights (ἡ καλοῦσι λυχνοκαίαν)." This usage was general, and the temples were, like our churches, lighted with lamps. The papyrus of the Louvre, No. 2,423, entitled. "the Antigraph of lights," mentions a gift of oil "for the forty-two lamps of the great goddess Astarte" (Revillout, *Rev. d'Égypte.*, 1881, p. 79). In Persia the magi bore the ever-burning fire before the kings; at Rome it was carried before the Empresses. torches were lighted on occasion of a monarch's entry, his triumph or festival (Vol. VI. p. 446, note 4, and p. 112 of this volume), and at the marriage or funeral of private individuals; a lamp always burned before the altar of the Lares, and often before the statues of the gods. When Constantine entered the Council of Nicaea, his approach was announced by the flambeaux borne before him (Eusebius, *Life of Const.* iii. 10). The poet Corippus, in a poem in honor of Justinian, explains this signal, –

. . . *Praenuntius ante*
Signa dedit cursor, posita de more lucerna.

On Julian's entrance into Sirmium the people and the soldiers came out to meet him with torches and flowers. *cum lumine multo et floribus* (Amm. Marcellinus, xxi. 10). The Church wished to pay to the King of Heaven the honors commonly offered to earthly rulers. Even to this day the bishop enters the church preceded by a chorister carrying a lighted candle. A passage of Amm. Marcellinus (xiv. 1) shows that the great cities were lighted by night . . . *ubi* (at Antioch) *pernoctantium luminum claritudo dierum solet imitari fulgorem.*

[3] *Ne quod colitur et adoratur in parietibus depingatur* (Council of Elvira, Canon 33). Eusebius (*Letter to Constantia*) blames as profane the desire to have a figure of Christ (*ap.* Migne, ii. 1,545. Cf. *id., Hist. eccl.* vii. 18). Macarius Magnus objects to painted representations of angels (Tillemont, iv. 309). This fear of recalling paganism will die away as paganism itself disappears, and the churches will be covered with paintings which will make

great, silent, severe Christ of the Byzantine churches does not
yet appear; neither are there sumptuous garments for the priests,
nor harmonious, solemn singing,[1] nor even incense, — a pagan offering that the true God refuses; this religion of death has not yet
begun to love the splendors of life. But upon the walls, upon the
lamps, perhaps even upon the vases of the altar, pious inscriptions,
and at the entrance of the sanctuary a promise of peace. — *Pax
intranti*; as on the threshold of certain temples of Aesculapius, who
was represented as a healer of maladies of the soul also, the
worshipper read these words: "Enter good, go out better."[2]   At
the altar the rites are simple and pure; instead of bloodshed and
a moaning victim and the coarsely abundant repast set out near
the pagan temple, the God who has made the harvests and the
vine gives himself under the form of wine and bread, and all
believers, in token of brotherhood, eat of the same bread and drink
from the same cup. As the preparation for these holy mysteries,
there was the dogmatic and moral instruction of the Scriptures,
the tragic story of the Passion, and the beautiful parables of the
Gospels; then followed the silent prayer of the believers, the
Sursum corda of the celebrant, which should be humanity's perpetual cry, and the faith of the whole assembly finding expression
in the rhythmic recitation of the psalms,[3] — that lyric poetry of
the Hebrews, the most beautiful that the world has ever known,

their walls like a religious volume open before the eyes of the devout. The symbolism of the
catacombs, with its vague impersonal figures, will give place to a fruitful realism ; that is to say,
to fixed types which the most ignorant man can recognize. The transition from one system to
the other is well indicated by the description of his church which Paulinus of Nola sends to
his friend Sulpicius Severus. (See Muntz, *La Peinture et l'iconographie chrétienne*.) Sculpture
also does not appear upon Christian sarcophagi until the fourth century. The Chevalier de
Rossi has gathered in the Museum of the Lateran a very curious collection of these, and M.
Le Blant has described and explained those of the city of Arles.

[1] It was Saint Ambrose who, near the close of the fourth century, organized sacred
singing; but it had early become the practice in the churches of the East, for the purpose of
sustaining the attention of the congregation, whom silent prayer could not occupy for a long
time, to divide the worshippers into two groups, who chanted the psalms responsively (Saint
Basil, *Letters*, Nos. 63 and 64). The psalms were sung, he says (*Homily upon the First Psalm*),
to the end that the sweetness of the harmony might gently insinuate the precepts into men's
hearts.

[2] *Bonus intra, melior exi* (*C. I. L.* vol. viii. No. 2,584) ; and for the Christian formula,
ibid., No. 9,712).

[3] *Primitiva Ecclesia ita psallebat, ut vox pronunciauti viciuior esset quam canenti* (Isidore
of Seville, *De eccles. offic.* i. 5). The younger Pliny (*Epist.* x. 94) shows that this usage was
very ancient: . . . *Carmen Christo . . . dicere secum invicem*. Music and singing also made
part of the religious ceremonies of the Jews and pagans. Ancient Egypt had among its clergy

BYZANTINE CHRIST (MOSAIC FROM THE CHAPEL OF MARTORANA AT PALERMO)

What attractions were these for refined and delicate souls, or even for those sinful women who would gladly, like her of Scripture,

SILVER VASE.[1]

have washed the Saviour's feet with their tears! Many thoroughly accepted the Christian doctrine, and derived from it those rules of conduct which are the condition of salvation; they lived in the shadow, in silence and meditation, and history knows not their names: such were the true flock of the Good Shepherd. But many also, not having the

THE GOOD SHEPHERD.[2]

strength to submit their character to their belief, will content themselves with taking the exterior forms of the faith, and let

INSCRIPTION, MAGNIFIED, ON VASE ABOVE.

passion still remain supreme in their souls, while with their lips they murmur the new prayers. Such were the politic and worldly Christians whom we shall now meet at every step in this history. In the case of still others the faith took a character of aggressiveness; and these will stir up religious quarrels and let loose upon the Empire a new form of domestic strife.

priestesses who were singers (Revillout, *Rec. d'Égypt.*, 1881, p. 100), and in Alexandria there was a great school, where choristers and musicians were trained for the solemnities of worship. See Miller, *Décret de Canope*, lines 58, 59; Julian, in a letter which will be quoted later; and Amm. Marcellinus, xxii. 16.

[1] Silver vase of the fourth century, bearing a Christian inscription. (*Cabinet de France*, No. 3,881.) This vase is about 14 inches high and 17 in circumference.

[2] Intaglio in the *Cabinet de France* (onyx 10 millim. by 07; No. 2,166 of the Catalogue).

II. — THE DONATISTS.

THE Church of Africa was already disturbed by the Donatists, — ardent sectaries and great disputers, hard of heart and violent in disposition, as that land of fire has always brought forth. This was the most rigid of the sects which, under the names of Montanists, Novatians, Meletians, etc., protested against the relaxation of discipline and a too facile indulgence towards sinners. They rejected from their communion the *traditores*, who in times of persecution had given up the Holy Scriptures to the pagan officials, and the *lapsi*, who had denied the faith. Their fierce pride would not admit that the Church could rightly pardon those who had shown weakness in times of danger. Under pretext that the deacon Caecilianus, raised by the people of Carthage to the see of that city, had been ordained by a *traditor*, seventy Numidian bishops consecrated in his stead the deacon Majorinus, and after him, in 313, Donatus. Carthage and many Numidian cities had at that time two bishops. This schism gave rise to acts of violence. An offer of conference being made by Caecilianus, one of the seventy replied : " Let him come, and instead of laying upon him hands of consecration, we will break his head as a penance." [1] These men, who yesterday were themselves persecuted, began an interminable war among themselves. They were scarcely less bold towards the authorities of the state. Hearing that the governor was about to set on foot an investigation into their conduct : " What is there in common," they said, " between Christians and kings, between bishops and the court ? "

However, neither party was as yet strong enough itself to settle the case, and each applied to Constantine to give them as judges the bishops of Gaul, among whom *traditores* had never been known. The Emperor was extremely averse to deviations from the established order : it was his wish that there should be throughout the

---

[1] *Exeat huc . . . . et quassetur illi caput de poenitentia* (Optatus Milevitanus, pp. 20–21, edit. of 1679). This Optatus, bishop of Milevi, one of the four cities of the Cirtensian Confederation, wrote, according to Saint Jerome, his treatise *De Schismate Donatistarum* before the year 375.

Empire but one religion, the worship of the supreme God, as there was but one human will, his own. These clamors, which threw a whole province into confusion on account of the election of a bishop, angered him; he resolved to put an end to them, without, however, causing the public authorities to interpose in the affair. Imitating the wise conduct of Aurelian in the case of Paul of Samosata,[1] he laid the matter before a commission of Italian and Gallic bishops, whom he constituted judges by a letter, in which he said: "The bishops are at variance, the people are separated into two factions and driven to extremes. It has pleased me to command Caecilianus, with ten of his partisans and ten of his adversaries, to come to Rome. I have moreover ordered Reticius, Maternus, and Marinus, your colleagues, to present themselves also, that the cause may be heard." Three Gallic and fifteen Italian bishops formed a tribunal; they reversed the action of the seventy, justified Caecilianus, and sent their decision, with all the documents in the case, to the Emperor, who maintained Caecilianus in his see.[2]

The Donatists, however, refused to accept the decision of the council, and incriminated another person, the Bishop of Apthonga. As it was in this case a question, not of doctrine, but of fact, — namely, whether the bishop had been a *traditor* and whether Caecilianus was the author of a certain letter, — the Emperor sent them before the proconsul of Africa, who treated them all, as ordinary persons amenable to his jurisdiction, with the haughty coldness of the Roman magistrate.[3] The Donatists were again the losing party.

---

[1] Page 301.

[2] Euseb., *Hist. eccl.* x. 5. Cf. Optatus Milevitanus, *De Schismate Donatist.* i. 28, and *Gesta purgationis Caecil.* The Donatists had asked to have their judges selected from among the Gallic bishops. Constantine, in part deferring to this desire, designated three from Gaul, but added to them bishops from Italy and Rhaetia under the supremacy of the Bishop of Rome. We have the letter addressed by Constantine to the Roman bishop *Miltiadi episcopo urbis Romae et Marco;* similar letters were doubtless despatched to all the bishops convoked for this first Roman council. The Fathers sat in the palace of the Lateran, — an imperial domain which Constantine gave to the Bishop of Rome probably after the death of Fausta, who occupied it when she came to the city. (Cf. Tillemont, iv. 141.) We have seen (p. 31) that towards the close of the second century a primacy of honor had already been recognized in the Bishop of Rome: Amm. Marcellinus (xv. 7) says, in the fourth, that the bishops of the Eternal City enjoyed greater consideration: . . . *Potiores aeternae Urbis episcopi;* although he also says that Constantius II. caused Pope Liberius to be arrested *tamquam imperatoriis jussis et plurimorum sui consortium decretis obsistens.*

[3] Optatus Milevitanus, *Gesta purgationis,* pp. 97, 98. Neither in the *Acta* of the proconsul of Africa nor in the laws and authentic letters of Constantine do we find the pious

But they were numerous and tenacious : they petitioned the Emperor with such vehemence to obtain new judges that he convoked a second assembly of bishops in the city of Arles, authorizing persons thus summoned to employ the imperial post for their journey.[1]   This was giving them the character of public functionaries; and in his eyes they became so, for he proposed by means of them to rule their turbulent communities.

The Council of Arles (314), where, according to some authorities, thirty-three bishops[2] were assembled, according to others a much greater number, condemned the Donatists and prepared twenty-two canons, of which only three concern political history.

Mixed marriages have always, and justly, been displeasing to the Church, since they imperil the faith of believers. But at this time, the Christians being a minority, and an ardent minority, these unions became a means of extending the gospel. The Council regarded them very mercifully ; it condemned to but a brief penitence the Christian maiden who had married a pagan (tenth canon), —evidently hoping that she would attract her husband into the Church. This was, moreover, Saint Paul's teaching.[3]

We know how Tertullian and Origen regarded the military life, and we have seen that the last persecution began upon the refusal of the Christians to enter the service or to remain in it. But from the moment when the Church obtained an equality with paganism, she naturally desired that all offices, and especially military ones, should be open to them. By a skilful change of front the Council of Arles, renouncing the early teaching, decided that those who abandoned the standards should be excommunicated from the Church (third canon).

affectations which Eusebius and the ecclesiastical historians attribute to this Emperor when he speaks to the bishops.

[1] The right of using the *cursus publicus* involved also that of being lodged and fed in the *mansiones* at the expense of the state, — or rather of those provincials upon whom the burden fell. To each group of two bishops Constantine granted (*Letter* to the Bishop of Syracuse) three public slaves to serve them. These favors, which were continued by Constantius, Amm. Marcellinus considers ruinous to the imperial post and the public treasury (xxi. 16, *ad ann.* 361).

[2] Many of the bishops sent priests or deacons as their representatives.

[3] The Apostle indeed counselled the Christian husband or wife in no case to abandon his or her pagan companion if the latter were content to dwell in the marriage state (1 *Cor.* vii. 10–16) ; but a letter of Saint Ambrose shows that towards the close of the century the Church felt herself strong enough to have no further need of compromises.

The members of each Christian community were subject to the spiritual jurisdiction of the bishop; the Church aspired to follow them into the public functions they were called to fill, however high the station might be. "A Christian appointed governor," says the seventh canon, "will take letters of recommendation to the bishop of the country which is intrusted to his care, and the bishop will watch over him, assist him with his advice, and, if he should violate Christian discipline, may exclude him from the Church." These men, yesterday proscribed, already looked forward to a conquest of the army and the government. What confidence, what audacity was this! With it also what a marvellous spirit of government they possessed, and how evident it is that the world cannot resist them!

Constantine brought the council to an end by ordering the bishops to return to their episcopal cities.[1] The Benedictines say : "It is noteworthy that at the close of this council the bishops did not sign in the order of the rank of their sees, but according to their seniority. . . . There was, therefore, nothing determined in Gaul touching the pre-eminence of certain sees; all the bishops were regarded as equal, age alone making a difference among them."[2]

CONSTANTINE.[3]

It was usual for the assemblies to communicate to absent bishops the decisions which had been made, so that uniformity of teaching might be secured. Before separating, the council sent its canons to the Pope, "who could," says the œcumenical letter, "more readily cause them to be accepted by all."[4] Rome, the sole apostolic see of the West, was accord-

---

[1] *Proficiscemini et redite ad proprias sedes* (Letter of Constantine to the Council of Arles). -- *Tædians, jussit omnes ad suas sedes redire* (Letter of the Council to Pope Sylvester).

[2] *Art de vérifier les dates*, ii. 267.

[3] Constantine wearing the casque, with the monogram. (*Cabinet de France*, Collection of the Duc de Luynes.) Intaglio, 12 millim. by 10 (much enlarged in our representation), which probably served for a seal to some religious dignitary. It is plainly not of the time of Constantine, and seems to be the work of an artist of the Renaissance. Cf. *Revue numism.*, 1866, pp. 78-110.

[4] *Per te potissimum omnibus insinuari.* See the twenty-two canons of the Council of Arles in Routh. *Reliquiæ sacrae*, iv. 307. The Bishop of Arles was the first to sign the letter, which gives reason to believe that he presided at the council. The Fathers at Arles

ingly its religious metropolis. By their deference, the **Fathers** confirmed the primacy of honor long accorded to the Roman bishop in the Latin provinces; but this was not an acknowledgment of primacy of jurisdiction.

The Donatists were no more submissive to the Council of Arles than they had been to that of Rome. Again they appealed to the Emperor. Vexed by these quarrels, which seemed to him futile, he exclaimed sadly: *O rabida furoris audacia!*[1] But he had put his hand upon the affairs of the Church, and could not withdraw it He sided now with the orthodox, now with their adversaries, imprisoning some, banishing others; and at last, tired of the dispute, sent the bishops home to their churches.[2]

III. — THE COUNCIL OF NICAEA (325).

In proclaiming liberty of worship, the edict of Milan had placed the government outside of and above the religious quarrels of the time, — an excellent attitude, which Constantine had not been able to maintain. The interests of public peace soon forced him to return to the old Roman doctrine of religion under the control of the state. But it was no longer a question of those cults without dogmas or teaching, without mutual ties, without authority outside the cities where they were established, and all having for their head the master of the Empire, the priest-monarch. The Christian Church was an immense body, having her discipline and her hierarchy. With her doctrine of divine inspiration, believed to be always active, she drew her rules of conduct from a higher sphere than that of the civil law; and hence acknowledged the latter only so far as she was forced to do so, or as she could bend it to her own interests. Graeco-Latin antiquity had never known a power like this, and long

address the Pope as *Pater dilectissime*, and they clearly mark the character of the Roman see when they say to him: "Thou couldst not be absent *a partibus illis in quibus et Apostoli quotidie sedent et error ipsorum sine intermissione Dei gloriam testatur*" (Optatus Milevitanus. *Gesta purgat.* p. 290).

[1] Optatus Milev., *De Schism. Donatist.* p. 28.

[2] Imprisonment of Caecilianus at Brixia, then his re-establishment in the see of Carthage in November, 316; exile of the Donatists about this time; their recall in 220. Cf. Routh. *Reliquiae sacrae*, iv. 307.

to control it was a thing impossible for the public authority. But
the belief of the intervention of the Holy Spirit caused in this
great body continual perturbations. The Church had already had
innumerable sects, who pursued each other with anathemas, and
was destined to have many more. In proposing to establish unity
and peace in the midst of this violent and irascible world, where
each party always believed itself the sole possessor of the truth,
Constantine undertook a formidable task. All his reign was destined to be disturbed by it; and his successors suffered like himself
until the time when the Christian clergy succeeded in withdrawing
religious questions from the decision of the civil power, and after
having rejoiced to welcome the entrance of the Church into the
State, became strong enough to attempt to place the State within
the Church. Was it possible for Constantine to act otherwise than
as he did? The honest and quiet deism which was the whole of
his religion, did not suffice for those fiery souls. We shall see that
he was compelled to give the Church her most formidable weapon
when he called together the first of those œcumenical councils
which later turned against his successors.

After the defeat of Licinius had made Constantine master of
Asia, he promulgated two edicts: one, to annul all the effects of
the late persecution; the other, a truly episcopal letter, full of gentleness and unction, exhorting all nations to adore the Supreme God,
" who, showing through his Son his own resplendent face, has bidden
the world to worship his divinity." This letter, which is a profession of the Christian faith, has in it nothing of the imperious and
hasty style of Constantine. It was evidently written by a bishop, and
this bishop must have been he whom, since the edict of Milan, the
Emperor had employed as secretary for ecclesiastical affairs, Hosius
of Cordova.[1] But Constantine appears through it, with the advice
many times repeated, that all live in peace, and cherish a spirit of
mutual toleration.[2]

Alas! toleration was in the policy of the Emperor; it was not,
and it could not be, in the conduct of men who believed themselves masters of the future of humanity, dispensing the salvation

---

[1] See p. 497. To him is addressed the ordinance concerning *manumissionibus in ecclesia*
(*Codex Theod.* iv. 7, anno 321).

[2] Euseb., *Life of Const.* 48–60, especially sect. 56.

or the eternal destruction of men's souls. At the moment when
Constantine was publishing his pacific rescript of 324, the most
violent of all the quarrels which ever agitated the Church broke
out in Alexandria, and spread through all the East.

There had been in Egypt revolts against discipline. Meletius,
bishop of Lycopolis, a partisan of rigid doctrines, had refused to
submit to his metropolitan, Alexander, and Colluthus strove to
defend the ancient rights of the presbyters, or elders, against the
encroachments of episcopal authority. Far greater in importance
was the question raised by Arius, an Alexandrian priest renowned
for his learning, for the austerity of his life, and for his powerful
logic. "If the Son," he said, "is begotten of the Father, as the
Church teaches, the Father existed before the Son, and these two
Persons of the Trinity are not equal." The reasoning was
accurate; but to bring reason into the mysteries of religion is to
destroy them.[1] Arius maintained indeed the God of the mind
whom philosophers place alone upon the throne of the universe;
but he abandoned the God of the heart, him whom the imagination
delighted to behold walking over the plains of Galilee and on the
banks of the Jordan surrounded by children and by holy women,
in the glorious Transfiguration upon Mount Tabor and upon the
blood-stained cross, and then breaking the stone from his sepulchre,
—a token of the universal resurrection which he had promised.
To make a religion, this was the God to be taught. The men of
administrative ability in the Church, who have been in large
numbers side by side with the men of faith, made no mistake
at this point; they knew that all Christianity centres in the
Christ, that his divinity was the great and novel feature of the
teaching, and that if it were abandoned, the entire edifice would
give way. Now, to represent Jesus as only the first of created
beings, and not eternally existent, would be opening the door to
those who saw in him a mere man, as Cerinthus, the Ebionites,
and Paul of Samosata had already taught. There was another
consequence even more dangerous; this would give satisfaction to
many pagans or converts whom the idea of the Trinity disturbed,

---

[1] In respect to the antecedents of Arianism, which had deep roots in the human mind,
and even in the Christian faith, see the *Pastor* of Hermas, the pseudo-Clementines, and in
this volume pp. 10 (note 3) and 38. The doctrine recurs again with the Nominalists of the
Middle Ages, and exists at the present day.

and who in Arianism recovered their one God, him whom the Emperor himself worshipped. Orthodox believers were therefore extremely troubled by the reappearance of this tenacious heresy, which under the veil of theological phraseology was an offensive return of conquered rationalism against triumphant Christianity. Alexander excommunicated Arius; and a hundred Libyan and African bishops united in council ratified the sentence of their metropolitan, and with the heresiarch they also condemned eleven deacons and two bishops, his adherents (321).[1]

But Arius had many other adherents, for he had illustrious predecessors: Plato and Aristotle, — that is to say, almost all Greek philosophy, — Philo the great Alexandrian Jew, and the Neo-Platonists, who had represented the Divine Being as divided, from a repugnance to make the world proceed directly from God, the multiform from unity, the imperfect from perfection, movement from the immovable. This famous ancestry explains the long popularity of Arianism in the Oriental provinces, where Hellenic subtlety took delight in these insoluble questions, and the indifference on this subject of the Western provinces, where the human mind, less disposed to meditation, as yet cared not to wander in the darkness of metaphysics. "Among pagans," was the observation of the Greek Themistius, "there are more than three hundred opinions concerning the divinity; it is not, therefore, wonderful if Christians do not agree upon this subject."[2] Vainly Alexander repeated to his opponents: "Abide by the gospels. The blessed Saint John says that the Word is above human knowledge, even above the knowledge of the angels. Inquire no further on this subject, and do not try to understand that which is above human comprehension."[3] "Concerning the mysteries of faith," says another, "inquire neither how nor why."[4] Words of wisdom are these, to which our insatiable curiosity will never listen. The infinite attracts us, and we always desire to measure its impenetrable depths. This fruitless endeavor is at once the honor and the despair of the human soul.

[1] Socrates, Hist. eccl. i. 6.

[2] Themistius, apud Socrates, Hist. eccl. iv. 32. Philo said a true thing when he maintained that we could know of God only what he is not (Vacherot, Hist. de l'École d'Alexandrie, i. 405).

[3] Letter of Alexander to the Bishop of Byzantium, apud Theodoret, Hist. eccl. i. 3: χαλεπώτεραί σου μὴ ζήτει καὶ ὑψηλότεραί σου μὴ ἐξέταζε.

[4] Gelasius of Cyzicus, Πρακτικὸν τῆς πρώτης συνόδου, ii. 25.

Arius had taken shelter with Eusebius of Nicomedeia (322). Some bishops supported him; to one council another was opposed. The Arians were again allowed to perform the rites of religion, which was equivalent to annulling the sentence of the Egyptian bishops; and Alexander was advised again to receive into his church those whom he had expelled. The Church was divided on the question; there were everywhere discussions concerning the Father and the Son, — even in the shops and public places; and the pagans represented the Trinity upon the stage, in order to turn the subject into ridicule.[1]

This tumult at last came to the ears of Constantine, and displeased him. He wrote to the two adversaries thus: "I understand that you, Alexander, asked the priests concerning the interpretation of a certain place in Scripture, and stirred up many vain and curious questions to know their opinion therein; and that you, Arius, said inconsiderately and rashly things that you should have concealed; whence discord arose between you, and the people, being disturbed by your factions, did fall away and forsook the Universal Church. . . . Questions like these which no law prescribes, the idle cobwebs of contention spun by curious wits, are propounded to try the strength of reason and the sharpness of understanding; yet they ought to be suppressed, not to distract the common people, or make them more factious. . . . Is it becoming that brethren should strive with brethren in a vain and idle contention about words, to the disturbance of the universal peace? . . . Seeing that your contentions arise from points not concerning the main structure of religion, and of small moment, they should breed no disagreement in your affections. . . . Agree, therefore, and let there be harmony between you, that the people may live in peace and unity, and that I may spend my days quietly and enjoy the happiness of a tranquil reign."[2] Constantine, who treated so lightly the great problem of Christianity, had nothing of the theologian in his character, but everything of the ruler; his religion was the public peace.

---

[1] Socrates, *Hist. eccl.* i. 6, and, for a later period, many passages of Gregory Nazianzen. Arius, to spread his ideas, composed verses upon well-known airs, "which were sung by travellers, millers, and artisans" (Philostorgius, ii. 2). Later, Gregory and Ephraem employed the same methods of religious instruction. The Psalms also were sung, and certain hymns of Gregory were even received, in the East, among the canticles of the Church.

[2] Eusebius, *Life of Const.* ii. 69, and Socrates, *Hist. eccl.* i. 7.

and his God a deity whom it seemed to him that every man might accept.

Hosius, his secretary, carried this letter to Alexandria, and vainly strove to restore tranquillity. Egypt was in a blaze; the bishops accused each other of heresy, and the congregations took sides with their pastors.[1] Then Constantine conceived a great political idea. He resolved to call together the bishops of all Christendom and have them prepare a *Credo*, which, after discussion and approbation by the majority, should become a law of the Empire. Then he himself would undertake to have this law respected by all the nations subject to his sway, and by all recalcitrant doctors and bishops of the Church.[2]

When Constantine said to the bishops: "Come to an agreement in the matter of your faith, and submit yourselves to the decision of your majority," the measure was one of supreme good sense; but when he added that he would have their decision executed, he went counter to his edict of Milan, which he ought far rather to have observed. To this statesman the toleration of 313 had been an administrative measure; the intolerance of 325 was another. He proposed to employ the council and its *Credo* as tools of government, to use the expression of Tacitus.

More than two hundred and fifty bishops,[3] belonging to the

---

[1] It is difficult to admit as genuine the long and singular letter that Constantine is said to have addressed to Arius. (See Baronius, *Ann. eccl.* 318, or Labbe, *Conc. gen.* ii. 270.) That later writers speak of this letter, or quote portions of it, is no proof of authenticity, for even the contemporaries of Constantine misrepresent his edicts and attribute to him speeches which he never made. The very judicious Roman Catholic author Lebeau (*Hist. du Bas-Empire*, i. 211) cannot persuade himself to accept it. It is proper to say, however, that the letters of Constantine quoted by Athanasius in his *Apologia* are equally verbose, and that the imperial secretaries of this period made their masters speak with but little dignity, — as preachers, and not as monarchs.

[2] The proconsul Gellius had called upon the philosophers of Athens to come to an agreement on the question of the Supreme Good, and had said to them that if they would only interest themselves in doing this, the question would be quickly settled. Gellius and Constantine are good representatives of that administrative spirit, hostile to subtle abstractions, and in every way wishing for exact statements, in order to know what conduct would be suitable in the case, and upon what opinion it would be proper to decide. (See Havet, *Le Christianisme*, ii. 70.)

[3] Eusebius, *Life of Const.* ii. 8. Athanasius (*Against Arius*) says three hundred and eighteen bishops, — doubtless for the reason that this was the number of servants assigned in Scripture to Abraham. The second œcumenical council, that of Constantinople in 381, has the same number. Each bishop brought with him several priests and deacons. The imperial post had been put at the service of the fathers, and Constantine supplied them with provi-

provinces which were to form the Eastern Empire, responded to the
call; one even came from Persia, and another from the country of
the Goths, — a proof that Christianity had long before this crossed the
frontiers of the Empire.[1] The Bishop of Rome, or, as Socrates calls
him, "the Bishop of the Imperial City," sent two priests to represent him. It was possible, therefore, without being too ambitious, to
call this gathering the œcumenical council, or assembly of bishops
from all the habitable earth. Hosius, the Emperor's confidential
secretary, appears to have had charge of the discussions,[2] in which
the priest Athanasius, the great adversary of Arius, took the most

sions. Socrates, Theodoret, and Sozomenus assert that the bishops, disagreeing among themselves, sent to Constantine a quantity of documents, which he, in the interests of peace, threw
into the fire.

[1] See p. 211, note 2. Philostorgius, however, calls Ulfilas the first bishop of the Goths;
it is possible, therefore, that he who is mentioned in the text was some person in holy orders
who had been sent to evangelize the Goths established in the Empire, and for this function
elevated to the rank of bishop.

[2] The delegation of authority by the Bishop of Rome to Hosius is an hypothesis which
nothing confirms. Eusebius (Life of Const. iii. 7) says only: "The Bishop of the Imperial
City did not attend, on account of his advanced age, but certain of his priests represented
him (πρεσβύτεροι δ' αὐτοῦ παρόντες τὴν αὐτοῦ τάξιν ἐπλήρουν)." It is entirely comprehensible,
on the other hand, that the Emperor should have given the charge of a discussion, so important
in a political point of view, to a man who had long enjoyed his confidence. It was Hosius
who signed first when the bishops attached their names to the creed. As to the objection that
Hosius, only a Bishop of Cordova, would not have taken precedence over those of Antioch and
Alexandria, it has been forgotten that this council was, to the Emperor, much more a matter
of State than of the Church. Anxious to put an end to the disputes which disturbed his
provinces, he cared but little whether Arius were justified, or Alexander; the object for which
he did care was to have the majority reach a conclusion which he could then employ to silence
the opponents, whichever party it might be. He therefore needed to influence in this assembly,
either personally or by some one upon whom he could rely; and this he did. Theodosius,
later, did the same in the case of the second œcumenical council, — that of Constantinople in
381, where was present neither Roman legate nor any one bishop from the West. Eusebius
says (Life of Constantine, iii. 13) that the Emperor, after his address, gave the presidents of
the council opportunity to speak (τοῖς τῆς συνόδου προέδροις). By this must be understood
those who later were called "patriarchs," or "primates." In this matter of Arianism, which
decided the fate of Christendom, the Bishop of Rome played no part whatever. The letter
sent by Hosius to the Western bishops to communicate to them the decisions of the council
was addressed sanctis Dei ecclesiis quae Romae sunt et in Italia et Hispania totâ et in reliquis
ulterius notiondum usque ad Oceanum commorantibus (Labbe, Conc. gén. ii. 267). Theologians only became aware of the importance of introducing unity into the Church, and
consequently of connecting the episcopal sees with the Roman see (pp. 30-31); but the
Emperors were much less concerned in this regard. The founder of Constantinople and the
Emperors who succeeded him in that city had no wish to give the clergy of the Oriental provinces an Italian head. In the famous edict of Theodosius for the suppression of paganism,
the bishops of Rome and Alexandria are again placed in the same rank (Codex Theod. xvi. 1.
2, anno 380). The younger Theodosius seems to make no difference between the patriarchs
of Rome and of Constantinople: "for the two cities ought to have the same rights" . . .
Constantinopolis quae Romae veteris praerogatica laetatur (ibid. 2, 45, anno 421).

active part.[1]   By order of the Emperor the council held its sessions
in the Basilica of Nicaea,—a vast edifice usually employed, as in
all the Graeco-Roman cities, for purposes of traffic and law

A great cause, indeed, was about to be pleaded in this basilica,
—that of the religious future of the world. In our days we wonder

GATES OF NICAEA, FROM PEYSSONNEL.[2]

at the audacity of men who dare to say to God what he is and
what he is not, forgetting that they may hear the Jehovah burst-
ing forth above their heads to ask of them, as he did the patriarch
Job: "Where wast thou . . . when the morning stars sang together, and all the sons of God shouted for joy? . . . Hast thou
commanded the morning since thy days; and caused the day-

[1] Athanasius, born at Alexandria about 296, was at this time twenty-nine years of age.
It should be observed that this great defender of the dogma of a God one in essence though
not one in person, was of a country where this belief held an important part in the national
religion; in reality, however, the Egyptian triad was very different from the Christian trinity.
In 326 Alexander was succeeded by Theonas, who occupied the episcopal throne but three
months, to which Athanasius was then raised by an orthodox minority. A Roman Catholic
author, in a learned book on the great bishop, recognizes the fact that in this election "the
canons were violated" (Fialon, *Saint Athanase*, p. 110).

[2] These gates, constructed from the débris of ancient edifices, have inscriptions arranged
without order, which marks them as belonging to the mediæval period. The MS. of the
Voyage de Peyssonnel à Nicée is in the Library of the Institute (Paris).

spring to know his place? . . . Hast thou entered into the springs
of the sea? or hast thou walked in the search of the depth?"

But in that time no man wondered at this rashness, for philosophers and theologians alike claimed to measure the infinite and

CHRIST ON THE CROSS.[1]

see the invisible. The nations listened to them eagerly, and believed
with those who from the open heaven represented a God of flesh
and blood descending to the earth and giving his flesh to be

[1] From a Syriac MS. of 586 (Laurentian Library at Florence). The engraving on the
next page represents the upper part of the carved wooden door of the Church of Santa Sabina
upon the Aventine at Rome. In one of the sections is the earliest-known representation of the
Crucifixion. The Christians of the earliest centuries had a great repugnance to delineating
scenes of martyrdom. At a considerably later period history prevailed over symbolism, and
the scenes of the New Testament were represented, for example at Santa Sabina (fifth century),
in the mosaics of Sant' Apollinare Nuovo at Ravenna (sixth century), and in the frescos of Pope
Formosus (891–896). The once-celebrated mosaic of the oratory of John VII. (705–707), which
represented the crucifixion of Saint Peter, is now lost. To show the details on the door of
Santa Sabina we give only the upper panels. On the left, at the top, is represented the Crucifixion; then follow in order: the Holy Women at the Tomb; the Healing of a Sick Man at
the Gate of the Temple; the Miracle of the Loaves; the Water changed to Wine; Moses
receiving the Tables of the Law (?); the Supper at Emmaus; the Visit of the Angels to
Abraham; Moses striking the Rock.

FRAGMENT OF A DOOR OF CARVED WOOD (FROM THE CHURCH OF SANTA SABINA AT ROME).

bruised and his blood to flow. The divine hypostases of the Neo-Platonists left them indifferent and cold; while the Christ, suffering, scourged, and dying on the cross to save them, was present to their eyes, with pierced hands and wounded side and head bowed in the agony of death. In the last beating of his heart they felt that vast love of the human race which their gods of marble and bronze had never known, and they could not reduce to common prose the splendid poem of the Passion. They did not say: If Jesus is only a man, his death is sublime; if he is God, it is but an illusion, a sleep of brief duration.[1] Christ, the conqueror of death, lifting mankind, with the hope of eternal compensation, far above the miseries of the present life, was the triumphant vision which set them free from their greatest dread, — the horror of destruction. This was the God to whom men now turned eagerly; and when their faith was attacked by metaphysical arguments, it became the business of metaphysics to defend it. The Emperor had no liking for such discussions, but they gratified the popular taste, and he was obliged to endure them.

The Fathers began to arrive about the middle of June, 325. Constantine had summoned Arius to be present;[2] and it is said that the philosophers also gathered eagerly at this great assize of philosophy and religion, with their belief in the Logos, holding the place of the Word, and in the Demiurgos of the Timeos, seeming to correspond to the Son of God, the Executor of the Divine Will. Bishops and philosophers joined in argument; but we have the history of these debates only from Christian authors, and they naturally ended with the defeat of the pagans, sometimes by aid of the argument which was perfectly legitimate in this case, and had been used by Tertullian: "Faith needs no demonstration."[3] It would, in fact, be nothing but reason if it asked for reasons.

Jesus had taught thus: "Blessed are the meek: for they shall inherit the earth. Blessed are they that mourn: for they shall be

---

[1] The Manichaeans and the Marcionites maintained that the Passion was only an appearance (Saint Epiphanes, *Hær.* lxix. 51 and 64). At that period it was believed that this world was the centre of the universe, which seemed to have been made expressly for man, king of all nature. No one then thought of the sidereal humanity which doubtless peoples infinitude, or asked whether the Redemption concerned it also.

[2] *Evocabatur frequenter Arius in concilium* (Rufin., *Hist. eccl.* i. 5).

[3] Sozomenus, *Hist. eccl.* i. 18.

comforted.   Blessed are they that hunger and thirst after righteousness : for they shall be filled. . . . Ye have heard that it was said
to them of old time. Thou shalt not kill : . . . but I say unto you,
that every one who is angry with his brother shall be in danger
of the judgment. . . . If, therefore, thou art offering thy gift at
the altar, and there rememberest that thy brother hath aught against
thee, leave there thy gift before the altar, and go thy way, first
be reconciled to thy brother, and then come and offer thy gift. . . .
Ye have heard that it was said, Thou shalt not commit adultery :
but I say unto you, that every one that looketh on a woman to lust
after her hath committed adultery with her already in his heart. . . .
Ye have heard that it was said, An eye for an eye, and a tooth for
a tooth : but I say unto you . . . Whosoever smiteth thee on thy
right cheek, turn to him the other also.   And if any man would
go to law with thee, and take away thy coat, let him have thy
cloke also. . . . Ye have heard that it was said, Thou shalt love
thy neighbor, and hate thine enemy : but I say unto you, Love your
enemies, and pray for them that persecute you. . . . For if ye
love them that love you, what reward have ye ? Judge not, that
ye be not judged. . . . Why beholdest thou the mote that is in
thy brother's eye, but considerest not the beam that is in thine
own eye ? . . . All things whatsoever ye would that men should
do unto you, even so do ye also unto them : for this is the law and
the prophets. . . . Take heed that ye do not your righteousness
before men, to be seen of them : else ye have no reward with your
Father which is in heaven.   When therefore thou doest alms, sound
not a trumpet before thee, as the hypocrites do in the synagogues
and in the streets. . . Verily I say unto you, They have received
their reward. . . . And when ye pray, ye shall not be as the hypocrites : for they love to stand and pray in the synagogues and in the
corners of the streets, that they may be seen of men. . . . But thou,
when thou prayest, enter into thine inner chamber, and having
shut thy door, pray to thy Father which is in secret. . . . And in
praying use not vain repetitions, as the Gentiles do : for they think
that they shall be heard for their much speaking . . . for your
Father knoweth what things ye have need of, before ye ask him.
After this manner therefore pray ye : Our Father which art in
heaven, hallowed be thy name.   Thy kingdom come.   Thy will be

done on earth as it is in heaven. Give us this day our daily
bread. And forgive us our trespasses, as we forgive those who tres-
pass against us. And lead us not into temptation, but deliver us
from evil."

Simple and beautiful words are these, which conquered men's
souls because they touch the heart. To make a church, a discipline,
something very different was needed, — a dogma, mystery, and the
supernatural. At this task the apostles and theologians had labored
for nearly three centuries; but the Christian Church had not yet
a constitution expressed in brief terms and accepted by all the
bishops. This the Council of Nicaea was now about to give
her.

The assembly began its labors on the 5th or 6th of July, in
the presence of Constantine. Hosius, who sat at his right hand,
opened the session by some words of gratitude to the Emperor.
Constantine then announced to the bishops that he had called them
together to re-establish harmony in the Church. In doing this
they would please God, he said, and would do a great service to
himself, their brother in the worship of God.[1]

It is not within the province of this history to relate in detail
the debates which took place in the assembly, — the passionate excitement of the orthodox believers, the wily reticence of the Eusebians, as the secret partisans of Arius were called, and their efforts
to prevent an official condemnation; withal, the embarrassment
of the Emperor in the midst of these subtleties which the old
soldier either did not comprehend, or despised when he was able
to perceive their meaning.[2] It will suffice us to recall the argument of Arius, and the response of the council contained in its

[1] Eusebius, *Life of Const.* iii. 11-12. The historian does not name the bishop who sat at
the Emperor's right, — perhaps to leave his hearers to infer that it was himself. The probability is that the bishop was Hosius, who signed first the Canons and the *Credo*. See on this
subject p. 497, n. 2. In Theodoret (ii. 15) Athanasius says: "Was there a council in which
Hosius did not preside, that most illustrious bishop of the time?" Constantine spoke in Latin,
the official language, which continued until 397 to be the language used in courts throughout
the Empire (*Code, Just.* vii. 45, 12). *Decreta a praetoribus latine interponi debent* (*Dig.* XLII.
i. 48). A bishop translated his very short address into Greek.

[2] Constantine is represented as interposing very learnedly in these theological discussions.
We may doubt this; for had he so well handled the subject of consubstantiality, he would not,
soon after, have favored those who denied it, and sent their adversaries into exile. Eusebius
(*Life of Const.* iii. 13) speaks only of his efforts to tranquillize men's minds; *universos ad
concordiam incitat.*

Credo. Arius maintained that God had not always been a Father; that there was a time when the Son was not; that he was made by the will of God, as others are, having no previous existence at all; that he is not of the same substance with the Father, since the divine substance could not beget a substance equal to itself. — that is to say, unbegotten; that he is mutable by nature, but by his free will chose to remain virtuous. The great heresiarch asserted further that the Father is invisible to the Son, and the Son cannot know him perfectly, nor can even know his own substance.

Athanasius, with a train of reasoning contrary in purport but kindred in character, opposed this theogony born of the brain of Arius; and both arguments were logical, for logic is the instrument whereby men draw from premises conclusions which were placed therein. These subtilties interested the more learned Fathers, but did not touch the majority, composed of simple and devout men, many of whom bore marks of the persecution they had suffered, and had no need of so much argument to make them believe in their God. It was for the sake of the Christ that they had suffered torture and that so many of their kindred and friends had perished as martyrs, — for the Christ, the Son of God, himself the very God; when they were told that Jesus Christ could not be God except he were formed of the substance of the Father, they were ready to vote against this Arius who represented him as a kind of subordinate divinity little more than a man. The Greek language, with its infinite resources, gave the necessary word to designate this unity of substance, ὁμοούσιος, " homoousion," which has been translated "consubstantial."

Thus the divinity of Christ was distinctly recognized. There was still another danger to be guarded against: the Son must not be confounded with the Father. After establishing the identity of substance, the council preserved the distinction of persons by repeating the anathema against the Sabellians, who had in the acts of the Trinity seen only the working of one Divine Being, thus representing the historic Christ as only a temporary manifestation of God in the form of man. The decision of the council was really much more a matter of sentiment than of reason; but, after all, is it not sentiment that rules the world?

The *Credo* of Nicaea, which after fifteen centuries the Catholic Church still professes, is thus expressed: "We believe in one God, the Father Almighty, Maker of all things visible and invisible; and in one Lord Jesus Christ the Son of God, the only begotten of the Father, that is, of the substance of the Father; God of God,

THE RAISING OF LAZARUS (FROM A GILT GLASS).[1]

light of light, true God of true God, begotten not made, consubstantial with the Father; by whom all things were made both in heaven and in earth; who, for us men and for our salvation, descended, was incarnate and was made man, and suffered, and rose again the third day; he ascended into heaven, and shall come to judge the living and the dead; and in the Holy Spirit."[2] And

---

[1] The Christ represented beardless, having in his hand a wand with which he touches Lazarus (Ach. Deville, *Histoire de la verrerie dans l'antiquité*, pl. 29).

[2] The *Credo* of the Mass [the Nicene Creed of the Church] is that which was determined upon by the second œcumenical council, at Constantinople in 381. To oppose heresies which had arisen since 325, this council made some addition to the original creed

the council added: " But the holy catholic and apostolic Church
of God anathematizes those who affirm that there was a time when
the Son was not, or that he was not before he was begotten, or
that he was made of things not existing; or who say that the
Son of God was of any other substance or essence, or created, or
liable to change."

All the bishops but two accepted this creed, and a synodal letter
addressed by the thirteen archbishops or metropolitan bishops,
Hosius at their head, transmitted it to all the churches " under
heaven." [1]

This brief declaration was the greatest event of history; for
in fixing the doctrinal unity of the Church, the Nicaean Fathers
secured her supremacy, and Constantine by this institution of general
councils gave her the means of following the developments of Christian thought, and even of accelerating them. Up to this time the
citizen's religious and civil duties had coincided; henceforward
they became divergent, each order having its own law and its own
master. The social unity was therefore about to be destroyed, and
prolonged wars were to be waged between Pope and Emperor, — the
representatives of these antagonistic principles, — who, by turns
victor and vanquished, will, one of them suffer the humiliation of
Canossa,[2] and the other finally shut himself up in his solitary
Vatican.

established by the first council, which remains the basis of the Catholic faith. The words in
italics were added in 381 : " I believe in one God the Father Almighty, *Maker of heaven and
earth, and of* all things visible and invisible : And in one Lord Jesus Christ, the only-begotten
Son of God, begotten of his Father *before all worlds,* God of God, Light of Light, very God of
very God, begotten, not made, being of one substance with the Father : by whom all things
were made, who for us men, and for our salvation, came down from heaven, and was incarnate *by the Holy Ghost of the Virgin Mary,* and was made man, *and was crucified also for us
under Pontius Pilate.* He suffered and was buried, and the third day he rose again *according
to the Scriptures,* and ascended into heaven, *and sitteth on the right hand of the Father.* And he
shall come again *with glory* to judge both the quick and the dead; *whose kingdom shall have no
end.* And I believe in the Holy Ghost, *the Lord and Giver of life, who proceedeth from the
Father (and the Son), who with the Father and the Son together is worshipped and glorified, who
spake by the Prophets. And I believe one Catholic and Apostolic Church. I acknowledge one
Baptism for the remission of sins, and I look for the Resurrection of the dead, and the life of
the world to come. Amen."* (Père Le Brun, of the Oratory, *Explication de la messe,* p. 249.)

[1] Labbe, *Conc. générale,* ii. 267.

[2] [The fortress of Canossa, in northern Italy, was the scene of the great humiliation of the
Emperor Henry IV. before Pope Gregory VII. (Hildebrand.) It will be remembered that
after a protracted quarrel between the two potentates on questions of their respective juris-
dictions, the Pope finally excommunicated his antagonist, thus releasing all the latter's subjects from their obligations of obedience, and arming the whole world against him. Upon this

After the creed of the Church the council undertook its discipline. It timidly disposed of the case of Meletius, leaving him the title of bishop, but forbidding him to exercise the functions of the office. It fixed the date of Easter on the Sunday following the full moon nearest to the vernal equinox, and it also established twenty canons, or general rules of discipline. We shall mention only those important in general history.

Canon II. forbids the hasty ordination of new converts to Christianity.

Canon III. forbids the clergy to have women residing in their houses other than their nearest relatives or such as are beyond the reach of slander.[1]

Canon IV. decrees that all the bishops of a province shall unite to constitute and ordain a bishop. But if this is inconvenient, through great necessity or the length of the journey, three at least shall be present to ordain a candidate, and then it shall be necessary that those absent consent thereto by letter; and the metropolitan bishop shall confirm what has been done.

---

the Emperor became alarmed, and crossing the Alps in midwinter (January, 1077), hastened to the castle where the Pope made his abode at the time. He was allowed to enter within the two outer of the three walls surrounding the fortress; but before the gate of the inner wall he was obliged to stand three whole days, fasting, bare-footed, bare-headed, clad in the thin white linen garb of the penitent, before the Pope deigned to admit him; and he finally received absolution only on conditions which rendered him the vassal of the Holy See.]

[1] [" The third canon guarded against the scandals which might arise from the ancient practice of the intimate companionship of the clergy with religious women not bound to them by the ties of close kindred. But connected with this decree was an abortive attempt, which discloses to us one of the most interesting scenes of the council " (Stanley's *Hist. of the Eastern Church*, pp. 257–58). " It seemed fit to the bishops," says Socrates (*Hist. eccl.* i. 11), " to introduce a new law into the Church, that those who were in holy orders — I speak of bishops, presbyters, and deacons — should have no conjugal intercourse with the wives whom they had married previous to their ordination: and when it was proposed to deliberate on this matter, Paphnutius, bishop of Upper Thebais, a man of such eminent piety that extraordinary miracles were done by him, having arisen in the midst of the assembly of bishops, earnestly entreated them not to impose so heavy a yoke on the ministers of religion, asserting that 'marriage is honorable among all,' so that they ought not to injure the Church by too stringent restrictions. . . . It would be sufficient, he thought, that such as had previously entered on their sacred calling should abjure matrimony, according to the ancient tradition of the Church, but that none should be separated from her to whom, while yet unordained, he had been legally united. And these sentiments he expressed, although himself without experience of marriage; for from a boy he had been brought up in a monastery, and was specially renowned above all men for his chastity. The whole assembly of the clergy assented to the reasoning of Paphnutius: wherefore they silenced all further debate on this point, leaving it to those who were husbands to exercise their own discretion in reference to their wives."]

Canon V. orders that they who have been separated from the Church by their own bishop shall not be received into communion elsewhere; also that a provincial synod shall be held twice every year to examine into such sentences of excommunication.[1]

Canons VI. and VII. are decrees in respect to the primacy of certain churches — namely, Alexandria, Antioch, and Jerusalem — over their respective provinces; and mention is made of Rome as "always holding the first rank."[2]

Canons IX. and X. require that presbyters who had *lapsed*, or had committed crimes before their ordination, such as would disqualify them for ordination, should be deprived of their offices as soon as such offences were discovered.

Canons XI., XII., and XIII. deal with the penances imposed upon apostates.[3]

Canons XV. and XVI. decree that bishops, presbyters, and deacons should remain in their own several churches, and not be transferred to others.[4]

---

[1] [" The fifth canon breathes an air of Anti-Nicene simplicity. It is intended to act as a check on the tyranny of individual bishops, to guard against the unjust exclusion of any one from the Church through the party spirit (φιλονεικία) or the narrow-mindedness (μικροψυχία) or the personal dislike (ἀηδία) of the bishop of any particular diocese. . . . The whole of this machinery has necessarily passed away; but the decree renders a striking testimony to the care with which the rights of individuals were guarded, and to the belief in the ancient evangelical doctrine of forbearance and forgiveness" (Stanley, *Hist. of the Eastern Church*, pp. 258, 259).]

[2] [" In this canon," says Dean Stanley (*op. cit.* pp. 259, 260), " we see the first germ of the yet undeveloped patriarchates of the East; and in the one precedent selected for such a jurisdiction we see the organization of what was to become the patriarchate of the West. ' This,' the council says, ' is to be laid down as is the custom in the parallel case of the Bishop of Rome.' In later times, and especially at the Council of Chalcedon, this decree was made the ground of exalting the primacy of the Roman see above that of Constantinople, which of course had not been mentioned at Nicaea. But it is a remarkable instance of the cautious and deliberate spirit of the Nicene Council that the settlement of the jurisdiction refers to no grounds, historical or doctrinal, for its decision, but simply appeals to established usages in words which have since become almost proverbial, ' Let ancient customs prevail.' "]

[3] These were graduated as follows: the *flentes* wept outside the church; the *audientes* listened to the exhortations, but withdrew when the prayers began; the *prostrati* remained kneeling while the assembly prayed for them; the *consistentes* were present at the celebration of the eucharist, but were not allowed to partake of it. Each of these penances lasted for a period of years.

[4] [" The fifteenth canon struck at a custom which prevailed, as it would seem, largely even at that early time, and which, in spite of this canon, was continued and probably will continue as long as the Church itself. It prohibits absolutely the translation of any bishop, presbyter, or deacon from one city to another. . . . There were at least two high personages in the council who must have winced under this decree, — the orthodox Eustathius of Antioch (translated from Berrhoea), and the heterodox Eusebius of Nicomedeia (translated from Berytus). But they would have had their revenge if they could have seen how soon the decree

Canon XVII. decrees that all clergymen guilty of usury be deposed.[1]

Canon XIX. makes mention of deaconesses. who were consecrated to their office by prayer and the laying on of hands. There is some uncertainty in respect to this office ; but deaconesses would seem to have performed the same duties towards women that deacons fulfilled towards men ; namely. assisting the poor and sick, and instructing those who desired to be baptized.

The simple and beautiful words of the Sermon on the Mount had suffered transformation into an elaborate system of dogmas. Instead of the twelve disciples, there were now millions of men : and the Church. the successor of those early believers who had not known where to lay their heads. was now building that vast spiritual edifice which has for so many centuries sheltered the noblest portion of humanity.

The Church had condemned Arius ; Constantine now banished him and ordered his books to be burned, threatening the death-penalty against any who should dare to keep them.[2] The bishops, his religious functionaries. having pronounced the sentence. the Emperor gave it a penal sanction in the same spirit that he caused the decrees of his judicial functionaries to be executed. Both were to him the guardians of the public peace.[3] A few years later he

would have spent its force. Eusebius himself. who had subscribed this very decree, was translated, a few years later. from Nicomedia to Constantinople. and it was thought so heroic a virtue in Eusebius of Caesarea to have declined a translation to the see of Antioch that Constantine declared him in consequence fit to be a bishop. not of a single city. but of the whole world. By the close of the century it was set aside as if it had never existed : and there is probably no Church in Europe in which the convenience or the ambition of men has not proved too strong for its adoption " (Stanley. *Hist. of the Eastern Church*, pp. 261. 262).]

[1] The civil law at this time in force authorized the rate of twelve per cent interest, and even of thirty-three per cent in the case of provisions . . . *duas medios qui accepit, tertium reddat* (*Codex theod.* ii. 33, 1).

[2] Socrates, *Hist. eccl.* i. 9, *ad fin.* ; Sozomenus, i. 21. Two bishops of the Arian party. Eusebius of Nicomedia and Theognis of Nicaea, received sentence of exile three months later (Philostorgius, i. 9-10). Constantine sent letters to the Nicaeans and Nicomedeians, directing them to proceed to the election of other bishops (Gelasius of Cyzicus, iii. 2-3, and Theodoret. i. 20), and forbidding them to call this procedure disorderly. since they would be obliged to give account of their conduct to him as guardian *suis debitaque erga Deum reverentiae*. Rufinus (*Hist. eccl.* i. 5) enumerates seventeen dissidents. of whom six were exiled with Arius ; the others signed the creed of Nicaea. — *manu sola, non mente.*

[3] Constantine exiled bishops who displeased him, as Eusebius and Theognis, caused others to be chosen in their stead, and deposed these in turn, in order to reinstate the former (Sozomenus, ii. 27). That Constantine, after banishing Athanasius to Trèves, refrained from filling the vacant see of Alexandria, seems to have been due to the fact that the Emperor

issued, against the Valentinian, Marcionite, and Paulinian heretics, an edict closing their places of prayer and prohibiting their assemblies.[1] It was thus that the persecution had begun in the reign of Diocletian; happily Constantine did not proceed to such extremities. In placing the secular arm at the service of a creed, — an example which was never to be forgotten, — the Emperor was false to his promises of 313; but he did not inaugurate a new policy. Amid the ruins of that past which the Church had just destroyed, he made haste to restore the old doctrine of the Republican Senate, that the rites and ceremonies of religion were under the control of the state. The exterior aspect was different; instead of Jupiter there was Jehovah, and Christianity had become the official religion. But while the belief was different, the feeling was the same. Scarcely had the council separated when men saw enacted in the imperial palace one of the most odious tragedies in history, and in the year 326 Constantine promulgated three laws which were diametrically opposed to the spirit of Christianity, and even to the merciful character of the Antonine legislation.[2] The gods of Rome were dead; but the old Roman harshness still existed, and the penal laws of the first Christian Emperor are among the most severe in Roman legislation.

In dismissing the Nicaean Fathers Constantine gave them this order: "Let there be but little talking, and no disputing; it would give cause for laughter."[3] The recommendation was wise, but not easy to follow. Men kept silence for a time; then discussions and concealed intrigues began, and an unlooked-for event was approach-

---

dreaded the tumults which an episcopal election might occasion in that great and turbulent city.

[1] Eusebius, *Life of Const.*, iii. 64-65. The text of Eusebius seems to be an amplification of the two edicts of 326 contained in the *Theodosian Code*, xvi. 5, 1 and 2, whereby the advantages given to the orthodox believers are refused to heretics and schismatics.

[2] A female servant in an inn, or even the hostess herself, cannot be accused of adultery. *. . . quas viltas vitae dignas honore observatione non credidit* (*Codex Theod.* ix. 7, 1). The master whose slave perishes under the rod is not guilty of homicide if he declares that he did not intend to kill the man, *inter emendatos non censetur ad crimen* (*ibid.*, ix. 12, 2). The woman who had criminal intercourse with her slave was put to death, and the slave burned at the stake (*ibid.*, ix. 9, 1). By a law of 319 the decurion marrying a slave was condemned to banishment, with confiscation of property; the woman was sent to the mines, and her former master lost by confiscation one half of his possessions (*Codex Theod.*, xii. 1, 6, and *Codex Just.*, v. 5, 3). Theodosius, much more Christian than Constantine, still spoke of the *servili faece*. On the laws of Constantine in regard to the exposure of children, see chap. cii. sect. 2.

[3] *Sermonum copia landquaquam . . . utilitatem afferre . . . ridendi praebeatur occasio* (Euseb., *De Vita Const.*, iii. 21).

ing, — he who had been defeated at the council was soon to return triumphant, and those who had driven him out were themselves to be sent into exile.

In Egypt the Meletians did not observe a rule which the council had made in respect to the succession of their bishops, for it required a self-abnegation of which these men were not capable. Athanasius, raised to the episcopal throne of Alexandria, combated them with his habitual vigor; they retorted by attacking the validity of his election, so that at the same time schism and episcopal competitions broke out. The Arians, on the contrary, with the skill appropriate to defeated minorities, sent to the Emperor submissive letters, which gratified his desire for religious peace. Eusebius of Caesarea despatched to him a pastoral order in which the bishops had explained the use of the word "consubstantial" in the Nicene Creed as an unimportant novelty which had pleased the Emperor, and should therefore be accepted; Constantia on her death-bed implored the Emperor to consider well lest he should incur the wrath of God and suffer great temporal calamities since he had been induced to condemn good men to perpetual banishment; and Arius himself at last addressed to the Emperor a very orthodox profession of faith, lacking only the one word about which all this debate centred.[1] "Wherefore we beseech your piety, most devout Emperor, that we who are persons consecrated to the ministry, and holding the faith and sentiments of the Church and of the Holy Scriptures, may by your pacific and devoted piety be reunited to our mother the Church, all superfluous questions and disputes being avoided, that so both we and the whole Church, being at peace, may in common offer our accustomed prayers for your tranquil reign and on behalf of your whole family."[2]

Constantine thought that the Eusebian party was decidedly the party of peace, and that they would be more satisfactory auxiliaries than the intractable orthodox, who were already so arrogant towards the temporal power. He recalled from exile Eusebius and Theognis, restored to them their bishoprics, expelling those who had been elected in their stead,[3] and wrote to Athanasius to receive Arius

---

[1] The word was there, indeed, but with the addition of a letter; and this changed the entire doctrine: *homoiousion*, instead of *homoousion*, — the former signifying "of like substance," the latter, "of the same substance."

[2] Socrates, i. 26; Sozomenus, ii. 27.

[3] Socrates, i. 14.

into his church. The bishop replied curtly that he could not do this.
To the Emperor, proposing to govern the Christian clergy as he had
ruled the pagan priesthood, this reply was a scandalous act of
disobedience. He at once sent two of his guards to Alexandria
with this message: "You will freely admit to the church those
who desire to enter; otherwise you shall be deposed from your
office and banished from the city."

In Syria Eustathius, the bishop of Antioch, had, like Athanasius,
attacked the Arians with great vigor, and offended many bishops by
his theological warmth, his imperious zeal, and his claim to interfere
in the government of their churches. The path to be followed in
these subtle discussions is very narrow, and to slip aside is extremely
easy: a word or a letter out of its place is heresy. Eustathius,
accused of Sabellianism, was deposed by a synod in which the Eusebians were the majority. The people of Antioch taking part with
their bishop, the Emperor sent one of his officers to repress these
tumults and to present for the vacant see two candidates between
whom the synod should decide. The sedition was evidently serious,
for Eustathius was exiled, with many of his priests and deacons, and
part of the people long remained attached to him.[1]

At this time the Goths and Sarmatians threatened the Empire,
and a war with Persia seemed imminent. Constantine abandoned
the affairs of the Church for negotiations and for arms. He left
undisturbed in Alexandria the bishop who had dared to oppose his
will, and appeared to forget the Eustathians in Antioch who refused
to accept their new prelate. Quarrels, however, still continued
among heretics, schismatics, and the orthodox believers. While the
Emperor was waging war upon the Danube and exchanging messages
with Sapor, the work of his council was beginning to be undermined
throughout the East. Arianism gratified the very rational tendency,
which has reappeared in modern times in certain Protestant sects,
to bring Jesus nearer to humanity: accordingly it made great
progress in the Asiatic provinces; it invaded the episcopal sees,
and even reached the imperial court. But the true author of the
Nicene Creed, he who was the pillar of the Orthodox Church, still

---

[1] Perhaps we may place at this time the revolt of one Caloretus, of whom it is known only
that he raised an insurrection in the Island of Cyprus, assumed the title of emperor, and was
burned to death. This person may be the same with Philumenes, to whom Athanasius was
said to have sent money.

remained in his place, and the Eusebians resolved to cast him down. Frauds and crimes were imputed to him; he was summoned to appear at Caesarea, and later at Tyre, before a synod in which his adversaries were the majority;[1] he was accused before the Emperor of sacrilege and sorcery, and — a more serious charge in the eyes of Constantine — of crimes against the state: he had, it was said, by incessant appeals impoverished his diocese in order to amass great sums of money, and he had hoarded up in Alexandria the corn of Egypt while Constantinople was suffering from famine. In the case of a man like Athanasius, such charges are stupid calumnies. That his episcopal sway was stern, his orthodoxy uncompromising, his estimate of the rights of the Church very different from that held by the Emperor, is undoubtedly true. But this was not enough for those to say whom his great fame offended; they accepted the slanders of folly, hatred, or envy with that singular facility which religious parties always have had in conscientiously welcoming the most abominable imputations against their adversaries. "Our enemy," says Gregory Nazianzen, "is always a heretic." Where the greatest charity should be manifested is found the greatest vindictiveness; and for the reason that in these contests earth and heaven are both at stake.

Constantine had sent to the Synod of Tyre Dionysius, a man of consular rank, to make known to the bishops the imperial will and to exercise surveillance over their proceedings. Dionysius was the bearer of a haughty letter, in which Constantine said: "If any refuse to obey me, they shall learn by exile that no man is permitted to resist the orders of the Emperor."[2] These words show what attitude the Emperor assumed towards the bishops, — he proposed to remain their master; and those who were the adherents of Athanasius were unwilling to have a master. "How could such men" (the Eusebians), they wrote later, speaking of the Synod of Tyre, in a letter addressed to the whole body of bishops, "entertain the purpose of holding a meeting against us? How can they have the boldness to call that a council at which a single count presided, which an

---

[1] They came even from Egypt; for Athanasius had but forty-nine bishops on his side, and there were present more than a hundred in all.

[2] Eusebius, *Life of Constantine*, iv. 42; ἀπέστειλα Διονύσιον . . . ὃς καὶ τοὺς ὀφείλοντας εἰς τὴν σύνοδον ἀφιχέσθαι μεθ' ὑμῶν ὑπομνήσει καὶ τῶν πραττομένων ἐξαιρέτως δὲ τῆς εὐταξίας κατάσκοπος παρέσται . . ., etc.

executioner attended, and where a chief jailer, instead of the deacons
of the Church, introduced us into court, and where only the count

FRAGMENTS OF A MOSAIC FOUND NEAR TYRE.[1]

spoke, and all present held their peace, or rather obeyed his direc-
tions? The removal of those bishops who seemed to deserve it was

[1] In 1860 M. Renan discovered in the neighborhood of Sour (Tyre), at Kahiheram,
a mosaic which had been used as the pavement of a church. "The work," he says, "is
neither pagan nor Christian; it belongs, as the Chevalier Rossi has shown, to that tran-
sitional period when a sort of realism was leading insensibly from pagan to Christian art,
when the gods of the ancient world were giving place to the months and seasons personified.
Jupiter, Venus, Mars, Saturn no longer figure as gods, but as planets, or else represent
days." For the explanation of this curious mosaic, — a copy of which, made by an Italian
by order of Napoleon III., is now in the Louvre, — see M. Renan's *Mission de Phénicie*,
pp. 611-626. Rossi and Longpérier believe that this work dates from the fourth century,
but that it was appropriated to a Christian use in the sixth or seventh. The details given
on this page form part of the border.

prevented at his desire; and when he gave the order we were dragged about by soldiers. To conclude, dear brethren, what manner of council was this, the object of which was banishment and murder at the pleasure of the Emperor?"[1]

These men who spoke so scornfully of the civil power, and claimed with so much pride "a free church," which they proposed to rule, had a legitimate ambition; for the religious conscience can be subjected to no other law than that which it gives itself. But the religious dominion is not clearly separated from the temporal, and he who holds the former, frequently aspires to seize upon the latter. What an overthrow of ancient principles, and for the imperial government what a sacrilegious innovation! The Emperors of the East could never submit to it, and the Czar, their successor, has followed in their track.

A few years after the publication of the edict which gave the Christians a right to live, the partisans of Athanasius proposed to their liberator the great problem which was to distract the Middle Ages and the modern world. It is easy to see how Constantine, regarding this haughty independence as a dangerous opposition to his government, should have passed over to the Arian side, and banished Athanasius to the city of Trèves in Gaul, — an exile doubly severe for this Egyptian.

Arius was victorious; the bishop of Constantinople was ordered to admit him to the Communion. But on the day when, accompanied by his friends, he went through the streets of the city to the church, he was taken suddenly ill, and died. A legend quickly gathered about this event. It was related that the old bishop, filled with horror at the order which he had received from the Emperor's own lips, had fallen, weeping, before an altar, praying the Lord to avert the sacrilege in any way that seemed to him good. Whereupon Arius, on his way to the church, was seized with mortal sickness, and fell dead before his feet had profaned its

[1] This letter is given by Saint Athanasius in his *Apologia*. In the next chapter (sect. 4) we shall see that debates on this important question, "Shall the Church be free, or in subjection to the Emperor?" filled the entire reign of Constantine. The Emperor never yielded, as Athanasius wished, the right to direct the councils. Even in 411, under the feeble and very orthodox Honorius, the Comes Marcellinus, not a very well-established Christian, presided over the famous conference at Carthage, at which were present Saint Augustine and four hundred African bishops. After three days of discussion, Marcellinus declared that the orthodox had vanquished the Donatists.

threshold (336).   The orthodox believers then caused him to suffer
death a second time, in the destruction of his works; and of the
writings of this vigorous thinker nothing has been left to posterity.

Athanasius derived no advantage from his rival's death. Certain Alexandrians solicited his recall; Saint Antonius even, whose
austerities in the Egyptian deserts had given him great popularity,
was persuaded to write to the Emperor in his behalf. Constantine replied to the former that he was weary of their follies and
frivolities, and to the monk that Athanasius was a seditious person
justly condemned by an ecclesiastical sentence.[1]

On their side the Donatists, passing from schism to heresy, no
longer recognized the validity of the sacraments administered by the
Catholics, and re-baptized the Christians who came to them. They
invaded a great number of the African bishoprics; they even strove
to deprive the orthodox party of the Roman see, one of them going
so far as to dispute Saint Peter's chair with the Pope. From the
midst of this chaos of religious passions and holy animosities came
forth a sect, the *circumcelliones* (*circa villas euates*), who called themselves "God's soldiers against the devil," and in the name of
Heaven made savage war upon society. They went through the
country armed with huge clubs, seeking martyrdom and inflict-
ing it. They set the slaves at liberty, abolished debts, and attacked
masters and creditors everywhere. When their war-cry, "Praise
be to God!" was heard outside a village, all men fled or concealed
themselves, but did not always escape the blows of these fanatics.[2]

With anarchy like this in doctrines and in the social conditions,
ended the reign of that Emperor who adopted Christianity for the
sake of giving peace to the Empire.

---

[1] Sozomenus, *Hist. eccl.* ii. 31.

[2] *Des landes.* These words are found in inscriptions (*C. I. L.* vol. viii. Nos. 2,046, 2,223,
2,308). Saint Augustine frequently mentions the circumcellions (Cf. *Enarratio in Psalm
CXXXII.* 6), and in modern times their history has been written by Tillemont in his *Mémoires
ecclés.* vii. 147–165. This sect lasted until the Arab invasion in the seventh century uprooted
Christianity in Africa.

IV. — LAST YEARS OF CONSTANTINE (326–337); FOUNDATION
OF CONSTANTINOPLE.

To his ecclesiastical biographer, Constantine is a monk always
at his prayers or engaged in devout exercises with his bishops, a
preaching friar who catechises his courtiers daily and passes his
days and nights in preparing sermons on impiety and falsehood,
on God's unity and providence, on the last judgment, and on the
chastisements reserved for wicked and selfish men,[1] Of the head
of a great Empire in process of reconstruction, of the legislator
who filled the codes with his laws, of the soldier kept on the
alert by the Barbarians who surrounded his provinces, not a word
is said. In the first portion of the present sketch of Constantine
we have seen the emperor, his military talents, his ambition, and
his cruelty; in the two succeeding, we have followed the statesman
bringing about a religious transformation in the Roman world: it
remains to us to examine the domestic tragedies of his reign, his
foreign wars, and the laws or institutions which owe their origin
to him.

In the year following the Council of Nicaea, Constantine went
to Rome, for the first time since his victory over Maxentius. He
arrived there about the middle of July, 326. It was at the time
when the *transvectio equitum* took place.[2] The knights, mounted
on fine horses and clad in splendid armor, traversed the city in
procession and went up to the Capitol, there to offer to Jupiter
the prayers of the Roman youth, — a solemnity originally patriotic
and military, but now merely a pagan festival. The Emperor remained upon the Palatine, and with contempt watched the passage
of this half-obliterated image of the conquering Rome of early days.

---

[1] Eusebius, *Life of Const.* iv. 29. Burckhardt (*Die Zeit Constantins*, p. 357) is inclined to
take in good faith these theological lectures delivered by Constantine to his court and people;
he compares them to the communications which modern governments make to the Press for the
purpose of guiding public opinion. The remark is ingenious, but, in my judgment, it contains
too much ingenuity.

[2] Suetonius, *Oct.* 38; Zosimus, ii. 29. This review of the equestrian order occurred on
the 15th of July.

The people revenged themselves by sarcasms for this disdain of the ancient customs, and the insolence of the crowd went so far that some of the imperial counsellors suggested a military repression.

Constantine had the good sense not to inflict punishment. He had, moreover, many other and heavier anxieties, oppressed as he

CONSTANTINE'S BATHS, AT ROME.[1]

was with the gloomy thoughts which were to lead him shortly to put to death his eldest son and the mother of his younger children. From the month of September preceding, a few weeks after the closing of the Council of Nicaea, we find him pre-occupied and uneasy; at a moment when he had reason to rejoice over a great political achievement, he addresses an edict to all the provinces of the Empire, calling for the denunciation of criminals.[2] He speaks only of *praevaricationes*, because he could not speak publicly of

---

[1] *Etiam periere ruinae.* These baths occupied a space on the Quirinal 2,625 feet in circumference. Nothing of them remains, except some scattered fragments in the cellars of the Palazzo Rospigliosi and in the Aldobrandini Gardens. In these thermae were found the reclining statues of the Nile and the Tiber, and the two colossal statues of Constantine now in the Piazza Campidoglio; these are given facing pages 440 and 464, from drawings made at Rome by M. Fritel. The cut given above represents the condition of the Baths in 1575 (from Du Pérac).

[2] *Ad universos provinciales*, XV *Kal. oct.* (325). *Codex Theod.* ix. 1, 4.

THE GATES OF ANTIOCH (FROM A PHOTOGRAPH BY CAPTAIN BAREY).

any other offences; but he desires all men to bring to him, in perfect security, any complaint against his judges, his *comites*, his friends even, and perhaps especially against the soldiers of his guard and his household officers. "Let any man come without fear," he says; "let him speak to me alone. I will hear everything; I will make investigation myself. If the accuser prove his charge, he shall receive reward; and thus may the Supreme God be propitious to me and to the state."

This appeal to the divine protection for the safety of the Emperor and the Empire is not made in cases of obscure and trivial offences. This professed desire for the public weal conceals the anxiety of a ruler who calls for denunciations and proposes to receive them personally, because in so doing he hopes to find and grasp the clew to an intrigue by which he feels that he is surrounded.

We are reduced to conjectures in respect to this mysterious affair.

Shall we suppose that the great catholic solemnity of the previous year had angered his pagan subjects against this Emperor who pre-

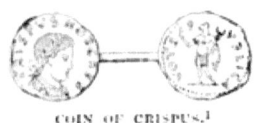

COIN OF CRISPUS.[1]

sides over an assembly of bishops? Is it possible that a plot had been formed to replace the monarch, apostate from the national religion, by his eldest son, who might be brought back to the ancestral cult? Pro-

longed reigns give rise to much impatience, and Diocletian had established the rule of abdication after twenty years. Now, Constantine had just celebrated his *vicesima*; was it not time to end this reign at its constitutional limit? At the court, two factions were certainly formed at a very early period, — one surrounding Crispus, who by his age and by his victories in Gaul and on the Hellespont

THE EMPRESS FAUSTA (BRONZE MEDALLION).

appeared to have the first claim; the other gathering about the sons of Fausta, much younger, but protected by their mother's influence. The Empress, who could not but dread the idea that her sons should one day have for master the son of Minervina, doubtless often—

---

[1] The obverse bears the laurelled head of the prince and the words CRISPVS NOB[ilissimus] CAES[ar]. On the reverse is a figure of Anubis, standing, and VOTA PVBLICA. (Bronze coin.)

daughter, sister, and wife of emperors that she was — contrasted the noble blood of her children with the inferior race of Crispus. Family ties are not strong in Oriental courts, and those nearest the throne are often peculiarly in danger. Crispus, who may have been called the concubine's son, by way of contesting his right to the paternal inheritance, perhaps replied to these concealed attacks by imprudently encouraging the hopes of his friends. In times of violence, when two parties exist in the state, each faction desires and aims at the extermination of the other. Should we go too far if we suppose Constantine rendered uneasy by the young reputation of his son, and the dangers it caused to the sons of Fausta?

These reasons are all only conjectural; but none more probable have ever been offered, and if the evil light which shines from this tragedy does not make clear its details, it at least shows causes clearly enough.

As the children of Fausta grew older, the importance of Crispus manifestly diminished. Constantine, the eldest, had long been Caesar; Constantius, the second, had received this title in 323, with the government of the Gallic provinces,[1] and though scarcely ten years of age, had just been associated with his father in the consulship (326). These reiterated marks of the affection of Constantine for his younger sons, the inaction in which Crispus appeared to be designedly retained, and, finally, the insults of the Roman populace to the Emperor, which made it seem probable that these pagans would willingly place a popular riot at the service of an intrigue, determined the Empress. Crispus was accused of meditating parricide; all the officers of the palace who had attached their fortunes to his, were represented as being his accomplices; witnesses were brought forward, either suborned or truthful; and the Emperor gave the order for his son's arrest, as guilty of treason. The young man was for a time imprisoned at Pola in Istria. But captives of this sort are not long kept alive; Crispus shortly perished, either by the sword or by poison.[2] At the same time a number of important persons who had been guilty of the imprudence of being devoted to the Emperor's eldest son were also put to death.[3] Lactantius, the preceptor of Crispus, seems to

---

[1] Julian, *Orat.* i. 12.   [2] Zosimus, ii. 29; Philostorgius, ii. 4.

[3] *Interfecit numerosos amicos* (Eutropius, x. 6). Eutropius places these murders after the death of Fausta; in my judgment, they preceded it.

have been involved in this disaster. This most eloquent of the Christian apologists, whose style has been compared to that of Cicero, shortly after ended his life in exile and penury. "He suffered from hunger," says Saint Jerome.[1]

A boy twelve years of age, Licinianus Caesar, appeared to Constantine likely at some future time to cause trouble. He was the son of a sister, Constantia, whom the Emperor loved. We cannot say whether or not Crispus was guilty of treasonable designs;[2] but it is quite certain that the only fault of Licinianus was that he existed. The man who had caused the death of his father-in-law, his nephew, the young son of Maxentius, his sister's husband, and the two Caesars of Licinius, did not hesitate at the murder of a boy, to make a clear space for his remaining sons. Whether pagan or Christian, he manifested always the same cold and implacable cruelty.

GOLD COIN.[3]

The tragedy was not yet ended. In the imperial palace lived Helena, the aged mother of the Emperor, a rough-mannered, energetic woman, to whom the murder of Crispus was a horrible crime. Repudiated by Constantius Chlorus, she had seen the imperial title and honors pass to a rival; when policy expelled Minervina, as it had driven out herself, from an Emperor's dwelling, this similarity in misfortune attached her to the son whom that daughter-in-law had borne to Constantine, and who was to grow up with a stepmother in his father's house. Helena watched over the boy with anxiety, and towards the children of Fausta she felt the same aversion that the latter manifested towards Crispus. Between these two women no doubt a mutual hatred existed. How did Helena succeed in making Fausta appear the author of abominable machinations?[4] This we do not know; but we have the fact that, by order of Constantine, the Empress was seized by her women, shut up in a hot bath, and smothered.

[1] *Chron. ad ann.* 318: . . . *Adeo in hac vita pauper est, ut plerumque etiam necessariis indiguerit.*

[2] A tradition to this effect is preserved by Gregory of Tours; but it was for the interest of the Flavians to have it believed.

[3] Licinianus Caesar, helmeted and cuirassed.

[4] On the subject of this interposition of Helena, Zosimus and Aurelius Victor unite their testimony: . . . ἐπὶ τῷ τηλικούτῳ πάθει δυσχεραινούσης καὶ ἀσχέτως τὴν ἀναίρεσιν τοῦ νέου φεροίσης . . . says one; *Cum cum mater Helena dolore nimio nepotis increparet,* says the other.

She was at an age when women have no further passion except for power and for the future of their children. Certain writers, however, have represented Fausta as another Phaedra, revenging herself for the disdain of a second Hippolytus, and finally put to death by her husband on discovery of her intrigue with a slave of the imperial stables.[1] This was a method of exculpating Con-

INTERIOR OF ST. JOHN LATERAN.[3]

stantine; but in estimating the character of Fausta we should remember that Julian speaks of her with respect. Amid the uncertainty produced by the silence ordered in respect to these executions, the historian passes by the victims and reserves his reprobation for their murderer. In the space of a few days Constantine had rivalled Nero: *Saturni aurea secla quis requiret? Sunt haec gemmea sed Neroniana;*[2] or rather, he had made himself the precursor of rulers who, in his city of Constantinople, were to make it a maxim of state policy to murder their nearest kindred.

Constantine bestowed upon the Bishop of Rome the palace of Fausta, upon the site of which now stands the church of St. John Lateran, with the baptistery which is said to be, but is not, the one wherein Constantine was baptized. Shall we regard this gift as one of those easy expiations of which the Middle Ages saw so many, or did remorse hinder the murderer from keeping possession of the abode in which his victim had lived? We cannot say; but for the second time this palace was the price of blood.[4]

---

[1] τοῦ κατ᾽ ἐστὶ, etc. (Philostorgius, ii. 4). According to usage, the names of Crispus and of Fausta were effaced from the public edifices (*Bull. épigr. de la Gaule*, for 1883, p. 141).

[2] These two lines were put up on the gates of the palace (Sidon. Apol. *Ep.* v. 19), making allusion to the double murder and to the effeminate splendor of the Emperor's dress, which was covered with pearls and gems.

[3] Rohault de Fleury, *Le Latran*, pl. xix.

[4] See, in Tacitus, the execution of Lateranus, under Nero. The account given by Zosimus (ii. 29), quite untrue though it is, shows in the Emperor's mind an inquietude which did perhaps exist.

The double tragedy which we have just related, marks for Constantine the close of his prosperous days, and nearly the close of his reign. He lived, indeed, eleven years after this; but these years are void of events; one only is of importance, the founding of Constantinople. For forty years Rome, abandoned by her Emperors, had been in disgrace with them for her captious spirit and her pagan zeal. An Asiatic court would have been ill at ease in the midst of the memories awakened by the words "Senate," and "Roman people," and "Forum," and a Christian Emperor could not dwell in the midst of all these pagan temples and in the presence of that Capitol where Jupiter was forever enthroned. Military reasons were added to political and religious in commanding this desertion of Rome. On the west, the Empire had reached the extremities of the world; on the south it bordered the desert, whence nothing disturbing could come; on the north it had its old German neighbor, which, so many times smitten by the legions, seemed now more troublesome than formidable. But in the East it was adjacent, along an immense frontier from the lower Danube to the Euphrates, to two menacing Barbaric powers, — a new Germany, that of the Goths, and a young empire, that of the Sassanidae. The city of Rome was too remote from the Tigris, beyond which Persia was again maturing ambitious schemes, too remote from the shores of the Euxine and of the lower Danube, where were gathering formidable Barbaric masses. Lastly, and chiefly, for a new religion there was needed a new capital.

At the entrance of the Propontis, between the Thracian Bosphorus and the Hellespont, on the shore of a deep and narrow bay which stretches far into the land, stood an ancient and renowned city, whose strength of resistance had been proved by the two great sieges in which it had held out against Septimius Severus and Constantine. Thence the Roman fleets might keep guard over the Asiatic and the European coasts of the Euxine, and give opportunity to fall upon the rear of Barbarians whom a rapid march of the legions upon the lower Danube should arrest in their advance. If the attack came from Asia, European troops transported to Sinope and to Trebizond easily reached the upper valley of the Euphrates and the provinces across the Tigris. For a century the Empire had leaned towards the East, whence its religious beliefs came

to it, and its most serious dangers; it was needful to follow its fortunes thither. Diocletian had sought a new capital at Nicomedeia;
Constantine did better in placing his at Byzantium.

His resolution taken, he hurried forward the work with that impatient activity manifested by him in all things, — an activity that
led him to write to his governors of provinces: "Send me word, not
that your edifices are begun, but that they are finished." He built a

HIPPODROME AT CONSTANTINOPLE.[1]

new wall, five leagues in length, to include the hillocks that were designated the Seven Hills of the New Rome; for himself he constructed
an immense palace; for the inhabitants baths, public fountains, a
hippodrome,[2] a forum surrounded by two-storied porticos; for the
Christians a church, that of the Holy Apostles, where he intended to
be buried; possibly that of the Holy Peace (Saint Irene), — a charac-
teristic devotion, indeed, for peace had been the life-long aim of this

[1] From a plan anterior to the capture of Constantinople by the Turks (Rich, *Dict. of
Antiq.*, at the word "circus").

[2] The hippodrome had been begun by Septimius Severus, and was finished by Constantine;
two obelisks, still standing, indicate the direction of the *spina*. As to the palace, the one which
was yet standing in the tenth century, and had been much enlarged by the successors of Constantine, "covered a space of 100,000 metres, — a little larger than that covered by the Louvre
and the Tuileries, buildings, courts, carrousel, and gardens." (Labarte, *Le Palais impérial de
Constantinople*, etc. p. 217.)

man of violence. The pagans retained their temples,[1] and saw the most revered statues of the ancient gods brought to decorate the public buildings and squares.

As the consuls and Emperors in earlier times had plundered Greece and Asia to adorn their capital, so now he ornamented his at the expense of the ancient sanctuaries. Olympia indeed retained the Pheidian Jupiter up to the time of Theodosius, and the Minerva Promachos of Athens caused Alaric to shrink back in awe; but the Pallas of Lindos, the Zeus of Dodona, the Muses of the Helicon, came to ornament the gates of the senatorial palace.[2] Castor and Pollux, Apollo and the Delphic tripod, were placed in the Hippodrome; Cybele and the Roman Fortuna, near the Forum. From Rome alone Constantine carried off sixty statues.[3] When, in other days, the masterpieces of

MINERVA.[4]

Greek genius were transported to the capital of the world, it had been at least after a victory, and the statues of the gods paid the ransom of men.

---

[1] See p. 506. Constantine did not destroy Byzantium, the rich and important city; he merely aggrandized it (Socrates, i. 16). The Emperor's edifices were built in the new quarters of the city, as the older part of Byzantium kept all that it had before, — the baths of Severus, for instance, which Constantine enlarged and embellished, and its temples, where later Julian sacrificed.

[2] Zosimus, v. 24.

[3] Banduri, *Antiq. Constantin.* i. 100. He took from Cybele her lions, and changed the position of her hands, to give her the attitude of prayer (Zosimus, ii. 31).

[4] Marble statue from the Museum of Naples.

The New Rome, called officially Constantinople, had, like the earlier one, its mysterious name, Flora, or ᾿Ανθοῦσα ;[1] it had also a senate, which long remained poor and obscure, although Constantine had attracted thither some of the Conscript Fathers of Rome by the gifts of palaces in the city, and domains in Thrace or Bithynia.[2] It had also knights, —as Rome still had, although they no longer did military service,[3]—and it obtained for its territory privileges of the *jus italicum*,[4] and for its inhabitants distributions of corn, wine, and oil, which had the effect of depopulating the adjacent country, as those of Rome

PHEIDIAN JUPITER.[5]

CASTOR AND POLLUX, ON A CHRISTIAN SARCOPHAGUS AT ARLES.[6]

had desolated its suburban region :[7] but Constantinople had not yet the urban prefect, who was given it later, in 359. Constantine

[1] Lydus, *De Mens.* iv. 51; *Chron. Paschale*, p. 528, ed. of Bonn.

[2] Later it had an urban prefect and one of the two consuls, the other remaining at Rome (Tillemont, iv. 240).

[3] What remained of the equestrian order continued to rank next to the senatorial order (*Codex Theod.* vi. 35; xiii. 5, 16; and *Codex Just.* xii. 32, 1, *anno* 364).

[4] *Codex Theod.* xiv. 13, 1. The peculiarities of the *jus italicum* were to give,—1st, quiritarian ownership, that is to say, special methods of acquiring property, peculiar to the ancient Romans, and since Caracalla's time no longer existing; 2d, exemption from the land-tax. Cf. Baudin, the *Jus Italicum*, p. 141.

[5] On a bronze coin of Athens.

[6] *Gazette archéol.*, 1878, pl. i. M. E. Le Blant has a monograph on this sarcophagus (*ibid.*, pp. 1–6) ; he calls attention to the circumstance that the two Dioscuri are represented of different ages, the one beardless, the other bearded, which is contrary to the traditions of mythologic art. The two compartments of the centre represent a husband and wife parting in this world or meeting in another. (See F. Ravaisson, *Les Monuments funéraires des Grecs*.)

[7] Socrates (ii. 13) says that at Constantinople 80,000 *measures* of corn were distributed daily; he gives no indication whether he speaks of *medii*, about a peck of our measure, or of *medimni*, six times as much. Procopius, speaking of the frumentary benefactions of Diocletian at Alexandria, states them in *medimni* : but in the time of Procopius, the sixth century,

did not venture to place the New Rome absolutely on an equal footing with the Old.[1]

In order to hasten the work of building, he prohibited every land-owner in the districts of Asia and Pontus from making a will unless he had a house in Constantinople.[2] This was a violation of one of the oldest rights of the Roman citizen; but the Emperor expected laws and customs to bend before his impatience. He changed also, in his favorite city, the character of the *frumentationes*; he assigned a share in the distributions to the houses built in Constantinople, which was sold along with the house itself.[3]

everything was put in Greek at Constantinople, while in the fourth century the metric system of Rome was still in use. When Constantine gave the inhabitants of Byzantium the advantages which the people of Rome enjoyed, the *modius* was the measure in use in distributions. Now, 80,000 *modii* daily make 29,200,000 a year, or two and a half times as much as the 12,000,000 given at Alexandria (p. 577), and these figures justify in a degree the words of Eunapius (*Lives of the Sophists*, s. v. Aedesius): "Neither the ships of Egypt nor the frumentary contributions of Asia, Syria, Phoenicia, and the other provinces suffice to satisfy the multitude in Constantinople." We have seen that the distributions at Rome in the time of Septimius Severus were 75,000 *modii* daily, or 27,375,000 a year; this is very nearly the amount distributed by Constantine; whence we may infer that the number of recipients was about the same, namely, 200,000. Besides these gratuitous distributions, Constantinople had also, like Rome, the sale at a reduced price. Theodosius II. in 409 expended 500 pounds of gold annually in this liberality (*Codex Theod.* xiv. 1; cf. Godefroy, vi. 264). A law of Constantine (*Codex Theod.* xi. 3, 1) seems to prove that before his time all the provinces had been rendered annonary; an ordinance of Anastasius in 494 shows that all *possessores* were subjected to it, except those of the province of Thrace, which was ravaged by the Barbarians (*Codex*, x. 27, 1), and it must have been necessary to make this tax universal, for the expense was increasing every day. To the gifts made at Rome, Alexandria, Carthage (*ibid.* xiv. 25, anno 315), and Athens (Julian, 1st *Paneg.* 8), were added distributions to the members of the provincial administration and of the court, — a list every day growing longer, — not to speak of those made to the soldiers. Soon after this, indeed, if not already, the *annona* and the *cellaria* were given to the sacerdotal body (see above, p. 598, n. 2). The transportation of all this grain occupied a great number of vessels, whose value was not included in the census of the *naviculari* (Tac., *Ann.* xiii. 51), which was so much more lost to the public treasury; and the owners of those vessels were *a civilibus muneribus et oneribus et obsequiis immunes*: a further burden to the cities (*Codex Theod.* xiii. 5, 7). These advantages had been granted by the first Emperors to the ship-owners and merchants who provisioned Rome. (See in the *Dig.* L, sect. 5, *de vacatione et excusatione munerum*.) The provincials had the further obligation of carrying the provisions destined for the army to the military magazines or to storehouses adjacent to the camps (*Codex Theod.* vii. 4, 15, anno 369). Forage must also be brought to the *mansiones* of the *cursus publicus*. — It has been said in the text that the distributions of corn and oil and lard had depopulated the country around Rome and Constantinople; this is true for the time when the distributions were first established; the list of beneficiaries being once made out, however, new names were inscribed only in the place of those of persons who had died, and the invasion of the poor from the outside ended. (See Vol. IV. pp. 115 *et seq.*)

[1] Socrates says (i. 16) : . . . ἴσην τε τῇ βασιλευούσῃ Ῥώμῃ ἀποδείξας.

[2] *Nov. Theod.* v. 1, sect. 1.

[3] . . . *Integer canon mancipibus consignetur, annona in pane cocto domibus exhibenda* (*Codex Theod.* xiv. 16, 2, and sect. 17, laws 1 and 12; Sozomenus, ii. 3).

These liberalities were no longer due to the haughty feeling of the Republic that to the conquerors belong the proceeds of the labor of the conquered; nor did they arise from the charitable sentiment of the Early Empire. — a relief to the poor. It was an advantage offered to the rich, who had no need of it, and the provinces were forced to gratify, at heavy cost to themselves, the ostentatious vanity of the monarch who wished to create in a few months a city which should eclipse all others. But Rome has well avenged herself: of her pagan Emperors she has preserved grand memories, and their buildings have left to her ruins which are the world's admiration; of the first Christian Emperor, her hastily created rival has retained nothing but the name.

Although art, at this time far in its decline, adorned Constantinople with no beautiful structures, men's imagination, which then was extremely active in the religious sphere, surrounded the city's origin with circumstances of marvel. The earliest days of the new capital were made witnesses of prodigies more wonderful than those the city by the Tiber had beheld. The god Mars had determined the site of the older city by arresting there the floating cradle of his sons; Constantine received from the Almighty the order to build. Twelve vultures had given Romulus the right to call the city by his own name; the birds were eagles that showed Constantine the way to Byzantium. The son of Rhea Sylvia had traced the line of his wall with a ploughshare; Constantine marked out his with the point of a lance, and when those attending him wondered at its length, he made answer: "I shall stop when He stops who goes before me." [1] Thus we find ourselves again in the mythologic age.

Constantinople was built in four years. [2] With haste like this,

[1] Ducange has made a collection of the texts relative to all these legends in his *Constantinopolis sacra*, pp. 23 *et seq.*

[2] The inauguration of the city took place on the 11th of May, 330. The so-called Constantinian sarcophagus, one of the finest of the Christian Museum of the Lateran, presents on the façade, represented on the opposite page, several distinct scenes. In the centre, the Christ, seated upon a *cathedra* between two apostles, holds out to one of them a *volumen*. The Sacrifice of Abraham and Pilate's Judgment occupy the two extremities. On one of the sides Jesus predicts Saint Peter's denial; on the other, he heals the sick woman kneeling at his feet, while a symbolic figure is striking a rock from which grows a tree bearing fruits. On the two sides are also represented a circular baptistery and one or two basilicas, of which the entrance is closed, according to the custom of the time, by veils or draperies. There has been

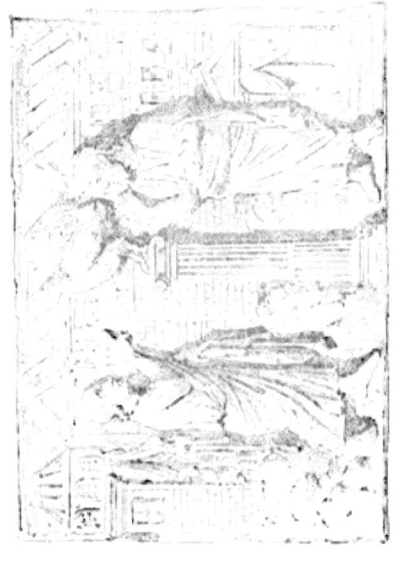

solid structures are not reared. Julian compares Constantinople
to the gardens of Adonis, which, growing up in the morning and
withered at night, last but a single day;[1] twenty years after its
consecration, the Church of the Apostles fell into ruins. It was
not because Constantine was sparing of his money; his buildings
at Antioch, at Jerusalem, at Constantinople, at Reims, and elsewhere
cost largely. An estimate, manifestly below the fact, states the
expenses in the transformation of Byzantium at a sum equal to
twelve million dollars of our money.[2] The taxes were increased,
and their burden became the heavier because the clergy, every day
more numerous, paid nothing at all, and because a portion of the
public wealth was employed in giving this cult, emerged from its
catacombs, the splendor which its victory deserved, each priest his
support, and each community its church. Soon it will be thought
necessary to have the new temples rival the old in magnificence.
The enormous amount of wealth which ten centuries had heaped
up in the latter became in a degree useless, and it was necessary,
amid the general impoverishment, to make a corresponding expen-
diture for the former; without counting also that the ancient expenses for games and festivals were not at all diminished.

It has been usual to date back to Constantine the institution
of those pious brotherhoods which, at Rome and in the South of
France, still undertake the burial of the dead. The pagans also
paid honor to the departed. Throughout the Empire associations
had long existed, societies of private individuals who guaranteed
that the last rites should be paid their members;[3] and in every
city there were *sandapilarii* and *respillones* to carry the bodies of
the poor to the funeral pile or to the tomb. The Church imitated this custom; its *fossores* even belonged to the inferior clergy.
The Emperor organized in Constantinople a body of nine hundred
and eighty *lecticarii*, whom he exempted " from all public charges."[4]

---

much discussion in regard to the interpretation of this sarcophagus. We only know that
it probably represents buildings of the time of Constantine or of his sons.

[1] *The Cæsars*, 24. Julian applies this comparison to the exploits of Constantine against
the Barbarians, " which were merely ridiculous."

[2] Manso, from the work of Codinus Curopalates, *Antiq. Constant.* viii. 14. This estimate,
made sixty years ago, should be doubled for the present day. Wietersheim (*op. cit.* i. 593,
note 2) says sixty millions of marks for the walls, porticos, and aqueducts.

[3] Vol. VI. p. 98.

[4] *Nov. Justin.* xliii., vol. xxii., chap. i. In Saint Jerome (*Epist.* 29, *Ad Innocentium*), and

His piety in so doing has been lauded : in reality it was a municipal service which he could not refuse to his new city.

While these marvels to which we have referred were taking place at Constantinople, others had occurred at Jerusalem. Saint Helena,

A FOSSOR (GRAVE-DIGGER).[1]

the Emperor's mother, had gone thither to distract her grief by a pious pilgrimage (327). When she asked to see the place where Jesus had been buried, it could not be shown her ; even the bishop himself had no idea of the locality. The entire ground had been for three centuries overturned by war and by peace ; buildings had been erected and then destroyed ; and Jews and Christians, driven out of Jerusalem, which had become a pagan city under Hadrian, were alike entirely unable to fix the site of the scenes of the Passion. On the hill of Calvary houses were now torn down in the search ; the ruins and the ground itself were examined, and the spot thoroughly cleared, but in vain. Helena was determined, however, that some traces should be found : and by dint of search, the holy grotto was discovered underneath a temple of Venus : suddenly three wooden crosses were brought to light. The work had been under the direction of a Jew, a shrewd man, who professed to have inherited from his ancestors a document in which were described the localities hallowed by the Passion. But of the three crosses discovered, which was that

in many places in the Theodosian Code, they are called "clergy." The Chevalier Rossi is of opinion that in the earliest centuries the *lecticarius* was identical with the "guardian of the catacombs."

[1] The inscription reads : "Diogenes, gravedigger, was laid in peace the eighth of the kalends of October." The *fossor* carries in one hand the pick, his instrument of labor, and in the other the lamp of the catacombs. Three crosses ornament his clothing. Tools are represented around him. This figure was found under an *arcosolium* of Saint Nereus in the catacomb of Calixtus. The *fossores* had for their patron Tobias.

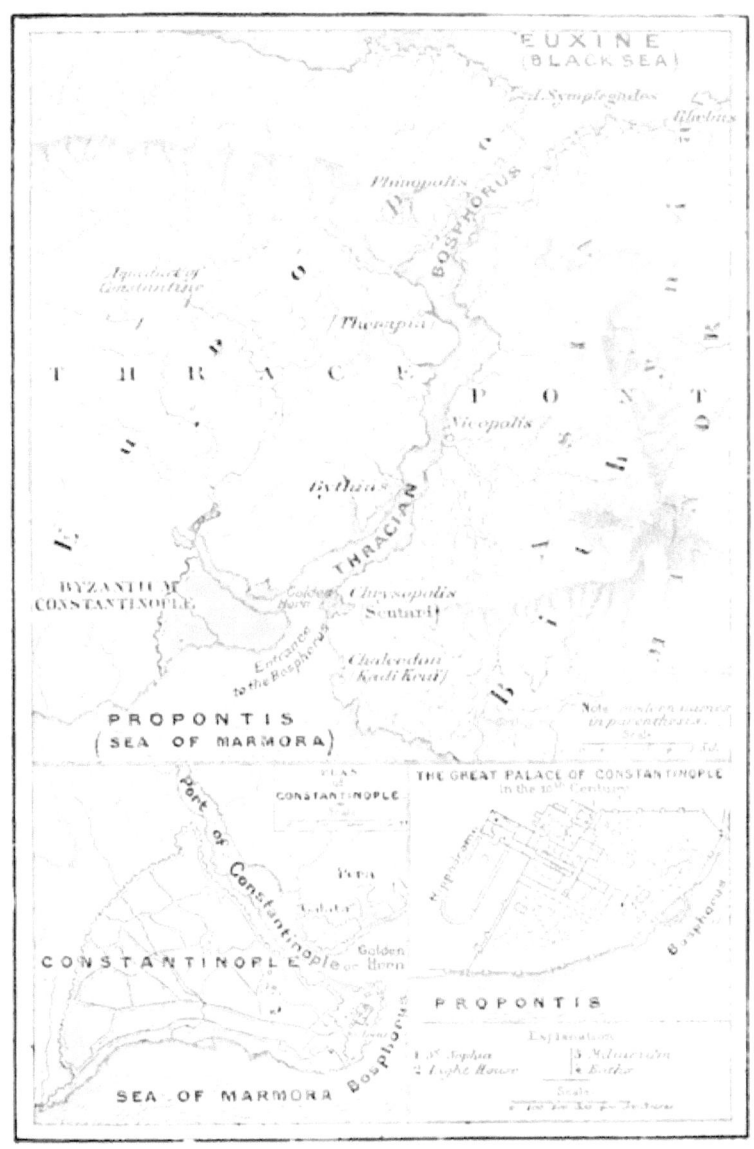

PLAN OF CONSTANTINOPLE, MAP OF THE BOSPHORUS, AND PLAN OF THE PALACE.

of the Lord? The Bishop of Jerusalem caused a woman afflicted with mortal illness to be brought to the spot; then kneeling in prayer with the Empress, he begged from Heaven a miracle. Two crosses held close to the dying woman left her still insensible; at the touch of the third she rose and walked: the virtue of the true cross had resuscitated her.[1]

Eusebius of Caesarea was the metropolitan of the Bishop of Jerusalem, and, if he was not present at the restoration of the sanctuary of Christendom, he would be sure, as historian of the Church and the Emperor, to inform himself carefully of all that was done in order to restore the holy places to the Christian believers. And, in fact, he does at great length relate how the Holy Sepulchre was discovered; but he knows nothing of the finding of the true cross.[2]

NEIGHBORHOOD OF JERUSALEM.

He, who attaches so much importance to the sacred monogram, to the *labarum*, and to the cross inscribed by Constantine on the shields of his soldiers, — how could it be that he did not celebrate that discovery which justified the enthusiasm which so many of his pages testify for the ineffable merits of the *signum salutare et vivi-*

[1] Socrates (*Hist. eccl.* i. 17) and Sozomenus (ii. 1) say that Helena also found the nails of the cross, and that Constantine made of them a bit for his horse and a helmet for himself, — which would certainly have been most irreverent. Once on the road to holy discoveries, there was no hesitation in going forward. The remains of Saint Andrew, Saint Luke, and Saint Timothy were discovered and sent to Constantinople, where they were solemnly enshrined in the Church of the Holy Apostles. Thus began the worship of saints, — needful to these populations, who required a new polytheism to take the place of the one they had abandoned; and it was certainly much purer and more consoling than the other had been.

[2] *Life of Constantine*, iii. 25.

ficum?[1] He does not omit it from his narrative because Saint Helena
was made to find a cross much in the way that an inexperienced visi-

THE HOLY SEPULCHRE, ON AN IVORY BUCKLE.[2]

tor to some famous historic locality is made to find a coin recently
buried,—this ingenuity would not have caused him a scruple; he leaves the story untold for the reason that the legend was not formed till after his death. — which event closely followed the Emperor's decease.

FRAGMENT OF A MOSAIC FROM THE CHURCH IN BETHLEHEM.[3]

In his narrative all is connected with Constantine, who orders the clearing away of the hill of Calvary and the construction of churches at the Holy Sepulchre, upon the Mount of Olives, at Bethlehem,

---

[1] Eusebius, *Life of Const.* ii. 16.

[2] M. Edmond Le Blant, *Études sur les sarcophages chrétiens antiques de la ville d'Arles,* p. 49. It is believed that this ivory buckle, preserved in a church of Arles, and used originally to fasten a leathern belt, belonged to Saint Caesarius, who died in 542.

[3] De Vogüé, *Les Églises de la Terre Sainte,* p. 96. Jesus seated upon an ass, his hand lifted in benediction. Behind him, an apostle; before him, children casting their garments in the road for him to pass over; another child climbing a tree to obtain palm-leaves; at the right, the people of Jerusalem awaiting the approach of the Christ, among them a woman carrying her child on her shoulder, after the manner of the Arab women of the present day.

CHURCH OF THE HOLY SEPULCHRE, SOUTHERN PORTAL (DE VOGÜÉ, LES ÉGLISES DE LA TERRE SAINTE).

and under the oak of Mamre. To him the pilgrimage of Helena
is a royal progress through Asia. The Empress carefully provides
for the wants of the cities and provinces through which she passes,
and arriving at Jerusalem, examines the work done by her son's
orders.[1] But at whatever date the *inventio crucis* took place, the
legend was timely. Men's minds were at that time borne forward

INTERIOR OF THE BASILICA OF BETHLEHEM.

by a too rapid movement into the higher regions of the Christian
ideal not to accept eagerly whatever supported and strengthened
their faith. The generation following did not doubt the authenticity of the miracle,[3] and the Holy Cross became the most precious of relics. By the effect it has more than once produced upon
the minds of kings and peoples, it even belongs to history.

[1] . . . Βασιλικῇ προμηθείᾳ ἐπεφραίνετο (Eusebius, *Life of Constantine*, iii. 42). Wilmanns'
inscription, No. 1,079, gives to Helena the title of Augusta. The soldiers saluted her thus, and
her effigy was on gold coins (*ibid.* iii. 47).

[2] De Vogüé, *Les Églises de la Terre Sainte*, p. 49. M. de Vogüé believes this basilica to
belong to the Constantinian epoch, or, at latest, to the sixth century.

[3] There remain two curious manifestations of this love of men's minds at that time for the
marvellous, — the poem of Juvencus, who put the gospel into verse (Saint Jerome, *ad ann.* 329:
. . . *Evangelia heroicis versibus explicat*), and that of Sedulius, who in the next century wrote
the *Paschale carmen*, entirely upon the miracles of Christ. Their works were included in the
decree of Pope Gelasius *de libris recipiendis* (494).

Aside from religious affairs, there remain, to complete the history of this reign, only an unimportant war with the Sarmatians and Goths (332), the division of the Empire among the sons and nephews of Constantine (335), and, lastly, the negotiations with Sapor II. for the protection of the Christians in Persia, and the beginning of a war with that monarch (337).

The war against the Sarmatians and Goths was not very heroic. Julian speaks of it with derision; Zosimus represents it as ending with reverses; Aurelius Victor and Eutropius, with successes; Jordanes, with a treaty which placed forty thousand Barbarians at the service of the Empire (332). This treaty supposes more negotiations than battles, and we must understand from it an alliance between the Emperor and the whole Gothic nation. This great body of *fœderati*, which henceforth made part of the Roman army, and appears to have kept at its full number, was

GOLD COIN.[1]

by no means composed of captives, but of warriors whose their kings, Araric and Aoric, ceded to the Empire on the double condition of pay for their compatriots and gifts for themselves.[2] We cannot doubt this when we read in Eutropius that Constantine had a great reputation for bounty among these Barbarians, and in Eusebius that he gave offices and rank to the most

GOLD COIN.[3]

famous among them. Themistius speaks even of a statue erected to a Gothic chief near the entrance to the Senate. That which concerns the Sarmatians or Vandals is very obscure and uninteresting, except the fact that, driven out of their own country by tribes whom they believed they had subjugated (334), they sought shelter from Constantine, who thereupon gave them an asylum in the provinces adjacent. It was the same policy, and it had the same results; twenty years later the Sarmatians ravaged Pannonia.[4] The fidelity of the Goths held out longer; but there is no doubt that many of them aided their kindred in gaining, in 378, the battle of Adrianople, where Valens with his whole army perished.

[1] Constantine II., wearing the diadem.
[2] In respect to these wars, see Wietersheim, i. 386 *et seq.*, ed. of 1880.
[3] Constantius II., wearing the diadem. FL. IVL. CONSTANTIVS PERP. AVG.
[4] Sozomenus, iii. 1; *et seq.*, 255.

Two years before his death Constantine, without abandoning the supreme control, made a division of his provinces. His three sons were already Caesars: to the eldest, Constantine II., he assigned Spain, Gaul, and Britain; to the second, Constantius II., Asia, Syria, and Egypt; and to Constans, the youngest, he gave Italy, Africa, and Illyria. Of Thrace, Macedon, and Achaia he made a kingdom for his nephew, the Caesar Delmatius; the other, Hannibalianus, received Pontus, Cappadocia, and Lesser Armenia, with the title of king.[1] The Empire had come to be a family estate, divided up at will among his heirs by the proprietor. This is very unlike the great policy of Diocletian. Constantine had made three wars, he had shed torrents of blood, and killed two Emperors, in order to reconstitute the Empire single and indivisible, and he now tore it into five fragments, without preparing in his lifetime ties which after his death should unite the chiefs of the new pentarchy. It seems, in fact, though this we cannot certainly say, that it was an actual dismemberment. The names of the Emperors will indeed be inscribed at the beginning of laws, and probably in the general measures of government the two kings will remain, one under the orders of the sovereign of Asia, the other under those of the master of Illyricum. But of the three Emperors, which one will take the chief command? Evidently no one of the three. How will the four prefectures be divided among them? Who will hold the new capital? Will it be the master of Thrace, Delmatius, one of the subordinate kings? Only the sword can decide these questions. Constantine had left to his sons the example of his own life, counselling them to ambition and civil war with far more energy than his testament counselled them to moderation and peace. We shall shortly see the results of this inconsiderate policy.

Since their great defeat by Diocletian, in 297, the Persians had shown a respectful fear of the Romans. At the date of which we are now speaking, Sapor II., the son of Hormisdas and grandson of Narses, a young man twenty-seven years of age, was full of military ardor

HORMISDAS.[2]

---

[1] We have coins with the legend: *Fl. Hannib. regi.* (Eckhel, viii. 201).

[2] Diademed head of the king, and the legend: "The worshipper of Ormuzd the excellent Hormisdas, the king of Iran and Turan, a celestial soul."   (Gold coin.)

and religious zeal.   The magi had just completed the work they
had begun by the destruction of the Arsacidae.[1] About the time
when Constantine was causing his bishops to prepare the *Credo* of
Nicaea, Sapor promulgated as the law of Iran the *Avesta*, or Book
of the Magi.   " Since our law is now clearly set forth," he says
in his edict, " let no man again fall into a false doctrine." [2]   Thus
the two Empires accomplished almost at the same moment a religious revolution.   It was the signal for furious wars to break out
between them.

Sapor at first tried his strength against the Arabs.   He defeated
the hordes who were in the neighborhood of Babylonia, ravaged
Yemen, and terrified his enemies by his cruelty.   The *rôle* of conqueror, attractive to his pride, was needful also for his security.
Christianity had made great advances in the Persian provinces
all along the eastern and southern frontier ; Armenia had been
Christianized, and the Persians could no longer count upon the
tribes of the Caucasus for assistance in case of need, for the Ibe-
rians, having adopted the new faith, were allied more closely than
ever to Rome.   This evangelization made the magi anxious for
their religion, and Sapor for his crown.   He was aware that the
conversion of Constantine gave the Romans auxiliaries in the very
heart of Asia : the relations of the Emperor with the Hindoos seemed
to prepare other perils on the eastern frontier ;[3] and Hormisdas,
a Persian prince who had taken refuge at Constantinople, might
prove in the hands of the Roman party a dangerous tool.   A letter of Constantine commending to Sapor the Christian subjects
of the latter, excited further distrust.[4]   Before entering upon open
hostilities with his powerful neighbor, Sapor sought to make sure
of Armenia, whose king, Diran, was the vassal or ally of the Romans.
The Persian governor of Atropatene allured this monarch to a conference, seized him, and put out one of his eyes.   This kingdom,
so long desired, having thus fallen into his power, Sapor again
demanded from Constantine the five provinces across the Tigris :

---

[1] See p. 132.

[2] De Harlez, *Avesta*, p. 36.

[3] Eusebius (*Life of Const.* ii. 50) speaks of an Indian embassy which came to Constantinople, and Cedrenus of a journey into India made by an agent of the Emperor, the philosopher
Metrodorus, to which Amm. Marcellinus makes allusion (xxv. 4).

[4] Eusebius, *ibid.* iv. 8.

the Emperor, like Trajan, replied to the envoys that he would
carry his answer in person. This was a declaration of war. While
the ponderous Roman army was gathering, the swift horsemen
of Sapor entered Mesopotamia; but hearing of the great prepara-

SARCOPHAGUS OF SAINT HELENA (SO CALLED), OF RED PORPHYRY.[1]

tions making in Syria, they returned across the Tigris with their
spoils (337).

Eusebius, terminating his most untrustworthy narrative by a
falsehood, represents the Persians imploring peace and Constantine generously granting it.[2] Sapor had more pride, and Constantine less confidence. At this moment, moreover, the latter was

[1] Vatican, Hall of the Sarcophagi. No. 589. The four sides represent a battle; the conquerors occupy the upper part, the prisoners are trodden under foot by the horses, or are
closely bound, their hands behind their backs, etc. M. Barbier de Montault, the Papal cham-
berlain, says, in the Catalogue of the Museo Pio-Clementino, that the body of Helena was
deposited in this sarcophagus. For the tomb of a woman and a saint, the decoration is
singular.

[2] *Life of Const.* iv. 57.

drawing near to the tomb, — whither emperors and peasants alike descend; and the road was sad to him, for he was to bequeath to his successors on the Oriental frontier a war destined to last a quarter of a century, and in the interior anarchy which his heretical baptism caused. As death approached, he accepted this rite from Eusebius of Nicomedeia, the friend and partisan of Arius. He who summoned the Council of Nicaea died, therefore, a Christian, but a Christian of the Arian faith, — that faith which most resembled the religion of his fathers; that also which has been most vigorously combated by the Church.

The Emperor died on the 22d of May, 337. His body was carried from Nicomedeia to Constantinople with the usual pomp. He was buried, as his mother had been, in a porphyry tomb in the Church of the Holy Apostles which he had built. Constantius, the only one of his sons who was present at the funeral, had not received baptism: he was therefore obliged to leave the church with his pagan guards before the religious ceremony began, — which brings to notice the singular fact that Constantine himself, remaining so long unbaptized, was never able, up to his latest day, to be present at a service of the Church.[1]

---

[1] The first canon of the Council of Valentia (374) refers to the custom of requiring the catechumens to leave the church before the celebration of the Mass. Saint Ambrose, shortly after this, wrote to his sister: "When I had sent away the catechumens and given baptism to those who were to receive it, I began" (*Epist. ad Marcell. sor.*). Saint Jerome enumerates five orders in the Church, — bishops, priests, deacons, believers, and catechumens. "The catechumens," says the Abbé Corblet (*Hist. dogmatique . . . du baptême*, i. 411), "occupy a middle place between the believers and the unbelievers; they are neither in the Church nor out of the Church, but midway."

Reverse of a coin of Constantine II. representing the serpent transfixed by the staff of the *labarum*.

COIN OF CONSTANTINE II.[2]

www.ingramcontent.com/pod-product-compliance
Lightning Source LLC
Chambersburg PA
CBHW020935030726
47496CB00005B/1204